Montaigne's

ESSAYS AND SELECTED WRITINGS

ST MARTIN'S PRESS   NEW YORK

Montaigne's

ESSAYS AND SELECTED WRITINGS

A Bilingual Edition

TRANSLATED AND EDITED BY

Donald M. Frame

COLUMBIA UNIVERSITY

Introduction

On the very first page of the *Essays* Montaigne warns his
reader that "I am myself the matter of my book," "a
book," he later elaborates, "consubstantial with its author,
concerned with my own self, an integral part of my life
. . ." (3, 281).[1] The first essayist, he meant by "essays" not
so much a literary genre as the tests or trials of his judgment, his natural faculties, and indeed his life. He com-
bined insatiable curiosity about himself with remarkable
detachment.

This is not to say that he is completely candid. To be
sure, he sometimes claims to be: "If I seemed to myself
good and wise or nearly so, I would shout it out at the
top of my voice." Or "I do not find so much good in
myself that I cannot tell it without blushing" (191, 279).
But these statements themselves reveal, by their self-dis-
paraging humor, a witness not so much candid as faithful.
Montaigne's aim is not confession but communication.
A Gascon, he loves paradox and exaggeration. To fail to
portray these in action would be—as he is well aware—to
falsify his portrait. Furthermore, a faithful portrait must
be not static but kinetic: "I do not portray being: I por-

---

[1] All references in this Introduction to passages by Montaigne
that are included in this volume will be located simply by the page
numbers alone—in this case (3,281)—in parentheses.

tray passing. . . . I may presently change, not only by chance, but also by intention. . . . So, all in all, I may indeed contradict myself now and then; but truth, as Demades said, I do not contradict" (313–5).

He also knew that the act of observation affects the process observed. In one way self-portrayal changes us: "Painting myself for others, I have painted my inward self with colors clearer than my original ones. I have no more made my book than my book has made me . . ." (281). In another way it holds us firm and stable: "I feel this unexpected profit from the publication of my behavior, that to some extent it serves me as a rule. . . . This public declaration obliges me to keep on my path, and not to give the lie to the picture of my qualities . . ." (365).

Montaigne's self-portrait is both individual and extraordinarily universal. Unlike the Romantics later, he considered himself typical and sought mankind in himself: "I set forth a humble and inglorious life; that does not matter. You can tie up all moral philosophy with a common and private life just as well as with a life of richer stuff. Each man bears the entire form of man's estate" (315). He believed that long study of self made him a passable judge of others: "It often happens that I see and distinguish the characters of my friends more exactly than they do themselves. I have astonished at least one by the pertinence of my description, and have given him information about himself" (421). His readers have gone him one better by recognizing themselves in him. His book reminds Virginia Woolf in *The Common Reader* of a portrait in a gallery: "As the centuries go by, there is

always a crowd before that picture, gazing into its depths, seeing their own faces reflected in it, seeing more the longer they look . . ." Of his own first reading of Montaigne Emerson wrote: "It seemed to me as if I had myself written the book, in some former life, so sincerely it spoke to my thought and experience."

To Montaigne, among many other things, his book was a way of seeking a friend to replace the one he had lost: "I hope . . . that if my humors happen to please and suit some worthy man before I die, he will try to meet me. . . . If . . . I knew of a man who was suited to me, truly I would go very far to find him. . . . Oh, a friend! How true is that old saying, that the enjoyment of one is sweeter and more necessary than that of the elements of water and fire!" (367). No wonder countless readers have found in him not only an author but a friend.

The self-portrait is, of course, often incidental to the ideas. The skeptical arguments of Montaigne's longest chapter ("Apology for Raymond Sebond"), his demonstration of human inanity and presumption, were long considered his principal message and had great impact on European thought. His ideal of the *honnête homme* and his concern with human nature as the proper and most fascinating study for man are important legacies to Frenchmen of the next two centuries. In the great line of French *moralistes* he is the first and the greatest.

Montaigne's style is one of his greatest charms. An important part of his self-portrait, it is oral, associative, substantive, concrete, and personal. His main aim is to make it truly represent him:

When I have been told, or have told myself: "You are too thick in figures of speech. . . . Here is a dangerous phrase." (I do not avoid any of those that are used in the streets of France; those who would combat usage with grammar make fools of themselves.) ". . . This is paradoxical reasoning. . . . You are often playful: people will think you are speaking in earnest when you are making believe." "Yes," I say, "but I correct the faults of inadvertence, not those of habit. Isn't this the way I speak everywhere? Don't I represent myself to the life? Enough, then. I have done what I wanted. Everyone recognizes me in my book, and my book in me.

Formal eloquence he mistrusts as deceptive and somehow charlatanic: "Fie on the eloquence that leaves us craving itself, not things!" His main concern is that style shall not obfuscate substance but serve it:

It is for words to serve and follow; and let Gascon get there if French cannot. I want the substance to stand out, and so to fill the imagination of the listener that he will have no memory of the words. The speech I love is a simple, natural speech, the same on paper as in the mouth . . . succulent and sinewy, brief and compressed . . . vehement and brusque . . . rather difficult than boring, remote from affectation, irregular, disconnected and bold . . . not pedantic, not monkish, not lawyer-like, but rather soldierly . . . (71).

He prefers an oral style, presumably because speech is more natural and spontaneous than writing. This quality is hard to demonstrate, but one aspect is not: his fondness for dialogue, usually with himself or man in general. An example of the first sort shows him as first spontaneous, then comically self-deprecatory, then resolutely honest: "I will have tossed off some subtle remark as I write. (I mean,

of course, dull for anyone else, sharp for me.—Let's leave aside all these amenities. Each man states this kind of thing according to his powers.)" In another we see him drop naturally into a dialogue between himself and "us":

We are great fools. "He has spent his life in idleness," we say; "I have done nothing today." What, have you not lived? That is not only the fundamental but the most illustrious of your occupations. "If I had been placed in a position to manage great affairs, I would have shown what I could do." Have you been able to think out and manage your own life? You have done the greatest task of all (435).

Montaigne defends his rambling order in the name of freedom, a kind of poetry, and the author's right to an attentive reader:

I go out of my way, but rather by license than carelessness. My ideas follow one another, but sometimes it is from a distance. . . . I love the poetic gait, by leaps and gambols. . . . It is the inattentive reader who loses my subject, not I. . . .

I want the matter to make its own divisions. It shows well enough where it changes, where it concludes, where it begins, where it resumes, without my interlacing it with words, with links and seams introduced for the benefit of weak or heedless ears, and without writing glosses on myself (373–5).

Montaigne's style is above all savory and concrete with images. As Sainte-Beuve wrote, "His style is a perpetual figure. . . . Thought and image, with him, it is all one." Emerson put it admirably: "Cut these words, and they would bleed; they are vascular and alive." Whatever he touches he vivifies. Here is life in retrospect: "I have seen the grass, the flower, and the fruit; now I see the dryness—

happily, since it is naturally" (351). Since age "puts more wrinkles in our minds than on our faces" (353), here is how the mind should fight back: "Let it grow green, let it flourish meanwhile, if it can, like mistletoe on a dead tree." Here is the effect of little and much learning on our pride: "To really learned men has happened what happens to ears of wheat: they rise high and lofty, heads erect and proud, as long as they are empty; but when they are full and swollen with grain in their ripeness, they begin to grow humble and lower their horns" (227).

Michel de Montaigne was born in 1533 in his father's pleasant château on a vine-covered hill just north of the Dordogne about thirty miles east of Bordeaux. He came from a prominent old Bordeaux family, the Ey-quems, ennobled fifty-six years earlier by the purchase of this "noble house" with the earnings from an international business in fish, woad, and wine. Equally prosperous were his maternal ancestors the Louppes (Lopez), originally Spanish Jews, who numbered more than one victim of the Inquisition and took refuge in Bordeaux and Toulouse as "New Christians." One brother and one sister of Montaigne became Protestants, though he and his parents and the other five children remained Catholic; in an age of religious violence the family atmosphere was tolerant.

Religious controversy formed a dark background to Montaigne's entire life. When he was born, the moderate humanistic reform typified by Erasmus seemed triumphant in France: Francis I, patron of arts and letters, had recently founded the first French nontheological school of higher

education, and Rabelais' best-selling *Pantagruel* had hailed the advent of a new golden age. Within a few years, however, King Francis was persecuting even peaceful Reformists and Calvin was building a stronghold of militant Reform in Geneva. Despite redoubled persecution under Henry II, Protestantism continued to grow, especially in Montaigne's Gascon homeland. Before he was thirty, religious strife had flared into civil war, which continued, active or latent, throughout his life.

Pierre Eyquem de Montaigne, "the best father that ever was," brought up his eldest son with strenuous mildness and hired a tutor and two assistants to see that the boy spoke and heard nothing but Latin until he was six. For the next seven years he shone at the excellent Collège de Guyenne in Bordeaux, where eminent Latinists feared to accost him, and he took leading parts in their Latin plays. However, his main memory is of the seamy side of education: boredom, imprisonment, sadistic cruelty.

In 1554 Montaigne's uncle Pierre de Gaujac bought himself (in the manner of the time) a councillor's post in a new tax court, the Cour des Aides of Périgueux, which he later passed on to Michel. In 1557 the Aides were incorporated into the Parlement of Bordeaux, one of the eight regional branches of *the* Parlement, the king's judicial arm. There Montaigne served for thirteen years, conscientiously but without enthusiasm, increasingly disenchanted with the laws and other products of the human mind. He resigned in 1570.

The only bright spot in the Parlement was his friendship with Etienne de La Boétie, ended after four or five years by the latter's death in 1563. With this high-minded

Christian humanist Montaigne enjoyed a full and frank communication which he keenly missed in later life. The stoical flavor of the earliest essays shows a strong influence of his dead friend.

In 1565 Montaigne married the daughter of a president in the Parlement, Françoise de La Chassaigne. Of the six children she bore him, only one, Léonor (1571–1616), lived beyond infancy. Marriage he never sought; it seemed to him a useful institution for the perpetuation of humanity in which love had no place. He appears to have given and received loyalty—and a little annoyance.

In 1568 Montaigne's father died, leaving him at thirty-five head of the family and lord of the estate. Not long before, he had set him the task of translating into French the Latin *Book of Creatures, or Natural Theology* of the fifteenth-century Spaniard Raymond Sebond, an attempt to demonstrate the existence and nature of God, and man's duties, by analogies drawn from the four levels—inanimate, vegetable, animal, human—of creation. A faithful and skilled translator, Montaigne showed his orthodoxy and his reservations about Sebond by sharply reducing, in translation, the extravagant claims of his author's Prologue that had placed it on the Index of Forbidden Books.[2]

After resigning from the Parlement, Montaigne published many of La Boétie's works, severally, with his own dedications to important persons, then returned to his château and his tower, solemnizing his retirement on his thirty-eighth birthday with a Latin inscription (468) next to his study. His retirement was not complete; he presum-

---

[2] See below, pp. 464–7.

ably earned the Order of Saint Michael and the position of gentleman in ordinary of the chamber to Charles ix, Henry iii, and later Henry of Navarre. Some time between 1572 and 1576 he sought to mediate at court between Navarre and Henri de Guise. Mainly, however, he settled himself in the third-floor book-lined study in his tower, to think and write.

Books i and ii of the *Essays*, in their original form, were written between 1571 and 1580; Book iii and many additions to Books i and ii between 1580 and 1588. From 1588 to his death in 1592 Montaigne wrote no new chapters, but made additions, which constitute nearly one-third of the total bulk of the *Essays*, to those of all three books.

Starting apparently with no clear plan, he found the title of his book, like its central concept, as he wrote, probably around 1577. Many of the earliest chapters, composed around 1572, are impersonal: a few anecdotes and a brief comment. Some, however, such as "That to Philosophize Is to Learn to Die" (8–17), "Of Solitude" (118–31), and "Of the Inconsistency of Our Actions" (142–63), show Montaigne's rather stoical concern with fashioning his character and preparing to meet death bravely with the help of reason and will. Soon, however, he criticizes stoical (and other) heroics as incompatible with consistency, and deflates man's vain notions about his powers. This criticism culminates around 1576 with his vast "Apology for Raymond Sebond" (196–253), in which, largely by the arguments of Pyrrhonistic skepticism, he humbles the presumption of man—at least of man without divine grace—and shows him to be little better or wiser than the animals, devoid and indeed incapable of true knowledge.

The destructiveness of Montaigne's skepticism is partly illusory, however. His Pyrrhonism is more a weapon than a conviction. His point is that we cannot have perfect knowledge, especially of externals; but our capacity for a practical understanding of our nature is clearly implied in his remark: "At least we must become wise at our own expense" (235). If there is anything we can know, it is ourselves. We must learn that we are fallible creatures of flux; but to know this much is something. From now on Montaigne will make himself the main subject of his study and of his book.

Already around 1573 (185) he had proclaimed the value of his study for his life. In "Democritus and Heraclitus" (130–41) he gives a clear account of his new-found "essay" method of self-scrutiny and self-portrayal. "Of Presumption" (254–75) is his first full self-portrait. In the late 1570's, as he looks more and more to himself for guidance, he shows a new optimism. In "The Education of Children" (16–79), faith in our ability to learn replaces the apparent pessimism of the "Apology" and philosophy appears no longer as learning how to die but (61) as learning how to live. Montaigne's confidence that he can meet pain courageously, tested by the onset of the kidney stone in 1578, rings out in the early pages (290–9) of "The Resemblance of Children to Fathers," the final chapter of the first (1580) edition of the *Essays*.

His book published, Montaigne set out on a seventeen-month trip to Rome via the mineral baths of Switzerland, Germany, and Italy. For his own satisfaction, he kept an account—partly with the help of a secretary, partly in Italian—that was discovered and published two centuries

later as the *Travel Journal* (470–9). Called back from Italy to serve as mayor of Bordeaux, he returned expecting to decline; but a polite order from Henry III induced him to accept.

Though Montaigne's account (384–95) of his two terms as mayor (1581–85) defends his detachment, his letters reveal him as a vigilant and conscientious magistrate in a treacherous time when loyalist Bordeaux was constantly threatened by Leaguers and Protestants alike. His term of office was soon followed by a painful period in 1586 while a royal army under the Leaguer Mayenne besieged Protestant Castillon only a few miles away: "I was belabored from every quarter; to the Ghibelline I was a Guelph, to the Guelph a Ghibelline" (397). Then the plague forced him to flee with his family for six months before returning to his château and his book. Busy as the years 1580 to 1588 were, he found time to write the thirteen long chapters of Book III and considerable additions to Books I and II.

Montaigne was in Paris when the first three-book edition of the *Essays* was published there in 1588. His arrival that February on a mission from Henry of Navarre to Henry III was reported as important news by both the English and the Spanish ambassadors. Navarre, the Protestant leader, was heir apparent to the throne of France. Henry III supported his claim but sought his conversion. The League opposed Navarre and pressed the king to disown him. Montaigne, a friend of Navarre and a loyal servant of Henry III, sought to cement the uneasy understanding between the two.

For most of 1588 Montaigne followed the court from

Paris to Chartres, Rouen, and finally Blois, where the king, frustrated at Guise's control over the Estates-General, had his League rival assassinated—as the king himself was soon to be. Montaigne's last few years were spent mainly at home, though two letters of 1590 to Henry IV (484–93) show that only accident and illness kept him from joining his new king, whom he had hoped to serve as a candid, untitled adviser. He wrote a great deal in his *Essays*—no new chapters but many massive additions. In his sixtieth year his health gave out; a throat inflammation, added to the kidney stone and other ailments, brought him on September 13, 1592, to a peaceful and Christian death.

Montaigne's final writings—Book III of the *Essays* and the additions to the chapters of Books I and II—are full of slowly won confidence in himself, in man, and in life. Before 1580 he had been almost obsessed by diversity, finding little else in individuals and in mankind. Now he finds a constant "ruling pattern" in each man and with it "the entire form of man's estate" (333, 315). Now he sees nature's ingenious balance between diversity and unity: "If our faces were not similar, we could not distinguish man from beast; if they were not dissimilar, we could not distinguish man from man" (411). Now he has reached many conclusions, for others as well as for himself.

These cover a wide range, but center in human life and how it should be lived. "The main responsibility of each of us is his own conduct; and that is what we are here for" (389). For Montaigne the basic fact about us is that we are neither brutes nor angels, but men; neither body nor soul, but both. These two parts which constitute our being are equals and should be friends. Our capacity

for change is very limited; we cannot even wholly will to become very different; yet we perversely set ourselves standards that we cannot meet. "They want to get out of themselves and escape from the man. That is madness: instead of changing into angels, they change into beasts . . ." (457–9).

Montaigne never ceases to recognize the absurdity of man, "the investigator without knowledge, the magistrate without jurisdiction, and all in all, the fool of the farce" (379). Not only are our pleasures "virtually nothing but wind"; alas, "we are all wind." But this must lead us to accept, not to reject, ourselves: "the most barbarous of our maladies is to despise our being" (433, 443). We must learn that pleasure and pain are interdependent, receive them contentedly, and harmonize them. A grateful acceptance of human nature and human life on their own terms is, for Montaigne, the key to our greatest achievement, appropriate living: "There is nothing so beautiful and legitimate as to play the man well and properly. . . . It is an absolute perfection and virtually divine to know how to enjoy our being rightfully. . . . Our great and glorious masterpiece is to live appropriately" (443, 459, 435–7). It is also the key to wisdom and happiness:

As for me, then, I love life and cultivate it just as God has been pleased to grant it to us. . . . We wrong that great and all-powerful Giver by refusing his gift, nullifying it, and disfiguring it. Himself all good, he has made all things good (451).

DONALD M. FRAME
Columbia University

xvii

Note on the Text

The basic text used here is the Bordeaux Copy of the fifth (1588) edition of the *Essais*, which Montaigne, with his own hand, marked "sixth edition" and covered with handwritten additions. It has been reproduced phototypically by Fortunat Strowski (Paris: Hachette, 1912). Since a heedless binder long ago cut out some of Montaigne's additions in trimming the pages of the Bordeaux Copy, the 1595 edition by Marie de Gournay, based on a copy of Montaigne's additions but not always completely reliable, has been used to supplement the other. The Municipal Edition by Strowski and others (Bordeaux: Pech, 1906–33, 5 vols.) gives all the variants of the manuscript additions and the 1588 text, and much of the 1580 text, which may be found in full in the Dezeimeris and Barckhausen edition (Bordeaux: Gounouilhou, 1870–3, 2 vols.). A few of the most interesting variants are given in the notes of the present volume.

The superscript letters $^{A\ B\ C}$ in the text introduce and distinguish material belonging to the three main and certain strata in which the *Essais* were composed:

^{A} introduces material published before 1588, mainly in 1580;

^{B} introduces material first published in 1588;

^{C} introduces material first published after 1588.

xix

Thus the original text of Books I and II (published 1580) is the ^A^ stratum, that of Book III (published 1588) part of the ^B^ stratum. All ^C^ material and all ^B^ material in Books I and II constitute additions to Montaigne's original text. Since many of his views and attitudes changed during the twenty years (1572-92) from when he started to write the *Essais* until his death, and since he intended his book as a record of change, making it his principle to add to but not to alter what he had once written, his additions sometimes clash with his initial text and—for the attentive reader who is unaware of the strata of composition— give a false impression that Montaigne is irresponsibly inconsistent.

The French text of the selections offered here follows very closely that of my *Selected Works* of Montaigne, now out of print, in Harper's French Masterworks series (New York: Harper & Brothers, 1953). The English translation, which is my own, first appeared entire in Montaigne, *The Complete Works* (Stanford, Calif.: Stanford University Press, 1957). Parts of it had been published earlier in the Classics Club edition of *Selected Essays* (New York: Walter J. Black, 1943) and the Crofts Classics edition of *Selections from the Essays* of Montaigne (New York: Appleton-Century-Crofts, 1948). I am indebted to all these publishers for their courtesy in allowing me to republish these materials in the present form.

The spelling of the French has been modernized—except for respecting Montaigne's preference for approximately the original forms of Greek and Latin proper names—and so has the punctuation. A glossary at the end lists the most frequently found French words now obsolete

or changed in meaning. The following table shows some of the main ways in which Montaigne's sixteenth-century French differs from modern usage.

Adjectives more often precede nouns.

Adjectives and adverbs often form the superlative with *plus* alone (not *le plus*) or *moins* (not *le moins*).

Articles (definite or indefinite) are more often omitted.

Genders of nouns are often different, often variable. (Arbitrarily, I have usually changed these to the modern gender when only one other word was affected; otherwise not.)

Infinitives are very often used as masculine nouns.

In negations, either *ne* or *pas* is often omitted.

Past participle agreement is freer and more capricious.

Personal pronoun subjects are often omitted.

Prepositions linking inflected verbs with infinitives are more optional and variable. (Montaigne uses both *jouir* and *jouir de*, and sometimes follows the same verb in the same sentence with both *à* and *de*.)

Pronoun objects of infinitives that directly follow other verbs usually precede both verbs.

Relative and interrogative pronouns as objects of prepositions are more variable, with *quoi* very common.

The subjunctive is often used after affirmative verbs of opinion; in the imperfect and pluperfect it is very common in both parts of contrary-to-fact conditional sentences. In some constructions (like concessive clauses) it is often not used.

Verbs: agreement in number with subject is much freer.

Word order: inversion of subject and verb is very common.

Selected Bibliography

EDITIONS

Essais. Ed. by Fortunat Strowski *et al*. 5 vols. Bordeaux: Pech, 1906–33 ("Edition Municipale"). Gives text of the Bordeaux Copy, with all 1588 variants and MS corrections.

Essais. Ed. by Fortunat Strowski. 1024 plates. Paris: Hachette, 1912. Phototypic reproduction of Bordeaux Copy showing all Montaigne's MS additions of 1588–92.

Essais. Ed. by Dezeimeris and Barckhausen. 2 vols. Bordeaux: Gounouilhou, 1870–3. Gives text of 1580 edition, shows place of later variants.

Essais. Ed. by Albert Thibaudet. Paris: Gallimard, 1934; reprinted, with different pagination, 1950. Pléiade edition. The handiest of all and the best all-round edition currently available.

Journal de voyage, Traduction de la Théologie naturelle de Raimond Sebond, Lettres. Ed. by Arthur Armaingaud. 5 vols. Paris: Conard, 1928–39. (Vols. VII–XI of Œuvres complètes.)

The Complete Works. Tr. by Donald M. Frame. Stanford, Calif.: Stanford University Press, 1957.

The Essays. Tr. by Jacob Zeitlin. 3 vols. New York: Knopf, 1934–6. Excellent introduction and notes.

xxiii

Auerbach, Erich. "L'Humaine Condition," in *Mimesis,* tr. by Willard R. Trask. Princeton University Press, 1953. Pp. 285–311.

Buffum, Imbrie. *Studies in the Baroque from Montaigne to Rotrou.* New Haven: Yale University Press, 1957.

Dreano, Mathurin. *La Pensée religieuse de Montaigne.* Paris: Beauchesne, 1936.

Emerson, Ralph Waldo. "Montaigne; or, the Skeptic," in *Representative Men.*

Frame, Donald M. *Montaigne's Discovery of Man: The Humanization of a Humanist.* New York: Columbia University Press, 1955.

Friedrich, Hugo. *Montaigne.* Bern: Francke, 1949. (In German.)

Gide, André. "Presenting Montaigne," tr. by Dorothy Bussy, in *The Living Thoughts of Montaigne.* New York and Toronto: Longmans, Green, 1939. Pp. 1–27.

Lanson, Gustave, *Les Essais de Montaigne: étude et analyse.* Paris: Mellottée [1930].

Lüthy, Herbert. "Montaigne, or the Art of Being Truthful," *Encounter,* November, 1953, pp. 33–44.

Moreau, Pierre. *Montaigne, l'homme et l'œuvre.* Paris: Boivin [1939].

Plattard, Jean. *Montaigne et son temps.* Paris: Boivin, 1933.

Poulet, Georges. "Montaigne," in *Studies in Human Time,* tr. by Elliott Coleman. Baltimore: Johns Hopkins University Press, 1956.

Sainte-Beuve C.-A. Chapters and articles on Montaigne in *Port-Royal*, Vol. II; *Causeries du lundi*, Vol. IV; *Nouveaux Lundis*, Vols. II, VI.

Strawn, Richard R., and Samuel F. Will. "Michel Eyquem de Montaigne," in Vol. II (*Sixteenth Century*) of D. C. Cabeen, *A Critical Bibliography of French Literature* (Syracuse, N. Y.: Syracuse University Press, 1956). Pp. 155–87, 314.

Strowski, Fortunat. *Montaigne*. Paris: Alcan, 1906. 2nd ed. 1931.

—— *Montaigne, sa vie publique et privée*. Paris: Nouvelle Revue Critique, 1938.

Villey, Pierre. *Les Essais de Michel de Montaigne*. Paris: Sfelt, 1932.

——— *Les Sources et l'évolution des Essais de Montaigne*. 2 vols. Paris: Hachette, 1908. 2nd ed. 1933.

Woolf, Virginia. "Montaigne," in *The Common Reader*. New York: Harcourt, Brace, 1948. Pp. 87–100.

Table

ESSAIS

Au Lecteur   2

LIVRE PREMIER

Chapitre

8	De l'oisiveté	4
20	Que philosopher c'est apprendre à mourir †	8
26	De l'institution des enfants †	16
31	Des cannibales	78
39	De la solitude †	118
50	De Démocritus et Héraclitus	130

LIVRE SECOND

1	De l'inconstance de nos actions	142
6	De l'exercitation	162
12	Apologie de Raimond Sebond †	198
17	De la présomption †	254
18	Du démentir	274
37	De la ressemblance des enfants aux pères †	288

xxvi

Contents

INTRODUCTION   v

NOTE ON THE TEXT   xix

SELECTED BIBLIOGRAPHY   xxiii

ESSAYS

To the Reader   3

BOOK ONE

Chapter

8   *Of Idleness*   5
20   *That to Philosophize Is to Learn to Die* †   9
26   *Of the Education of Children* †   17
31   *Of Cannibals*   79
39   *Of Solitude* †   119
50   *Of Democritus and Heraclitus*   131

BOOK TWO

1   *Of the Inconsistency of Our Actions*   143
6   *Of Practice*   163
12   *Apology for Raymond Sebond* †   199
17   *Of Presumption* †   255
18   *Of Giving the Lie*   275
37   *Of the Resemblance of Children to
      Fathers* †   289

LIVRE TROISIÈME

2   *Du repentir*   312
9   *De la vanité* †   354
10   *De ménager sa volonté* †   378
12   *De la physionomie* †   394
13   *De l'expérience* †   406

PAGES CHOISIES

Traduction de la Théologie Naturelle de
  Raimond Sebond †   464
Inscription latine commémorant la
  retraite de Montaigne   468
Journal de Voyage †   470
Lettres
  À *son père: Sur la mort de La Boétie* † 480
  Au Roi Henri IV   484
  Au Roi Henri IV   490

† Extracts.

xxviii

BOOK THREE

2	*Of Repentance*	313
9	*Of Vanity* †	355
10	*Of Husbanding Your Will* †	379
12	*Of Physiognomy* †	395
13	*Of Experience* †	407

SELECTED WRITINGS

Translation of the Natural Theology of Raymond Sebond †	465
Latin Inscription Commemorating Montaigne's Retirement	469
Travel Journal †	471
Letters	
To His Father: On the Death of La Boétie †	481
To King Henry IV	485
To King Henry IV	491

GLOSSARY 494

† Extracts.

Essais

Essays

[A]C'est ici un livre de bonne foi, lecteur. Il t'avertit dès l'entrée que je ne m'y suis proposé aucune fin, que domestique et privée. Je n'y ai eu nulle considération de ton service, ni de ma gloire. Mes forces ne sont pas capables d'un tel dessein. Je l'ai voué à la commodité particulière de mes parents et amis: à ce que m'ayant perdu (ce qu'ils ont à faire bientôt) ils y puissent retrouver aucuns traits de mes conditions et humeurs, et que par ce moyen ils nourrissent plus entière et plus vive la connaissance qu'ils ont eue de moi.

Si c'eût été pour rechercher la faveur du monde, je me fusse mieux paré, et me présenterais en une marche étudiée. Je veux qu'on m'y voie en ma façon simple, naturelle et ordinaire, sans contention et artifice: car c'est moi que je peins. Mes défauts s'y liront au vif, et ma forme naïve, autant que la révérence publique me l'a permis. Que si j'eusse été entre ces nations qu'on dit vivre encore sous la douce liberté des premières lois de nature, je t'assure que je m'y fusse très volontiers peint tout entier, et tout nu.

Ainsi, lecteur, je suis moi-même la matière de mon livre: ce n'est pas raison que tu emploies ton loisir en un sujet si frivole et si vain.

A Dieu donc, de Montaigne, ce premier de mars mil cinq cent quatre-vingts.

---

[1] Montaigne's preface was presumably written at the 1580 date that he gives. Therefore it tells us not his original plan but his final one before publication.

TO THE READER [1]

[A]This book was written in good faith, reader. It warns you from the outset that in it I have set myself no goal but a domestic and private one. I have had no thought of serving either you or my own glory. My powers are inadequate for such a purpose. I have dedicated it to the private convenience of my relatives and friends, so that when they have lost me (as soon they must), they may recover here some features of my habits and temperament, and by this means keep the knowledge they have had of me more complete and alive.

If I had written to seek the world's favor, I should have bedecked myself better, and should present myself in a studied posture. I want to be seen here in my simple, natural, ordinary fashion, without straining or artifice; for it is myself that I portray. My defects will here be read to the life, and also my natural form, as far as respect for the public has allowed. Had I been placed among those nations which are said to live still in the sweet freedom of nature's first laws, I assure you I should very gladly have portrayed myself here entire and wholly naked.

Thus, reader, I am myself the matter of my book; you would be unreasonable to spend your leisure on so frivolous and vain a subject.

So farewell. Montaigne, this first day of March, fifteen hundred and eighty.

Livre Premier

8 De l'oisiveté [1]

^AComme nous voyons des terres oisives, si elles sont grasses et fertiles, foisonner en cent mille sortes d'herbes sauvages et inutiles, et que pour les tenir en office, il les faut assujettir et employer à certaines semences, pour notre service; et comme nous voyons que les femmes produisent bien toutes seules des amas et pièces de chair informes, mais que pour faire une génération bonne et naturelle, il les faut embesogner d'une autre semence: ainsi est-il des esprits. Si on ne les occupe à certain sujet, qui les bride et contraigne, ils se jettent déréglés, par-ci par-là, dans le vague champ des imaginations,

> ^BSicut aquæ tremulum labris ubi lumen ahenis
> Sole repercussum, aut radiantis imagine Lunæ
> Omnia pervolitat late loca, jamque sub auras
> Erigitur, summique ferit laquearia tecti.[2]

---

[1] Composed around 1572, this chapter may have been in effect Montaigne's first preface.

4

Book One

8   Of Idleness [1]

^AJust as we see that fallow land, if rich and fertile, teems with a hundred thousand kinds of wild and useless weeds, and that to set it to work we must subject it and sow it with certain seeds for our service; and as we see that women, all alone, produce mere shapeless masses and lumps of flesh, but that to create a good and natural offspring they must be made fertile with a different kind of seed; so it is with minds. Unless you keep them busy with some definite subject that will bridle and control them, they throw themselves in disorder hither and yon in the vague field of imagination.

> ^BThus, in a brazen urn, the water's light
> Trembling reflects the sun's and moon's bright rays,
> And, darting here and there in aimless flight,
> Rises aloft, and on the ceiling plays. [2]

---

[2] Virgil, *Aeneid*, VIII, 22–25.

ᴬEt n'est folie ni rêverie, qu'ils ne produisent en cette agitation,

> velut ægri somnia, vanæ
> Finguntur species.³

L'âme qui n'a point de but établi, elle se perd: car comme on dit, c'est n'être en aucun lieu que d'être partout.

ᴮQuisquis ubique habitat, Maxime, nusquam habitat.⁴

ᴬDernièrement que je me retirai chez moi, délibéré, autant que je pourrais, ne me mêler d'autre chose que de passer en repos et à part ce peu qui me reste de vie, il me semblait ne pouvoir faire plus grande faveur à mon esprit que de le laisser, en pleine oisiveté, s'entretenir soi-même, et s'arrêter et rasseoir en soi: ce que j'espérais qu'il pût meshui faire plus aisément, devenu avec le temps plus pesant et plus mûr. Mais je trouve—

> variam semper dant otia mentem ⁵

—qu'au rebours, faisant le cheval échappé, il se donne cent fois plus d'affaire à soi-même qu'il n'en prenait pour autrui; et m'enfante tant de chimères et monstres fantasques les uns sur les autres, sans ordre et sans propos, que pour en contempler à mon aise l'ineptie et l'étrangeté, j'ai commencé de les mettre en rôle, espérant avec le temps lui en faire honte à lui-même.

---

³ Horace, *Ars Poetica*, 7–8.
⁴ Martial, *Epigrams*, vii, lxxiii, 6.

^AAnd there is no mad or idle fancy that they do not bring forth in this agitation:

> Like a sick man's dreams,
> They form vain visions.[3]

The soul that has no fixed goal loses itself; for as they say, to be everywhere is to be nowhere:

^BHe who dwells everywhere, Maximus, nowhere dwells.[4]

^ALately when I retired to my home, determined so far as possible to bother about nothing except spending the little life I have left in rest and seclusion, it seemed to me I could do my mind no greater favor than to let it entertain itself in full idleness and stay and settle in itself, which I hoped it might do more easily now, having become weightier and riper with time. But I find—

> Ever idle hours breed wandering thoughts [5]

—that, on the contrary, like a runaway horse, it gives itself a hundred times more trouble than it took for others, and gives birth to so many chimeras and fantastic monsters, one after another, without order or purpose, that in order to contemplate their ineptitude and strangeness at my pleasure, I have begun to put them in writing, hoping in time to make my mind ashamed of itself.

---

[5] Lucan, *Pharsalia*, IV, 704.

[I:8] *Of Idleness*

[A]Cicéron dit que philosopher ce n'est autre chose que s'apprêter à la mort. C'est d'autant que l'étude et la contemplation retirent aucunement notre âme hors de nous et l'embesognent à part du corps, qui est quelque apprentissage et ressemblance de la mort; ou bien c'est que toute la sagesse et discours du monde se résout enfin à ce point, de nous apprendre à ne craindre point à mourir.

. . . Toutes les règles se rencontrent et conviennent à cet article. Et bien qu'elles nous conduisent aussi toutes d'un commun accord à mépriser la douleur, la pauvreté, et autres accidents à quoi la vie humaine est sujette, ce n'est pas d'un pareil soin, tant parce que ces accidents ne sont pas de telle nécessité (la plupart des hommes passent leur vie sans goûter de la pauvreté, et tels encore sans sentiment de douleur et de maladie, comme Xénophilus le Musicien, qui vécut cent et six ans d'une entière santé), qu'aussi d'autant qu'au pis aller la mort peut mettre fin, quand il nous plaira, et couper broche à tous autres inconvénients. Mais quant à la mort, elle est inévitable.

[B]Omnes eodem cogimur, omnium
Versatur urna, serius ocius
Sors exitura et nos in æter-
Num exitium impositura cymbæ.[2]

[A]Et par conséquent, si elle nous fait peur, c'est un sujet

---

[1] A statement of Montaigne's clearly dates part, and probably most, of this essay at 1572.

20 *That to Philosophize Is to Learn to Die* [1]

ᴬCicero says that to philosophize is nothing else but to pre-
pare for death. This is because study and contemplation
draw our soul out of us to some extent and keep it busy
outside the body; which is a sort of apprenticeship and
semblance of death. Or else it is because all the wisdom
and reasoning in the world boils down finally to this
point: to teach us not to be afraid to die.

. . . All rules meet and agree at this point. And though
they all with one accord lead us also to scorn pain, poverty,
and other accidents to which human life is subject, it is
not with equal insistence; partly because these accidents
are not so inevitable (most men spend their life without
tasting poverty, and some also without feeling pain and
illness, like Xenophilus the musician, who lived a hundred
and six years in complete health), and also because at
worst, whenever we please, death can put an end, and
deny access, to all our other woes. But as for death itself,
it is inevitable.

> ᴮWe are all forced down the same road. Our fate,
> Tossed in the urn, will spring out soon or late,
> And force us helpless into Charon's bark,
> Passengers destined for eternal dark.[2]

ᴬAnd consequently, if it frightens us, it is a continual

---

[2] Horace, *Odes*, ɪɪ, iii, 25–28.

continuel de tourment, et qui ne se peut aucunement soulager. ^CIl n'est lieu d'où elle ne nous vienne; nous pouvons tourner sans cesse la tête çà et là comme en pays suspect: *quæ quasi saxum Tantalo semper impendet.*[3] ^ANos parlements renvoient souvent exécuter les criminels au lieu où le crime est commis: durant le chemin, promenez-les par des belles maisons, faites-leur tant de bonne chère qu'il vous plaira,

> ^Bnon Siculæ dapes
> Dulcem elaborabunt saporem,
> Non avium cytharæque cantus
> Somnum reducent,[3a]

^Apensez-vous qu'ils s'en puissent réjouir, et que la finale intention de leur voyage, leur étant ordinairement devant les yeux, ne leur ait altéré et affadi le goût à toutes ces commodités?

> ^BAudit iter, numeratque dies, spacioque viarum
> Metitur vitam, torquetur peste futura.[4]

^ALe but de notre carrière, c'est la mort, c'est l'objet nécessaire de notre visée: si elle nous effraie, comme est-il possible d'aller un pas en avant, sans fièvre? Le remède du vulgaire, c'est de n'y penser pas. Mais de quelle brutale stupidité lui peut venir un si grossier aveuglement? Il lui faut faire brider l'âne par la queue,

> Qui capite ipse suo instituit vestigia retro.[5]

---

3 Cicero, *De Finibus*, I, xviii.
3a Horace, *Odes*, III, i, 18–21.

source of torment which cannot be alleviated at all. ᶜThere is no place from which it may not come to us; we may turn our heads constantly this way and that as in a suspicious country: *death always hangs over us, like the stone over Tantalus.*³ ᴬOur law courts often send criminals to be executed at the place where the crime was committed. On the way, take them past beautiful houses, give them as good a time as you like—

> ᴮNot even a Sicilian feast
> Can now produce for him a pleasant taste,
> Nor song of birds, nor music of the lyre
> Restore his sleep ³ᵃ

—ᴬdo you think that they can rejoice in these things, and that the final purpose of their trip, being steadily before their eyes, will not have changed and spoiled their taste for all these pleasures?

> ᴮHe hears it as it comes, counts days, measures the breath
> Of life upon their length, tortured by coming death.⁴

ᴬThe goal of our career is death. It is the necessary object of our aim. If it frightens us, how is it possible to go a step forward without feverishness? The remedy of the common herd is not to think about it. But from what brutish stupidity can come so gross a blindness! They have to bridle the ass by the tail,

> Who sets his mind on moving only backward.⁵

---

⁴ Claudian, *In Rufinum*, ɪɪ, 137–8.
⁵ Lucretius, *De Rerum Natura*, ɪv, 472.

[I:20] *That to Philosophize*

Ce n'est pas de merveille s'il est si souvent pris au piège. . . .

Qu'importe-t-il, me direz-vous, comment que ce soit, pourvu qu'on ne s'en donne point de peine? Je suis de cet avis, et en quelque manière qu'on se puisse mettre à l'abri des coups, fût-ce sous la peau d'un veau, je ne suis pas homme qui y reculasse. Car il me suffit de passer à mon aise; et le meilleur jeu que je me puisse donner, je le prends, si peu glorieux au reste et exemplaire que vous voudrez,

> præterim delirus inersque videri,
> Dum mea delectent mala me, vel denique fallant,
> Quam sapere et ringi.[6]

Mais c'est folie d'y penser arriver par là. Ils vont, ils viennent, ils trottent, ils dansent, de mort nulles nouvelles. Tout cela est beau. Mais aussi quand elle arrive, ou à eux, ou à leurs femmes, enfants et amis, les surprenant en dessoude et à découvert, quels tourments, quels cris, quelle rage, et quel désespoir les accable! Vîtes-vous jamais rien si rabaissé, si changé, si confus? Il y faut pourvoir de meilleure heure: et cette nonchalance bestiale, quand elle pourrait loger en la tête d'un homme d'entendement, ce que je trouve entièrement impossible, nous vend trop cher ses denrées. Si c'était ennemi qui se peut éviter, je conseillerais d'emprunter les armes de la couardise. Mais puisqu'il ne se peut, Bpuisqu'il vous attrape fuyant et poltron aussi bien qu'honnête homme,

> ANempe et fugacem persequitur virum,
> Nec parcit imbellis juventæ
> Poplitibus, timidoque tergo,[7]

---

[6] Horace, *Epistles*, ii, ii, 126–8.

It is no wonder they are so often caught in the trap. . . .

What does it matter, you will tell me, how it happens, provided we do not worry about it? I am of that opinion; and in whatever way we can put ourselves in shelter from blows, even under a calf's skin, I am not the man to shrink from it. For it is enough for me to spend my life comfortably; and the best game I can give myself I'll take, though it be as little glorious and exemplary as you like:

> If but my faults could trick and please
> My wits, I'd rather seem a fool, at ease,
> Than to be wise and rage.[6]

But it is folly to expect to get there that way. They go, they come, they trot, they dance—of death no news. All that is fine. But when it comes, either to them or to their wives, children, or friends, surprising them unprepared and defenseless, what torments, what cries, what frenzy, what despair overwhelms them! Did you ever see anything so dejected, so changed, so upset? We must provide for this earlier; and this brutish nonchalance, even if it could lodge in the head of a man of understanding—which I consider entirely impossible—sells us its wares too dear. If it were an enemy we could avoid, I would advise us to borrow the arms of cowardice. But since that cannot be, ^Bsince it catches you just the same, whether you flee like a coward or act like a man—

> ^AAs surely it pursues the man that flees,
> Nor does it spare the haunches slack
> Of warless youth, or its timid back [7]

---

[7] Horace, *Odes*, III, ii, 14–16.

[I:20] *That to Philosophize*

^Bet que nulle trempe de cuirasse vous couvre,

> Ille licet ferro cautus se condat ære,
> Mors tamen inclusum protrahet inde caput,[8]

^Aapprenons à le soutenir de pied ferme, et à le combattre. Et pour commencer à lui ôter son plus grand avantage contre nous, prenons voie toute contraire à la commune. Otons-lui l'etrangeté, pratiquons-le, accoutumons-le, n'ayons rien si souvent en la tête que la mort. A tous instants représentons-la à notre imagination et en tous visages.

. . . Il n'est rien de quoi je me sois dès toujours plus entretenu que des imaginations de la mort: voire en la saison la plus licencieuse de mon âge,

> ^BJucundum cum ætas florida ver ageret,[9]

^Aparmi les dames et les jeux, tel me pensait empêché à digérer à part moi quelque jalousie, ou l'incertitude de quelque espérance, cependant que je m'entretenais de je ne sais qui, surpris les jours précédents d'une fièvre chaude et de sa fin, au partir d'une fête pareille, et la tête pleine d'oisiveté, d'amour et de bon temps, comme moi, et qu'autant m'en pendait à l'oreille:

> ^BJam fuerit, nec post unquam revocare licebit.[10]

^AJe ne ridais non plus le front de ce pensement-là que

---

⁸ Propertius, *Elegies*, iii, xviii, 25–26.
⁹ Catullus, *Poems*, lxviii, 16.

—^Band since no kind of armor protects you—

> Hide as he will, cautious, in steel and brass,
> Still death will drag his head outside at last [8]

—^Alet us learn to meet it steadfastly and to combat it. And to begin to strip it of its greatest advantage against us, let us take an entirely different way from the usual one. Let us rid it of its strangeness, come to know it, get used to it. Let us have nothing on our minds as often as death. At every moment let us picture it in our imagination in all its aspects.

. . . Since my earliest days, there is nothing with which I have occupied my mind more than with images of death. Even in the most licentious season of my life,

> ^BWhen blooming youth enjoyed a gladsome spring, [9]

^Aamid ladies and games, someone would think me involved in digesting some jealousy by myself, or the uncertainty of some hope, while I was thinking about I don't remember whom, who had been overtaken a few days before by a hot fever and by death, on leaving a similar feast, his head full of idleness, love, and a good time, like myself; and thinking that the same chance was hanging from my ear:

> ^BAnd soon it will have been, past any man's recall. [10]

^AI did not wrinkle my forehead any more over that

---

[10] Lucretius, *De Rerum Natura*, III, 915.

[I:20] *That to Philosophize*

d'un autre. Il est impossible que d'arrivée nous ne sentions des piqûres de telles imaginations. Mais en les maniant et repassant, au long aller, on les apprivoise sans doute. Autrement de ma part je fusse en continuelle frayeur et frénésie: car jamais homme ne se défia tant de sa vie, jamais homme ne fit moins d'état de sa durée. . . .

26 De l'institution des enfants [1]

A MADAME DIANE DE FOIX, *Comtesse de Gurson*

ᴬJe ne vis jamais père, pour teigneux ou bossé que fût son fils, qui laissât de l'avouer. Non pourtant, s'il n'est du tout enivré de cette affection, qu'il ne s'aperçoive de sa défaillance; mais tant y a qu'il est sien. Aussi moi je vois mieux que tout autre que ce ne sont ici que rêveries d'homme qui n'a goûté des sciences que la croûte première, en son enfance, et n'en a retenu qu'un général et informe visage: un peu de chaque chose et rien du tout, à la française. Car en somme, je sais qu'il y a une Médecine, une Jurisprudence, quatre parties en la Mathématique, et grossièrement ce à quoi elles visent. ᶜEt à l'aventure encore sais-je la prétention des sciences en général au

---

[1] Composed in 1579 or 1580.

thought than any other. It is impossible that we should fail to feel the sting of such notions at first. But by handling them and going over them, in the long run we tame them beyond question. Otherwise for my part I should be in continual fright and frenzy; for never did a man so distrust his life, never did a man set less faith in his duration. . . .

26 *Of the Education of Children* [1]

TO MADAME DIANE DE FOIX, *Comtesse de Gurson*

[A]I have never seen a father who failed to claim his son, however mangy or hunchbacked he was. Not that he does not perceive his defect, unless he is utterly intoxicated by his affection; but the fact remains that the boy is his. And so I myself see better than anyone else that these are nothing but reveries of a man who has tasted only the outer crust of sciences in his childhood, and has retained only a vague general picture of them: a little of everything and nothing thoroughly, French style. For to sum up, I know that there is such a thing as medicine, jurisprudence, four parts in mathematics, and roughly what they aim at. [C]And perhaps I also know the service that the sciences in general

service de notre vie. ᴬMais d'y enfoncer plus avant, de m'être rongé les ongles à l'étude d'Aristote, ᶜmonarque de la doctrine moderne, ᴬou opiniâtré après quelque science, je ne l'ai jamais fait; ᶜni n'est art de quoi je susse peindre seulement les premiers linéaments. Et n'est enfant des classes moyennes qui ne se puisse dire plus savant que moi, qui n'ai seulement pas de quoi l'examiner sur sa première leçon, au moins selon icelle. Et si l'on m'y force, je suis contraint, assez ineptement, d'en tirer quelque matière de propos universel, sur quoi j'examine son jugement naturel: leçon qui leur est autant inconnue, comme à moi la leur.

Je n'ai dressé commerce avec aucun livre solide, sinon Plutarque et Sénèque,[2] où je puise comme les Danaïdes, remplissant et versant sans cesse. J'en attache quelque chose à ce papier; à moi, si peu que rien.

ᴬL'histoire, c'est plus mon gibier, ou la poésie, que j'aime d'une particulière inclination. Car, comme disait Cléanthès, tout ainsi que la voix, contrainte dans l'étroit canal d'une trompette, sort plus aiguë et plus forte, ainsi me semble-t-il que la sentence, pressée aux pieds nombreux de la poésie, s'élance bien plus brusquement et me fiert d'une plus vive secousse. Quant aux facultés naturelles qui sont en moi, de quoi c'est ici l'essai, je les sens fléchir sous la charge. Mes conceptions et mon jugement ne marche[3] qu'à tâtons, chancelant, bronchant et choppant; et quand je suis allé le plus avant que je puis, si ne me suis-

---

2 Plutarch of Chaeronea (c. 46–c. 120) and the younger Lucius Annaeus Seneca ("the Philosopher": c. 4 B.C.–65 A.D.) were Montaigne's favorite authors. The latter's *Epistles* he read in the original Latin, the former's *Lives* and *Moralia* in Jacques Amyot's French

aim to contribute to our life. ᴬBut as for plunging in deeper, or gnawing my nails over the study of Aristotle, ᶜmonarch of modern learning, ᴬor stubbornly pursuing some part of knowledge, I have never done it; ᶜnor is there an art of which I could sketch even the outlines. There is not a child halfway through school who cannot claim to be more learned than I, who have not even the equipment to examine him on his first lesson, at least according to that lesson. And if they force me to, I am constrained, rather ineptly, to draw from it some matter of universal scope, on which I test the boy's natural judgment: a lesson as strange to them as theirs is to me.

I have not had regular dealings with any solid book, except Plutarch and Seneca,[2] from whom I draw like the Danaïds, incessantly filling up and pouring out. Some of this sticks to this paper; to myself, little or nothing.

ᴬHistory is more my quarry, or poetry, which I love with particular affection. For as Cleanthes said, just as sound, when pent up in the narrow channel of a trumpet, comes out sharper and stronger, so it seems to me that a thought, when compressed into the numbered feet of poetry, springs forth much more violently and strikes me a much stiffer jolt. As for the natural faculties that are in me, of which this book is the essay, I feel them bending under the load. My conceptions and my judgment move [3] only by groping, staggering, stumbling, and blundering; and when I have gone ahead as far as I can, still I am

translations (1559 and 1572) from the Greek.

[3] As will often be seen in these pages, but generally not explained, Montaigne frequently makes his verb agree with the last-named subject, disregarding earlier ones.

[I:26] *Education of Children*

je aucunement satisfait: je vois encore du pays au delà, mais d'une vue trouble et en nuage, que je ne puis démêler. Et, entreprenant de parler indifféremment de tout ce qui se présente à ma fantaisie et n'y employant que mes propres et naturels moyens, s'il m'advient, comme il fait souvent, de rencontrer de fortune dans les bons auteurs ces mêmes lieux que j'ai entrepris de traiter, comme je viens de faire chez Plutarque tout présentement son discours de la force de l'imagination: à me reconnaître, au prix de ces gens-là, si faible et si chétif, si pesant et si endormi, je me fais pitié ou dédain à moi-même. Si me gratifié-je de ceci, que mes opinions ont cet honneur de rencontrer souvent aux leurs; ᶜet que je vais au moins de loin après, disant que voire. ᴬAussi que j'ai cela, qu'un chacun n'a pas, de connaître l'extrême différence d'entre eux et moi. Et laisse ce néanmoins courir mes inventions ainsi faibles et basses, comme je les ai produites, sans en replâtrer et recoudre les défauts que cette comparaison m'y a découvert. ᶜIl faut avoir les reins bien fermes pour entreprendre de marcher front à front avec ces gens-là. ᴬLes écrivains indiscrets de notre siècle, qui, parmi leurs ouvrages de néant, vont semant des lieux entiers des anciens auteurs pour se faire honneur, font le contraire. Car cette infinie dissemblance de lustres rend un visage si pâle, si terni et si laid à ce qui est leur qu'ils y perdent beaucoup plus qu'ils n'y gagnent.

ᶜC'était deux contraires fantaisies. Le philosophe Chrysippus mêlait à ses livres non les passages seulement, mais des ouvrages entiers d'autres auteurs, et en un la *Médée* d'Euripidès: et disait Apollodorus que, qui en

not at all satisfied: I can still see country beyond, but with a dim and clouded vision, so that I cannot clearly distinguish it. And when I undertake to speak indiscriminately of everything that comes to my fancy without using any but my own natural resources, if I happen, as I often do, to come across in the good authors those same subjects I have attempted to treat—as in Plutarch I have just this very moment come across his discourse on the power of imagination—seeing myself so weak and puny, so heavy and sluggish, in comparison with those men, I hold myself in pity and disdain.

Still I am pleased at this, that my opinions have the honor of often coinciding with theirs, ᶜand that at least I go the same way, though far behind them, saying "How true!" ᴬAlso that I have this, which not everyone has, that I know the vast difference between them and me. And nonetheless I let my thoughts run on, weak and lowly as they are, as I have produced them, without plastering and sewing up the flaws that this comparison has revealed to me. ᶜOne needs very strong loins to undertake to march abreast of those men. ᴬThe undiscerning writers of our century who amid their nonexistent works scatter whole passages of the ancient authors to do themselves honor, do just the opposite. For this infinite difference in brilliance gives so pale, tarnished, and ugly an aspect to the part that is their own that they lose in this way much more than they gain.

ᶜThere were two contrasting fancies. The philosopher Chrysippus mixed into his books, not merely passages, but entire works of other authors, and in one the *Medea* of Euripides; and Apollodorus said that if you cut out of

[I:26] *Education of Children*

retrancherait ce qu'il y avait d'étranger, son papier demeurerait en blanc. Épicurus au rebours, en trois cents volumes qu'il laissa, n'avait pas semé une seule allégation étrangère.

ᴬIl m'advint l'autre jour de tomber sur un tel passage. J'avais traîné languissant après des paroles françaises, si exsangues, si décharnées et si vides de matière et de sens, que ce n'était voirement que paroles françaises. Au bout d'un long et ennuyeux chemin, je vins à rencontrer une pièce haute, riche, et élevée jusqu'aux nues. Si j'eusse trouvé la pente douce et la montée un peu allongée, cela eût été excusable: c'était un précipice si droit et si coupé que, des six premières paroles, je connus que je m'envolais en l'autre monde. De là je découvris la fondrière d'où je venais, si basse et si profonde que je n'eus onques plus le cœur de m'y ravaler. Si j'étoffais l'un de mes discours de ces riches dépouilles, il éclairerait par trop la bêtise des autres.

ᶜReprendre en autrui mes propres fautes ne me semble non plus incompatible que de reprendre, comme je fais souvent, celles d'autrui en moi. Il les faut accuser partout et leur ôter tout lieu de franchise. Si sais-je bien combien audacieusement j'entreprends moi-même à tous coups de m'égaler à mes larcins, d'aller pair à pair quand et eux, non sans une téméraire espérance que je puisse tromper les yeux des juges à les discerner. Mais c'est autant par le bénéfice de mon application que par le bénéfice de mon invention et de ma force. Et puis je ne lutte point en gros ces vieux champions-là, et corps à corps: c'est par reprises, menues et légères atteintes. Je ne m'y aheurte pas; je ne fais que les tâter; et ne vais point tant

them all the foreign matter, the paper he used would be left blank. Epicurus, on the contrary, in three hundred volumes that he left, put in not a single borrowed quotation.

ᴬI happened the other day to come upon such a passage. I had dragged along languidly after French words so bloodless, fleshless, and empty of matter and sense that they really were nothing but French words. At the end of a long and tedious road I came upon a bit that was sublime, rich, and lofty as the clouds. If I had found the slope gentle and the climb a bit slower, it would have been excusable; but it was a precipice so straight and steep that after the first six words I realized that I was flying off into another world. From there I saw the bog I had come out of, so low and deep that I never again had the stomach to go back down into it. If I stuffed one of my chapters with these rich spoils, it would show up too clearly the stupidity of the others.

ᶜTo criticize my own faults in others seems to me no more inconsistent than to criticize, as I often do, others' faults in myself. We must denounce them everywhere and leave them no place of refuge. Still, I well know how audaciously I always attempt to match the level of my pilferings, to keep pace with them, not without a rash hope that I may deceive the eyes of the judges who try to discover them. But this is as much by virtue of my use of them as by virtue of my inventiveness or my power. And then, I do not wrestle with those old champions wholesale and body against body; I do so by snatches, by little light attacks. I don't go at them stubbornly; I only feel them out; and I don't go nearly as much as I think about

comme je marchande d'aller.

Si je leur pouvais tenir palot je serais honnête homme, car je ne les entreprends que par où ils sont les plus raides.

De faire ce que j'ai découvert d'aucuns, se couvrir des armes d'autrui jusqu'à ne montrer pas seulement le bout de ses doigts, conduire son dessein, comme il est aisé aux savants en une matière commune, sous les inventions anciennes rapiécées par-ci par-là: à ceux qui les veulent cacher et faire propres, c'est premièrement injustice et lâcheté, que n'ayant rien en leur vaillant par où se produire, ils cherchent à se présenter par une valeur étrangère; et puis grande sottise, se contentant par piperie de s'acquérir l'ignorante approbation du vulgaire, se décrier envers les gens d'entendement, qui hochent du nez notre incrustation empruntée, desquels seuls la louange a du poids. De ma part il n'est rien que je veuille moins faire. Je ne dis les autres, sinon pour d'autant plus me dire. Ceci ne touche pas des centons qui se publient pour centons: et j'en ai vu de tres ingénieux en mon temps, entre autres un sous le nom de Capilupus, outre les anciens. Ce sont des esprits qui se font voir et par ailleurs et par là, comme Lipsius [4] en ce docte et laborieux tissu de ses *Politiques*.

[A]Quoi qu'il en soit, veux-je dire, et quelles que soient ces inepties, je n'ai pas délibéré de les cacher, non plus qu'un mien portrait chauve et grisonnant, où le peintre aurait mis non un visage parfait, mais le mien. Car aussi

---

[4] The Belgian Justus Lipsius (1547–1606), one of the most learned scholars of his time, was an early admirer and correspondent of Montaigne, whom he called "the French Thales."

going. If I were a match for them I would be a good man, for I take them on only at their stiffest points.

As for doing what I have discovered others doing, covering themselves with other men's armor until they don't show even their finger tips, and carrying out their plan, as is easy for the learned in common subjects, with ancient inventions pieced out here and there—for those who want to hide their borrowings and appropriate them, this is first of all injustice and cowardice, that, having nothing of their own worth bringing out, they try to present themselves under false colors; and second, it is stupid of them to content themselves with gaining deceitfully the ignorant approbation of the common herd, while discrediting themselves in the eyes of men of understanding, whose praise alone has any weight, and who turn up their nose at our borrowed incrustations. For my part, there is nothing I want less to do. I do not speak the minds of others except to speak my own mind better. This does not apply to the compilations that are published as compilations; and I have seen some very ingenious ones in my time; among others, one under the name of Capilupus, besides the ancients. The minds of these authors are such that they stand out in this sort of writing as well as in other kinds, as does Lipsius [4] in the learned and laborious web of his *Politics*.

ᴬHowever that may be, I mean to say, and whatever these absurdities may be, I have had no intention of concealing them, any more than I would a bald and graying portrait of myself, in which the painter had drawn not a perfect face, but mine. For likewise these are my humors

ce sont ici mes humeurs et opinions; je les donne pour
ce qui est en ma croyance, non pour ce qui est à croire.
Je ne vise ici qu'à découvrir moi-même, qui serai par
aventure autre demain, si nouvel apprentissage me change.
Je n'ai point l'autorité d'être cru, ni ne le désire, me sen-
tant trop mal instruit pour instruire autrui.

Quelqu'un donc, ayant vu l'article précédent,[5] me
disait chez moi l'autre jour que je me devais être un peu
étendu sur le discours de l'institution des enfants. Or,
Madame, si j'avais quelque suffisance en ce sujet, je ne
pourrais la mieux employer que d'en faire un présent à ce
petit homme qui vous menace de faire tantôt une belle
sortie de chez vous (vous êtes trop généreuse pour commencer autrement que par un mâle). Car, ayant eu tant de
part à la conduite de votre mariage, j'ai quelque droit et
intérêt à la grandeur et prospérité de tout ce qui en
viendra; outre ce que l'ancienne possession que vous avez
sur ma servitude m'obligent[6] assez à désirer honneur, bien,
et avantage à tout ce qui vous touche. Mais à la vérité
je n'y entends sinon cela, que la plus grande difficulté et
importante de l'humaine science semble être en cet endroit
où il se traite de la nourriture et institution des enfants.

cTout ainsi qu'en l'agriculture les façons qui vont
avant le planter sont certaines et aisées, et le planter
même; mais depuis que ce qui est planté vient à prendre
vie, à l'élever il y a une grande variété de façons et difficulté: pareillement aux hommes. Il y a peu d'industrie
à les planter, mais depuis qu'ils sont nés on se charge

---

[5] The chapter "Du pédantisme" ("Of Pedantry": 1: 25).

and opinions; I offer them as what I believe, not what is to be believed. I aim here only at revealing myself, who will perhaps be different tomorrow, if I learn something new which changes me. I have no authority to be believed, nor do I want it, feeling myself too ill-instructed to instruct others.

Well, someone who had seen the preceding article [5] was telling me at my home the other day that I should have enlarged a bit on the subject of the education of children. Now, Madame, if I had some competence in this matter, I could not use it better than to make a present of it to the little man who threatens soon to come out so bravely from within you (you are too noble-spirited to begin otherwise than with a male). For having had so great a part in bringing about your marriage, I have a certain rightful interest in the greatness and prosperity of whatever comes out of it; besides that, the ancient claim that you have on my servitude is enough to oblige [6] me to wish honor, good, and advantage to all that concerns you. But in truth I understand nothing about it except this, that the greatest and most important difficulty in human knowledge seems to lie in the branch of knowledge which deals with the upbringing and education of children.

ᶜJust as in agriculture the operations that come before the planting, as well as the planting itself, are certain and easy; but as soon as the plant comes to life, there are various methods and great difficulties in raising it; so it is with men: little industry is needed to plant them, but it is quite a different burden we assume from the moment of their

---

[6] This plural verb (subject: *possession*) seems to be simply absent-mindedness.

[I:26] *Education of Children*

d'un soin divers, plein d'embesognement et de crainte, à les dresser et nourrir.

ᴬLa montre de leurs inclinations est si tendre en ce bas âge et si obscure, les promesses si incertaines et fausses, qu'il est malaisé d'y établir aucun solide jugement. ᴮVoyez Cimon, voyez Thémistoclès et mille autres, combien ils se sont disconvenus à eux-mêmes. Les petits des ours, des chiens, montrent leur inclination naturelle; mais les hommes, se jetant incontinent en des accoutumances, en des opinions, en des lois, se changent ou se déguisent facilement.

ᴬSi est-il difficile de forcer les propensions naturelles. D'où il advient que, par faute d'avoir bien choisi leur route, pour néant se travaille-t-on souvent et emploie l'on beaucoup d'âge à dresser les enfants aux choses auxquelles ils ne peuvent prendre pied. Toutefois, en cette difficulté, mon opinion est de les acheminer toujours aux meilleures choses et plus profitables, et qu'on se doit peu appliquer à ces légères divinations et pronostics que nous prenons des mouvements de leur enfance. ᶜPlaton même, en sa *République*, me semble leur donner beaucoup d'autorité.

ᴬMadame, c'est un grand ornement que la science, et un outil de merveilleux service, notamment aux personnes élevées en tel degré de fortune comme vous êtes. A la vérité, elle n'a point son vrai usage en mains viles et basses. Elle est bien plus fière de prêter ses moyens à conduire une guerre, à commander un peuple, à pratiquer l'amitié d'un prince ou d'une nation étrangère, qu'à dresser un argument dialectique, ou à plaider un appel, ou ordonner une masse de pilules. Ainsi, Madame, parce que je crois que vous n'oublierez pas cette partie en l'institution des vôtres, vous qui en avez savouré la douceur et

birth, a burden full of care and fear—that of training them and bringing them up.

ᴬThe manifestation of their inclinations is so slight and so obscure at that early age, the promises so uncertain and misleading, that it is hard to base any solid judgment on them. ᴮLook at Cimon, look at Themistocles and a thousand others, how they belied themselves. The young of bears and dogs show their natural inclination, but men, plunging headlong into certain habits, opinions, and laws, easily change or disguise themselves.

ᴬStill it is difficult to force natural propensities. Whence it happens that, because we have failed to choose their road well, we often spend a lot of time and effort for nothing, training children for things in which they cannot get a foothold. At all events, in this difficulty, my advice is to guide them always to the best and most profitable things, and to pay little heed to those trivial conjectures and prognostications which we make from the actions of their childhood. ᶜEven Plato, in his *Republic*, seems to me to give them too much authority.

ᴬMadame, learning is a great ornament and a wonderfully serviceable tool, notably for people raised to such a degree of fortune as you are. In truth, it does not receive its proper use in mean and lowborn hands. It is much prouder to lend its resources to conducting a war, governing a people, or gaining the friendship of a prince or a foreign nation, than to constructing a dialectical argument, pleading an appeal, or prescribing a mass of pills. Thus, Madame, because I think you will not forget this element in the education of your children, you who have

qui êtes d'une race lettrée (car nous avons encore les écrits de ces anciens comtes de Foix, d'où Monsieur le Comte, votre mari, et vous êtes descendus; et François, Monsieur de Candale, votre oncle, en fait naître tous les jours d'autres, qui étendront la connaissance de cette qualité de votre famille à plusieurs siècles), je vous veux dire là-dessus une seule fantaisie que j'ai contraire au commun usage. C'est tout ce que je puis conférer à votre service en cela.

La charge du gouverneur que vous lui donnerez, du choix duquel dépend tout l'effet de son institution, elle a plusieurs autres grandes parties; mais je n'y touche point, pour n'y savoir rien apporter qui vaille; et de cet article, sur lequel je me mêle de lui donner avis, il m'en croira autant qu'il y verra d'apparence. A un enfant de maison qui recherche les lettres, non pour le gain (car une fin si abjecte est indigne de la grâce et faveur des muses, et puis elle regarde et dépend d'autrui), ni tant pour les commodités externes que pour les siennes propres, et pour s'en enrichir et parer au dedans, ayant plutôt envie d'en tirer un habile homme qu'un homme savant, je voudrais aussi qu'on fût soigneux de lui choisir un conducteur qui eût plutôt la tête bien faite que bien pleine; et qu'on y requît tous les deux, mais plus les mœurs et l'entendement que la science; et qu'il se conduisît en sa charge d'une nouvelle manière.

On ne cesse de criailler à nos oreilles, comme qui verserait dans un entonnoir; et notre charge ce n'est que redire ce qu'on nous a dit. Je voudrais qu'il corrigeât cette partie, et que, de belle arrivée, selon la portée de l'âme qu'il a en main, il commençât à la mettre sur la

tasted its sweetness and who are of a literary race (for we still have the writings of those ancient counts of Foix from whom his lordship the count your husband and yourself are descended; and François, Monsieur de Candale, your uncle, every day brings forth others, which will extend for many centuries the knowledge of this quality in your family), I want to tell you a single fancy of mine on this subject, which is contrary to common usage; it is all that I can contribute to your service in this matter.

The task of the tutor that you will give your son, upon whose choice depends the whole success of his education, has many other important parts, but I do not touch upon them, since I cannot offer anything worth while concerning them; and in this matter on which I venture to give him advice, he will take it only as far as it seems good to him. For a child of noble family who seeks learning not for gain (for such an abject goal is unworthy of the graces and favor of the Muses, and besides it looks to others and depends on them), or so much for external advantages as for his own, and to enrich and furnish himself inwardly, since I would rather make of him an able man than a learned man, I would also urge that care be taken to choose a guide with a well-made rather than a well-filled head; that both these qualities should be required of him, but more particularly character and understanding than learning; and that he should go about his job in a novel way.

Our tutors never stop bawling into our ears, as though they were pouring water into a funnel; and our task is only to repeat what has been told us. I should like the tutor to correct this practice, and right from the start, according to the capacity of the mind he has in hand, to

montre, lui faisant goûter les choses, les choisir et discerner d'elle-même; quelquefois lui ouvrant chemin, quelquefois le lui laissant ouvrir. Je ne veux pas qu'il invente et parle seul, je veux qu'il écoute son disciple parler à son tour. ^cSocratès, et depuis, Arcésilas, faisaient premièrement parler leurs disciples, et puis ils parlaient à eux. *Obest plerumque iis qui discere volunt authoritas eorum qui docent.*[7]

Il est bon qu'il le fasse trotter devant lui pour juger de son train, et juger jusqu'à quel point il se doit ravaler pour s'accommoder à sa force. A faute de cette proportion nous gâtons tout; et de la savoir choisir, et s'y conduire bien mesurément, c'est l'une des plus ardues besognes que je sache; et est l'effet d'une haute âme et bien forte, savoir condescendre à ses allures puériles et les guider. Je marche plus sûr et plus ferme amont qu'aval.

Ceux qui, comme porte notre usage, entreprennent d'une même leçon et pareille mesure de conduite régenter plusieurs esprits de si diverses mesures et formes, ce n'est pas merveille si, en tout un peuple d'enfants, ils en rencontrent à peine deux ou trois qui rapportent quelque juste fruit de leur discipline.

^AQu'il ne lui demande pas seulement compte des mots de sa leçon, mais du sens et de la substance, et qu'il juge du profit qu'il aura fait non par le témoignage de sa mémoire, mais de sa vie. Que ce qu'il viendra d'apprendre, il le lui fasse mettre en cent visages et accommoder à autant de divers sujets, pour voir s'il l'a encore bien pris et bien fait sien, ^cprenant l'instruction de son progrès

---

[7] Cicero, *De Natura Deorum*, i, v.

begin putting it through its paces, making it taste things, choose them, and discern them by itself; sometimes clearing the way for him, sometimes letting him clear his own way. I don't want him to think and talk alone, I want him to listen to his pupil speaking in his turn. ^CSocrates, and later Arcesilaus, first had their disciples speak, and then they spoke to them. *The authority of those who teach is often an obstacle to those who want to learn.* ⁷

It is good that he should have his pupil trot before him, to judge the child's pace and how much he must stoop to match his strength. For lack of this proportion we spoil everything; and to be able to hit it right and to go along in it evenly is one of the hardest tasks that I know; it is the achievement of a lofty and very strong soul to know how to come down to a childish gait and guide it. I walk more firmly and surely uphill than down.

If, as is our custom, the teachers undertake to regulate many minds of such different capacities and forms with the same lesson and a similar measure of guidance, it is no wonder if in a whole race of children they find barely two or three who reap any proper fruit from their teaching.

^ALet him be asked for an account not merely of the words of his lesson, but of its sense and substance, and let him judge the profit he has made by the testimony not of his memory, but of his life. Let him be made to show what he has just learned in a hundred aspects, and apply it to as many different subjects, to see if he has yet properly grasped it and made it his own, ^Cplanning his progress

des pédagogismes de Platon. ᴬC'est témoignage de crudité et indigestion que de regorger la viande comme on l'a avalée. L'estomac n'a pas fait son opération s'il n'a fait changer la façon et la forme à ce qu'on lui avait donné à cuire.

ᴮNotre âme ne branle qu'à crédit, liée et contrainte à l'appétit des fantaisies d'autrui, serve et captivée sous l'autorité de leur leçon. On nous a tant assujettis aux cordes que nous n'avons plus de franches allures. Notre vigueur et liberté est éteinte. ᶜ*Numquam tutelæ suæ fiunt.*[8] ᴮJe vis privément à Pise un honnête homme, mais si aristotélicien que le plus général de ses dogmes est: que la touche et règle de toutes imaginations solides et de toute vérité c'est la conformité à la doctrine d'Aristote; que hors de là ce ne sont que chimères et inanité; qu'il a tout vu et tout dit. Cette proposition, pour avoir été un peu trop largement et iniquement interprétée, le mit autrefois et tint longtemps en grand accessoire à l'inquisition à Rome.

ᴬQu'il lui fasse tout passer par l'étamine et ne loge rien en sa tête par simple autorité et à crédit; les principes d'Aristote ne lui soient principes, non plus que ceux des stoïciens ou épicuriens. Qu'on lui propose cette diversité de jugements: il choisira s'il peut, sinon il en demeurera en doute. ᶜIl n'y a que les fous certains et résolus.

ᴬChe non men che saper dubbiar m'aggrada.[9]

Car s'il embrasse les opinions de Xénophon et de Platon

---

[8] Seneca, *Epistles,* xxxiii, 10.

according to the pedagogical method of Plato. ᴬIt is a sign of rawness and indigestion to disgorge food just as we swallowed it. The stomach has not done its work if it has not changed the condition and form of what has been given it to cook.

ᴮOur mind moves only on faith, being bound and constrained to the whim of others' fancies, a slave and a captive under the authority of their teaching. We have been so well accustomed to leading strings that we have no free motion left; our vigor and liberty are extinct. ᶜ*They never become their own guardians.*⁸ ᴮI had a private talk with a man at Pisa, a good man, but such an Aristotelian that the most sweeping of his dogmas is that the touchstone and measure of all solid speculations and of all truth is conformity with the teaching of Aristotle; that outside of this there is nothing but chimeras and inanity; that Aristotle saw everything and said everything. This proposition, having been interpreted a little too broadly and unfairly, put him once, and kept him long, in great danger of the Inquisition at Rome.

ᴬLet the tutor make his charge pass everything through a sieve and lodge nothing in his head on mere authority and trust: let not Aristotle's principles be principles to him any more than those of the Stoics or Epicureans. Let this variety of ideas be set before him; he will choose if he can; if not, he will remain in doubt. ᶜOnly the fools are certain and assured.

ᴬFor doubting pleases me no less than knowing.⁹

For if he embraces Xenophon's and Plato's opinions by his

---

⁹ Dante, *Inferno*, xi, 93.

[I:26] *Education of Children*

par son propre discours, ce ne seront plus les leurs, ce seront les siennes. ^CQui suit un autre, il ne suit rien. Il ne trouve rien, voire il ne cherche rien. *Non sumus sub rege; sibi quisque se vindicet.*[10] Qu'il sache qu'il sait, au moins. ^AIl faut qu'il emboive leurs humeurs, non qu'il apprenne leurs préceptes. Et qu'il oublie hardiment, s'il veut, d'où il les tient, mais qu'il se les sache approprier. La vérité et la raison sont communes à un chacun, et ne sont non plus à qui les a dites premièrement qu'à qui les dit après. ^CCe n'est non plus selon Platon que selon moi, puisque lui et moi l'entendons et voyons de même. ^ALes abeilles pillotent deçà delà les fleurs, mais elles en font après le miel, qui est tout leur; ce n'est plus thym ni marjolaine. Ainsi les pièces empruntées d'autrui, il les transformera et confondra pour en faire un ouvrage tout sien: à savoir, son jugement. Son institution, son travail et étude ne vise qu'à le former.

^CQu'il cèle tout ce de quoi il a été secouru, et ne produise que ce qu'il en a fait. Les pilleurs, les emprunteurs mettent en parade leurs bâtiments, leurs achats, non pas ce qu'ils tirent d'autrui. Vous ne voyez pas les épices d'un homme de parlement, vous voyez les alliances qu'il a gagnées et honneurs à ses enfants. Nul ne met en compte public sa recette: chacun y met son acquêt.

Le gain de notre étude, c'est en être devenu meilleur et plus sage.

^AC'est, disait Épicharmus, l'entendement qui voit et qui oit, c'est l'entendement qui approfite tout, qui dispose tout, qui agit, qui domine et qui règne; toutes autres

---

[10] Seneca, *Epistles,* xxxiii, 4.

own reasoning, they will no longer be theirs, they will be his. ^CHe who follows another follows nothing. He finds nothing; indeed he seeks nothing. *We are not under a king; let each one claim his own freedom.*[10] Let him know that he knows, at least. ^AHe must imbibe their ways of thinking, not learn their precepts. And let him boldly forget, if he wants, where he got them, but let him know how to make them his own. Truth and reason are common to everyone, and no more belong to the man who first spoke them than to the man who says them later. ^CIt is no more according to Plato than according to me, since he and I understand and see it in the same way. ^AThe bees plunder the flowers here and there, but afterward they make of them honey, which is all theirs; it is no longer thyme or marjoram. Even so with the pieces borrowed from others; he will transform and blend them to make a work that is all his own, to wit, his judgment. His education, work, and study aim only at forming this.

^CLet him hide all the help he has had, and show only what he has made of it. The pillagers, the borrowers, parade their buildings, their purchases, not what they get from others. You do not see the gratuities of a member of a Parlement, you see the alliances he has gained and honors for his children. No one makes public his receipts; everyone makes public his acquisitions.

The gain from our study is to have become better and wiser by it.

^AIt is the understanding, Epicharmus used to say, that sees and hears; it is the understanding that makes profit of everything, that arranges everything, that acts, domi-

choses sont aveugles, sourdes et sans âme. Certes nous le rendons servile et couard, pour ne lui laisser la liberté de rien faire de soi. Qui demanda jamais à son disciple ce qu'il lui semble ᴮde la rhétorique et de la grammaire, ᴬde telle ou telle sentence de Cicéron? On nous les plaque en la mémoire toutes empennées, comme des oracles où les lettres et les syllabes sont de la substance de la chose. ᶜSavoir par cœur n'est pas savoir: c'est tenir ce qu'on a donné en garde à sa mémoire. Ce qu'on sait droitement, on en dispose, sans regarder au patron, sans tourner les yeux vers son livre. Fâcheuse suffisance qu'une suffisance pure livresque! Je m'attends qu'elle serve d'ornement, non de fondement; suivant l'avis de Platon, qui dit la fermeté, la foi, la sincérité, être la vraie philosophie; les autres sciences qui visent ailleurs n'être que fard.

ᴬJe voudrais que le Paluël ou Pompée,[11] ces beaux danseurs de mon temps, apprissent des cabrioles à les voir seulement faire, sans nous bouger de nos places, comme ceux-ci veulent instruire notre entendement sans l'ébranler; ᶜou qu'on nous apprît à manier un cheval, ou une pique, ou un luth, ou la voix, sans nous y exercer, comme ceux-ci nous veulent apprendre à bien juger et à bien parler sans nous exercer ni à parler ni à juger.

ᴬOr, à cet apprentissage, tout ce qui se présente à nos yeux sert de livre suffisant: la malice d'un page, la sottise d'un valet, un propos de table, ce sont autant de nouvelles matières.

A cette cause, le commerce des hommes y est merveil-

---

[11] Ludovico Palvalli and Pompeo Diobono, famous Milanese dancing masters at the French court.

nates, and reigns; all other things are blind, deaf, and soul-
less. Truly we make it servile and cowardly, by leaving it
no freedom to do anything by itself. Who ever asked his
pupil what he thinks ᴮof rhetoric or grammar, or ᴬof such-
and-such a saying of Cicero? They slap them into our memory with all their feathers on, like oracles in which the
letters and syllables are the substance of the matter. ᶜTo
know by heart is not to know; it is to retain what we have
given our memory to keep. What we know rightly we dispose of, without looking at the model, without turning our
eyes toward our book. Sad competence, a purely bookish
competence! I intend it to serve as decoration, not as
foundation, according to the opinion of Plato, who says
that steadfastness, faith, and sincerity are the real philosophy, and the other sciences which aim at other things
are only powder and rouge.

ᴬI wish Paluel or Pompey,[11] those fine dancers of my
time, could teach us capers just by performing them before
us and without moving us from our seats, as those people
want to train our understanding without setting it in motion; ᶜor that we could be taught to handle a horse, or a
pike, or a lute, or our voice, without practicing at it, as
those people want to teach us to judge well and to speak
well, without having us practice either speaking or judging.

ᴬNow, for this apprenticeship, everything that comes to
our eyes is book enough: a page's prank, a servant's
blunder, a remark at table, are so many new materials.

For this reason, mixing with men is wonderfully useful,

leusement propre, et la visite des pays étrangers, non pour en rapporter seulement, à la mode de notre noblesse française, combien de pas a Santa Rotonda, ou la richesse des caleçons de la Signora Livia,[12] ou, comme d'autres, combien le visage de Néron de quelque vieille ruine de là est plus long ou plus large que celui de quelque pareille médaille; mais pour en rapporter principalement les humeurs de ces nations et leurs façons, et pour frotter et limer notre cervelle contre celle d'autrui. Je voudrais qu'on commençât à le promener dès sa tendre enfance, et premièrement, pour faire d'une pierre deux coups, par les nations voisines où le langage est plus éloigné du nôtre, et auquel, si vous ne la formez de bonne heure, la langue ne se peut plier.

Aussi bien est-ce une opinion reçue d'un chacun que ce n'est pas raison de nourrir un enfant au giron de ses parents. Cette amour [13] naturelle les attendrit trop et relâche, voire les plus sages. Ils ne sont capables ni de châtier ses fautes, ni de le voir nourri grossièrement, comme il faut, et hasardeusement. Ils ne le sauraient souffrir revenir suant et poudreux de son exercice, Cboire chaud, boire froid, Ani le voir sur un cheval rebours, ni contre un rude tireur, le fleuret au poing, ni la première arquebuse. Car il n'y a remède: qui en veut faire un homme de bien, sans doute il ne le faut épargner en cette jeunesse, et souvent choquer les règles de la médecine:

> Bvitamque sub dio et trepidis agat
> In rebus.[14]

---

[12] Presumably a popular dancer of Montaigne's time.
[13] The gender of *amour*, like that of many other words, was

and visiting foreign countries, not merely to bring back, in the manner of our French noblemen, knowledge of the measurements of the Santa Rotonda, or of the richness of Signora Livia's [12] drawers, or, like some others, how much longer or wider Nero's face is in some old ruin there than on some similar medallion; but to bring back knowledge of the characters and ways of those nations, and to rub and polish our brains by contact with those of others. I should like the tutor to start taking him abroad at a tender age, and first, to kill two birds with one stone, in those neighboring nations where the language is farthest from our own and where the tongue cannot be bent to it unless you train it early.

Likewise it is an opinion accepted by all, that it is not right to bring up a child in the lap of his parents. This natural love [13] makes them too tender and lax, even the wisest of them. They are capable neither of chastising his faults nor of seeing him brought up roughly, as he should be, and hazardously. They could not endure his returning sweating and dusty from his exercise, ^cdrinking hot, drinking cold, ^Aor see him on a skittish horse, or up against a tough fencer, foil in hand, or with his first harquebus. For there is no help for it: if you want to make a man of him, unquestionably you must not spare him in his youth, and must often clash with the rules of medicine:

> ^BLet him live beneath the open sky
> And dangerously.[14]

variable in Montaigne's time.
[14] Horace, *Odes*, iii, ii, 5–6.

[I:26] *Education of Children*

^CCe n'est pas assez de lui raidir l'âme; il lui faut aussi raidir les muscles. Elle est trop pressée si elle n'est secondée, et a trop à faire de seule fournir à deux offices. Je sais combien ahane la mienne en compagnie d'un corps si tendre, si sensible, qui se laisse si fort aller sur elle. Et aperçois souvent en ma leçon qu'en leurs écrits mes maîtres font valoir pour magnanimité et force de courage des exemples qui tiennent volontiers plus de l'épaisseur de la peau et dureté des os. J'ai vu des hommes, des femmes et des enfants ainsi nés qu'une bastonnade leur est moins qu'à moi une chiquenaude; qui ne remuent ni langue ni sourcil aux coups qu'on leur donne. Quand les athlètes contrefont les philosophes en patience, c'est plutôt vigueur de nerfs que de cœur.

. . . ^AOn lui apprendra de n'entrer en discours ou contestation qu'où il verra un champion digne de sa lutte, et là même à n'employer pas tous les tours qui lui peuvent servir, mais ceux-là seulement qui lui peuvent le plus servir. Qu'on le rende délicat au choix et triage de ses raisons, et aimant la pertinence, et par conséquent la brièveté. Qu'on l'instruise surtout à se rendre et à quitter les armes à la vérité tout aussitôt qu'il l'apercevra; soit qu'elle naisse ès mains de son adversaire, soit qu'elle naisse en lui-même par quelque ravisement. Car il ne sera pas mis en chaire pour dire un rôle prescrit. Il n'est engagé à aucune cause, que parce qu'il l'approuve. Ni ne sera du métier où se vend à purs deniers comptants la liberté de se pouvoir repentir et reconnaître. ^C*Neque, ut omnia quæ præscripta et imperata sint, defendat, necessitate ulla cogitur.*[15]

---

[15] Cicero, *Academica*, II, iii.

cIt is not enough to toughen his soul; we must also toughen his muscles. The soul is too hard pressed unless it is seconded, and has too great a task doing two jobs alone. I know how much mine labors in company with a body so tender and so sensitive, which leans so hard upon it. And I often perceive in my reading that in their writings my masters give weight, as examples of great spirit and stoutheartedness, to acts that are likely to owe more to thickness of skin and toughness of bones. I have seen men, women, and children naturally so constituted that a beating is less to them than a flick of the finger to me; who move neither tongue nor eyebrow at the blows they receive. When athletes imitate philosophers in endurance, their strength is that of sinews rather than of heart.

. . . AHe will be taught not to enter into discussion or argument except when he sees a champion worth wrestling with, and even then not to use all the tricks that can help him, but only those that can help him most. Let him be made fastidious in choosing and sorting his arguments, and fond of pertinence, and consequently of brevity. Let him be taught above all to surrender and throw down his arms before truth as soon as he perceives it, whether it be found in the hands of his opponents, or in himself through reconsideration. For he will not be set in a professor's chair to deliver a prepared lecture. He is pledged to no cause, except by the fact that he approves of it. Nor will he take up the trade in which men sell for ready cash the liberty to repent and acknowledge their mistakes. *cNor is he forced by any necessity to defend everything that has been prescribed and commanded.*[15]

Si son gouverneur tient de mon humeur, il lui formera la volonté à être très loyal serviteur de son prince et très affectionné et très courageux; mais il lui refroidira l'envie de s'y attacher autrement que par un devoir public. Outre plusieurs autres inconvénients qui blessent notre franchise par ces obligations particulières, le jugement d'un homme gagé et acheté, ou il est moins entier et moins libre, ou il est taché et d'imprudence et d'ingratitude. Un courtisan ne peut avoir ni loi ni volonté de dire et penser que favorablement d'un maître qui, parmi tant de milliers d'autres sujets, l'a choisi pour le nourrir et élever de sa main. Cette faveur et utilité corrompent non sans quelque raison sa franchise, et l'éblouissent. Pourtant voit-on coutumièrement le langage de ces gens-là divers à tout autre langage d'un état, et de peu de foi en telle matière.

ᴬQue sa conscience et sa vertu reluisent en son parler, ᶜet n'aient que la raison pour guide. ᴬQu'on lui fasse entendre que de confesser la faute qu'il découvrira en son propre discours, encore qu'elle ne soit aperçue que par lui, c'est un effet de jugement et de sincérité, qui sont les principales parties qu'il cherche; ᶜque l'opiniâtrer et contester sont qualités communes, plus apparentes aux plus basses âmes; que se raviser et se corriger, abandonner un mauvais parti sur le cours de son ardeur, ce sont qualités rares, fortes et philosophiques.

ᴬOn l'avertira, étant en compagnie, d'avoir les yeux partout; car je trouve que les premiers sièges sont communément saisis par les hommes moins capables, et que les grandeurs de fortune ne se trouvent guère mêlées à la suffisance. J'ai vu, cependant qu'on s'entretenait au haut bout

If his tutor is of my disposition, he will form his will to be a very loyal, very affectionate, and very courageous servant of his prince; but he will cool in him any desire to attach himself to that prince otherwise than by sense of public duty. Besides several other disadvantages which impair our freedom by these private obligations, the judgment of a man who is hired and bought is either less whole and less free, or tainted with imprudence and ingratitude. A courtier can have neither the right nor the will to speak and think otherwise than favorably of a master who among so many thousands of other subjects has chosen him to train and raise up with his own hand. This favor and advantage corrupt his freedom, not without some reason, and dazzle him. Therefore we generally find the language of those people different from any other language in a state, and little to be trusted in such matters.

ᴬLet his conscience and his virtue shine forth in his speech, ᶜand be guided only by reason. ᴬLet him be made to understand that to confess the flaw he discovers in his own argument, though it be still unnoticed except by himself, is an act of judgment and sincerity, which are the principal qualities he seeks; ᶜthat obstinacy and contention are vulgar qualities, most often seen in the meanest souls; that to change his mind and correct himself, to give up a bad position at the height of his ardor, are rare, strong, and philosophical qualities.

ᴬHe will be warned, when he is in company, to have his eyes everywhere; for I find that the chief places are commonly seized by the least capable men, and that greatness of fortune is rarely found in combination with ability. While people at the upper end of a table were talking

d'une table de la beauté d'une tapisserie ou du goût de la malvoisie, se perdre beaucoup de beaux traits à l'autre bout. Il sondera la portée d'un chacun: un bouvier, un maçon, un passant: il faut tout mettre en besogne, et emprunter chacun selon sa marchandise, car tout sert en ménage; la sottise même et faiblesse d'autrui lui sera instruction. A contrôler les grâces et façons d'un chacun, il s'engendrera envie des bonnes et mépris des mauvaises.

Qu'on lui mette en fantaisie une honnête curiosité de s'enquérir de toutes choses; tout ce qu'il y aura de singulier autour de lui, il le verra: un bâtiment, une fontaine, un homme, le lieu d'une bataille ancienne, le passage de Cæsar ou de Charlemagne:

^BQuæ tellus sit lenta gelu, quæ putris ab æstu
    Ventus in Italiam quis bene vela ferat.[16]

^AIl s'enquerra des mœurs, des moyens et des alliances de ce prince, et de celui-là. Ce sont choses très plaisantes à apprendre et très utiles à savoir.

En cette pratique des hommes, j'entends y comprendre, et principalement, ceux qui ne vivent qu'en la mémoire des livres. Il pratiquera, par le moyen des histoires, ces grandes âmes des meilleurs siècles. C'est un vain étude, qui veut; mais qui veut aussi, c'est un étude de fruit inestimable, ^Cet le seul étude, comme dit Platon, que les Lacédémoniens eussent réservé à leur part. ^AQuel profit ne fera-t-il en cette part-là à la lecture des vies de notre Plutarque? Mais que mon guide se souvienne où

---

[16] Propertius, *Elegies*, iv, iii, 39–40.

about the beauty of a tapestry or the flavor of the malmsey, I have seen many fine sallies wasted at the other end. He will sound the capacity of each man: a cowherd, a mason, a passer-by; he must put everything to use, and borrow from each man according to his wares, for everything is useful in a household; even the stupidity and weakness of others will be an education to him. By taking stock of the graces and manners of others, he will create in himself desire of the good ones and contempt for the bad.

Put into his head an honest curiosity to inquire into all things; whatever is unusual around him he will see: a building, a fountain, a man, the field of an ancient battle, the place where Caesar or Charlemagne passed:

ᴮWhich land is parched with heat, which numb with frost,
What wind drives sails to the Italian coast.¹⁶

ᴬHe will inquire into the conduct, the resources, and the alliances of this prince and that. These are things very pleasant to learn and very useful to know.

In this association with men I mean to include, and foremost, those who live only in the memory of books. He will associate, by means of histories, with those great souls of the best ages. It is a vain study, if you will; but also, if you will, it is a study of inestimable value, ᶜand the only study, as Plato tells us, in which the Lacedaemonians had kept a stake for themselves. ᴬWhat profit will he not gain in this field by reading the *Lives* of our Plutarch? But let my guide remember the object of his

vise sa charge; et qu'il n'imprime pas tant à son disciple
Cla date de la ruine de Carthage que les mœurs d'Hannibal et de Scipion, ni tant A où mourut Marcellus que pourquoi il fut indigne de son devoir qu'il mourût là. Qu'il
ne lui apprenne pas tant les histoires qu'à en juger. . . .

Il se tire une merveilleuse clarté, pour le jugement humain, de la fréquentation du monde. Nous sommes tous
contraints et amoncelés en nous, et avons la vue raccour-
cie à la longueur de notre nez. On demandait à Socratès
d'où il était. Il ne répondit pas "D'Athènes," mais "Du
monde." Lui, qui avait son imagination plus pleine et
plus étendue, embrassait l'univers comme sa ville, jetait
ses connaissances, sa société et ses affections à tout le
genre humain, non pas comme nous qui ne regardons
que sous nous. Quand les vignes gèlent en mon village,
mon prêtre en argumente l'ire de Dieu sur la race humaine, et juge que la pépie en tienne déjà les Cannibales.
A voir nos guerres civiles, qui ne crie que cette machine
se bouleverse et que le jour du jugement nous prend au
collet, sans s'aviser que plusieurs pires choses se sont
vues, et que les dix mille parts du monde ne laissent pas
de galler le bon temps cependant? BMoi, selon leur
licence et impunité, admire de les voir si douces et molles.
AA qui il grêle sur la tête, tout l'hémisphère semble
être en tempête et orage. Et disait le Savoyard que, si ce
sot de roi de France eût su bien conduire sa fortune, il
était homme pour devenir maître d'hôtel de son duc. Son
imagination ne concevait autre plus élevée grandeur que
celle de son maître. CNous sommes insensiblement tous

48

task, and let him not impress on his pupil so much ᶜthe date of the destruction of Carthage as the characters of Hannibal and Scipio, nor so much ᴬwhere Marcellus died as why his death there showed him unworthy of his duty. Let him be taught not so much the histories as how to judge them. . . .

Wonderful brilliance may be gained for human judgment by getting to know men. We are all huddled and concentrated in ourselves, and our vision is reduced to the length of our nose. Socrates was asked where he was from. He replied not "Athens," but "The world." He, whose imagination was fuller and more extensive, embraced the universe as his city, and distributed his knowledge, his company, and his affections to all mankind, unlike us who look only at what is underfoot. When the vines freeze in my village, my priest infers that the wrath of God is upon the human race, and judges that the cannibals already have the pip. Seeing our civil wars, who does not cry out that this mechanism is being turned topsy-turvy and that the judgment day has us by the throat, without reflecting that many worse things have happened, and that ten thousand parts of the world, to our one, are meanwhile having a gay time? ᴮMyself, considering their licentiousness and impunity, I am amazed to see our wars so gentle and mild. ᴬWhen the hail comes down on a man's head, it seems to him that the whole hemisphere is in tempest and storm. And a Savoyard said that if that fool of a French king had known how to play his cards right, he would have had it in him to become chief steward to the duke of Savoy. His imagination conceived no higher dignity than that of his master. ᶜWe are all unconsciously

en cette erreur: erreur de grande suite et préjudice. ^Mais qui se présente, comme dans un tableau, cette grande image de notre mère nature en son entière majesté; qui lit en son visage une si générale et constante variété; qui se remarque là-dedans, et non soi, mais tout un royaume, comme un trait d'une pointe très délicate: celui-là seul estime les choses selon leur juste grandeur.

Ce grand monde, que les uns multiplient encore comme espèces sous un genre, c'est le miroir où il nous faut regarder pour nous connaître de bon biais. Somme, je veux que ce soit le livre de mon écolier. Tant d'humeurs, de sectes, de jugements, d'opinions, de lois et de coutumes nous apprennent à juger sainement des nôtres, et apprennent notre jugement à reconnaître son imperfection et sa naturelle faiblesse: qui n'est pas un léger apprentissage. Tant de remuements d'état et changements de fortune publique nous instruisent à ne faire pas grand miracle de la nôtre. Tant de noms, tant de victoires et conquêtes ensevelies sous l'oubliance rendent ridicule l'espérance d'éterniser notre nom par la prise de dix argoulets et d'un poulailler qui n'est connu que de sa chute. L'orgueil et la fierté de tant de pompes étrangères, la majesté si enflée de tant de cours et de grandeurs, nous fermit et assure la vue à soutenir l'éclat des nôtres sans ciller les yeux. Tant de milliasses d'hommes enterrés avant nous nous encouragent à ne craindre d'aller trouver si bonne compagnie en l'autre monde. Ainsi du reste. . . .

Aux exemples se pourront proprement assortir tous les plus profitables discours de la philosophie, à laquelle se doivent toucher les actions humaines comme à leur règle.

in this error, an error of great consequence and harm. ᴬBut whoever considers as in a painting the great picture of our mother Nature in her full majesty; whoever reads such universal and constant variety in her face; whoever finds himself there, and not merely himself, but a whole kingdom, as a dot made with a very fine brush; that man alone estimates things according to their true proportions.

This great world, which some multiply further as being only a species under one genus, is the mirror in which we must look at ourselves to recognize ourselves from the proper angle. In short, I want it to be the book of my student. So many humors, sects, judgments, opinions, laws, and customs teach us to judge sanely of our own, and teach our judgment to recognize its own imperfection and natural weakness, which is no small lesson. So many state disturbances and changes of public fortune teach us not to make a great miracle out of our own. So. many names, so many victories and conquests, buried in oblivion, make it ridiculous to hope to perpetuate our name by the capture of ten mounted archers and some chicken coop known only by its fall. The pride and arrogance of so many foreign displays of pomp, the puffed-up majesty of so many courts and dignities, strengthens our sight and makes it steady enough to sustain the brilliance of our own without blinking. So many millions of men buried before us encourage us not to be afraid of joining such good company in the other world. And likewise for other things. . . .

To the examples may properly be fitted all the most profitable lessons of philosophy, by which human actions

[I:26] *Education of Children*

On lui dira

> ^Bquid fas optare, quid asper
> Utile nummus habet; patriæ charisque propinquis
> Quantum elargiri deceat; quem te Deus esse
> Jussit, et humana qua parte locatus es in re;
> Quid sumus, aut quidnam victuri gignimur; [17]

^Aque c'est que savoir et ignorer; qui doit être le but de l'étude; que c'est que vaillance, tempérance et justice; ce qu'il y a à dire entre l'ambition et l'avarice, la servitude et la subjection, la licence et la liberté; à quelles marques on connaît le vrai et solide contentement; jusqu'où il faut craindre la mort, la douleur et la honte,

> ^BEt quo quemque modo fugiatque feratque laborem; [18]

^Aquels ressorts nous meuvent, et le moyen de tant de divers branles en nous. Car il me semble que les premiers discours de quoi on lui doit abreuver l'entendement, ce doivent être ceux qui règlent ses mœurs et son sens, qui lui apprendront à se connaître, et à savoir bien mourir et bien vivre. ^CEntre les arts libéraux, commençons par l'art qui nous fait libres. . . .

^AC'est grand cas que les choses en soient là en notre siècle que la philosophie, ce soit, jusqu'aux gens d'entendement, un nom vain et fantastique, qui se trouve de nul usage et de nul prix, ^Cet par opinion et par effet. ^AJe crois que ces ergotismes en sont cause, qui ont saisi ses ave-

---

[17] Persius, *Satires*, III, 69–72, 67.

must be measured as their rule. He will be told:

^BWhat you may justly wish; the use and ends
Of hard-earned coin; our debt to country and to friends;
What heaven has ordered us to be, and where our stand,
Amid humanity, is fixed by high command;
What we now are, what destiny for us is planned; ¹⁷

^Awhat it is to know and not to know, and what must be the aim of study; what are valor, temperance, and justice; what the difference is between ambition and avarice, servitude and submission, license and liberty; by what signs we may recognize true and solid contentment; how much we should fear death, pain, and shame:

^BWhat hardships to avoid, what to endure, and how; ¹⁸

^Awhat springs move us, and the cause of such different impulses in us. For it seems to me that the first lessons in which we should steep his mind must be those that regulate his behavior and his sense, that will teach him to know himself and to die well and live well. ^CAmong the liberal arts, let us begin with the art that liberates us. . . .

^AIt is a strange fact that things should be in such a pass in our century that philosophy, even with people of understanding, should be an empty and fantastic name, a thing of no use and no value, ^Cboth in common opinion and in fact. ^AI think those quibblings which have taken possession of all the approaches to her are the cause of this.

---

¹⁸ Virgil, *Aeneid*, III, 459.

[I:26] *Education of Children*

nues. On a grand tort de la peindre inaccessible aux enfants, et d'un visage renfrogné, sourcilleux et terrible. Qui me l'a masquée de ce faux visage, pâle et hideux? Il n'est rien plus gai, plus gaillard, plus enjoué, et à peu que je ne dise folâtre. Elle ne prêche que fête et bon temps. Une mine triste et transie montre que ce n'est pas là son gîte. Démétrius le Grammairien rencontrant dans le temple de Delphes une troupe de philosophes assis ensemble, il leur dit: "Ou je me trompe, ou, à vous voir la contenance si paisible et si gaie, vous n'êtes pas en grand discours entre vous." A quoi l'un d'eux, Héracléon le Mégarien, répondit: "C'est à faire à ceux qui cherchent si le futur du verbe βάλλω a double λ, ou qui cherchent la dérivation des comparatifs χεῖρον et βέλτιον, et des superlatifs χεῖοιστον et βέλτιστον,[19] qu'il faut rider le front, s'entretenant de leur science. Mais quant aux discours de la philosophie, ils ont accoutumé d'égayer et réjouir ceux qui les traitent, non les renfrogner et contrister."

> [B]Deprendas animi tormenta latentis in ægro
> Corpore, deprendas et gaudia; sumit utrumque
> Inde habitum facies.[20]

[A]L'âme qui loge la philosophie doit par sa santé rendre sain encore le corps. Elle doit faire luire jusqu'au dehors son repos et son aise; doit former à son moule le port extérieur, et l'armer par conséquent d'une gracieuse fierté, d'un maintien actif et allègre, et d'une contenance con-

---

[19] The Greek words are βάλλω (to throw), χεῖρον (worse), βέλτιον (better), χεῖοιστον (worst), βέλτιστον (best).

It is very wrong to portray her as inaccessible to children, with a surly, frowning, and terrifying face. Who has masked her with this false face, pale and hideous? There is nothing more gay, more lusty, more sprightly, and I might almost say more frolicsome. She preaches nothing but merrymaking and a good time. A sad and dejected look shows that she does not dwell there. Demetrius the grammarian, finding a group of philosophers seated together in the temple of Delphi, said to them: "Either I am mistaken, or, judging by your peaceful and gay countenances, you are not engaged in any deep discussion." To which one of them, Heracleon the Megarian, replied: "It is for those who are inquiring whether the future of the verb βάλλω has a double λ, or seeking the derivation of the comparatives χεῖρον and βέλτιον and the superlatives χείριστον and βέλτιστον,[19] to knit their brows when discussing their science. But as for the teachings of philosophy, they are wont to delight and rejoice those who discuss them, not to make them sullen and sad."

> [B]You'll find the hidden torments of the mind
> Shown in the body, and the joys you'll find;
> The face puts on a cloak of either kind.[20]

[A]The soul in which philosophy dwells should by its health make even the body healthy. It should make its tranquillity and gladness shine out from within; should form in its own mold the outward demeanor, and consequently arm it with graceful pride, an active and joyous

_____

[20] Juvenal, *Satires*, IX, 18–20.

tente et débonnaire. ᶜLa plus expresse marque de la sagesse, c'est une éjouissance constante: son état est comme des choses au-dessus de la lune, toujours serein. ᴬC'est "Barroco" et "Baralipton" ²¹ qui rendent leurs suppôts ainsi crottés et enfumes, ce n'est pas elle; ils ne la connaissent que par ouïr dire. Comment? elle fait état de séréner les tempêtes de l'âme, d'apprendre la faim et les fièvres à rire, non par quelques épicycles imaginaires, mais par raisons naturelles et palpables.

ᶜElle ²² a pour son but la vertu, qui n'est pas, comme dit l'école, plantée à la tête d'un mont coupé, raboteux et inaccessible. Ceux qui l'ont approchée la tiennent, au rebours, logée dans une belle plaine fertile et fleurissante, d'où elle voit bien sous soi toutes choses; mais si peut-on y arriver, qui en sait l'adresse, par des routes ombrageuses, gazonnées et doux-fleurantes, plaisamment, et d'une pente facile et polie, comme est celle des voûtes célestes. Pour n'avoir hanté cette vertu suprême, belle, triomphante, amoureuse, délicieuse pareillement et courageuse, ennemie professe et irréconciliable d'aigreur, de déplaisir, de crainte et de contrainte, ayant pour guide nature, fortune et volupté pour compagnes: ils sont allés, selon leur faiblesse, feindre cette sotte image, triste, querelleuse, dépite, menaceuse, mineuse, et la placer sur un rocher, à l'écart, emmi des ronces, fantôme à étonner les gens.

Mon gouverneur, qui connaît devoir remplir la volonté de son disciple autant ou plus d'affection que de révérence

---

²¹ Artificial words in scholastic logic whose vowels represent forms of syllogisms.

bearing, and a contented and good-natured countenance. ᶜThe surest sign of wisdom is constant cheerfulness; her state is like that of things above the moon, ever serene. ᴬIt is *Baroco* and *Baralipton* ²¹ that make their disciples dirt-caked and smoky, and not she; they know her only by hearsay. Why, she makes it her business to calm the tempests of the soul and to teach hungers and fevers to laugh, not by some imaginary epicycles, but by natural and palpable reasons.

ᶜShe ²² has virtue as her goal, which is not, as the schoolmen say, set on the top of a steep, rugged, inaccessible mountain. Those who have approached virtue maintain, on the contrary, that she is established in a beautiful plain, fertile and flowering, from where, to be sure, she sees all things beneath her; but you can get there, if you know the way, by shady, grassy, sweetly flowering roads, pleasantly, by an easy smooth slope, like that of the celestial vaults. It is because they have not associated with this virtue—this supreme, beautiful, triumphant, loving virtue, as delightful as she is courageous, a professed and implacable enemy of sourness, displeasure, fear, and constraint, having nature for her guide, fortune and pleasure for companions—that there are men who in their weakness have made up this stupid, sad, quarrelsome, sullen, threatening, scowling image and set it on a rock, in a solitary place, among the brambles: a phantom to frighten people.

My tutor, who knows he must fill his pupil's mind as much, or more, with affection as with reverence for virtue,

---

²² *Elle* is still *la philosophie*, to which is equated in the 1588–92 addition *la sagesse*.

[I:26] *Education of Children*

envers la vertu, lui saura dire que les poètes suivent les humeurs communes, et lui faire toucher au doigt que les dieux ont mis plutôt la sueur aux avenues des cabinets de Vénus que de Pallas. Et quand il commencera de se sentir, lui présentant Bradamante ou Angélique [23] pour maîtresse à jouir, et d'une beauté naïve, active, généreuse, non hommasse mais virile, au prix d'une beauté molle, affétée, délicate, artificielle; l'une travestie en garçon, coiffée d'un morion luisant, l'autre vêtue en garce, coiffée d'un attifet emperlé: il jugera mâle son amour même, s'il choisit tout diversement à cet efféminé pasteur de Phrygie.[24] Il lui fera cette nouvelle leçon, que le prix et hauteur de la vraie vertu est en la facilité, utilité et plaisir de son exercice, si éloigné de difficulté que les enfants y peuvent comme les hommes, les simples comme les subtils. Le règlement c'est son outil, non pas la force. Socratès, son premier mignon, quitte à escient sa force pour glisser en la naïveté et aisance de son progrès. C'est la mère nourrice des plaisirs humains. En les rendant justes elle les rend sûrs et purs. Les modérant, elle les tient en haleine et en goût. Retranchant ceux qu'elle refuse, elle nous aiguise envers ceux qu'elle nous laisse; et nous laisse abondamment tous ceux que veut nature, et jusqu'à la satiété, maternellement, sinon jusqu'à la lasseté (si d'aventure nous ne voulons dire que le régime qui arrête le buveur avant l'ivresse, le mangeur avant la crudité, le paillard avant la pelade, soit ennemi de nos plaisirs).

---

[23] The two heroines of Ariosto's *Orlando Furioso* (1532).

[24] Paris, whose awarding of the golden apple for beauty to Aphrodite rather than to Hera or Athena led ultimately to the Trojan War.

will be able to tell him that the poets agree with the common view, and to set his finger on the fact that the gods make men sweat harder in the approaches to the chambers of Venus than of Pallas. And when he begins to feel his oats, and the choice is offered him between Bradamante and Angelica [23] as a mistress to be enjoyed—a natural, active, spirited, manly but not mannish beauty, next to a soft, affected, delicate, artificial beauty; one disguised as a boy, wearing a shining helmet, the other dressed as a girl, wearing a headdress of pearls—the tutor will think his pupil manly even in love if he chooses quite differently from that effeminate shepherd of Phrygia.[24]

He will teach him this new lesson, that the value and height of true virtue lies in the ease, utility, and pleasure of its practice, which is so far from being difficult that children can master it as well as men, the simple as well as the subtle. Virtue's tool is moderation, not strength. Socrates, her prime favorite, deliberately gives up his strength, to slip into the naturalness and ease of her gait. She is the nursing mother of human pleasures. By making them just, she makes them sure and pure. By moderating them, she keeps them in breath and appetite. By withdrawing the ones she refuses, she makes us keener for the ones she allows us; and she allows us abundantly all those that nature wills, even to satiety, in maternal fashion, if not to the point of lassitude (unless perchance we want to say that the regimen that stops the drinker short of drunkenness, the eater short of indigestion, the lecher short of baldness, is an enemy of our pleasures). If she lacks the

Si la fortune commune lui faut, elle lui échappe ou elle s'en passe, et s'en forge une autre toute sienne, non plus flottante et roulante. Elle sait être riche et puissante et savante, et coucher dans des matelas musqués. Elle aime la vie, elle aime la beauté et la gloire et la santé. Mais son office propre et particulier c'est savoir user de ces biens-là réglément et les savoir perdre constamment: office bien plus noble qu'âpre, sans lequel tout cours de vie est dénaturé, turbulent et difforme, et y peut-on justement attacher ces écueils, ces halliers et ces monstres. . . .

ᴬPuisque la philosophie est celle qui nous instruit à vivre, et que l'enfance y a sa leçon comme les autres âges, pourquoi ne la lui communique-t-on? . . . On nous apprend à vivre quand la vie est passée. . . . ᶜNotre enfant est bien plus pressé. . . . Employons un temps si court aux instructions nécessaires. . . . ᴬLa philosophie a des discours pour la naissance des hommes, comme pour la décrépitude. . . .

Au nôtre un cabinet, un jardin, la table et le lit, la solitude, la compagnie, le matin et le vêpre, toutes heures lui seront unes, toutes places lui seront étude; car la philosophie, qui comme formatrice des jugements et des mœurs sera sa principale leçon, a ce privilège de se mêler partout. . . . Ainsi sans doute il chômera moins que les autres. Mais comme les pas que nous employons à nous promener dans une galerie, quoiqu'il y en ait trois fois autant, ne nous lassent pas comme ceux que nous mettons à quelque chemin désigné, aussi notre leçon, se passant comme par rencontre, sans obligation de temps et de lieu, et se mêlant à toutes nos actions, se coulera sans se faire sentir. Les jeux mêmes et les exercices seront une bonne

fortune of ordinary men, she rises above it or does without it, and makes herself a different sort of fortune that is all her own, and no longer fluctuating and unsteady. She knows how to be rich and powerful and learned, and lie on perfumed mattresses. She loves life, she loves beauty and glory and health. But her own particular task is to know how to enjoy those blessings with temperance, and to lose them with fortitude: a task far more noble than harsh, without which the course of any life is denatured, turbulent, and deformed, and fit to be associated with those dangers, those brambles, and those monsters. . . .

ᴬSince it is philosophy that teaches us to live, and since there is a lesson in it for childhood as well as for the other ages, why is it not imparted to children? They teach us to live, when life is past. . . . ᶜOur child is in much more of a hurry. . . . Let us use so short a time for the necessary teachings. . . . ᴬPhilosophy has lessons for the birth of men as well as for their decrepitude. . . .

For our boy, a closet, a garden, the table and the bed, solitude, company, morning and evening, all hours will be the same, all places will be his study; for philosophy, which, as the molder of judgment and conduct, will be his principal lesson, has this privilege of being everywhere at home. . . . Thus he will doubtless be less idle than others. But, as the steps we take walking back and forth in a gallery, though there be three times as many, do not tire us like those we take on a set journey, so our lesson, occurring as if by chance, not bound to any time or place, and mingling with all our actions, will slip by without being felt. Even games and exercises will be a good

partie de l'étude: la course, la lutte, ^Cla musique, ^Ala danse, la chasse, le maniement des chevaux et des armes. Je veux que la bienséance extérieure, et l'entregent, ^Cet la disposition de la personne, ^Ase façonne quand et quand l'âme. Ce n'est pas une âme, ce n'est pas un corps qu'on dresse, c'est un homme; il n'en faut pas faire à deux. Et, comme dit Platon, il ne faut pas les dresser l'un sans l'autre, mais les conduire également, comme une couple de chevaux attelés à même timon. ^CEt à l'ouïr, semble-t-il pas prêter plus de temps et plus de sollicitude aux exercices du corps, et estimer que l'esprit s'en exerce quand et quand, et non au rebours?

^AAu demeurant, cette institution se doit conduire par une sévère douceur, non comme il se fait. Au lieu de convier les enfants aux lettres, on ne leur présente, à la vérité, qu'horreur et cruauté. Ôtez-moi la violence et la force: il n'est rien à mon avis qui abâtardisse et étourdisse si fort une nature bien née. Si vous avez envie qu'il craigne la honte et le châtiment, ne l'y endurcissez pas. Endurcissez-le à la sueur et au froid, au vent, au soleil et aux hasards qu'il lui faut mépriser; ôtez-lui toute mollesse et délicatesse au vêtir et coucher, au manger et au boire; accoutumez-le à tout. Que ce ne soit pas un beau garçon et dameret, mais un garçon vert et vigoureux.

^CEnfant, homme, vieil, j'ai toujours cru et jugé de même. Mais entre autres choses, cette police de la plupart de nos collèges m'a toujours déplu. On eût failli à l'aventure moins dommageablement, s'inclinant vers l'indulgence. C'est une vraie geôle de jeunesse captive. On la rend débauchée, l'en punissant avant qu'elle le soit. Arrivez-y sur le point de leur office: vous n'oyez que cris et

part of his study: running, wrestling, ^Cmusic, ^Adancing, hunting, handling horses and weapons. I want his outward behavior and social grace ^Cand his physical adaptability ^Ato be fashioned at the same time with his soul. It is not a soul that is being trained, not a body, but a man; these parts must not be separated. And, as Plato says, they must not be trained one without the other, but driven abreast like a pair of horses harnessed to the same pole. ^CAnd, to hear him, does he not seem to give more time and care to exercises of the body, and to think that the mind gets its exercise at the same time, and not the other way around?

^AFor the rest, this education is to be carried on with severe gentleness, not as is customary. Instead of being invited to letters, children are shown in truth nothing but horror and cruelty. Away with violence and compulsion! There is nothing to my mind which so depraves and stupefies a wellborn nature. If you would like him to fear shame and chastisement, don't harden him to them. Harden him to sweat and cold, wind and sun, and the dangers that he must scorn; wean him from all softness and delicacy in dressing and sleeping, eating and drinking; accustom him to everything. Let him not be a pretty boy and a little lady, but a lusty and vigorous youth.

^CAs a boy, a man, and a graybeard, I have always thought and judged in the same way. But, among other things, I have always disliked the discipline of most of our schools. They might have erred less harmfully by leaning toward indulgence. They are a real jail of captive youth. They make them slack, by punishing them for slackness before they show it. Go in at lesson time: you hear nothing

d'enfants suppliciés et de maîtres enivrés en leur colère. Quelle manière pour éveiller l'appétit envers leur leçon à ces tendres âmes et craintives, de les y guider d'une trogne effroyable, les mains armées de fouets! Inique et pernicieuse forme! Joint ce que Quintilien en a très bien remarqué, que cette impérieuse autorité tire des suites périlleuses, et nommément à notre façon de châtiment. Combien leurs classes seraient plus décemment jonchées de fleurs et de feuillée que de tronçons d'osier sanglants! J'y ferais portraire la joie, l'allégresse, et Flora et les Grâces, comme fit en son école le philosophe Speusippus. Où est leur profit, que ce fût aussi leur ébat. On doit ensucrer les viandes salubres à l'enfant, et enfieller celles qui lui sont nuisibles. . . .

^AToute étrangeté et particularité en nos mœurs et conditions est évitable comme ennemie de communication et de société ^cet comme monstrueuse. Qui ne s'étonnerait de la complexion de Démophon, maître d'hôtel d'Alexandre, qui suait à l'ombre et tremblait au soleil? ^AJ'en ai vu fuir la senteur des pommes plus que les arquebusades, d'autres s'effrayer pour une souris, d'autres rendre la gorge à voir de la crème, d'autres à voir brasser un lit de plume, comme Germanicus ne pouvait souffrir ni la vue ni le chant des coqs. Il y peut avoir, à l'aventure, à cela quelque propriété occulte; mais on l'éteindrait, à mon avis, qui s'y prendrait de bonne heure. L'institution a gagné cela sur moi, il est vrai que ce n'a point été sans quelque soin, que, sauf la bière, mon appétit est accommodable indifféremment à toutes choses de quoi on se paît.

Le corps encore souple, on le doit, à cette cause, plier

but cries, both from tortured boys and from masters drunk with rage. What a way to arouse zest for their lesson in these tender and timid souls, to guide them to it with a horrible scowl and hands armed with rods! Wicked and pernicious system! Besides, as Quintilian very rightly remarked, this imperious authority brings on dangerous consequences, and especially in our manner of punishment. How much more fittingly would their classes be strewn with flowers and leaves than with bloody stumps of birch rods! I would have portraits there of Joy and Gladness, and Flora and the Graces, as the philosopher Speusippus had in his school. Where their profit is, let their frolic be also. Healthy foods should be sweetened for the child, and harmful ones dipped in gall. . . .

ᴬAny strangeness and peculiarity in our conduct and ways is to be avoided as inimical to social intercourse, ᶜand unnatural. Who would not be astonished at the constitution of Demophon, Alexander's steward, who sweated in the shade and shivered in the sun? ᴬI have seen men flee from the smell of apples more than from harquebus fire, others take fright at a mouse, others throw up at the sight of cream, and others at the plumping of a feather bed; and Germanicus could not endure either the sight or the crowing of cocks. There may perhaps be some occult quality in this; but a man could exterminate it, in my opinion, if he set about it early. Education has won this much from me—it is true that it was not without some trouble—that, except for beer, my appetite adapts itself indiscriminately to everything people eat.

While the body is still supple, it should for that reason

à toutes façons et coutumes. Et pourvu qu'on puisse tenir l'appétit et la volonté sous boucle, qu'on rende hardiment un jeune homme commode à toutes nations et compagnies, voire au dérèglement et aux excès, si besoin est. ᶜSon exercitation suive l'usage. ᴬQu'il puisse faire toutes choses, et n'aime à faire que les bonnes. Les philosophes mêmes ne trouvent pas louable en Callisthénès d'avoir perdu la bonne grâce du grand Alexandre, son maître, pour n'avoir voulu boire d'autant à lui. Il rira, il folâtrera, il se débauchera avec son prince. Je veux qu'en la débauche même il surpasse en vigueur et en fermeté ses compagnons, et qu'il ne laisse à faire le mal ni à faute de force ni de science, mais à faute de volonté. . . .

Allant un jour à Orléans, je trouvai dans cette plaine au deçà de Cléry deux régents qui venaient à Bordeaux, environ à cinquante pas l'un de l'autre. Plus loin, derrière eux, je découvris une troupe et un maître en tête, qui était feu Monsieur le comte de La Rochefoucault. Un de mes gens s'enquit au premier de ces régents qui était ce gentilhomme qui venait après lui. Lui, qui n'avait pas vu ce train qui le suivait, et qui pensait qu'on lui parlât de son compagnon, répondit plaisamment: "Il n'est pas gentilhomme; c'est un grammairien, et je suis logicien."

Or, nous qui cherchons ici, au rebours, de former non un grammairien ou logicien mais un gentilhomme, laissons-les abuser de leur loisir; nous avons affaire ailleurs. Mais que notre disciple soit bien pourvu de choses, les paroles ne suivront que trop; il les traînera si elles ne veulent suivre. J'en ois qui s'excusent de ne se pouvoir exprimer, et font contenance d'avoir la tête pleine de plusieurs belles choses, mais, à faute d'éloquence, ne les pou-

be bent to all fashions and customs. And provided his appetite and will can be kept in check, let a young man boldly be made fit for all nations and companies, even for dissoluteness and excess, if need be. ^CLet his training follow usage. ^ALet him be able to do all things, and love to do only the good. The philosophers themselves do not think it praiseworthy in Callisthenes to have lost the good graces of his master Alexander the Great by refusing to keep pace with him in drinking. He will laugh, he will carouse, he will dissipate with his prince. Even in dissipation I want him to outdo his comrades in vigor and endurance; and I want him to refrain from doing evil, not for lack of power or knowledge, but for lack of will. . . .

Going to Orléans one day, I met, in that plain this side of Cléry, two teachers coming to Bordeaux, about fifty yards apart. Further off, behind them, I perceived a company and a lord at the head, who was the late Count de La Rochefoucauld. One of my men inquired of the first of these teachers who was the gentleman that came behind him. He, not having seen the retinue that was following him, and thinking that my man was talking about his companion, replied comically: "He is not a gentleman; he is a grammarian, and I am a logician."

Now, we who are trying on the contrary to make not a grammarian or a logician, but a gentleman, let us allow them to misuse their free time; we have business elsewhere. Provided our pupil is well equipped with substance, words will follow only too readily; if they won't follow willingly, he will drag them. I hear some making excuses for not being able to express themselves, and pretending to have their heads full of many fine things, but to be unable to

voir mettre en évidence: c'est une baye. Savez-vous, à
mon avis, que c'est que cela? Ce sont des ombrages qui
leur viennent de quelques conceptions informes, qu'ils ne
peuvent démêler et éclaircir au dedans ni par conséquent
produire au dehors: ils ne s'entendent pas encore eux-
mêmes. Et voyez-les un peu bégayer sur le point de l'en-
fanter, vous jugez que leur travail n'est point à l'accou-
chement mais ^Cà la conception, et ^Aqu'ils ne font que
lécher cette matière imparfaite. De ma part je tiens, ^Cet
Socratès l'ordonne, ^Aque qui a en l'esprit une vive imagination et claire, il la produira, soit en Bergamasque, soit
par mines s'il est muet:

Verbaque prævisam rem non invita sequentur.[25]

Et comme disait celui-là aussi poétiquement en sa prose,
cum res animum occupavere, verba ambiunt.[26] ^CEt cet
autre: *Ipsæ res verba rapiunt.*[27] ^AIl ne sait pas ablatif,
conjonctif, substantif, ni la grammaire; ne fait pas son
laquais ou une harengère du Petit Pont; et si vous en-
tretiendront tout votre soûl, si vous en avez envie, et se
déferreront aussi peu à l'aventure que le meilleur maître
ès arts de France. Il ne sait pas la rhétorique, ni, pour
avant-jeu, capter la bénévolence du candide lecteur, ni
ne lui chaut de le savoir. De vrai, toute cette belle
peinture s'efface aisément par le lustre d'une vérité simple
et naïve. . . .

---

[25] Horace, *Ars Poetica*, 311.
[26] Seneca the Elder, *Controversiæ*, III, Proem.

express them for lack of eloquence. That is all bluff. Do you know what I think those things are? They are shadows that come to them of some shapeless conceptions, which they cannot untangle and clear up within, and consequently cannot set forth without: they do not understand themselves yet. And just watch them stammer on the point of giving birth; you will conclude that they are laboring not for delivery, but Cfor conception, and Athat they are only trying to lick into shape this unfinished matter. For my part I hold, Cand Socrates makes it a rule, Athat whoever has a vivid and clear idea in his mind will express it, if necessary in Bergamask dialect, or, if he is dumb, by signs:

Master the stuff, and words will freely follow.[25]

And as another said just as poetically in his prose: *When things have taken possession of the mind, words come thick and fast.*[26] C And another: *The things themselves carry the words along.*[27]

AHe knows no ablatives, conjunctives, substantives, or grammar; nor does his lackey, or a fishwife of the Petit Pont, and yet they will talk your ear off, if you like, and will perhaps stumble as little over the rules of their language as the best master of arts in France. He does not know rhetoric, or how in a preface to capture the benevolence of the gentle reader; nor does he care to know it. In truth, all this fine painting is easily eclipsed by the luster of a simple natural truth. . . .

---

[27] Cicero, *De Finibus*, III, v.

[I:26] *Education of Children*

Voire, mais que fera-t-il si on le presse de la subtilité sophistique de quelque syllogisme: le jambon fait boire, le boire désaltère, par quoi le jambon désaltère? ᶜQu'il s'en moque. Il est plus subtil de s'en moquer que d'y répondre.

. . . Je tords bien plus volontiers une bonne sentence pour la coudre sur moi que je ne tords mon fil pour l'aller quérir. ᴬAu rebours c'est aux paroles à servir et à suivre; et que le gascon y arrive si le français n'y peut aller. Je veux que les choses surmontent, et qu'elles remplissent de façon l'imagination de celui qui écoute, qu'il n'ait aucune souvenance des mots. Le parler que j'aime, c'est un parler simple et naïf, tel sur le papier qu'à la bouche: un parler succulent et nerveux, court et serré, ᶜnon tant délicat et peigné comme véhément et brusque:

Hæc demum sapiet dictio, quæ feriet,[28]

ᴬplutôt difficile qu'ennuyeux, éloigné d'affectation, déréglé, décousu et hardi: chaque lopin y fasse son corps; non pédantesque, non fratesque, non plaideresque, mais plutôt soldatesque. . . .

C'est un bel et grand agencement sans doute que le grec et latin, mais on l'achète trop cher. Je dirai ici une façon d'en avoir meilleur marché que de coutume, qui a été essayée en moi-même. S'en servira qui voudra.

Feu mon père, ayant fait toutes les recherches qu'homme peut faire parmi les gens savants et d'entendement, d'une forme d'institution exquise, fut avisé de cet inconvé-

---

[28] Epitaph of Lucan.

True, but what will he do if someone presses him with the sophistic subtlety of some syllogism? "Ham makes us drink; drinking quenches thirst; therefore ham quenches thirst." ^CLet him laugh at it; it is subtler to laugh at it than to answer it.

. . . I much more readily twist a good saying to sew it on me than I twist the thread of my thought to go and fetch it. ^AOn the contrary, it is for words to serve and follow; and let Gascon get there if French cannot. I want the substance to stand out, and so to fill the imagination of the listener that he will have no memory of the words. The speech I love is a simple, natural speech, the same on paper as in the mouth; a speech succulent and sinewy, brief and compressed, ^Cnot so much dainty and well-combed as vehement and brusque:

The speech that strikes the mind will have most taste; [28]

^Arather difficult than boring, remote from affectation, irregular, disconnected and bold; each bit making a body in itself; not pedantic, not monkish, not lawyer-like, but rather soldierly. . . .

There is no doubt that Greek and Latin are great and handsome ornaments, but we buy them too dear. I shall tell you here a way to get them cheaper than usual, which was tried out on myself. Anyone who wants to can use it.

My late father, having made all the inquiries a man can make, among men of learning and understanding, about a superlative system of education, became aware of the

nient qui était en usage; et lui disait-on que cette longueur que nous mettions à apprendre les langues, ^cqui ne leur coûtaient rien, ^Aest la seule cause pourquoi nous ne pouvions arriver à la grandeur d'âme et de connaissance des anciens Grecs et Romains. Je ne crois pas que c'en soit la seule cause. Tant y a que l'expédient que mon père y trouva ce fut que, en nourrice et avant le premier dénouement de ma langue, il me donna en charge à un Allemand, qui depuis est mort fameux médecin en France, du tout ignorant de notre langue, et très bien versé en la latine.[29] Celui-ci, qu'il avait fait venir exprès et qui était bien chèrement gagé, m'avait continuellement entre les bras. Il en eut aussi avec lui deux autres moindres en savoir pour me suivre, et soulager le premier. Ceux-ci ne m'entretenaient d'autre langue que latine. Quant au reste de sa maison, c'était une règle inviolable que ni lui-même, ni ma mère, ni valet, ni chambrière, ne parlaient en ma compagnie qu'autant de mots de latin que chacun avait appris pour jargonner avec moi.

C'est merveille du fruit que chacun y fit. Mon père et ma mère y apprirent assez de latin pour l'entendre, et en acquirent à suffisance pour s'en servir à la nécessité, comme firent aussi les autres domestiques qui étaient plus attachés à mon service. Somme, nous nous latinisâmes tant qu'il en regorgea jusqu'à nos villages tout autour, où il y a encore, et ont pris pied par l'usage, plusieurs appellations latines d'artisans et d'outils. Quant à moi, j'avais plus de six ans avant que j'entendisse non plus de français ou de périgourdin que d'arabesque. Et sans art, sans livre, sans

---

[29] Doctor Horstanus, later a professor at the Collège de Guyenne at Bordeaux.

drawbacks that were prevalent; and he was told that the long time we put into learning languages ᶜwhich cost the ancient Greeks and Romans nothing ᴬwas the only reason we could not attain their greatness in soul and in knowledge. I do not think that that is the only reason. At all events, the expedient my father hit upon was this, that while I was nursing and before the first loosening of my tongue, he put me in the care of a German, who has since died a famous doctor in France, wholly ignorant of our language and very well versed in Latin.²⁹ This man, whom he had sent for expressly, and who was very highly paid, had me constantly in his hands. There were also two others with him, less learned, to attend me and relieve him. These spoke to me in no other language than Latin. As for the rest of my father's household, it was an inviolable rule that neither my father himself, nor my mother, nor any valet or housemaid, should speak anything in my presence but such Latin words as each had learned in order to jabber with me.

It is wonderful how everyone profited from this. My father and mother learned enough Latin in this way to understand it, and acquired sufficient skill to use it when necessary, as did also the servants who were most attached to my service. Altogether, we Latinized ourselves so much that it overflowed all the way to our villages on every side, where there still remain several Latin names for artisans and tools that have taken root by usage. As for me, I was over six before I understood any more French or Perigordian than Arabic. And without artificial means, without a

grammaire ou précepte, sans fouet et sans larmes, j'avais appris du latin tout aussi pur que mon maître d'école le savait; car je ne le pouvais avoir mêlé ni altéré. Si par essai on me voulait donner un thème, à la mode des collèges, on le donne aux autres en français; mais à moi il me le fallait donner en mauvais latin pour le tourner en bon. Et Nicolas Grouchy, qui a écrit *De Comitiis Romanorum*, Guillaume Guérente, qui a commenté Aristote, George Buchanan, ce grand poète écossais, ᴮMarc-Antoine Muret, ᶜque la France et l'Italie reconnaît pour le meilleur orateur du temps,³⁰ ᴬmes précepteurs domestiques, m'ont dit souvent que j'avais ce langage en mon enfance si prêt et si à main qu'ils craignaient à m'accoster. Buchanan, que je vis depuis à la suite de feu Monsieur le maréchal de Brissac, me dit qu'il était après à écrire de l'institution des enfants, et qu'il prenait l'exemplaire de la mienne; car il avait lors en charge ce comte de Brissac que nous avons vu depuis si valeureux et si brave.

Quant au grec, duquel je n'ai quasi du tout point d'intelligence, mon père désigna me le faire apprendre par art, mais d'une voie nouvelle, par forme d'ébat et d'exercice. Nous pelotions nos déclinaisons à la manière de ceux qui, par certains jeux de tablier, apprennent l'arithmétique et la géométrie. Car entre autres choses il avait été conseillé de me faire goûter la science et le devoir par une volonté non forcée et de mon propre désir, et d'élever

---

³⁰ Two of these four distinguished Latin scholars were especially eminent: the Scotsman George Buchanan (1506–82), translator of Euripides into Latin and author of two Latin tragedies, *Jephthes* and *Baptistes*; and Marc-Antoine Muret (1526–85), author of a Latin

book, without grammar or precept, without the whip and without tears, I had learned a Latin quite as pure as what my schoolmaster knew, for I could not have contaminated or altered it. If as a test they wanted to give me a theme in the school fashion, where they give it to others in French, they had to give it to me in bad Latin, to turn it into good. And Nicolas Grouchy, who wrote *De Comitiis Romanorum*, Guillaume Guérente, who wrote a commentary on Aristotle, George Buchanan, that great Scottish poet, ^BMarc-Antoine Muret, ^Cwhom France and Italy recognize as the best orator of his time,[30] ^Amy private tutors, have often told me that in my childhood I had that language so ready and handy that they were afraid to accost me. Buchanan, whom I afterward saw in the suite of the late Marshal de Brissac, told me that he was writing on the education of children and that he was taking my education as a model; for he was then in charge of that Count de Brissac who later showed himself so valorous and brave.

As for Greek, of which I have practically no knowledge at all, my father planned to have me taught it artificially, but in a new way, in the form of amusement and exercise. We volleyed our conjugations back and forth, like those who learn arithmetic and geometry by such games as checkers and chess. For among other things he had been advised to teach me to enjoy knowledge and duty by my own free will and desire, and to educate my mind in all

tragedy, *Julius Cæsar*, and future commentator of Ronsard's *Amours*. Later in this chapter, in a passage not included in these excerpts, Montaigne tells how as a student at the Collège de Guyenne he played the leading roles in Latin tragedies of Buchanan, Guérente, and Muret.

[I:26] *Education of Children*

mon âme en toute douceur et liberté, sans rigueur et contrainte. Je dis jusqu'à telle superstition que parce qu'aucuns tiennent que cela trouble la cervelle tendre des enfants de les éveiller le matin en sursaut et de les arracher du sommeil (auquel ils sont plongés beaucoup plus que nous ne sommes) tout à coup et par violence, il me faisait éveiller par le son de quelque instrument; et ne fus jamais sans homme qui m'en servît.

Cet exemple suffira pour en juger le reste et pour recommander aussi et la prudence et l'affection d'un si bon père, auquel il ne se faut nullement prendre s'il n'a recueilli aucuns fruits répondant à une si exquise culture. Deux choses en furent cause: le champ stérile et incommode; car quoique j'eusse la santé ferme et entière et quand et quand un naturel doux et traitable, j'étais parmi cela si pesant, mol et endormi qu'on ne me pouvait arracher de l'oisiveté, non pas pour me faire jouer. Ce que je voyais je le voyais bien, et sous cette complexion lourde nourrissais des imaginations hardies et des opinions audessus de mon âge. L'esprit, je l'avais lent, et qui n'allait qu'autant qu'on le menait; l'appréhension, tardive; l'invention, lâche; et après tout un incroyable défaut de mémoire. De tout cela il n'est pas merveille s'il ne sut rien tirer qui vaille. Secondement, comme ceux que presse un furieux désir de guérison se laissent aller à toute sorte de conseil, le bon homme, ayant extrême peur de faillir en chose qu'il avait tant à cœur, se laissa enfin emporter à l'opinion commune, qui suit toujours ceux qui vont devant, comme les grues, et se rangea à la coutume, n'ayant plus autour de lui ceux qui lui avaient donné ces premières institutions, qu'il avait apportées d'Italie; et m'envoya,

gentleness and freedom, without rigor and constraint. He did this so religiously that because some hold that it troubles the tender brains of children to wake them in the morning with a start, and to snatch them suddenly and violently from their sleep, in which they are plunged much more deeply than we are, he had me awakened by the sound of some instrument; and I was never without a man to do this for me.

This example will be enough to let you judge the rest, and also to commend both the prudence and the affection of so good a father, who is not at all to be blamed if he reaped no fruit corresponding to such an excellent cultivation. Two things were the cause of this: first, the sterile and unfit soil; for though my health was sound and complete and my nature gentle and tractable, I was withal so sluggish, lax, and drowsy that they could not tear me from my sloth, not even to make me play. What I saw, I saw well, and beneath this inert appearance nourished bold ideas and opinions beyond my years. I had a slow mind, which would go only as far as it was led; a tardy understanding, a weak imagination, and on top of all an incredible lack of memory. It is no wonder if he could get nothing worth while from all this.

Second, just as people frantically eager to be cured will try any sort of advice, that good man, being extremely afraid of failing in a thing so close to his heart, at last let himself be carried away by the common opinion, which always follows the leader like a flock of cranes, and fell in line with custom, having no longer about him the men who had given him those first plans, which he had brought from Italy. And he sent me, when I was about six, to the

environ mes six ans, au Collège de Guyenne, très florissant pour lors et le meilleur de France. Et là il n'est possible de rien ajouter au soin qu'il eut et à me choisir des précepteurs de chambre suffisants et à toutes les autres circonstances de ma nourriture, en laquelle il réserva plusieurs façons particulières contre l'usage des collèges. Mais tant y a que c'était toujours collège. Mon latin s'abâtardit incontinent, duquel depuis par désaccoutumance j'ai perdu tout usage. Et ne me servit cette mienne nouvelle institution que de me faire enjamber d'arrivée aux premières classes; car à treize ans que je sortis du collège j'avais achevé mon cours (qu'ils appellent), et à la vérité sans aucun fruit que je pusse à présent mettre en compte. . . .

Pour revenir à mon propos, il n'y a tel que d'allécher l'appétit et l'affection, autrement on ne fait que des ânes chargés de livres. On leur donne à coups de fouet en garde leur pochette pleine de science, laquelle, pour bien faire, il ne faut pas seulement loger chez soi, il la faut épouser.

31   *Des cannibales* [1]

AQuand le roi Pyrrhus passa en Italie, après qu'il eut reconnu l'ordonnance de l'armée que les Romains lui envoyaient au devant: "Je ne sais," dit-il, "quels barbares sont ceux-ci," (car les Grecs appelaient ainsi toutes les

---

[1] Composed around 1579 or 1580.

Collège de Guyenne, which was then very flourishing and the best in France. And there, nothing could be added to the care he took, both to choose me competent personal tutors and in all the other aspects of my education, in which he held out for certain particular practices contrary to school usage. But for all that, it was still school. My Latin promptly degenerated, and since then, for lack of practice, I have lost all use of it. And all this novel education of mine did for me was to make me skip immediately to the upper classes; for when I left the school at thirteen, I had finished my course (as they call it), and in truth without any benefit that I can place in evidence now. . . .

ᴬTo return to my subject, there is nothing like arousing appetite and affection; otherwise all you make out of them is asses loaded with books. By dint of whipping, they are given their pocketful of learning for safekeeping; but if learning is to do us any good, we must not merely lodge it within us, we must espouse it.

31 *Of Cannibals* [1]

ᴬWhen King Pyrrhus passed over into Italy, after he had reconnoitered the formation of the army that the Romans were sending to meet him, he said: "I do not know what barbarians these are" (for so the Greeks called all foreign

nations étrangères) "mais la disposition de cette armée que je vois n'est aucunement barbare." Autant en dirent les Grecs de celle que Flaminius fit passer en leur pays; ^cet Philippus, voyant d'un tertre l'ordre et distribution du camp romain en son royaume, sous Publius Sulpicius Galba. ^AVoilà comment il se faut garder de s'attacher aux opinions vulgaires, et les faut juger par la voie de la raison, non par la voix commune.

J'ai eu longtemps avec moi un homme qui avait demeuré dix ou douze ans en cet autre monde qui a été découvert en notre siècle, en l'endroit où Villegaignon prit terre, qu'il surnomma la France Antarctique.[2] Cette découverte d'un pays infini semble être de considération. Je ne sais si je me puis répondre qu'il ne s'en fasse à l'avenir quelque autre, tant de personnages plus grands que nous ayant été trompés en celle-ci. J'ai peur que nous avons les yeux plus grands que le ventre, et plus de curiosité que nous n'avons de capacité. Nous embrassons tout, mais nous n'étreignons que du vent.

Platon introduit Solon racontant avoir appris des prêtres de la ville de Saïs en Égypte que, jadis et avant le déluge, il y avait une grande île, nommée Atlantide,[3] droit à la bouche du détroit de Gibraltar, qui tenait plus de pays que l'Afrique et l'Asie toutes deux ensemble; et que les rois de cette contrée-là, qui ne possédaient pas seulement cette île mais s'étaient étendus dans la terre ferme si avant qu'ils tenaient de la largeur d'Afrique jusqu'en Égypte et de la longueur de l'Europe jusqu'en la Toscane, entreprirent d'enjamber jusque sur l'Asie et subjuguer toutes

---

[2] Villegaignon reached Brazil in 1557.

nations), "but the formation of this army that I see is not at all barbarous." The Greeks said as much of the army that Flamininus brought into their country, ᶜand so did Philip, seeing from a knoll the order and distribution of the Roman camp, in his kingdom, under Publius Sulpicius Galba. ᴬThus we should beware of clinging to vulgar opinions, and judge them by reason's way, not by popular say.

I had with me for a long time a man who had lived for ten or twelve years in that other world which has been discovered in our century, in the place where Villegaignon landed, and which he called Antarctic France.[2] This discovery of a boundless country seems worthy of consideration. I don't know if I can guarantee that some other such discovery will not be made in the future, so many personages greater than ourselves having been mistaken about this one. I am afraid we have eyes bigger than our stomachs, and more curiosity than capacity. We embrace everything, but we clasp only wind.

Plato brings in Solon, telling how he had learned from the priests of the city of Saïs in Egypt that in days of old, before the Flood, there was a great island named Atlantis,[3] right at the mouth of the Strait of Gibraltar, which contained more land than Africa and Asia put together, and that the kings of that country, who not only possessed that island but had stretched out so far on the mainland that they held the breadth of Africa as far as Egypt, and the length of Europe as far as Tuscany, undertook to step over into Asia and subjugate all the nations that border on the

---

[3] Plato's account of Atlantis is in the *Timæus*.

[I:31] *Of Cannibals*

les nations qui bordent la mer Méditerranée jusqu'au golfe de la mer Majeure; et pour cet effet, traversèrent les Espagnes, la Gaule, l'Italie, jusqu'en la Grèce, où les Athéniens les soutinrent; mais que quelque temps après, et les Athéniens, et eux, et leur île, furent engloutis par le déluge. Il est bien vraisemblable que cet extrême ravage d'eaux ait fait des changements étranges aux habitations de la terre, comme on tient que la mer a retranché la Sicile d'avec l'Italie—

> [B]Hæc loca, vi quondam et vasta convulsa ruina,
> Dissiluisse ferunt, cum protinus utraque tellus
> Una foret,[4]

—[A]Chypre d'avec la Syrie, l'île de Nègrepont de la terre ferme de la Béotie; et joint ailleurs les terres qui étaient divisées, comblant de limon et de sable les fosses d'entre-deux:

> sterilisque diu palus aptaque remis
> Vicinas urbes alit, et grave sentit aratrum.[5]

Mais il n'y a pas grande apparence que cette île soit ce monde nouveau que nous venons de découvrir; car elle touchait quasi l'Espagne, et ce serait un effet incroyable d'inondation de l'en avoir reculée, comme elle est, de plus de douze cents lieues; outre ce que les navigations des modernes ont déjà presque découvert que ce n'est point une île, ains terre ferme et continente avec l'Inde orientale d'un côté et avec les terres qui sont sous les deux

---

[4] Virgil, *Aeneid*, III, 414–6.

Mediterranean, as far as the Black Sea; and for this purpose crossed the Spains, Gaul, Italy, as far as Greece, where the Athenians checked them; but that some time after, both the Athenians and themselves and their island were swallowed up by the Flood.

It is quite likely that that extreme devastation of waters made amazing changes in the habitations of the earth, as people maintain that the sea cut off Sicily from Italy—

> [B]'Tis said an earthquake once asunder tore
> These lands with dreadful havoc, which before
> Formed but one land, one coast [4]

—[A]Cyprus from Syria, the island of Euboea from the mainland of Boeotia; and elsewhere joined lands that were divided, filling the channels between them with sand and mud:

> A sterile marsh, long fit for rowing, now
> Feeds neighbor towns, and feels the heavy plow.[5]

But there is no great likelihood that that island was the new world which we have just discovered; for it almost touched Spain, and it would be an incredible result of a flood to have forced it away as far as it is, more than twelve hundred leagues; besides, the travels of the moderns have already almost revealed that it is not an island, but a mainland connected with the East Indies on one side, and elsewhere with the lands under the two poles; or, if it is sepa-

---

[5] Horace, *Ars Poetica*, 65–6.

[I:31] *Of Cannibals*

pôles d'autre part; ou, si elle en est séparée, que c'est d'un
si petit détroit et intervalle qu'elle ne mérite pas d'être
nommée île pour cela.

^BIl semble qu'il y ait des mouvements, ^cnaturels les
uns, les autres ^Bfiévreux, en ces grands corps comme aux
nôtres. Quand je considère l'impression que ma rivière
de Dordogne fait de mon temps vers la rive droite de sa
descente, et qu'en vingt ans elle a tant gagné, et dérobé le
fondement à plusieurs bâtiments, je vois bien que c'est
une agitation extraordinaire; car si elle fût allée ce train,
ou dût aller à l'avenir, la figure du monde serait renversée.
Mais il leur prend des changements: tantôt elles s'épan-
dent d'un côté, tantôt d'un autre, tantôt elles se contiennent. Je ne parle pas des soudaines inondations de quoi
nous manions les causes. En Médoc, le long de la mer,
mon frère, sieur d'Arsac, voit une sienne terre ensevelie
sous les sables que la mer vomit devant elle; le faîte d'aucuns bâtiments paraît encore; ses rentes et domaines se
sont échangés en pacages bien maigres. Les habitants
disent que depuis quelque temps la mer se pousse si fort
vers eux qu'ils ont perdu quatre lieues de terre. Ces sables
sont ses fourriers; ^cet voyons des grandes monts-joies
d'arène mouvante, qui marchent d'une demi-lieue devant
elle, et gagnent pays.

^AL'autre témoignage de l'antiquité auquel on veut rap-
porter cette découverte est dans Aristote, au moins si ce
petit livret *Des merveilles inouïes* est à lui. Il raconte là
que certains Carthaginois, s'étant jetés au travers de la mer
Atlantique hors le détroit de Gibraltar, et navigué longtemps, avaient découvert enfin une grande île fertile, toute
revêtue de bois et arrosée de grandes et profondes rivières,

rated from them, it is by so narrow a strait and interval that it does not deserve to be called an island on that account.

^BIt seems that there are movements, ^Csome natural, others ^Bfeverish, in these great bodies, just as in our own. When I consider the inroads that my river, the Dordogne, is making in my lifetime into the right bank in its descent, and that in twenty years it has gained so much ground and stolen away the foundations of several buildings, I clearly see that this is an extraordinary disturbance; for if it had always gone at this rate, or was to do so in the future, the face of the world would be turned topsy-turvy. But rivers are subject to changes: now they overflow in one direction, now in another, now they keep to their course. I am not speaking of the sudden inundations whose causes are manifest. In Médoc, along the seashore, my brother, the sieur d'Arsac, can see an estate of his buried under the sands that the sea spews forth; the tops of some buildings are still visible; his farms and domains have changed into very thin pasturage. The inhabitants say that for some time the sea has been pushing toward them so hard that they have lost four leagues of land. These sands are its harbingers; ^Cand we see great dunes of moving sand that march half a league ahead of it and keep conquering land.

^AThe other testimony of antiquity with which some would connect this discovery is in Aristotle, at least if that little book *Of Unheard-of Wonders* is by him. He there relates that certain Carthaginians, after setting out upon the Atlantic Ocean from the Strait of Gibraltar and sailing a long time, at last discovered a great fertile island, all clothed in woods and watered by great deep rivers, far

[I:31] *Of Cannibals*

fort éloignée de toutes terres fermes; et qu'eux et autres depuis, attirés par la bonté et fertilité du terroir, s'y en allèrent avec leurs femmes et enfants et commencèrent à s'y habituer. Les seigneurs de Carthage, voyant que leur pays se dépeuplait peu à peu, firent défense expresse, sur peine de mort, que nul n'eût plus à aller là, et en chassèrent ces nouveaux habitants, craignant, à ce que l'on dit, que par succession de temps ils ne vinssent à multiplier tellement qu'ils les supplantassent eux-mêmes et ruinassent leur état. Cette narration d'Aristote n'a non plus d'accord avec nos terres neuves.

Cet homme que j'avais était homme simple et grossier,[6] qui est une condition propre à rendre véritable témoignage. Car les fines gens remarquent bien plus curieusement et plus de choses, mais ils les glosent; et pour faire valoir leur interprétation et la persuader, ils ne se peuvent garder d'altérer un peu l'histoire: ils ne vous représentent jamais les choses pures, ils les inclinent et masquent selon le visage qu'ils leur ont vu; et, pour donner crédit à leur jugement et vous y attirer, prêtent volontiers de ce côté-là à la matière, l'allongent et l'amplifient. Ou il faut un homme très fidèle, ou si simple qu'il n'ait pas de quoi bâtir et donner de la vraisemblance à des inventions fausses; et qui n'ait rien épousé. Le mien était tel; et outre cela, il m'a fait voir à diverses fois plusieurs matelots et marchands qu'il avait connus en ce voyage. Ainsi je me contente de cette information sans m'enquérir de ce que les cosmographes en disent.

Il nous faudrait des topographes qui nous fissent narra-

---

[6] The traveler Montaigne spoke of at the beginning of the chapter.

remote from any mainland; and that they, and others since, attracted by the goodness and fertility of the soil, went there with their wives and children, and began to settle there. The lords of Carthage, seeing that their country was gradually becoming depopulated, expressly forbade anyone to go there any more, on pain of death, and drove out these new inhabitants, fearing, it is said, that in course of time they might come to multiply so greatly as to supplant their former masters and ruin their state. This story of Aristotle does not fit our new lands any better than the other.

This man I had was a simple, crude fellow [6]—a character fit to bear true witness; for clever people observe more things and more curiously, but they interpret them; and to lend weight and conviction to their interpretation, they cannot help altering history a little. They never show you things as they are, but bend and disguise them according to the way they have seen them; and to give credence to their judgment and attract you to it, they are prone to add something to their matter, to stretch it out and amplify it. We need a man either very honest, or so simple that he has not the stuff to build up false inventions and give them plausibility; and wedded to no theory. Such was my man; and besides this, he at various times brought sailors and merchants, whom he had known on that trip, to see me. So I content myself with his information, without inquiring what the cosmographers say about it.

We ought to have topographers who would give us an

tion particulière des endroits où ils ont été. Mais pour avoir cet avantage sur nous d'avoir vu la Palestine, ils veulent jouir de ce privilège de nous conter nouvelles de tout le demeurant du monde. Je voudrais que chacun écrivît ce qu'il sait et autant qu'il en sait, non en cela seulement mais en tous autres sujets: car tel peut avoir quelque particulière science ou expérience de la nature d'une rivière ou d'une fontaine, qui ne sait au reste que ce que chacun sait. Il entreprendra toutefois, pour faire courir ce petit lopin, d'écrire toute la physique. De ce vice sourdent plusieurs grandes incommodités.

Or je trouve, pour revenir à mon propos, qu'il n'y a rien de barbare et de sauvage en cette nation, à ce qu'on m'en a rapporté, sinon que chacun appelle barbarie ce qui n'est pas de son usage; comme de vrai il semble que nous n'avons autre mire de la vérité et de la raison que l'exemple et idée des opinions et usances du pays où nous sommes. Là est toujours la parfaite religion, la parfaite police, parfait et accompli usage de toutes choses. Ils sont sauvages, de même que nous appelons sauvages les fruits que nature, de soi et de son progrès ordinaire, a produits; là où à la vérité ce sont ceux que nous avons altérés par notre artifice et détournés de l'ordre commun que nous devrions appeler plutôt sauvages. En ceux-là sont vives et vigoureuses les vraies et plus utiles et naturelles vertus et propriétés, lesquelles nous avons abâtardies en ceux-ci, et les avons seulement accommodées au plaisir de notre goût corrompu. ᶜEt si pourtant la saveur même et délicatesse se trouve à notre goût excellente, à l'envi des nôtres, en divers fruits de ces contrées-là, sans culture. ᴬCe n'est pas raison que l'art gagne le point d'honneur

exact account of the places where they have been. But because they have over us the advantage of having seen Palestine, they want to enjoy the privilege of telling us news about all the rest of the world. I would like everyone to write what he knows, and as much as he knows, not only in this, but in all other subjects; for a man may have some special knowledge and experience of the nature of a river or a fountain, who in other matters knows only what everybody knows. However, to circulate this little scrap of knowledge, he will undertake to write the whole of physics. From this vice spring many great abuses.

Now, to return to my subject, I think there is nothing barbarous and savage in that nation, from what I have been told, except that each man calls barbarism whatever is not his own practice; for indeed it seems we have no other test of truth and reason than the example and pattern of the opinions and customs of the country we live in. *There* is always the perfect religion, the perfect government, the perfect and accomplished manners in all things. Those people are wild, just as we call wild the fruits that Nature has produced by herself and in her normal course; whereas really it is those that we have changed artificially and led astray from the common order, that we should rather call wild. The former retain alive and vigorous their genuine, their most useful and natural, virtues and properties, which we have debased in the latter in adapting them to gratify our corrupted taste. ^CAnd yet for all that, the savor and delicacy of some uncultivated fruits of those countries is quite as excellent, even to our taste, as that of our own. ^AIt is not reasonable that art should win the place of honor over our great and powerful mother Nature.

[I:31] *Of Cannibals*

sur notre grande et puissante mère nature. Nous avons tant rechargé la beauté et richesse de ses ouvrages par nos inventions que nous l'avons du tout étouffée. Si est-ce que, partout où sa pureté reluit, elle fait une merveilleuse honte à nos vaines et frivoles entreprises:

> [B]Et veniunt ederæ sponte sua melius,
> Surgit et in solis formosior arbutus antris,
> Et volucres nulla dulcius arte canunt.[7]

[A]Tous nos efforts ne peuvent seulement arriver à représenter le nid du moindre oiselet, sa contexture, sa beauté et l'utilité de son usage, non pas la tissure de la chétive araignée. [C]Toutes choses, dit Platon, sont produites par la nature, ou par la fortune, ou par l'art; les plus grandes et plus belles, par l'une ou l'autre des deux premières; les moindres et imparfaites, par la dernière.

[A]Ces nations me semblent donc ainsi barbares, pour avoir reçu fort peu de façon de l'esprit humain, et être encore fort voisines de leur naïveté originelle. Les lois naturelles leur commandent encore, fort peu abâtardies par les nôtres; mais c'est en telle pureté qu'il me prend quelquefois déplaisir de quoi la connaissance n'en soit venue plus tôt, du temps qu'il y avait des hommes qui en eussent su mieux juger que nous. Il me déplaît que Lycurgus et Platon ne l'aient eue; car il me semble que ce que nous voyons par expérience en ces nations-là surpasse non seulement toutes les peintures de quoi la poésie a embelli l'âge doré, et toutes ses inventions à feindre une heureuse condition d'hommes, mais encore la conception et le désir

---

[7] Propertius, *Elegies*, I, ii, 10–12.

We have so overloaded the beauty and richness of her works by our inventions that we have quite smothered her. Yet wherever her purity shines forth, she wonderfully puts to shame our vain and frivolous attempts:

> ^BIvy comes readier without our care;
> In lonely caves the arbutus grows more fair;
> No art with artless bird song can compare.⁷

^AAll our efforts cannot even succeed in reproducing the nest of the tiniest little bird, its contexture, its beauty and convenience; or even the web of the puny spider. ^CAll things, says Plato, are produced by nature, by fortune, or by art; the greatest and most beautiful by one or the other of the first two, the least and most imperfect by the last.

^AThese nations, then, seem to me barbarous in this sense, that they have been fashioned very little by the human mind, and are still very close to their original naturalness. The laws of nature still rule them, very little corrupted by ours; and they are in such a state of purity that I am sometimes vexed that they were unknown earlier, in the days when there were men able to judge them better than we. I am sorry that Lycurgus and Plato did not know of them; for it seems to me that what we actually see in these nations surpasses not only all the pictures in which poets have idealized the golden age and all their inventions in imagining a happy state of man, but also the conceptions and the very desire of philosophy. They could not

même de la philosophie. Ils n'ont pu imaginer une naïveté si pure et simple comme nous la voyons par expérience; ni n'ont pu croire que notre société se pût maintenir avec si peu d'artifice et de soudure humaine. C'est une nation, dirais-je à Platon,[8] en laquelle il n'y a aucune espèce de trafic; nulle connaissance de lettres; nulle science de nombres; nul nom de magistrat ni de supériorité politique; nul usage de service, de richesse ou de pauvreté; nuls contrats; nulles successions; nuls partages; nulles occupations qu'oisives; nul respect de parenté que commun; nuls vêtements; nulle agriculture; nul métal; nul usage de vin ou de blé. Les paroles mêmes qui signifient le mensonge, la trahison, la dissimulation, l'avarice, l'envie, la détraction, le pardon, inouïes. Combien trouverait-il la république qu'il a imaginée, éloignée de cette perfection: Cviri a diis recentes.[9]

BHos natura modos primum dedit.[10]

AAu demeurant, ils vivent en une contrée de pays très plaisante et bien tempérée: de façon qu'à ce que m'ont dit mes témoins il est rare d'y voir un homme malade; et m'ont assuré n'en y avoir vu aucun tremblant, chassieux, édenté, ou courbé de vieillesse. Ils sont assis le long de la mer, et fermés du côté de la terre de grandes et hautes montagnes, ayant entre-deux cent lieues ou environ d'étendue en large. Ils ont grande abondance de poisson et de chairs qui n'ont aucune ressemblance aux nôtres, et les mangent sans autre artifice que de les cuire. Le premier

---

[8] The passage that follows is imitated by Shakespeare in *The Tempest*, ii, i, 154 ff.

imagine a naturalness so pure and simple as we see by experience; nor could they believe that our society could be maintained with so little artifice and human solder. This is a nation, I should say to Plato,[8] in which there is no sort of traffic, no knowledge of letters, no science of numbers, no name for a magistrate or for political superiority, no custom of servitude, no riches or poverty, no contracts, no successions, no partitions, no occupations but leisure ones, no care for any but common kinship, no clothes, no agriculture, no metal, no use of wine or wheat. The very words that signify lying, treachery, dissimulation, avarice, envy, belittling, pardon—unheard of. How far from this perfection would he find the republic that he imagined: ^C*Men fresh sprung from the gods.*[9]

^BThese manners nature first ordained.[10]

^AFor the rest, they live in a country with a very pleasant and temperate climate, so that according to my witnesses it is rare to see a sick man there; and they have assured me that they never saw one palsied, bleary-eyed, toothless, or bent with age. They are settled along the sea and shut in on the land side by great high mountains, with a stretch about a hundred leagues wide in between. They have a great abundance of fish and flesh which bear no resemblance to ours, and they eat them with no other artifice than cooking. The first man who rode a horse there, though

---

9 Seneca, *Epistles*, xc, 44.
10 Virgil, *Georgics*, ii, 20.

qui y mena un cheval, quoiqu'il les eût pratiqués à plusieurs autres voyages, leur fit tant d'horreur en cette assiette qu'ils le tuèrent à coups de trait avant que le pouvoir reconnaître.

Leurs bâtiments sont fort longs et capables de deux ou trois cents âmes, étoffés d'écorce de grands arbres, tenant à terre par un bout et se soutenant et appuyant l'un contre l'autre par le faîte à la mode d'aucunes de nos granges, desquelles la couverture pend jusqu'à terre et sert de flanc. Ils ont du bois si dur qu'ils en coupent et en font leurs épées et des grils à cuire leur viande. Leurs lits sont d'un tissu de coton, suspendus contre le toit comme ceux de nos navires, à chacun le sien; car les femmes couchent à part des maris.

Ils se lèvent avec le soleil et mangent soudain après s'être levés, pour toute la journée; car ils ne font autre repas que celui-là. Ils ne boivent pas lors, comme Suidas dit de quelques autres peuples d'Orient qui buvaient hors du manger; ils boivent à plusieurs fois sur jour, et d'autant. Leur breuvage est fait de quelque racine et est de la couleur de nos vins clairets. Ils ne le boivent que tiède; ce breuvage ne se conserve que deux ou trois jours; il a le goût un peu piquant, nullement fumeux, salutaire à l'estomac, et laxatif à ceux qui ne l'ont accoutumé; c'est une boisson très agréable à qui y est duit. Au lieu du pain, ils usent d'une certaine matière blanche, comme du coriandre confit. J'en ai tâté: le goût en est doux et un peu fade.

Toute la journée se passe à danser. Les plus jeunes vont à la chasse des bêtes à tout des arcs. Une partie des fem-

he had had dealings with them on several other trips, so horrified them in this posture that they shot him dead with arrows before they could recognize him.

Their buildings are very long, with a capacity of two or three hundred souls; they are covered with the bark of great trees, the strips reaching to the ground at one end and supporting and leaning on one another at the top, in the manner of some of our barns, whose covering hangs down to the ground and acts as a side. They have wood so hard that they cut with it and make of it their swords and grills to cook their food. Their beds are of a cotton weave, hung from the roof like those in our ships, each man having his own; for the wives sleep apart from their husbands.

They get up with the sun, and eat immediately upon rising, to last them through the day; for they take no other meal than that one. Like some other Eastern peoples, of whom Suidas tells us, who drank apart from meals, they do not drink then; but they drink several times a day, and to capacity. Their drink is made of some root, and is of the color of our claret wines. They drink it only lukewarm. This beverage keeps only two or three days; it has a slightly sharp taste, is not at all heady, is good for the stomach, and has a laxative effect upon those who are not used to it; it is a very pleasant drink for any one who is accustomed to it. In place of bread they use a certain white substance like preserved coriander. I have tried it; it tastes sweet and a little flat.

The whole day is spent in dancing. The younger men go to hunt animals with bows. Some of the women busy

mes s'amusent cependant à chauffer leur breuvage, qui est leur principal office. Il y a quelqu'un des vieillards qui, le matin, avant qu'ils se mettent à manger, prêche en commun toute la grangée, en se promenant d'un bout à autre et redisant une même clause à plusieurs fois jusqu'à ce qu'il ait achevé le tour (car ce sont bâtiments qui ont bien cent pas de longueur). Il ne leur recommande que deux choses: la vaillance contre les ennemis et l'amitié à leurs femmes. Et ne faillent jamais de remarquer cette obligation, pour leur refrain, que ce sont elles qui leur maintiennent leur boisson tiède et assaisonnée.

Il se voit en plusieurs lieux, et entre autres chez moi, la forme de leurs lits, de leurs cordons, de leurs épées et bracelets de bois de quoi ils couvrent leurs poignets aux combats, et des grandes cannes, ouvertes par un bout, par le son desquelles ils soutiennent la cadence en leur danser. Ils sont ras partout, et se font le poil beaucoup plus nettement que nous, sans autre rasoir que de bois ou de pierre. Ils croient les âmes éternelles, et celles qui ont bien mérité des dieux être logées à l'endroit du ciel où le soleil se lève; les maudites, du côté de l'Occident.

Ils ont je ne sais quels prêtres et prophètes, qui se présentent bien rarement au peuple, ayant leur demeure aux montagnes. A leur arrivée il se fait une grande fête et assemblée solennelle de plusieurs villages (chaque grange, comme je l'ai décrite, fait un village; et sont environ à une lieue française l'une de l'autre). Ce prophète parle à eux en public, les exhortant à la vertu et à leur devoir; mais toute leur science éthique ne contient que ces deux articles, de la résolution à la guerre et affection à leurs femmes. Celui-ci leur pronostique les choses à venir et les

themselves meanwhile with warming their drink, which is their chief duty. Some one of the old men, in the morning before they begin to eat, preaches to the whole barnful in common, walking from one end to the other, and repeating one single sentence several times until he has completed the circuit (for the buildings are fully a hundred paces long). He recommends to them only two things: valor against the enemy and love for their wives. And they never fail to point out this obligation, as their refrain, that it is their wives who keep their drink warm and seasoned.

There may be seen in several places, including my own house, specimens of their beds, of their ropes, of their wooden swords and the bracelets with which they cover their wrists in combats, and of the big canes, open at one end, by whose sound they keep time in their dances. They are close shaven all over, and shave themselves much more cleanly than we, with nothing but a wooden or stone razor. They believe that souls are immortal, and that those who have deserved well of the gods are lodged in that part of heaven where the sun rises, and the damned in the west.

They have some sort of priests and prophets, but they rarely appear before the people, having their home in the mountains. On their arrival there is a great feast and solemn assembly of several villages—each barn, as I have described it, makes up a village, and they are about one French league from each other. The prophet speaks to them in public, exhorting them to virtue and their duty; but their whole ethical science contains only these two articles: resoluteness in war and affection for their wives. He prophesies to them things to come and the results they

événements qu'ils doivent espérer de leurs entreprises, les achemine ou détourne de la guerre; mais c'est par tel si que, où il faut à bien deviner, et s'il leur advient autrement qu'il ne leur a prédit, il est haché en mille pièces s'ils l'attrapent, et condamné pour faux prophète. A cette cause, celui qui s'est une fois mécompté, on ne le voit plus.

ᶜC'est don de Dieu que la divination: voilà pourquoi ce devrait être une imposture punissable, d'en abuser. Entre les Scythes, quand les devins avaient failli de rencontre, on les couchait, enforgés de pieds et de mains, sur des charrettes pleines de bruyère, tirées par des bœufs, en quoi on les faisait brûler. Ceux qui manient les choses sujettes à la conduite de l'humaine suffisance sont excusables d'y faire ce qu'ils peuvent. Mais ces autres qui nous viennent pipant des assurances d'une faculté extraordinaire qui est hors de notre connaissance, faut-il pas les punir de ce qu'ils ne maintiennent l'effet de leur promesse, et de la témérité de leur imposture?

ᴬIls ont leurs guerres contre les nations qui sont au delà de leurs montagnes, plus avant en la terre ferme, auxquelles ils vont tous nus, n'ayant autres armes que des arcs ou des épées de bois, appointées par un bout, à la mode des langues de nos épieus. C'est chose émerveillable que de la fermeté de leurs combats, qui ne finissent jamais que par meurtre et effusion de sang; car, de routes et d'effroi, ils ne savent que c'est.

Chacun rapporte pour son trophée la tête de l'ennemi qu'il a tué et l'attache à l'entrée de son logis. Après avoir longtemps bien traité leurs prisonniers, et de toutes les commodités dont ils se peuvent aviser, celui qui en est

are to expect from their undertakings, and urges them to war or holds them back from it; but this is on the condition that when he fails to prophesy correctly, and if things turn out otherwise than he has predicted, he is cut into a thousand pieces if they catch him, and condemned as a false prophet. For this reason, the prophet who has once been mistaken is never seen again.

^CDivination is a gift of God; that is why its abuse should be punished as imposture. Among the Scythians, when the soothsayers failed to hit the mark, they were laid, chained hand and foot, on carts full of heather and drawn by oxen, on which they were burned. Those who handle matters subject to the control of human capacity are excusable if they do the best they can. But these others, who come and trick us with assurances of an extraordinary faculty that is beyond our ken, should they not be punished for not making good their promise, and for the temerity of their imposture?

^AThey have their wars with the nations beyond the mountains, further inland, to which they go quite naked, with no other arms than bows or wooden swords ending in a sharp point, in the manner of the tongues of our boar spears. It is astonishing what firmness they show in their combats, which never end but in slaughter and bloodshed; for as to routs and terror, they know nothing of either.

Each man brings back as his trophy the head of the enemy he has killed, and sets it up at the entrance to his dwelling. After they have treated their prisoners well for a long time with all the hospitality they can think of, each

le maître fait une grande assemblée de ses connaissants. Il attache une corde à l'un des bras du prisonnier, ^cpar le bout de laquelle il le tient éloigné de quelques pas de peur d'en être offensé, ^Aet donne au plus cher de ses amis l'autre bras à tenir de même; et eux deux, en présence de toute l'assemblée, l'assomment à coups d'épée. Cela fait, ils le rôtissent et en mangent en commun et en envoient des lopins à ceux de leurs amis qui sont absents. Ce n'est pas, comme on pense, pour s'en nourrir, ainsi que faisaient anciennement les Scythes: c'est pour représenter une extrême vengeance. Et qu'il soit ainsi, ayant aperçu que les Portugais, qui s'étaient ralliés à leurs adversaires, usaient d'une autre sorte de mort contre eux quand ils les prenaient, qui était de les enterrer jusqu'à la ceinture et tirer au demeurant du corps force coups de trait, et les pendre après, ils pensèrent que ces gens-ci de l'autre monde, comme ceux qui avaient semé la connaissance de beaucoup de vices parmi leur voisinage et qui étaient beaucoup plus grands maîtres qu'eux en toute sorte de malice, ne prenaient pas sans occasion cette sorte de vengeance, et qu'elle devait être plus aigre que la leur, commencèrent de quitter leur façon ancienne pour suivre celle-ci.

Je ne suis pas marri que nous remarquons l'horreur barbaresque qu'il y a en une telle action, mais oui bien de quoi, jugeant bien de leurs fautes, nous soyons si aveuglés aux nôtres. Je pense qu'il y a plus de barbarie à manger un homme vivant qu'à le manger mort, à déchirer par tourments et par gênes un corps encore plein de sentiment, le faire rôtir par le menu, le faire mordre et meurtrir aux chiens et aux pourceaux (comme nous l'avons non seulement lu mais vu de fraîche mémoire, non entre

man who has a prisoner calls a great assembly of his acquaintances. He ties a rope to one of the prisoner's arms, ᶜby the end of which he holds him, a few steps away, for fear of being hurt, ᴬand gives his dearest friend the other arm to hold in the same way; and these two, in the presence of the whole assembly, kill him with their swords. This done, they roast him and eat him in common and send some pieces to their absent friends. This is not, as people think, for nourishment, as of old the Scythians used to do; it is to betoken an extreme revenge. And the proof of this came when they saw the Portuguese, who had joined forces with their adversaries, inflict a different kind of death on them when they took them prisoner, which was to bury them up to the waist, shoot the rest of their body full of arrows, and afterward hang them. They thought that these people from the other world, being men who had sown the knowledge of many vices among their neighbors and were much greater masters than themselves in every sort of wickedness, did not adopt this sort of vengeance without some reason, and that it must be more painful than their own; so they began to give up their old method and to follow this one.

I am not sorry that we notice the barbarous horror of such acts, but I am heartily sorry that, judging their faults rightly, we should be so blind to our own. I think there is more barbarity in eating a man alive than in eating him dead; and in tearing by tortures and the rack a body still full of feeling, in roasting a man bit by bit, in having him bitten and mangled by dogs and swine (as we have not only read but seen within fresh memory, not among ancient enemies, but among neighbors and fellow citizens,

des ennemis anciens mais entre des voisins et concitoyens, et, qui pis est, sous prétexte de piété et de religion), que de le rôtir et manger après qu'il est trépassé.

Chrysippus et Zénon, chefs de la secte stoïque, ont bien pensé qu'il n'y avait aucun mal de se servir de notre charogne à quoi que ce fût pour notre besoin, et d'en tirer de la nourriture; comme nos ancêtres, étant assiégés par Cæsar en la ville d'Alexia,[11] se résolurent de soutenir la faim de ce siège par les corps des vieillards, des femmes et autres personnes inutiles au combat.

> [B]Vascones, fama est, alimentis talibus usi
> Produxere animas.[12]

[A]Et les médecins ne craignent pas de s'en servir à toute sorte d'usage pour notre santé, soit pour l'appliquer au dedans, ou au dehors. Mais il ne se trouva jamais aucune opinion si déréglée qui excusât la trahison, la déloyauté, la tyrannie, la cruauté, qui sont nos fautes ordinaires.

Nous les pouvons donc bien appeler barbares, eu égard aux règles de la raison, mais non pas eu égard à nous, qui les surpassons en toute sorte de barbarie.

Leur guerre est toute noble et généreuse, et a autant d'excuse et de beauté que cette maladie humaine en peut recevoir: elle n'a autre fondement parmi eux que la seule jalousie de la vertu. Ils ne sont pas en débat de la conquête de nouvelles terres, car ils jouissent encore de cette liberté naturelle qui les fournit sans travail et sans peine de toutes choses nécessaires, en telle abondance qu'ils n'ont que faire

---

[11] Alésia, where in 52 B.C. Caesar besieged and finally captured Vercingetorix and brought his Gallic wars to an end.

and what is worse, on the pretext of piety and religion), than in roasting and eating him after he is dead.

Indeed, Chrysippus and Zeno, heads of the Stoic sect, thought there was nothing wrong in using our carcasses for any purpose in case of need, and getting nourishment from them; just as our ancestors, when besieged by Caesar in the city of Alésia,[11] resolved to relieve their famine by eating old men, women, and other people useless for fighting.

> [B]The Gascons once, 'tis said, their life renewed
> By eating of such food.[12]

[A]And physicians do not fear to use human flesh in all sorts of ways for our health, applying it either inwardly or outwardly. But there never was any opinion so disordered as to excuse treachery, disloyalty, tyranny, and cruelty, which are our ordinary vices.

So we may well call these people barbarians, in respect to the rules of reason, but not in respect to ourselves, who surpass them in every kind of barbarity.

Their warfare is wholly noble and generous, and as excusable and beautiful as this human disease can be; its only basis among them is their rivalry in valor. They are not fighting for the conquest of new lands, for they still enjoy that natural abundance that provides them without toil and trouble with all necessary things in such profusion that they have no wish to enlarge their boundaries. They

---

[12] Juvenal, *Satires*, xv, 93–4.

[I:31] *Of Cannibals*

d'agrandir leurs limites. Ils sont encore en cet heureux point de ne désirer qu'autant que leurs nécessités naturelles leur ordonnent; tout ce qui est au delà est superflu pour eux.

Ils s'entr'appellent généralement, ceux de même âge, frères; enfants, ceux qui sont au-dessous; et les vieillards sont pères à tous les autres. Ceux-ci laissent à leurs héritiers en commun cette pleine possession de biens par indivis, sans autre titre que celui tout pur que nature donne à ses créatures, les produisant au monde.

Si leurs voisins passent les montagnes pour les venir assaillir et qu'ils emportent la victoire sur eux, l'acquêt du victorieux c'est la gloire, et l'avantage d'être demeuré maître en valeur et en vertu; car autrement ils n'ont que faire des biens des vaincus, et s'en retournent à leur pays, où ils n'ont faute d'aucune chose nécessaire ni faute encore de cette grande partie, de savoir heureusement jouir de leur condition et s'en contenter. Autant en font ceux-ci à leur tour. Ils ne demandent à leurs prisonniers autre rançon que la confession et reconnaissance d'être vaincus; mais il ne s'en trouve pas un, en tout un siècle, qui n'aime mieux la mort que de relâcher, ni par contenance ni de parole, un seul point d'une grandeur de courage invincible: il ne s'en voit aucun qui n'aime mieux être tué et mangé que de requérir seulement de ne l'être pas. Ils les traitent en toute liberté, afin que la vie leur soit d'autant plus chère; et les entretiennent communément des menaces de leur mort future, des tourments qu'ils y auront à souffrir, des apprêts qu'on dresse pour cet effet, du détranchement de leurs membres, et du festin qui se fera à leurs dépens. Tout cela se fait pour cette seule fin d'arracher de

are still in that happy state of desiring only as much as their natural needs demand; anything beyond that is superfluous to them.

They generally call those of the same age, brothers; those who are younger, children; and the old men are fathers to all the others. These leave to their heirs in common the full possession of their property, without division or any other title at all than just the one that Nature gives to her creatures in bringing them into the world.

If their neighbors cross the mountains to attack them and win a victory, the gain of the victor is glory, and the advantage of having proved the master in valor and virtue; for apart from this they have no use for the goods of the vanquished, and they return to their own country, where they lack neither anything necessary nor that great thing, the knowledge of how to enjoy their condition happily and be content with it. These men of ours do the same in their turn. They demand of their prisoners no other ransom than that they confess and acknowledge their defeat. But there is not one in a whole century who does not choose to die rather than to relax a single bit, by word or look, from the grandeur of an invincible courage; not one who would not rather be killed and eaten than so much as ask not to be. They treat them very freely, so that life may be all the dearer to them, and usually entertain them with threats of their coming death, of the torments they will have to suffer, the preparations that are being made for that purpose, the cutting up of their limbs, and the feast that will be made at their expense. All this is done for the sole purpose of extorting from their lips some weak

[I:31] *Of Cannibals*

leur bouche quelque parole molle ou rabaissée, ou de leur donner envie de s'enfuir, pour gagner cet avantage de les avoir épouvantés et d'avoir fait force à leur constance. Car aussi, à le bien prendre, c'est en ce seul point que consiste la vraie victoire:

^cvictoria nulla est
Quam quæ confessos animo quoque subjugat hostes.¹³

Les Hongrois, très belliqueux combattants, ne poursuivaient jadis leur pointe outre avoir rendu l'ennemi à leur merci. Car, en ayant arraché cette confession, ils le laissaient aller sans offense, sans rançon, sauf pour le plus d'en tirer parole de ne s'armer dès lors en avant contre eux.

^AAssez d'avantages gagnons-nous sur nos ennemis qui sont avantages empruntés, non pas nôtres. C'est la qualité d'un portefaix, non de la vertu, d'avoir les bras et les jambes plus raides; c'est une qualité morte et corporelle que la disposition; c'est un coup de la fortune de faire broncher notre ennemi et de lui éblouir les yeux par la lumière du soleil; c'est un tour d'art et de science, et qui peut tomber en une personne lâche et de néant, d'être suffisant à l'escrime. L'estimation et le prix d'un homme consiste au cœur et en la volonté; c'est là où gît son vrai honneur; la vaillance, c'est la fermeté non pas des jambes et des bras mais du courage et de l'âme; elle ne consiste pas en la valeur de notre cheval ni de nos armes, mais en la nôtre. Celui qui tombe obstiné en son courage, ^csi succiderit, de genu pugnat.¹⁴ ^AQui pour quelque danger

---

¹³ Claudian, De Sexto Consulatu Honorii, xxviii, 248–9.

or base word, or making them want to flee, so as to gain the advantage of having terrified them and broken down their firmness. For indeed, if you take it the right way, it is in this point alone that true victory lies:

^CIt is no victory
Unless the vanquished foe admits your mastery.¹³

The Hungarians, very bellicose fighters, did not in olden times pursue their advantage beyond putting the enemy at their mercy. For having wrung a confession from him to this effect, they let him go unharmed and unransomed, except, at most, for exacting his promise never again to take up arms against them.

^AWe win enough advantages over our enemies that are borrowed advantages, not really our own. It is the quality of a porter, not of valor, to have sturdier arms and legs; agility is a dead and corporeal quality; it is a stroke of luck to make our enemy stumble, or dazzle his eyes by the sunlight; it is a trick of art and technique, which may be found in a worthless coward, to be an able fencer. The worth and value of a man is in his heart and his will; there lies his real honor. Valor is the strength, not of legs and arms, but of heart and soul; it consists not in the worth of our horse or our weapons, but in our own. He who falls obstinate in his courage, ^C*if he has fallen, he fights on his knees.*¹⁴ ^AHe who relaxes none of his assurance, no matter

---

¹⁴ Seneca, *De Providentia,* ii.

de la mort voisine ne relâche aucun point de son assurance; qui regarde encore, en rendant l'âme, son ennemi d'une vue ferme et dédaigneuse; il est battu non pas de nous, mais de la fortune; ^cil est tué, non pas vaincu.

^BLes plus vaillants sont parfois les plus infortunés.

^CAussi y a-t-il des pertes triomphantes à l'envi des victoires. Ni ces quatre victoires sœurs, les plus belles que le soleil ait onques vu de ses yeux, de Salamine, de Platée, de Mycale, de Sicile, osèrent onques opposer toute leur gloire ensemble à la gloire de la déconfiture du roi Léonidas et des siens au pas des Thermopyles.

Qui courut jamais d'une plus glorieuse envie et plus ambitieuse au gain d'un combat, que le capitaine Ischolas à la perte? Qui plus ingénieusement et curieusement s'est assuré de son salut, que lui de sa ruine? Il était commis à défendre certain passage du Péloponnèse contre les Arcadiens. Pour quoi faire se trouvant du tout incapable, vu la nature du lieu et inégalité des forces, et se résolvant que tout ce qui se présenterait aux ennemis aurait de nécessité à y demeurer; d'autre part estimant indigne et de sa propre vertu et magnanimité et du nom lacédémonien, de faillir à sa charge; il prit entre ces deux extrémités un moyen parti, de telle sorte. Les plus jeunes et dispos de sa troupe, il les conserva à la tuition et service de leur pays, et les y renvoya; et avec ceux desquels le défaut était moindre, il délibéra de soutenir ce pas, et par leur mort en faire acheter aux ennemis l'entrée la plus chère qu'il lui serait possible; comme il advint. Car étant tantôt environné de toutes parts par les Arcadiens, après en avoir fait une grande boucherie, lui et les siens furent tous mis

how great the danger of imminent death; who, giving up his soul, still looks firmly and scornfully at his enemy—he is beaten not by us, but by fortune; ^Che is killed, not conquered.

^BThe most valiant are sometimes the most unfortunate. ^CThus there are triumphant defeats that rival victories. Nor did those four sister victories, the fairest that the sun ever set eyes on—Salamis, Plataea, Mycale, and Sicily—ever dare match all their combined glory against the glory of the annihilation of King Leonidas and his men at the pass of Thermopylae.

Who ever hastened with more glorious and ambitious desire to win a battle than Captain Ischolas to lose one? Who ever secured his safety more ingeniously and painstakingly than he did his destruction? He was charged to defend a certain pass in the Peloponnesus against the Arcadians. Finding himself wholly incapable of doing this, in view of the nature of the place and the inequality of the forces, he made up his mind that all who confronted the enemy would necessarily have to remain on the field. On the other hand, deeming it unworthy both of his own virtue and magnanimity and of the Lacedaemonian name to fail in his charge, he took a middle course between these two extremes, in this way. The youngest and fittest of his band he preserved for the defense and service of their country, and sent them home; and with those whose loss was less important, he determined to hold this pass, and by their death to make the enemy buy their entry as dearly as he could. And so it turned out. For he was presently surrounded on all sides by the Arcadians, and after slaughtering a large number of them, he and his men were

[I:31] *Of Cannibals*

au fil de l'épée. Est-il quelque trophée assigné pour les vainqueurs qui ne soit mieux dû à ces vaincus? Le vrai vaincre a pour son rôle l'estor, non pas le salut; et consiste l'honneur de la vertu à combattre, non à battre.

ᴬPour revenir à notre histoire, il s'en faut tant que ces prisonniers se rendent, pour tout ce qu'on leur fait, qu'au rebours, pendant ces deux ou trois mois qu'on les garde, ils portent une contenance gaie; ils pressent leurs maîtres de se hâter de les mettre en cette épreuve; ils les défient, les injurient, leur reprochent leur lâcheté et le nombre des batailles perdues contre les leurs. J'ai une chanson faite par un prisonnier où il y a ce trait: qu'ils viennent hardiment trèstous et s'assemblent pour dîner de lui; car ils mangeront quand et quand leurs pères et leurs aïeux, qui ont servi d'aliment et de nourriture à son corps. "Ces muscles," dit-il, "cette chair et ces veines, ce sont les vôtres, pauvres fous que vous êtes; vous ne reconnaissez pas que la substance des membres de vos ancêtres s'y tient encore: savourez-les bien, vous y trouverez le goût de votre propre chair." Invention qui ne sent aucunement la barbarie.

Ceux qui les peignent mourant et qui représentent cette action quand on les assomme, ils peignent le prisonnier crachant au visage de ceux qui le tuent et leur faisant la moue. De vrai, ils ne cessent jusqu'au dernier soupir de les braver et défier de parole et de contenance. Sans mentir, au prix de nous, voilà des hommes bien sauvages; car ou il faut qu'ils le soient bien à bon escient, ou que nous le soyons: il y a une merveilleuse distance entre leur forme et la nôtre.

Les hommes y ont plusieurs femmes, et en ont d'autant plus grand nombre qu'ils sont en meilleure réputation de

all put to the sword. Is there a trophy dedicated to victors that would not be more due to these vanquished? The role of true victory is in fighting, not in coming off safely; and the honor of valor consists in combating, not in beating.

ᴬTo return to our story. These prisoners are so far from giving in, in spite of all that is done to them, that on the contrary, during the two or three months that they are kept, they wear a gay expression; they urge their captors to hurry and put them to the test; they defy them, insult them, reproach them with their cowardice and the number of battles they have lost to the prisoners' own people.

I have a song composed by a prisoner which contains this challenge, that they should all come boldly and gather to dine off him, for they will be eating at the same time their own fathers and grandfathers, who have served to feed and nourish his body. "These muscles," he says, "this flesh and these veins are your own, poor fools that you are. You do not recognize that the substance of your ancestors' limbs is still contained in them. Savor them well; you will find in them the taste of your own flesh." An idea that certainly does not smack of barbarity.

Those that paint these people dying, and who show the execution, portray the prisoner spitting in the face of his slayers and scowling at them. Indeed, to the last gasp they never stop braving and defying their enemies by word and look. Truly here are real savages by our standards; for either they must be thoroughly so, or we must be; there is an amazing distance between their character and ours.

The men there have several wives, and the higher their reputation for valor the more wives they have. It is a re-

vaillance. C'est une beauté remarquable en leurs mariages que la même jalousie que nos femmes ont pour nous empêcher de l'amitié et bienveillance d'autres femmes, les leurs l'ont toute pareille pour la leur acquérir. Étant plus soigneuses de l'honneur de leurs maris que de toute autre chose, elles cherchent et mettent leur sollicitude à avoir le plus de compagnes qu'elles peuvent, d'autant que c'est un témoignage de la vertu du mari.

ᶜLes nôtres crieront au miracle; ce ne l'est pas: c'est une vertu proprement matrimoniale, mais du plus haut étage. Et en la Bible, Lia, Rachel, Sara et les femmes de Jacob fournirent leurs belles servantes à leurs maris; et Livia seconda les appétits d'Auguste, à son intérêt; et la femme du roi Déjotarus, Stratonice, prêta non seulement à l'usage de son mari une fort belle jeune fille de chambre qui la servait, mais en nourrit soigneusement les enfants et leur fit épaule à succéder aux états de leur père.

ᴬEt afin qu'on ne pense point que tout ceci se fasse par une simple et servile obligation à leur usance et par l'impression de l'autorité de leur ancienne coutume, sans discours et sans jugement, et pour avoir l'âme si stupide que de ne pouvoir prendre autre parti, il faut alléguer quelques traits de leur suffisance. Outre celui que je viens de réciter de l'une de leurs chansons guerrières, j'en ai une autre, amoureuse, qui commence en ce sens: "Couleuvre, arrête-toi; arrête-toi, couleuvre, afin que ma sœur tire sur le patron de ta peinture la façon et l'ouvrage d'un riche cordon que je puisse donner à m'amie: ainsi soit en tout temps ta beauté et ta disposition préférée à tous les autres serpents." Ce premier couplet, c'est le refrain de

markably beautiful thing about their marriages that the same jealousy our wives have to keep us from the affection and kindness of other women, theirs have to win this for them. Being more concerned for their husbands' honor than for anything else, they strive and scheme to have as many companions as they can, since that is a sign of their husbands' valor.

ᶜOur wives will cry "Miracle!" but it is no miracle. It is a properly matrimonial virtue, but one of the highest order. In the Bible, Leah, Rachel, Sarah, and Jacob's wives gave their beautiful handmaids to their husbands; and Livia seconded the appetites of Augustus, to her own disadvantage; and Stratonice, the wife of King Deiotarus, not only lent her husband for his use a very beautiful young chambermaid in her service, but carefully brought up her children, and backed them up to succeed to their father's estates.

ᴬAnd lest it be thought that all this is done through a simple and servile bondage to usage and through the pressure of the authority of their ancient customs, without reasoning or judgment, and because their minds are so stupid that they cannot take any other course, I must cite some examples of their capacity. Besides the warlike song I have just quoted, I have another, a love song, which begins in this vein: "Adder, stay; stay, adder, that from the pattern of your coloring my sister may draw the fashion and the workmanship of a rich girdle that I may give to my love; so may your beauty and your pattern be forever preferred to all other serpents." This first couplet is the refrain of the

la chanson. Or j'ai assez de commerce avec la poésie pour juger ceci, que non seulement il n'y a rien de barbarie en cette imagination, mais qu'elle est tout à fait anacréontique.[15] Leur langage, au demeurant, c'est un doux langage et qui a le son agréable, retirant aux terminaisons grecques.

Trois d'entre eux, ignorant combien coûtera un jour à leur repos et à leur bonheur la connaissance des corruptions de deçà et que de ce commerce naîtra leur ruine, comme je présuppose qu'elle soit déjà avancée, bien misérables de s'être laissés piper au désir de la nouveauté et avoir quitté la douceur de leur ciel pour venir voir le nôtre, furent à Rouen du temps que le feu roi Charles Neuvième y était.[16] Le roi parla à eux longtemps; on leur fit voir notre façon, notre pompe, la forme d'une belle ville. Après cela quelqu'un en demanda leur avis et voulut savoir d'eux ce qu'ils y avaient trouvé de plus admirable. Ils répondirent trois choses, d'où j'ai perdu la troisième et en suis bien marri; mais j'en ai encore deux en mémoire. Ils dirent qu'ils trouvaient en premier lieu fort étrange que tant de grands hommes, portant barbe, forts et armés, qui étaient autour du roi (il est vraisemblable qu'ils parlaient des Suisses de sa garde) se soumissent à obéir à un enfant, et qu'on ne choisissait plutôt quelqu'un d'entre eux pour commander. Secondement (ils ont une façon de leur langage telle qu'ils nomment les hommes moitiés les uns des autres) qu'ils avaient aperçu qu'il y

---

[15] The brilliant light poems of Anacreon of Teos (6th century B.C.) and his imitators were published in Greek by Henri Estienne in 1554 and translated into French two years later by Rémy Belleau. They

song. Now I am familiar enough with poetry to be a judge of this: not only is there nothing barbarous in this fancy, but it is altogether Anacreontic.[15] Their language, moreover, is a soft language, with an agreeable sound, somewhat like Greek in its endings.

Three of these men, ignorant of the price they will pay some day, in loss of repose and happiness, for gaining knowledge of the corruptions of this side of the ocean; ignorant also of the fact that of this intercourse will come their ruin (which I suppose is already well advanced; poor wretches, to let themselves be tricked by the desire for new things, and to have left the serenity of their own sky to come and see ours!)—three of these men were at Rouen, at the time the late King Charles IX was there.[16] The king talked to them for a long time; they were shown our ways, our splendor, the aspect of a fine city. After that, someone asked their opinion, and wanted to know what they had found most amazing. They mentioned three things, of which I have forgotten the third, and I am very sorry for it; but I still remember two of them. They said that in the first place they thought it very strange that so many grown men, bearded, strong, and armed, who were around the king (it is likely that they were talking about the Swiss of his guard) should submit to obey a child, and that one of them was not chosen to command instead. Second (they have a way in their language of speaking of men as halves of one another), they had noticed that there were among

---

were much admired by the Pléiade and in particular by Ronsard.

[16] In 1562 Guise recaptured Rouen from the Protestants, whereupon the French court went there, and with it Montaigne.

[I:31] *Of Cannibals*

avait parmi nous des hommes pleins et gorgés de toutes sortes de commodités, et que leurs moitiés étaient mendiants à leurs portes, décharnés de faim et de pauvreté; et trouvaient étrange comme ces moitiés-ci nécessiteuses pouvaient souffrir une telle injustice, qu'ils ne prissent les autres à la gorge ou missent le feu à leurs maisons.

Je parlai à l'un d'eux fort longtemps; mais j'avais un truchement qui me suivait si mal et qui était si empêché à recevoir mes imaginations par sa bêtise, que je n'en pus tirer guère de plaisir. Sur ce que je lui demandai quel fruit il recevait de la supériorité qu'il avait parmi les siens (car c'était un capitaine, et nos matelots le nommaient roi), il me dit que c'était marcher le premier à la guerre. De combien d'hommes il était suivi, il me montra une espace de lieu, pour signifier que c'était autant qu'il en pourrait en une telle espace; ce pouvait être quatre ou cinq mille hommes. Si hors la guerre toute son autorité était expirée, il dit qu'il lui en restait cela, que quand il visitait les villages qui dépendaient de lui on lui dressait des sentiers au travers des haies de leurs bois, par où il pût passer bien à l'aise.

Tout cela ne va pas trop mal. Mais quoi, ils ne portent point de haut-de-chausses.

us men full and gorged with all sorts of good things, and that their other halves were beggars at their doors, emaciated with hunger and poverty; and they thought it strange that these needy halves could endure such an injustice, and did not take the others by the throat, or set fire to their houses.

I had a very long talk with one of them; but I had an interpreter who followed my meaning so badly, and who was so hindered by his stupidity in taking in my ideas, that I could get hardly any satisfaction from the man. When I asked him what profit he gained from his superior position among his people (for he was a captain, and our sailors called him king), he told me that it was to march foremost in war. How many men followed him? He pointed to a piece of ground, to signify as many as such a space could hold; it might have been four or five thousand men. Did all his authority expire with the war? He said that this much remained, that when he visited the villages dependent on him, they made paths for him through the underbrush by which he might pass quite comfortably.

All this is not too bad—but what of it? They don't wear breeches.

[I:31] *Of Cannibals*

[A]Laissons à part cette longue comparaison de la vie solitaire à l'active; et quant à ce beau mot de quoi se couvre l'ambition et l'avarice, que nous ne sommes pas nés pour notre particulier, ains pour le public, rapportons-nous-en hardiment à ceux qui sont en la danse; et qu'ils se battent la conscience, si, au rebours, les états, les charges, et cette tracasserie du monde ne se recherche plutôt pour tirer du public son profit particulier. Les mauvais moyens par où on s'y pousse en notre siècle montrent bien que la fin n'en vaut guère. . . .

Or la fin, ce crois-je, en est tout une, d'en vivre plus à loisir et à son aise. Mais on n'en cherche pas toujours bien le chemin. Souvent on pense avoir quitté les affaires, on ne les a que changées. Il n'y a guère moins de tourment au gouvernement d'une famille que d'un état entier. Où que l'âme soit empêchée, elle y est toute; et, pour être les occupations domestiques moins importantes, elles n'en sont pas moins importunes. Davantage, pour nous être défaits de la cour ou du marché, nous ne sommes pas défaits des principaux tourments de notre vie:

ratio et prudentia curas,
Non locus effusi late maris arbiter, aufert.[2]

---

[1] The parts of this essay that are given here were probably written around 1572.

ᴬLet us leave aside the usual long comparison between the solitary and the active life; and as for that fine statement under which ambition and avarice take cover—that we are not born for our private selves, but for the public—let us boldly appeal to those who are in the midst of the dance. Let them cudgel their conscience and say whether, on the contrary, the titles, the offices, and the hustle and bustle of the world are not sought out to gain private profit from the public. The evil means men use in our day to push themselves show clearly that the end is not worth much. . . .

Now the aim of all solitude, I take it, is the same: to live more at leisure and at one's ease. But people do not always look for the right way. Often they think they have left business, and they have only changed it. There is scarcely less trouble in governing a family than in governing an entire state: whatever the mind is wrapped up in, it is all wrapped up in it, and domestic occupations are no less importunate for being less important. Furthermore, by getting rid of the court and the market place we do not get rid of the principal worries of our life:

> Reason and sense remove anxiety,
> Not villas that look out upon the sea.[2]

---

[2] Horace, *Epistles*, I, xi, 25–26.

[I:39] *Of Solitude*

L'ambition, l'avarice, l'irrésolution, la peur et les concupiscences ne nous abandonnent point pour changer de contrée.

> Et post equitem sedet atra cura.[3]

Elles nous suivent souvent jusque dans les cloîtres et dans les écoles de philosophie. Ni les déserts, ni les rochers creusés, ni la haire, ni les jeûnes ne nous en démêlent:

> hæret lateri letalis arundo.[4]

On disait à Socrates que quelqu'un ne s'était aucunement amendé en son voyage. "Je crois bien," dit-il; "il s'était emporté avec soi."

> Quid terras alio calentes
> Sole mutamus? patria quis exul
> Se quoque fugit? [5]

Si on ne se décharge premièrement, et son âme, du faix qui la presse, le remuement la fera fouler davantage. . . . Par quoi ce n'est pas assez de s'être écarté du peuple; ce n'est pas assez de changer de place; il se faut écarter des conditions populaires qui sont en nous: il se faut séquestrer et ravoir de soi. . . . Notre mal nous tient en l'âme; or elle ne se peut échapper à elle-même:

> In culpa est animus qui se non effugit unquam.[6]

---

[3] Horace, *Odes*, iii, i, 40.
[4] Virgil, *Aeneid*, iv, 73.

Ambition, avarice, irresolution, fear, and lust do not leave us when we change our country.

Behind the horseman sits black care.[3]

They often follow us even into the cloisters and the schools of philosophy. Neither deserts, nor rocky caves, nor hair shirts, nor fastings will free us of them:

The fatal shaft sticks in her side.[4]

Someone said to Socrates that a certain man had grown no better by his travels. "I should think not," he said; "he took himself along with him."

Why should we move to find
Countries and climates of another kind?
What exile leaves himself behind? [5]

If a man does not first unburden his soul of the load that weighs upon it, movement will cause it to be crushed still more. . . . Wherefore it is not enough to have gotten away from the crowd, it is not enough to move; we must get away from the gregarious instincts that are inside us, we must sequester ourselves and repossess ourselves. . . . Our illness grips us by the soul, and the soul cannot escape from itself:

The soul's at fault, which ne'er escapes itself.[6]

---

[5] Horace, *Odes*, ii, xvi, 18–20.
[6] Horace, *Epistles*, i, xiv, 13.

[I:39] *Of Solitude*

Ainsi il la faut ramener et retirer en soi. C'est la vraie solitude, et qui se peut jouir au milieu des villes et des cours des rois; mais elle se jouit plus commodément à part.

Or, puisque nous entreprenons de vivre seuls et de nous passer de compagnie, faisons que notre contentement dépende de nous; déprenons-nous de toutes les liaisons qui nous attachent à autrui, gagnons sur nous de pouvoir à bon escient vivre seuls et y vivre à notre aise.

Stilpon s'étant échappé de l'embrasement de sa ville, où il avait perdu femme, enfants et chevance, Démétrius Pcliorcétès, le voyant en une si grande ruine de sa patrie le visage non effrayé, lui demanda s'il n'avait pas eu du dommage. Il répondit que non, et qu'il n'y avait, Dieu merci, rien perdu du sien. . . .

Certes l'homme d'entendement n'a rien perdu s'il a soi-même. . . . Il faut avoir femmes, enfants, biens, et surtout de la santé, qui peut; mais non pas s'y attacher en manière que notre heur en dépende. Il se faut réserver une arrière-boutique toute nôtre, toute franche, en laquelle nous établissons notre vraie liberté et principale retraite et solitude. En celle-ci faut-il prendre notre ordinaire entretien de nous à nous-mêmes, et si privé que nulle accointance ou communication étrangère y trouve place; discourir et y rire comme sans femme, sans enfants et sans biens, sans train et sans valets, afin que quand l'occasion adviendra de leur perte il ne nous soit pas nouveau de nous en passer. Nous avons une âme contournable en soi-même; elle se peut faire compagnie; elle a de quoi

Therefore we must bring it back and withdraw it into itself: that is the real solitude, which may be enjoyed in the midst of cities and the courts of kings; but it is enjoyed more handily alone.

Now since we are undertaking to live alone and do without company, let us make our contentment depend on ourselves; let us cut loose from all the ties that bind us to others; let us win from ourselves the power to live really alone and to live that way at our ease.

After Stilpo escaped the burning of his city, in which he had lost wife, children, and property, Demetrius Poliorcetes, seeing him unperturbed in expression amid the great ruin of his country, asked him if he had not suffered loss. No, he replied; thanks to God he had lost nothing of his own. . . .

Certainly a man of understanding has lost nothing, if he has himself. . . . We should have wife, children, goods, and above all health, if we can; but we must not bind ourselves to them so strongly that our happiness depends on them. We must reserve a back shop all our own, entirely free, in which to establish our real liberty and our principal retreat and solitude. Here our ordinary conversation must be between us and ourselves, and so private that no outside association or communication can find a place; here we must talk and laugh as if without wife, without children, without possesssions, without retinue and servants, so that, when the time comes to lose them, it will be nothing new to us to do without them. We have a soul that can be turned upon itself; it can keep itself company; it has the means to attack and the means to

assaillir et de quoi défendre, de quoi recevoir et de quoi donner: ne craignons pas en cette solitude nous croupir d'oisiveté ennuyeuse. . . .

En nos actions accoutumées, de mille il n'en est pas une qui nous regarde. Celui que tu vois grimpant contremont les ruines de ce mur, furieux et hors de soi, en butte de tant d'arquebusades; et cet autre, tout cicatrisé, transi et pâle de faim, délibéré de crever plutôt que de lui ouvrir la porte, penses-tu qu'ils y soient pour eux? Pour tel, à l'aventure, qu'ils ne virent onques, et qui ne se donne aucune peine de leur fait, plongé cependant en l'oisiveté et aux délices. Celui-ci, tout pituiteux, chassieux et crasseux, que tu vois sortir après minuit d'une étude, penses-tu qu'il cherche parmi les livres comme il se rendra plus homme de bien, plus content et plus sage? Nulles nouvelles. Il y mourra, ou il apprendra à la postérité la mesure des vers de Plaute et la vraie orthographe d'un mot latin. Qui ne contre-change volontiers la santé, le repos et la vie à la réputation et à la gloire, la plus inutile, vaine et fausse monnaie qui soit en notre usage? Notre mort ne nous faisait pas assez de peur, chargeons-nous encore de celle de nos femmes, de nos enfants et de nos gens. Nos affaires ne nous donnaient pas assez de peine, prenons encore à nous tourmenter et rompre la tête de ceux de nos voisins et amis. . . .

C'est assez vécu pour autrui, vivons pour nous au moins ce bout de vie. Ramenons à nous et à notre aise nos pensées et nos intentions. Ce n'est pas une légère partie que de

defend, the means to receive and the means to give: let us not fear that in this solitude we shall stagnate in tedious idleness. . . .

Among our customary actions there is not one in a thousand that concerns ourselves. The man you see climbing atop the ruins of that wall, frenzied and beside himself, a mark for so many harquebus shots; and that other, all scarred, pale and faint with hunger, determined to die rather than open the gates to him—do you think they are there for their own sake? They are there for the sake of some man whom perhaps they never saw, who is not in the least concerned about their doings, and who at that very moment is plunged in idleness and pleasures.

This fellow, all dirty, with running nose and eyes, whom you see coming out of his study after midnight, do you think he is seeking among his books how to make himself a better, happier, and wiser man? No such news. He is going to teach posterity the meter of Plautus' verses and the true spelling of a Latin word, or die in the attempt. Who does not willingly exchange health, rest, and life for reputation and glory, the most useless, worthless, and false coin that is current among us? Our own death does not frighten us enough? Let us burden ourselves also with that of our wives, our children, and our servants. Our own affairs don't give us enough trouble? Let us also torment ourselves and get headaches over those of our neighbors and friends. . . .

We have lived enough for others; let us live at least this remaining bit of life for ourselves. Let us bring back our thoughts and plans to ourselves and our well-being. It

faire sûrement sa retraite; elle nous empêche assez sans y mêler d'autres entreprises. Puisque Dieu nous donne loisir de disposer de notre délogement, préparons-nous-y; plions bagage; prenons de bonne heure congé de la compagnie; dépêtrons-nous de ces violentes prises qui nous engagent ailleurs et éloignent de nous. Il faut dénouer ces obligations si fortes, et meshui aimer ceci et cela, mais n'épouser rien que soi. C'est-à-dire: le reste soit à nous, mais non pas joint et collé en façon qu'on ne le puisse déprendre sans nous écorcher et arracher ensemble quelque pièce du nôtre. La plus grande chose du monde, c'est de savoir être à soi. . . .

Or, quant à la fin que Pline et Cicéron [7] nous proposent, de la gloire, c'est bien loin de mon compte. . . . Ils se sont seulement reculés pour mieux sauter. . . . Mettons au contrepoids l'avis de deux philosophes, et de deux sectes très différentes, écrivant l'un à Idoménéus, l'autre à Lucilius, leurs amis, pour, du maniement des affaires et des grandeurs, les retirer à la solitude.[8]

"Vous avez," disent-ils, "vécu nageant et flottant jusqu'à présent, venez-vous-en mourir au port. . . . Quittez avec les autres voluptés celle qui vient de l'approbation d'autrui; et quant à votre science et suffisance, ne vous

---

[7] Montaigne had quoted Pliny the Younger and Cicero, in a passage not given here, on the glory of retirement.

[8] The philosophers in question are Epicurus (writing to Idomeneus)

is no small matter to arrange our retirement securely; it keeps us busy enough without mixing other undertakings with it. Since God gives us leisure to make arrangements for moving out, let us make them; let us pack our bags; let us take an early leave of the company; let us break free from the violent clutches that engage us elsewhere and draw us away from ourselves. We must untie these bonds that are so powerful, and henceforth love this and that, but be wedded only to ourselves. That is to say, let the other things be ours, but not joined and glued to us so strongly that they cannot be detached without tearing off our skin and some part of our flesh as well. The greatest thing in the world is to know how to belong to one-self. . . .

Now, as for glory, the goal that Pliny and Cicero [7] set up for us, it is very far from my reckoning. . . . They have only stepped back to make a better jump. . . . Let us put into the scales the advice of two philosophers of two very different sects, one writing to Idomeneus, the other to Lucilius, their friends, to persuade them to give up handling affairs and withdraw from their high positions into solitude.[8]

"You have," they say, "lived until now swimming and floating; come away and die in port. . . . Abandon with the other pleasures that which comes from the approbation of others; and as for your knowledge and ability, don't worry, it will not lose its effect if it makes you

___

and Seneca (writing to Lucilius). Most of what follows is taken from Seneca's *Epistles*.

[I:39] *Of Solitude*

chaille, elle ne perdra pas son effet si vous en valez mieux vous-même. Souvienne-vous [9] de celui à qui, comme on demandât [10] à quoi faire il se peinait si fort en un art qui ne pouvait venir à la connaissance de guère de gens: 'J'en ai assez de peu,' répondit-il, 'j'en ai assez d'un, j'en ai assez de pas un.' Il disait vrai: vous et un compagnon êtes assez suffisant théâtre l'un à l'autre, ou vous à vous-même. Que le peuple vous soit un, et un vous soit tout le peuple. C'est une lâche ambition de vouloir tirer gloire de son oisiveté et de sa cachette. Il faut faire comme les animaux qui effacent la trace à la porte de leur tanière.

"Ce n'est plus ce qu'il vous faut chercher, que le monde parle de vous, mais comme il faut que vous parliez à vous-même. Retirez-vous en vous, mais préparez-vous premièrement de vous y recevoir: ce serait folie de vous fier à vous-même si vous ne vous savez gouverner. Il y a moyen de faillir en la solitude comme en la compagnie. Jusqu'à ce que vous vous soyez rendu tel devant qui vous n'osiez clocher, et jusqu'à ce que vous ayez honte et respect de vous-même,—^C*observentur species honestæ animo*,[11]—^Aprésentez-vous toujours en l'imagination Caton, Phocion et Aristidès,[12] en la présence desquels les fous mêmes cacheraient leurs fautes, et établissez-les contrôleurs de toutes vos intentions: si elles se détraquent, leur révérence les remettra en train. Ils vous contiendront en

---

[9] *Souvienne-vous = qu'il vous souvienne.*
[10] This subjunctive seems to be simply a Latinism.
[11] Cicero, *Tusculans*, II, xxii.
[12] Cato is presumably Cato the Younger (95–46 B.C.), one of Montaigne's greatest heroes in the 1570's, whose brave opposition to Caesar finally led to defeat and suicide. Phocion was an Athenian

yourself a better man. Remember [9] the man who, when asked [10] why he took so much pains in an art which could come to the knowledge of so few people, replied: 'Few are enough for me, one is enough for me, none at all is enough for me.' He spoke truly: you and one companion are an adequate theater for each other, or you for yourself. Let the people be one to you, and let one be a whole people to you. It is a base ambition to want to derive glory from our idleness and our concealment. We must do like the animals that rub out their tracks at the entrance to their lairs.

"Seek no longer that the world should speak of you, but how you should speak to yourself. Retire into yourself, but first prepare to receive yourself there; it would be madness to trust in yourself if you do not know how to govern yourself. There are ways to fail in solitude as well as in company. Until you have made yourself such that you dare not trip up in your own presence, and until you feel both shame and respect for yourself, *let true ideals be kept before your mind,*[11] *keep ever in your mind Cato, Phocion, and Aristides,[12] in whose presence even fools would hide their faults; make them controllers of all your intentions; if these intentions get off the track, your reverence for those men will set them right again. They will keep you in a fair way to be content with yourself,

---

statesman and general of the time of Philip and Alexander of Macedon, killed on a charge of treason in 318 B.C. Aristides fought at Marathon and later became such a byword for his justice that he was ostracized, according to one story, on that account by the jealous Athenians.

[I:39] *Of Solitude*

cette voie de vous contenter de vous-même, de n'emprunter rien que de vous, d'arrêter et fermir votre âme en certaines et limitées cogitations où elle se puisse plaire; et ayant entendu les vrais biens, desquels on jouit à mesure qu'on les entend, s'en contenter, sans désir de prolongement de vie ni de nom."

Voilà le conseil de la vraie et naïve philosophie, non d'une philosophie ostentatrice et parlière, comme est celle des deux premiers.[13]

50   De Démocritus et Héraclitus [1]

[A]Le jugement est un outil à tous sujets, et se mêle partout. A cette cause, aux essais [2] que j'en fais ici, j'y emploie toute sorte d'occasion. Si c'est un sujet que je n'entende point, à cela même je l'essaie, sondant le gué de bien loin; et puis le trouvant trop profond pour ma taille, je me tiens à la rive; et cette reconnaissance de ne pouvoir passer outre, c'est un trait de son effet, voire de ceux de quoi il se vante le plus. Tantôt, à un sujet vain et de néant, j'essaie voir s'il trouvera de quoi lui donner corps, et de quoi l'appuyer et étançonner. Tantôt je le promène à un sujet noble et tracassé, auquel il n'a rien à trouver de soi, le chemin en étant si frayé qu'il ne peut marcher que sur la piste d'autrui. Là il fait son jeu à élire la route

---

[13] Pliny and Cicero.
[1] No date can be assigned with any assurance to this chapter.

to borrow nothing except from yourself, to arrest your mind and fix it on definite and limited thoughts in which it may take pleasure; and, after understanding the true blessings, which we enjoy in so far as we understand them, to rest content with them, without any desire to prolong life and reputation."

That is the counsel of true and natural philosophy, not of an ostentatious and talky philosophy like that of the first two.[13]

50 Of Democritus and Heraclitus [1]

[A]Judgment is a tool to use on all subjects, and comes in everywhere. Therefore in the tests [2] that I make of it here, I use every sort of occasion. If it is a subject I do not understand at all, even on that I essay my judgment, sounding the ford from a good distance; and then, finding it too deep for my height, I stick to the bank. And this acknowledgment that I cannot cross over is a token of its action, indeed one of those it is most proud of. Sometimes in a vain and nonexistent subject I try to see if it will find the wherewithal to give it body, prop it up, and support it. Sometimes I lead it to a noble and well-worn subject in which it has nothing original to discover, the road being so beaten that it can walk only in others' footsteps. There it plays its part by choosing the way

---

[2] Tests, trials, essays.

qui lui semble la meilleure, et, de mille sentiers, il dit que celui-ci ou celui-là a été le mieux choisi.

Je prends de la fortune le premier argument. Ils me sont également bons. Et ne désigne jamais de les produire entiers.³ ᶜCar je ne vois le tout de rien. Ne font pas, ceux qui promettent de nous le faire voir. De cent membres et visages qu'a chaque chose, j'en prends un tantôt à lécher seulement, tantôt à effleurer, et parfois à pincer jusqu'à l'os. J'y donne une pointe, non pas le plus largement, mais le plus profondément que je sais. Et aime plus souvent à les saisir par quelque lustre inusité. Je me hasarderais de traiter à fond quelque matière, si je me connaissais moins. Semant ici un mot, ici un autre, échantillons dépris de leur pièce, écartés, sans dessein et sans promesse, je ne suis pas tenu d'en faire bon, ni de m'y tenir moi-même sans varier quand il me plaît et me rendre au doute et incertitude, et à ma maîtresse forme, qui est l'ignorance.

Tout mouvement nous découvre. ᴬCette même âme de Cæsar, qui se fait voir à ordonner et dresser la bataille de Pharsale, elle se fait aussi voir à dresser des parties oisives et amoureuses. On juge un cheval non seulement à le voir manier sur une carrière, mais encore à lui voir aller le pas, voire et à le voir en repos à l'étable.

---

³ The next eight sentences, from "Car je ne vois" ("For I do not see") to "Tout mouvement nous découvre" ("Every movement reveals us") are an amplification by Montaigne, between 1588 and 1592, of the following version which had appeared in all earlier editions: ". . . de les traiter entiers et à fond de cuve: de mille visages qu'ils ont chacun, j'en prends celui qu'il me plaît; je les saisis volontiers par quelque lustre extraordinaire; j'en trierais bien de plus riches et pleins, si j'avais quelque autre fin proposée que

that seems best to it, and of a thousand paths it says that this one or that was the most wisely chosen.

I take the first subject that chance offers. They are all equally good to me. And I never plan to develop them completely.⁹ ᶜFor I do not see the whole of anything. Nor do those who promise to show it to us. Of a hundred members and faces that each thing has, I take one, sometimes only to lick it, sometimes to brush the surface, sometimes to pinch it to the bone. I give it a stab, not as wide but as deep as I know how. And most often I like to take them from some unaccustomed point of view. I would venture to treat some matter thoroughly, if I knew myself less well. Scattering a word here, there another, samples separated from their context, dispersed, without a plan and without a promise, I am not bound to make something of them or to adhere to them myself without varying when I please and giving myself up to doubt and uncertainty and my ruling quality, which is ignorance.

Every movement reveals us. ᴬThat same mind of Caesar's which shows itself in ordering and directing the battle of Pharsalia, shows itself also in arranging idle and amorous affairs. We judge a horse not only by seeing him handled on a racecourse, but also by seeing him walk, and even by seeing him resting in the stable.

---

celle que j'ai. Toute action est propre à nous faire connaître: cette même âme de Cæsar. . . ."—". . . to treat them entire and to the bottom of the vat: of a thousand facets that they each have, I take the one I please; I am prone to seize them by some extraordinary aspect. I would indeed pick out richer and fuller ones, if I had some other goal in mind than the one I have. Every action is fit to make us known; that same mind of Caesar's . . ."

[I:50] *Of Democritus and Heraclitus*

^cEntre les fonctions de l'âme il en est de basses: qui ne la voit encore par là, n'achève pas de la connaître. Et à l'aventure la remarque l'on mieux où elle va son pas simple. Les vents des passions la prennent plus en ces hautes assiettes. Joint qu'elle se couche entière sur chaque matière, et s'y exerce entière, et n'en traite jamais plus d'une à la fois. Et la traite, non selon elle, mais selon soi.

Les choses à part elles ont peut-être leurs poids et mesures et conditions; mais au dedans, en nous, elle les leur taille comme elle l'entend. La mort est effroyable à Cicéron, désirable à Caton, indifférente à Socratès. La santé, la conscience, l'autorité, la science, la richesse, la beauté et leurs contraires se dépouillent à l'entrée, et reçoivent de l'âme nouvelle vêture, et de la teinture qu'il lui plaît—brune, verte, claire, obscure, aigre, douce, profonde, superficielle—et qu'il plaît à chacune d'elles; car elles n'ont pas vérifié en commun leurs styles, règles et formes: chacune est reine en son état. Par quoi ne prenons plus excuse des externes qualités des choses: c'est à nous à nous en rendre compte. Notre bien et notre mal ne tient qu'à nous. Offrons-y nos offrandes et nos vœux, non pas à la fortune: elle ne peut rien sur nos mœurs: au rebours, elles l'entraînent à leur suite, et la moulent à leur forme.

Pourquoi ne jugerai-je d'Alexandre à table, devisant et buvant d'autant? Ou s'il maniait des échecs, quelle corde de son esprit ne touche et emploie ce niais et puérile jeu? Je le hais et fuis de ce qu'il n'est pas assez jeu, et qu'il

ᶜAmong the functions of the soul there are some lowly ones; he who does not see that side of her also, does not fully know her. And perhaps she is best observed when she goes at her simple pace. The winds of passion seize her more strongly on her lofty flights. Moreover, she gives all her being to each matter, and concentrates all her strength on it, and never treats more than one at a time. And she treats a matter not according to itself, but according to herself.

Things in themselves may have their own weights and measures and qualities; but once inside, within us, she allots them their qualities as she sees fit. Death is frightful to Cicero, desirable to Cato, a matter of indifference to Socrates. Health, conscience, authority, knowledge, riches, beauty, and their opposites—all are stripped on entry and receive from the soul new clothing, and the coloring that she chooses—brown, green, bright, dark, bitter, sweet, deep, superficial—and which each individual soul chooses; for they have not agreed together on their styles, rules, and forms; each one is queen in her realm. Wherefore let us no longer make the external qualities of things our excuse; it is up to us to reckon them as we will. Our good and our ill depend on ourselves alone. Let us offer our offerings and vows to ourselves, not to Fortune; she has no power over our character; on the contrary, it drags her in its train and molds her in its own form.

Why shall I not judge Alexander at table, talking and drinking his fill, or when he was playing chess? What sinew of his soul is not touched and employed in this silly and puerile game? I hate it and avoid it, because it is not

nous ébat trop sérieusement, ayant honte d'y fournir l'attention qui suffirait à quelque bonne chose. Il ne fut pas plus embesogné à dresser son glorieux passage aux Indes; ni cet autre à dénouer un passage duquel dépend le salut du genre humain. Voyez combien notre âme grossit et épaissit cet amusement ridicule; si tous ses nerfs ne bandent; combien amplement elle donne à chacun loi en cela de se connaître et de juger droitement de soi. Je ne me vois et retâte plus universellement en nulle autre posture. Quelle passion ne nous y exerce? la colère, le dépit, la haine, l'impatience et une véhémente ambition de vaincre, en chose en laquelle il serait plus excusable d'être ambitieux d'être vaincu. Car la précellence rare et au-dessus du commun messied à un homme d'honneur en chose frivole. Ce que je dis en cet exemple se peut dire en tous autres: chaque parcelle, chaque occupation de l'homme l'accuse et le montre également qu'un autre.

ᴬDémocritus et Héraclitus ont été deux philosophes, desquels le premier, trouvant vaine et ridicule l'humaine condition, ne sortait en public qu'avec un visage moqueur et riant; Héraclitus, ayant pitié et compassion de cette même condition nôtre, en portait le visage continuellement attristé, et les yeux chargés de larmes,

> ᴮalter
> Ridebat, quoties a limine moverat unum
> Protuleratque pedem; flebat contrarius alter.[4]

ᴬJ'aime mieux la première humeur, non parce qu'il

---

[4] Juvenal, *Satires*, x, 28–30.

enough a game, and too serious an amusement; I am ashamed to devote to it the attention that would suffice to accomplish something good. He was no more absorbed when he prepared his glorious expedition to India; nor is this other in unraveling a passage on which depends the salvation of the human race. See how our mind swells and magnifies this ridiculous amusement; how all its muscles grow tense; what ample opportunity it here gives everyone to know himself, and to judge himself rightly. In no other situation do I see and check up on myself more thoroughly. What passion does not excite us in this game: anger, vexation, hatred, impatience, and a vehement ambition to win in a thing in which ambition to be beaten would be more excusable. For rare and extraordinary excellence in frivolous things is unbecoming a man of honor. What I say of this example may be said of all others: each particle, each occupation, of a man betrays him and reveals him just as well as any other.

ᴬDemocritus and Heraclitus were two philosophers, of whom the first, finding the condition of man vain and ridiculous, never went out in public but with a mocking and laughing face; whereas Heraclitus, having pity and compassion on this same condition of ours, wore a face perpetually sad, and eyes filled with tears:

> ᴮOne always, when he o'er his threshold stepped,
> Laughed at the world; the other always wept.⁴

ᴬI prefer the first humor; not because it is pleasanter to

est plus plaisant de rire que de pleurer, mais parce qu'elle est plus dédaigneuse et qu'elle nous condamne plus que l'autre: et il me semble que nous ne pouvons jamais être assez méprisés selon notre mérite. La plainte et la commisération sont mêlées à quelque estimation de la chose qu'on plaint; les choses de quoi on se moque, on les estime sans prix. Je ne pense point qu'il y ait tant de malheur en nous comme il y a de vanité, ni tant de malice comme de sottise: nous ne sommes pas si pleins de mal comme d'inanité; nous ne sommes pas si misérables comme nous sommes vils.

Ainsi Diogénès, qui baguenaudait à part soi, roulant son tonneau et hochant du nez le grand Alexandre, nous estimant des mouches ou des vessies pleins de vent, était bien juge plus aigre et plus poignant, et par conséquent plus juste, à mon humeur, que Timon, celui qui fut surnommé le haïsseur des hommes. Car ce qu'on hait, on le prend à cœur. Celui-ci nous souhaitait du mal, était passionné du désir de notre ruine, fuyait notre conversation comme dangereuse, de méchants, et de nature dépravée; l'autre nous estimait si peu que nous ne pourrions ni le troubler ni l'altérer par notre contagion, nous laissait de compagnie, non pour la crainte, mais pour le dédain de notre commerce: il ne nous estimait capables ni de bien ni de mal faire.

De même marque fut la réponse de Statilius, auquel Brutus parla pour le joindre à la conspiration contre Cæsar: il trouva l'entreprise juste, mais il ne trouva pas les hommes dignes pour lesquels on se mit aucunement en peine, ^cconformément à la discipline d'Hégésias, qui disait le sage ne devoir rien faire que pour soi, d'autant

laugh than to weep, but because it is more disdainful, and condemns us more than the other; and it seems to me that we can never be despised as much as we deserve. Pity and commiseration are mingled with some esteem for the thing we pity; the things we laugh at we consider worthless. I do not think there is as much unhappiness in us as vanity, nor as much malice as stupidity. We are not so full of evil as of inanity; we are not as wretched as we are worthless.

Thus Diogenes, who pottered about by himself, rolling his tub and turning up his nose at the great Alexander, considering us as flies or bags of wind, was really a sharper and more stinging judge, and consequently juster, to my taste, than Timon, who was surnamed the hater of men. For what we hate we take seriously. Timon wished us ill, passionately desired our ruin, shunned association with us as dangerous, as with wicked men depraved by nature. Diogenes esteemed us so little that contact with us could neither disturb him nor affect him, and avoided our company, not through fear of association with us, but through disdain of it; he considered us incapable of doing either good or evil.

Of the same stamp was the reply of Statilius, whom Brutus asked to join the conspiracy against Caesar. He considered the enterprise just, but he did not believe that men were worth taking any trouble about. ᶜAnd this is in conformity with the teachings of Hegesias, who said that the wise man should do nothing except for himself, since

que seul il est digne pour qui on fasse; et à celle de Théodorus, que c'est injustice que le sage se hasarde pour le bien de son pays, et qu'il mette en péril la sagesse pour des fous.

Notre propre et péculière condition est autant ridicule que risible.

he alone is worth having anything done for him; and that of Theodorus, that it is unjust for a wise man to risk his life for the good of his country, and endanger wisdom for the sake of fools.

Our own peculiar condition is that we are as fit to be laughed at as able to laugh.

Livre Second

1 De l'inconstance de nos actions [1]

ᴬCeux qui s'exercent à contrôler les actions humaines ne se trouvent en aucune partie si empêchés qu'à les rapiécer et mettre à même lustre: car elles se contredisent communément de si étrange façon qu'il semble impossible qu'elles soient parties de même boutique. Le jeune Marius se trouve tantôt fils de Mars, tantôt fils de Vénus. Le pape Boniface Huitième entra, dit-on, en sa charge comme un renard, s'y porta comme un lion, et mourut comme un chien. Et qui croirait que ce fût Néron, cette vraie image de la cruauté, comme on lui présentait à signer, suivant le style, la sentence d'un criminel condamné, qui eût répondu: "Plût à Dieu que je n'eusse jamais su écrire!" Tant le cœur lui serrait de condamner un homme à mort. Tout est si plein de tels exemples, voire chacun en peut tant fournir à soi-même, que je trouve étrange de voir quelquefois des gens d'entendement se mettre en peine

---

[1] Written about 1572. Throughout the chapter, as the context shows, *inconstance* can mean both inconstancy and inconsistency, just as *constance* can mean both constancy and consistency.

Book Two

1 *Of the Inconsistency of Our Actions* [1]

ᴬThose who make a practice of comparing human actions
are never so perplexed as when they try to see them as a
whole and in the same light; for they commonly contradict
each other so strangely that it seems impossible that they
have come from the same shop. One moment young
Marius is a son of Mars, another moment a son of Venus.
Pope Boniface VIII, they say, entered office like a fox,
behaved in it like a lion, and died like a dog. And who
would believe that it was Nero, that living image of
cruelty, who said, when they brought him in customary
fashion the sentence of a condemned criminal to sign:
"Would to God I had never learned to write!" So much
his heart was wrung at condemning a man to death!

Everything is so full of such examples—each man, in
fact, can supply himself with so many—that I find it
strange to see intelligent men sometimes going to great
pains to match these pieces; seeing that irresolution seems

d'assortir ces pièces: vu que l'irrésolution me semble le plus commun et apparent vice de notre nature, témoin ce fameux verset de Publius le farceur:

Malum consilium est, quod mutari non potest.[2]

[B]Il y a quelque apparence de faire jugement d'un homme par les plus communs traits de sa vie; mais vu la naturelle instabilité de nos mœurs et opinions, il m'a semblé souvent que les bons auteurs mêmes ont tort de s'opiniâtrer à former de nous une constante et solide contexture. Ils choisissent un air universel, et suivant cette image vont rangeant et interprétant toutes les actions d'un personnage; et, s'ils ne les peuvent assez tordre, les vont renvoyant à la dissimulation. Auguste leur est échappé; car il se trouve en cet homme une variété d'actions si apparente, soudaine et continuelle, tout le cours de sa vie, qu'il s'est fait lâcher, entier et indécis, aux plus hardis juges. Je crois des hommes plus malaisément la constance que tout autre chose, et rien plus aisément que l'inconstance. Qui en jugerait en détail [c]et distinctement pièce à pièce, [B]rencontrerait plus souvent à dire vrai.

[A]En toute l'ancienneté il est malaisé de choisir une douzaine d'hommes qui aient dressé leur vie à un certain et assuré train, qui est le principal but de la sagesse. Car pour la comprendre toute en un mot, dit un ancien,[3] et pour embrasser en une toutes les règles de notre vie, c'est vouloir et ne vouloir pas, toujours, même chose. Je ne

---

[2] Publilius Syrus, quoted from Aulus Gellius, *Attic Nights*, xvii, 14.

144

to me the most common and apparent defect of our nature, as witness that famous line of Publilius, the farce writer:

> Bad is the plan that never can be changed.[2]

[B]There is some justification for basing a judgment of a man on the most ordinary acts of his life; but in view of the natural instability of our conduct and opinions, it has often seemed to me that even good authors are wrong to insist on fashioning a consistent and solid fabric out of us. They choose one general characteristic, and go and arrange and interpret all a man's actions to fit their picture; and if they cannot twist them enough, they go and set them down to dissimulation. Augustus has escaped them; for there is in this man throughout the course of his life such an obvious, abrupt, and continual variety of actions that even the boldest judges have had to let him go, intact and unsolved. Nothing is harder for me than to believe in men's consistency, nothing easier than to believe in their inconsistency. He who would judge them in detail [C]and distinctly, bit by bit, [B]would more often hit upon the truth.

[A]In all antiquity it is hard to pick out a dozen men who set their lives to a certain and constant course, which is the principal goal of wisdom. For, to comprise all wisdom in a word, says an ancient,[3] and to embrace all the rules of our life in one, it is "always to will the same things, and always to oppose the same things." I would not

---

[3] Seneca (*Epistles*, xx, 5).

daignerais, dit-il, ajouter: "pourvu que la volonté soit juste"; car si elle n'est juste il est impossible qu'elle soit toujours une.

De vrai, j'ai autrefois appris que le vice ce n'est que dérèglement et faute de mesure, et par conséquent il est impossible d'y attacher la constance. C'est un mot de Démosthénès, dit-on, que le commencement de toute vertu, c'est consultation et délibération; et la fin et perfection, constance. Si par discours nous entreprenions certaine voie, nous la prendrions la plus belle; mais nul n'y a pensé:

Quod petiit, spernit; repetit quod nuper omisit;
Æstuat, et vitæ disconvenit ordine toto.[4]

Notre façon ordinaire c'est d'aller après les inclinations de notre appétit, à gauche, à dextre, contremont, contrebas, selon que le vent des occasions nous emporte. Nous ne pensons ce que nous voulons qu'à l'instant que nous le voulons, et changeons comme cet animal qui prend la couleur du lieu où on le couche. Ce que nous avons à cette heure proposé, nous le changeons tantôt, et tantôt encore retournons sur nos pas: ce n'est que branle et inconstance:

Ducimur ut nervis alienis mobile lignum.[5]

Nous n'allons pas; on nous emporte, comme les choses qui flottent, ores doucement, ores avec violence, selon que l'eau est ireuse ou bonasse:

---

[4] Horace, *Epistles*, 1, i, 98–9.

deign, he says, to add "provided the will is just"; for if it is not just, it cannot always be whole.

In truth, I once learned that vice is only unruliness and lack of moderation, and that consequently consistency cannot be attributed to it. It is a maxim of Demosthenes, they say, that the beginning of all virtue is consultation and deliberation; and the end and perfection, consistency. If it were by reasoning that we settled on a particular course of action, we would choose the fairest course—but no one has thought of that:

> He spurns the thing he sought, and seeks anew
> What he just spurned; he seethes, his life's askew.[4]

Our ordinary practice is to follow the inclinations of our appetite, to the left, to the right, uphill and down, as the wind of circumstance carries us. We think of what we want only at the moment we want it, and we change like that animal which takes the color of the place you set it on. What we have just now planned, we presently change, and presently again we retrace our steps: nothing but oscillation and inconsistency:

> Like puppets we are moved by outside strings.[5]

We do not go; we are carried away, like floating objects, now gently, now violently, according as the water is angry or calm:

---

[5] Horace, *Satires*, ii, vii, 82.

[II:1] *Of the Inconsistency*

ᴮnonne videmus
Quid sibi quisque velit nescire, et quærere semper,
Commutare locum, quasi onus deponere possit? ⁶

ᴬChaque jour nouvelle fantaisie, et se meuvent nos humeurs avec les mouvements du temps:

Tales sunt hominum mentes, quali pater ipse
Juppiter auctifero lustravit lumine terras.ᵀ

ᶜNous flottons entre divers avis; nous ne voulons rien librement, rien absolument, rien constamment.

ᴬA qui aurait prescrit et établi certaines lois et certaine police en sa tête, nous verrions tout partout en sa vie reluire une égalité de mœurs, un ordre et une relation infaillible des unes choses aux autres.

ᶜEmpédoclès remarquait cette difformité aux Agrigentins, qu'ils s'abandonnaient aux délices comme s'ils avaient lendemain à mourir, et bâtissaient comme si jamais ils ne devaient mourir.

ᴬLe discours en ⁸ serait bien aisé à faire, comme il se voit du jeune Caton: qui en a touché une marche, a tout touché; c'est une harmonie de sons très accordants, qui ne se peut démentir. A nous, au rebours, autant d'actions, autant faut-il de jugements particuliers. Le plus sûr, à mon opinion, serait de les rapporter aux circonstances voisines, sans entrer en plus longue recherche et sans en conclure autre conséquence.

---

⁶ Lucretius, *De Rerum Natura*, ɪɪɪ, 1057–9.
⁷ Homer, *Odyssey*, xvɪɪɪ, 136–37, as translated by Cicero and quoted in St. Augustine, *City of God*, v, viii.

^BDo we not see all humans unaware
Of what they want, and always searching everywhere,
And changing place, as if to drop the load they bear? ⁶

^AEvery day a new fancy, and our humors shift with the shifts in the weather:

Such are the minds of men, as is the fertile light
That Father Jove himself sends down to make earth bright.⁷

^CWe float between different states of mind; we wish nothing freely, nothing absolutely, nothing constantly.

^AIf any man could prescribe and establish definite laws and a definite organization in his head, we should see shining throughout his life an evenness of habits, an order, and an infallible relation between his principles and his practice.

^CEmpedocles noticed this inconsistency in the Agrigentines, that they abandoned themselves to pleasures as if they were to die on the morrow, and built as if they were never to die.

^AThis man ⁸ would be easy to understand, as is shown by the example of the younger Cato: he who has touched one chord of him has touched all; he is a harmony of perfectly concordant sounds, which cannot conflict. With us, it is the opposite: for so many actions, we need so many individual judgments. The surest thing, in my opinion, would be to trace our actions to the neighboring circumstances, without getting into any further research and without drawing from them any other conclusions.

---

⁸ "En" refers to the disciplined man in the sentence before last.

[II:1] *Of the Inconsistency*

Pendant les débauches de notre pauvre état [9] on me rapporta qu'une fille, bien près de là où j'étais, s'était précipitée du haut d'une fenêtre pour éviter la force d'un bélître de soldat, son hôte. Elle ne s'était pas tuée à la chute, et pour redoubler son entreprise s'était voulu donner d'un couteau par la gorge, mais on l'en avait empêchée, toutefois après s'y être bien fort blessée. Elle-même confessait que le soldat ne l'avait encore pressée que de requêtes, sollicitations et présents, mais qu'elle avait eu peur qu'enfin il en vînt à la contrainte. Et là-dessus les paroles, la contenance, et ce sang témoin de sa vertu, à la vraie façon d'une autre Lucrèce. Or j'ai su, à la vérité, qu'avant et depuis elle avait été garce de non si difficile composition. Comme dit le conte: Tout beau et honnête que vous êtes, quand vous aurez failli votre pointe, n'en concluez pas incontinent une chasteté inviolable en votre maîtresse; ce n'est pas à dire que le muletier n'y trouve son heure.

Antigonus, ayant pris en affection un de ses soudards pour sa vertu et vaillance, commanda à ses médecins de le panser d'une maladie longue et intérieure qui l'avait tourmenté longtemps; et s'apercevant après sa guérison qu'il allait beaucoup plus froidement aux affaires, lui demanda qui l'avait ainsi changé et encouardi. "Vous-même, Sire," lui répondit-il, "m'ayant déchargé des maux pour lesquels je ne tenais compte de ma vie." Le soldat de Lucullus, ayant été dévalisé par les ennemis, fit sur eux, pour se revancher, une belle entreprise. Quand il se fut

---

[9] The religious civil wars between Catholics and Protestants, which lasted intermittently from 1562 to 1594.

During the disorders of our poor country,[9] I was told that a girl, living near where I then was, had thrown herself out of a high window to avoid the violence of a knavish soldier quartered in her house. Not killed by the fall, she reasserted her purpose by trying to cut her throat with a knife. From this she was prevented, but only after wounding herself gravely. She herself confessed that the soldier had as yet pressed her only with requests, solicitations, and gifts; but she had been afraid, she said, that he would finally resort to force. And all this with such words, such expressions, not to mention the blood that testified to her virtue, as would have become another Lucrece. Now, I learned that as a matter of fact, both before and since, she was a wench not so hard to come to terms with. As the story says: Handsome and gentlemanly as you may be, when you have had no luck, do not promptly conclude that your mistress is inviolably chaste; this does not prove that the mule driver may not have his chance with her.

Antigonus, having taken a liking to one of his soldiers for his virtue and valor, ordered his physicians to treat the man for a persistent internal malady that had long tormented him. After his cure, his master noticed that he was going about his business much less warmly, and asked him what had changed him so and made him such a coward. "You yourself, Sire," he answered, "by delivering me from the ills that made my life indifferent to me." A soldier of Lucullus who had been robbed of everything by the enemy made a bold attack on them to get revenge. When he had

[II:1] *Of the Inconsistency*

remplumé de sa perte, Lucullus, l'ayant pris en bonne opinion, l'employait à quelque exploit hasardeux par toutes les plus belles remontrances de quoi il se pouvait aviser,

Verbis quæ timido quoque possent addere mentem.[10]

"Employez-y," répondit-il, "quelque misérable soldat dévalisé";

quantumvis rusticus ibit,
Ibit eo, quo vis, qui zonam perdidit, inquit; [11]

et refusa résolument d'y aller.

ᶜQuand nous lisons que Mahomet ayant outrageusement rudoyé Chasan, chef de ses janissaires, de ce qu'il voyait sa troupe enfoncée par les Hongrois et lui se porter lâchement au combat, Chasan alla pour toute réponse se ruer furieusement, seul, en l'état qu'il était, les armes au poing, dans le premier corps des ennemis qui se présenta, où il fut soudain englouti: ce n'est à l'aventure pas tant justification que ravisement, ni tant sa prouesse naturelle qu'un nouveau dépit.

ᴬCelui que vous vîtes hier si aventureux, ne trouvez pas étrange de le voir aussi poltron le lendemain. Ou la colère, ou la nécessité, ou la compagnie, ou le vin, ou le son d'une trompette lui avait mis le cœur au ventre. Ce n'est pas un cœur ainsi formé par discours; ces circonstances le lui ont fermi; ce n'est pas merveille si le voilà devenu autre par autres circonstances contraires.

---

[10] Horace, *Epistles*, ii, ii, 36.

retrieved his loss, Lucullus, having formed a good opinion of him, urged him to some dangerous exploit with all the fine expostulations he could think of,

With words that might have stirred a coward's heart.[10]

"Urge some poor soldier who has been robbed to do it," he replied;

Though but a rustic lout,
"That man will go who's lost his money," he called out; [11]

and resolutely refused to go.

ᶜWe read that Sultan Mohammed outrageously berated Hassan, leader of his Janissaries, because he saw his troops giving way to the Hungarians and Hassan himself behaving like a coward in the fight. Hassan's only reply was to go and hurl himself furiously—alone, just as he was, arms in hand—into the first body of enemies that he met, by whom he was promptly swallowed up; this was perhaps not so much self-justification as a change of mood, nor so much his natural valor as fresh spite.

ᴬThat man whom you saw so adventurous yesterday, do not think it strange to find him just as cowardly today: either anger, or necessity, or company, or wine, or the sound of a trumpet, had put his heart in his belly. His was a courage formed not by reason, but by one of these circumstances; it is no wonder if he has now been made different by other, contrary circumstances.

---

[11] Horace, *Epistles*, ɪɪ, ii, 39–40.

[II:1] *Of the Inconsistency*

^CCette variation et contradiction qui se voit en nous, si souple, a fait qu'aucuns nous songent deux âmes, d'autres deux puissances qui nous accompagnent et agitent chacune à sa mode, vers le bien l'une, l'autre vers le mal; une si brusque diversité ne se pouvant bien assortir à un sujet simple.

^BNon seulement le vent des accidents me remue selon son inclination, mais en outre je me remue et trouble moi-même par l'instabilité de ma posture; et qui y regarde primement ne se trouve guère deux fois en même état. Je donne à mon âme tantôt un visage, tantôt un autre, selon le côté où je la couche. Si je parle diversement de moi, c'est que je me regarde diversement. Toutes les contrariétés s'y trouvent selon quelque tour et en quelque façon. Honteux, insolent; ^Cchaste, luxurieux; ^Bbavard, taciturne; laborieux, délicat; ingénieux, hébété; chagrin, débonnaire; menteur, véritable; ^Csavant, ignorant, et libéral, et avare, et prodigue: ^Btout cela je le vois en moi aucunement, selon que je me vire; et quiconque s'étudie bien attentivement trouve en soi, voire et en son jugement même, cette volubilité et discordance. Je n'ai rien à dire de moi entièrement, simplement et solidement, sans confusion et sans mélange, ni en un mot. *Distinguo* est le plus universel membre de ma logique.

^AEncore que je sois toujours d'avis de dire du bien le bien et d'interpréter plutôt en bonne part les choses qui le peuvent être, si est-ce que l'étrangeté de notre condition porte que nous soyons souvent par le vice même poussés à bien faire—si le bien faire ne se jugeait par la seule intention. Par quoi un fait courageux ne doit pas conclure un homme vaillant: celui qui le serait bien à

CThese supple variations and contradictions that are seen in us have made some imagine that we have two souls, and others that two powers accompany us and drive us, each in its own way, one toward good, the other toward evil; for such sudden diversity cannot well be reconciled with a simple subject.

BNot only does the wind of accident move me at will, but, besides, I am moved and disturbed as a result merely of my own unstable posture; and anyone who observes carefully can hardly find himself twice in the same state. I give my soul now one face, now another, according to which direction I turn it. If I speak of myself in different ways, that is because I look at myself in different ways. All contradictions may be found in me by some twist and in some fashion. Bashful, insolent; Cchaste, lascivious; Btalkative, taciturn; tough, delicate; clever, stupid; surly, affable; lying, truthful; Clearned, ignorant; liberal, miserly, and prodigal: Ball this I see in myself to some extent according to how I turn; and whoever studies himself really attentively finds in himself, yes, even in his judgment, this gyration and discord. I have nothing to say about myself absolutely, simply, and solidly, without confusion and without mixture, or in one word. *Distinguo* is the most universal member of my logic.

AAlthough I am always minded to say good of what is good, and inclined to interpret favorably anything that can be so interpreted, still it is true that the strangeness of our condition makes it happen that we are often driven to do good by vice itself—were it not that doing good is judged by intention alone.

Therefore one courageous deed must not be taken to

point, il le serait toujours et à toutes occasions. Si c'était une habitude de vertu et non une saillie, elle rendrait un homme pareillement résolu à tous accidents: tel seul qu'en compagnie, tel en camp clos qu'en une bataille; car quoi qu'on dise, il n'y a pas autre vaillance sur le pavé et autre au camp. Aussi courageusement porterait-il une maladie en son lit qu'une blessure au camp, et ne craindrait non plus la mort en sa maison qu'en un assaut. Nous ne verrions pas un même homme donner dans la brèche d'une brave assurance, et se tourmenter après comme une femme de la perte d'un procès ou d'un fils. ᶜQuand, étant lâche à l'infamie, il est ferme à la pauvreté; quand, étant mol entre les rasoirs des barbiers, il se trouve raide contre les épées des adversaires, l'action est louable, non pas l'homme.

Plusieurs Grecs, dit Cicéron, ne peuvent voir les ennemis et se trouvent constants aux maladies; les Cimbres et Celtibériens tout le rebours: *nihil enim potest esse æquabile, quod non a certa ratione proficiscatur.*[12]

ᴮIl n'est point de vaillance plus extrême en son espèce que celle d'Alexandre; mais elle n'est qu'en espèce, ni assez pleine partout et universelle. ᶜTout incomparable qu'elle est, si a-t-elle encore ses taches: ᴮqui fait que nous le voyons se troubler si éperdument aux plus légères soupçons qu'il prend des machinations des siens contre sa vie, et se porter en cette recherche d'une si véhémente et indiscrète injustice et d'une crainte qui subvertit sa raison naturelle. La superstition aussi, de quoi il était si fort atteint, porte quelque image de pusillanimité. ᶜEt l'excès

---

[12] Cicero, *Tusculans,* ɪɪ, xxvii.

prove a man valiant; a man who was really valiant would be so always and on all occasions. If valor were a habit of virtue, and not a sally, it would make a man equally resolute in any contingency, the same alone as in company, the same in single combat as in battle; for, whatever they say, there is not one valor for the pavement and another for the camp. As bravely would he bear an illness in his bed as a wound in camp, and he would fear death no more in his home than in an assault. We would not see the same man charging into the breach with brave assurance, and later tormenting himself, like a woman, over the loss of a lawsuit or a son. ᶜWhen, though a coward against infamy, he is firm against poverty; when, though weak against the surgeons' knives, he is steadfast against the enemy's swords, the action is praiseworthy, not the man.

Many Greeks, says Cicero, cannot look at the enemy, and are brave in sickness; the Cimbrians and Celtiberians, just the opposite; *for nothing can be uniform that does not spring from a firm principle.*[12]

ᴮThere is no more extreme valor of its kind than Alexander's; but it is only of one kind, and not complete and universal enough. ᶜIncomparable though it is, it still has its blemishes; ᴮwhich is why we see him worry so frantically when he conceives the slightest suspicion that his men are plotting against his life, and why he behaves in such matters with such violent and indiscriminate injustice and with a fear that subverts his natural reason. Also superstition, with which he was so strongly tainted, bears some stamp of pusillanimity. ᶜAnd the excessiveness of the penance he

de la pénitence qu'il fit du meurtre de Clytus est aussi témoignage de l'inégalité de son courage.

^ANotre fait, ce ne sont que pièces rapportées—^Cvoluptatem contemnunt, in dolore sunt molliores; gloriam negligunt, franguntur infamia [13]—^Aet voulons acquérir un honneur à fausses enseignes. La vertu ne veut être suivie que pour elle-même; et si on emprunte parfois son masque pour autre occasion, elle nous l'arrache aussitôt du visage. C'est une vive et forte teinture, quand l'âme en est une fois abreuvée, et qui ne s'en va qu'elle n'emporte la pièce. Voilà pourquoi pour juger d'un homme il faut suivre longuement et curieusement sa trace. Si la constance ne s'y maintient de son seul fondement, ^Ccui vivendi via considerata atque provisa est,[14] ^Asi la variété des occurrences lui fait changer de pas (je dis de voie, car le pas s'en peut ou hâter ou appesantir), laissez-le courir: celui-là s'en va à-vau-le-vent, comme dit la devise de notre Talbot.[15]

Ce n'est pas merveille, dit un ancien,[16] que le hasard puisse tant sur nous, puisque nous vivons par hasard. A qui n'a dressé en gros sa vie à une certaine fin, il est impossible de disposer les actions particulières. Il est impossible de ranger les pièces, à qui n'a une forme du total en sa tête. A quoi faire la provision des couleurs à qui ne sait ce qu'il a à peindre? Aucun ne fait certain dessein de sa vie, et n'en délibérons qu'à parcelles. L'archer doit premièrement savoir où il vise, et puis y accommoder

---

[13] Cicero, De Officiis, I, xxi.
[14] Cicero, Paradoxes, v, i.
[15] John Talbot, Earl of Shrewsbury, popular in pro-English Guy-

did for the murder of Clytus is also evidence of the un-
evenness of his temper.

ᴬOur actions are nothing but a patchwork—ᶜ*they despise pleasure, but are too cowardly in pain; they are indifferent to glory, but infamy breaks their spirit* [13]—ᴬand we
want to gain honor under false colors. Virtue will not be
followed except for her own sake; and if we sometimes
borrow her mask for some other purpose, she promptly
snatches it from our face. It is a strong and vivid dye, once
the soul is steeped in it, and will not go without taking the
fabric with it. That is why, to judge a man, we must follow
his traces long and carefully. If he does not maintain consistency for its own sake, ᶜ*with a way of life that has been
well considered and preconcerted,* [14] ᴬif changing circumstances make him change his pace (I mean his path, for
his pace may be hastened or slowed), let him go: that
man goes before the wind, as the motto of our Talbot [15]
says.

It is no wonder, says an ancient,[16] that chance has so
much power over us, since we live by chance. A man who
has not directed his life as a whole toward a definite goal
cannot possibly set his particular actions in order. A man
who does not have a picture of the whole in his head
cannot possibly arrange the pieces. What good does it
do a man to lay in a supply of paints if he does not know
what he is to paint? No one makes a definite plan of his
life; we think about it only piecemeal. The archer must

---

enne during the Hundred Years' War, was killed at the battle of
Castillon a few miles from Montaigne's estate.
[16] Seneca (*Epistles*, lxxi, 3).

[II:1] *Of the Inconsistency*

la main, l'arc, la corde, la flèche et les mouvements. Nos conseils fourvoient parce qu'ils n'ont pas d'adresse et de but. Nul vent fait pour celui qui n'a point de port destiné.

Je ne suis pas d'avis de ce jugement qu'on fit pour Sophoclès, de l'avoir argumenté suffisant au maniement des choses domestiques, contre l'accusation de son fils, pour avoir vu l'une de ses tragédies. ᶜNi ne trouve la conjecture des Pariens envoyés pour réformer les Milésiens suffisante à la conséquence qu'ils en tirèrent. Visitant l'île, ils remarquaient les terres mieux cultivées et maisons champêtres mieux gouvernées; et ayant enregistré le nom des maîtres d'icelles, comme ils eurent fait l'assemblée des citoyens en la ville, ils nommèrent ces maîtres-là pour nouveaux gouverneurs et magistrats; jugeant que, soigneux de leurs affaires privées, ils le seraient des publiques.

ᴬNous sommes tous de lopins, et d'une contexture si informe et diverse que chaque pièce, chaque moment fait son jeu. Et se trouve autant de différence de nous à nous-mêmes que de nous à autrui. ᶜ*Magnam rem puta unum hominem agere.*[17] ᴬPuisque l'ambition peut apprendre aux hommes et la vaillance, et la tempérance, et la libéralité, voire et la justice; puisque l'avarice peut planter au courage d'un garçon de boutique, nourri à l'ombre et à l'oisiveté, l'assurance de se jeter si loin du foyer domestique, à la merci des vagues et de Neptune courroucé, dans un frêle bateau; et qu'elle apprend encore la discrétion et la prudence; et que Vénus même fournit de résolution

first know what he is aiming at, and then set his hand, his bow, his string, his arrow, and his movements for that goal. Our plans go astray because they have no direction and no aim. No wind works for the man who has no port of destination.

I do not agree with the judgment given in favor of Sophocles, on the strength of seeing one of his tragedies, that it proved him competent to manage his domestic affairs, against the accusation of his son. ᶜNor do I think that the conjecture of the Parians sent to reform the Milesians was sufficient ground for the conclusion they drew. Visiting the island, they noticed the best-cultivated lands and the best-run country houses, and noted down the names of their owners. Then they assembled the citizens in the town and appointed these owners the new governors and magistrates, judging that they, who were careful of their private affairs, would be careful of those of the public.

ᴬWe are all patchwork, and so shapeless and diverse in composition that each bit, each moment, plays its own game. And there is as much difference between us and ourselves as between us and others. ᶜ*Consider it a great thing to play the part of one single man.*[17] ᴬAmbition can teach men valor, and temperance, and liberality, and even justice. Greed can implant in the heart of a shop apprentice, brought up in obscurity and idleness, the confidence to cast himself far from hearth and home, in a frail boat at the mercy of the waves and angry Neptune; it also teaches discretion and wisdom. Venus herself supplies resolution

---

[17] Seneca, *Epistles*, cxx, 22.

[II:1] *Of the Inconsistency*

et de hardiesse la jeunesse encore sous la discipline et la verge, et gendarme le tendre cœur des pucelles au giron de leurs mères:

> [B]Hac duce, custodes furtim transgressa jacentes,
> Ad Juvenem tenebris sola puella venit; [18]

[A]ce n'est pas tour de rassis entendement de nous juger simplement par nos actions de dehors. Il faut sonder jusqu'au dedans et voir par quels ressorts se donne le branle; mais d'autant que c'est une hasardeuse et haute entreprise, je voudrais que moins de gens s'en mêlassent.

6 De l'exercitation [1]

[A]Il est malaisé que le discours et l'instruction, encore que notre croyance s'y applique volontiers, soient assez puissantes pour nous acheminer jusqu'à l'action, si outre cela nous n'exerçons et formons notre âme par expérience au train auquel nous la voulons ranger; autrement, quand elle sera au propre des effets, elle s'y trouvera sans doute empêchée. Voilà pourquoi, parmi les philosophes, ceux qui ont voulu atteindre à quelque plus grande excellence ne se sont pas contentés d'attendre à couvert et en repos les rigueurs de la fortune, de peur qu'elle ne les surprît inexpérimentés et nouveaux au combat; ains ils lui sont

---

[18] Tibullus, *Elegies*, II, i, 75–6.

and boldness to boys still subject to discipline and the rod, and arms the tender hearts of virgins who are still in their mothers' laps:

ᴮFurtively passing sleeping guards, with Love as guide,
Alone by night the girl comes to the young man's side.[18]

ᴬIn view of this, a sound intellect will refuse to judge men simply by their outward actions; we must probe the inside and discover what springs set men in motion. But since this is an arduous and hazardous undertaking, I wish fewer people would meddle with it.

6 Of Practice [1]

ᴬReasoning and education, though we are willing to put our trust in them, can hardly be powerful enough to lead us to action, unless besides we exercise and form our soul by experience to the way we want it to go; otherwise, when it comes to the time for action, it will undoubtedly find itself at a loss. That is why, among the philosophers, those who have wanted to attain some greater excellence have not been content to await the rigors of Fortune in shelter and repose, for fear she might surprise them inexperienced and new to the combat; rather they have gone forth to meet her and have flung themselves deliberately

---

[1] Written no later than 1574, probably 1573–74.

allés au-devant et se sont jetés à escient à la preuve des difficultés. Les uns en ont abandonné les richesses pour s'exercer à une pauvreté volontaire; les autres ont recherché le labeur et une austérité de vie pénible pour se durcir au mal et au travail; d'autres se sont privés des parties du corps les plus chères, comme de la vue et des membres propres à la génération, de peur que leur service, trop plaisant et trop mou, ne relâchât et n'attendrît la fermeté de leur âme. Mais à mourir, qui est la plus grande besogne que nous ayons à faire, l'exercitation ne nous y peut aider. On se peut, par usage et par expérience, fortifier contre les douleurs, la honte, l'indigence et tels autres accidents; mais quant à la mort, nous ne la pouvons essayer qu'une fois; nous y sommes tous apprentis quand nous y venons.

Il s'est trouvé anciennement des hommes si excellents ménagers du temps qu'ils ont essayé en la mort même de la goûter et savourer, et ont bandé leur esprit pour voir que c'était de ce passage; mais ils ne sont pas revenus nous en dire les nouvelles:

nemo expergitus extat
Frigida quem semel est vitai pausa sequuta.[2]

Canius Julius, noble homme romain, de vertu et fermeté singulière, ayant été condamné à mort par ce maraud de Caligula, outre plusieurs merveilleuses preuves qu'il donna de sa résolution, comme il était sur le point de souffrir la main du bourreau, un philosophe, son ami, lui demanda: "Eh bien, Canius, en quelle démarche est à cette heure votre âme? que fait-elle? en quels pensements êtes-vous?"

---

[2] Lucretius, *De Rerum Natura*, iii, 929–30.

into the test of difficulties. Some of them have abandoned riches to exercise themselves in a voluntary poverty; others have sought labor and a painful austerity of life to toughen themselves against toil and trouble; others have deprived themselves of the most precious parts of the body, such as sight and the organs of generation, for fear that their services, too pleasant and easy, might relax and soften the firmness of their soul.

But for dying, which is the greatest task we have to perform, practice cannot help us. A man can, by habit and experience, fortify himself against pain, shame, indigence, and such other accidents; but as for death, we can try it only once: we are all apprentices when we come to it.

In ancient times there were men who husbanded their time so excellently that they tried to taste and savor it even at the point of death, and strained their minds to see what this passage was; but they have not come back to tell us news of it:

> No man awakes
> Whom once the icy end of living overtakes.[2]

Canius Julius, a Roman nobleman of singular virtue and firmness, after being condemned to death by that scoundrel Caligula, gave this among many prodigious proofs of his resoluteness. As he was on the point of being executed, a philosopher friend of his asked him: "Well, Canius, how stands your soul at this moment? What is it doing? What are your thoughts?" "I was thinking," he replied, "about

—"Je pensais," lui répondit-il, "à me tenir prêt et bandé de toute ma force pour voir si en cet instant de la mort, si court et si bref, je pourrai apercevoir quelque délogement de l'âme, et si elle aura quelque ressentiment de son issue, pour, si j'en apprends quelque chose, en revenir donner après, si je puis, avertissement à mes amis." Celui-ci, philosophe non seulement jusqu'à la mort, mais en la mort même. Quelle assurance était-ce, et quelle fierté de courage, de vouloir que sa mort lui servît de leçon, et avoir loisir de penser ailleurs en un si grand affaire!

^BJus hoc animi morientis habebat.³

^AIl me semble toutefois qu'il y a quelque façon de nous apprivoiser à elle et de l'essayer aucunement. Nous en pouvons avoir expérience, sinon entière et parfaite, au moins telle qu'elle ne soit pas inutile, et qui nous rende plus fortifiés et assurés. Si nous ne la pouvons joindre, nous la pouvons approcher, nous la pouvons reconnaître; et si nous ne donnons jusqu'à son fort, au moins verrons-nous et en pratiquerons les avenues.

Ce n'est pas sans raison qu'on nous fait regarder à notre sommeil même pour la ressemblance qu'il a de la mort. ^CCombien facilement nous passons du veiller au dormir! Avec combien peu d'intérêt nous perdons la connaissance de la lumière et de nous! A l'aventure pourrait sembler inutile et contre nature la faculté du sommeil qui nous prive de toute action et de tout sentiment, n'était que par icelui nature nous instruit qu'elle nous a pareillement fait pour mourir que pour vivre, et, dès la vie, nous pré-

---

₃ Lucan, *Pharsalia*, VIII, 636.

holding myself ready and with all my powers intent to see whether in that instant of death, so short and brief, I shall be able to perceive any dislodgment of the soul, and whether it will have any feeling of its departure; so that, if I learn anything about it, I may return later, if I can, to give the information to my friends." This man philosophizes not only unto death, but even in death itself. What assurance it was, and what proud courage, to want his death to serve as a lesson to him, and to have leisure to think about other things in such a great business!

^BSuch sway he had over his dying soul.[3]

^AIt seems to me, however, that there is a certain way of familiarizing ourselves with death and trying it out to some extent. We can have an experience of it that is, if not entire and perfect, at least not useless, and that makes us more fortified and assured. If we cannot reach it, we can approach it, we can reconnoiter it; and if we do not penetrate as far as its fort, at least we shall see and become acquainted with the approaches to it.

It is not without reason that we are taught to study even our sleep for the resemblance it has with death. ^CHow easily we pass from waking to sleeping! With how little sense of loss we lose consciousness of the light and of ourselves! Perhaps the faculty of sleep, which deprives us of all action and all feeling, might seem useless and contrary to nature, were it not that thereby Nature teaches us that she has made us for dying and living alike, and from the start of life presents to us the eternal state that she re-

sente l'éternel état qu'elle nous garde après icelle, pour nous y accoutumer et nous en ôter la crainte.

ᴬMais ceux qui sont tombés par quelque violent accident en défaillance de cœur et qui y ont perdu tous sentiments, ceux-là, à mon avis, ont été bien près de voir son vrai et naturel visage: car quant à l'instant et au point du passage, il n'est pas à craindre qu'il porte avec soi aucun travail ou déplaisir, d'autant que nous ne pouvons avoir nul sentiment sans loisir. Nos souffrances ont besoin de temps, qui est si court et si précipité en la mort qu'il faut nécessairement qu'elle soit insensible. Ce sont les approches que nous avons à craindre; et celles-là peuvent tomber en expérience.

Plusieurs choses nous semblent plus grandes par imagination que par effet. J'ai passé une bonne partie de mon âge en une parfaite et entière santé: je dis non seulement entière, mais encore allègre et bouillante. Cet état, plein de verdeur et de fête, me faisait trouver si horrible la considération des maladies que quand je suis venu à les expérimenter j'ai trouvé leurs pointures molles et lâches au prix de ma crainte.

ᴮVoici que j'éprouve tous les jours: suis-je à couvert chaudement dans une bonne salle pendant qu'il se passe une nuit orageuse et tempétueuse, je m'étonne et m'afflige pour ceux qui sont lors en la campagne; y suis-je moi-même, je ne désire pas seulement d'être ailleurs.

ᴬCela seul, d'être toujours enfermé dans une chambre, me semblait insupportable. Je fus incontinent dressé à y être une semaine, et un mois, plein d'émotion, d'altération et de faiblesse; et ai trouvé que lors de ma santé je plaignais les malades beaucoup plus que je ne me trouve

serves for us after we die, to accustom us to it and take away our fear of it.

ᴬBut those who by some violent accident have fallen into a faint and lost all sensation, those, in my opinion, have been very close to seeing death's true and natural face. For as for the instant and point of passing away, it is not to be feared that it carries with it any travail or pain, since we can have no feeling without leisure. Our sufferings need time, which in death is so short and precipitate that it must necessarily be imperceptible. It is the approaches that we have to fear; and these may fall within our experience.

Many things seem to us greater in imagination than in reality. I have spent a good part of my life in perfect and entire health; I mean not merely entire, but even blithe and ebullient. This state, full of verdure and cheer, made me find the thought of illnesses so horrible that when I came to experience them I found their pains mild and easy compared with my fears.

ᴮHere is what I experience every day: if I am warmly sheltered in a nice room during a stormy and tempestuous night, I am appalled and distressed for those who are then in the open country; if I am myself outside, I do not even wish to be anywhere else.

ᴬThe mere idea of being always shut up in a room seemed to me unbearable. Suddenly I had to get used to being there a week, or a month, full of agitation, alteration, and weakness. And I have found that in time of health I used to pity the sick much more than I now think

à plaindre moi-même quand j'en suis, et que la force de mon appréhension enchérissait près de moitié l'essence et vérité de la chose. J'espère qu'il m'en adviendra de même de la mort, et qu'elle ne vaut pas la peine que je prends à tant d'apprêts que je dresse et tant de secours que j'appelle et assemble pour en soutenir l'effort; mais à toutes aventures, nous ne pouvons nous donner trop d'avantage.

Pendant nos troisièmes troubles ou deuxièmes (il ne me souvient pas bien de cela), m'étant allé un jour promener à une lieue de chez moi, qui suis assis dans le moiau de tout le trouble des guerres civiles de France, estimant être en toute sûreté et si voisin de ma retraite que je n'avais point besoin de meilleur équipage, j'avais pris un cheval bien aisé mais non guère ferme. A mon retour, une occasion soudaine s'étant présentée de m'aider de ce cheval à un service qui n'était pas bien de son usage, un de mes gens, grand et fort, monté sur un puissant roussin qui avait une bouche désespérée, frais au demeurant et vigoureux, pour faire le hardi et devancer ses compagnons vint à le pousser à toute bride droit dans ma route et fondre comme un colosse sur le petit homme et petit cheval et le foudroyer de sa raideur et de sa pesanteur, nous envoyant l'un et l'autre les pieds contremont: si que voilà le cheval abattu et couché tout étourdi, moi dix ou douze pas au delà, mort, étendu à la renverse, le visage tout meurtri et tout écorché, mon épée que j'avais à la main, à plus de dix pas au delà, ma ceinture en pièces, n'ayant ni mouvement ni sentiment non plus qu'une souche. C'est le seul évanouissement que j'aie senti jusqu'à cette heure.

I deserve to be pitied when I am sick myself; and that the power of my apprehension made its object appear almost half again as fearful as it was in its truth and essence. I hope that the same thing will happen to me with death, and that it is not worth the trouble I take, the many preparations that I make, and all the many aids that I invoke and assemble to sustain the shock of it. But at all events, we can never be well enough prepared.

During our third civil war, or the second (I do not quite remember which), I went riding one day about a league from my house, which is situated at the very hub of all the turmoil of the civil wars of France. Thinking myself perfectly safe, and so near my home that I needed no better equipage, I took a very easy but not very strong horse. On my return, when a sudden occasion came up for me to use this horse for a service to which it was not accustomed, one of my men, big and strong, riding a powerful work horse who had a desperately hard mouth and was moreover fresh and vigorous—this man, in order to show his daring and get ahead of his companions, spurred his horse at full speed up the path behind me, came down like a colossus on the little man and little horse, and hit us like a thunderbolt with all his strength and weight, sending us both head over heels. So that there lay the horse bowled over and stunned, and I ten or twelve paces beyond, dead, stretched on my back, my face all bruised and skinned, my sword, which I had had in my hand, more than ten paces away, my belt in pieces, having no more motion or feeling than a log. It is the only swoon that I have experienced to this day.

[II:6] *Of Practice*

Ceux qui étaient avec moi, après avoir essayé par tous les moyens qu'ils purent de me faire revenir, me tenant pour mort, me prirent entre leurs bras, et m'emportaient avec beaucoup de difficulté en ma maison, qui était loin de là environ une demi-lieue française. Sur le chemin, et après avoir été plus de deux grosses heures tenu pour trépassé, je commençai à me mouvoir et respirer: car il était tombé si grande abondance de sang dans mon estomac que pour l'en décharger nature eut besoin de ressusciter ses forces. On me dressa sur mes pieds, où je rendis un plein seau de bouillons de sang pur; et plusieurs fois par le chemin il m'en fallut faire de même. Par là je commençai à reprendre un peu de vie, mais ce fut par les menus et par un si long trait de temps que mes premiers sentiments étaient beaucoup plus approchants de la mort que de la vie:

> ᴮPerche, dubbiosa anchor del suo ritorno,
> Non s'assecura attonita la mente.⁴

ᴬCette recordation que j'en ai fort empreinte en mon âme, me représentant son visage et son idée si près du naturel, me concilie aucunement à elle. Quand je commençai à y voir, ce fut d'une vue si trouble, si faible et si morte, que je ne discernais encore rien que la lumière,

> come quel ch' or apre or chiude
> Gli occhi, mezzo tra' l sonno e l' esser desto.⁵

Quant aux fonctions de l'âme, elles naissaient avec même progrès que celles du corps. Je me vis tout sanglant,

---

⁴ Tasso, *Jerusalem Delivered*, xii, stanza 74.

Those who were with me, after having tried all the means they could to bring me round, thinking me dead, took me in their arms and were carrying me with great difficulty to my house, which was about half a French league from there. On the way, and after I had been taken for dead for more than two full hours, I began to move and breathe; for so great an abundance of blood had fallen into my stomach that nature had to revive its forces to discharge it. They set me up on my feet, where I threw up a whole bucketful of clots of pure blood, and several times on the way I had to do the same thing. In so doing I began to recover a little life, but it was bit by bit and over so long a stretch of time that my first feelings were much closer to death than to life:

> ᴮBecause the shaken soul, uncertain yet
> Of its return, is still not firmly set.⁴

ᴬThis recollection, which is strongly implanted on my soul, showing me the face and idea of death so true to nature, reconciles me to it somewhat.

When I began to see anything, it was with a vision so blurred, weak, and dead, that I still could distinguish nothing but the light,

> As one 'twixt wakefulness and doze,
> Whose eyes now open, now again they close.⁵

As for the functions of the soul, they were reviving with the same progress as those of the body. I saw myself all

---

⁵ Tasso, *Jerusalem Delivered*, vɪɪɪ, stanza 26.

[II:6] *Of Practice*

car mon pourpoint était taché partout du sang que j'avais rendu. La première pensée qui me vint, ce fut que j'avais une arquebusade en la tête: de vrai, en même temps, il s'en tirait plusieurs autour de nous. Il me semblait que ma vie ne me tenait plus qu'au bout des lèvres: je fermais les yeux pour aider, ce me semblait, à la pousser hors, et prenais plaisir à m'alanguir et à me laisser aller. C'était une imagination qui ne faisait que nager superficiellement en mon âme, aussi tendre et aussi faible que tout le reste, mais à la vérité non seulement exempte de déplaisir, ains mêlée à cette douceur que sentent ceux qui se laissent glisser au sommeil.

Je crois que c'est ce même état où se trouvent ceux qu'on voit défaillant de faiblesse en l'agonie de la mort; et tiens que nous les plaignons sans cause, estimant qu'ils soient agités de grièves douleurs, ou avoir l'âme pressée de cogitations pénibles. Ç'a été toujours mon avis, contre l'opinion de plusieurs et même d'Étienne de La Boétie, que ceux que nous voyons ainsi renversés et assoupis aux approches de leur fin, ou accablés de la longueur du mal, ou par l'accident d'une apoplexie, ou mal caduc—

^Bvi morbi sæpe coactus
Ante oculos aliquis nostros, ut fulminis ictu,
Concidit, et spumas agit; ingemit, et fremit artus;
Desipit, extentat nervos, torquetur, anhelat,
Inconstanter et in jactando membra fatigat,[6]

—^Aou blessés en la tête, que nous oyons romeller et rendre parfois des soupirs tranchants, quoique nous en tirons

---

[6] Lucretius, *De Rerum Natura*, III, 487–91.

bloody, for my doublet was stained all over with the blood I had thrown up. The first thought that came to me was that I had gotten a harquebus shot in the head; indeed several were being fired around us at the time of the accident. It seemed to me that my life was hanging only by the tip of my lips; I closed my eyes in order, it seemed to me, to help push it out, and took pleasure in growing languid and letting myself go. It was an idea that was only floating on the surface of my soul, as delicate and feeble as all the rest, but in truth not only free from distress but mingled with that sweet feeling that people have who let themselves slide into sleep.

I believe that this is the same state in which people find themselves whom we see fainting with weakness in the agony of death; and I maintain that we pity them without cause, supposing that they are agitated by grievous pains or have their soul oppressed by painful thoughts. This has always been my view, against the opinion of many, and even of Etienne de La Boétie, concerning those whom we see thus prostrate and comatose as their end approaches, or overwhelmed by the length of the disease, or by a stroke of apoplexy, or by epilepsy—

> ^BThis do we often see:
> A man, struck, as by lightning, by some malady,
> Falls down all foaming at the mouth, shivers and rants;
> He moans under the torture, writhes his muscles, pants,
> And in fitful tossing exhausts his weary limbs ⁶

—^Aor wounded in the head: When we hear them groan and from time to time utter poignant sighs, or see them

aucuns signes par où il semble qu'il leur reste encore de la connaissance, et quelques mouvements que nous leur voyons faire du corps; j'ai toujours pensé, dis-je, qu'ils avaient et l'âme et le corps enseveli et endormi:

^BVivit, et est vitæ nescius ipse suæ.⁷

^AEt ne pouvais croire que, à un si grand étonnement de membres et si grande défaillance des sens, l'âme pût maintenir aucune force au dedans pour se reconnaître; et que, par ainsi, ils n'avaient aucun discours qui les tourmentât et qui leur pût faire juger et sentir la misère de leur condition; et que par conséquent ils n'étaient pas fort à plaindre.

^BJe n'imagine aucun état pour moi si insupportable et horrible que d'avoir l'âme vive et affligée sans moyen de se déclarer: comme je dirais de ceux qu'on envoie au supplice, leur ayant coupé la langue, si ce n'était qu'en cette sorte de mort la plus muette me semble la mieux séante, si elle est accompagnée d'un ferme visage et grave; et comme ces misérables prisonniers qui tombent ès mains des vilains bourreaux soldats de ce temps, desquels ils sont tourmentés de toute espèce de cruel traitement pour les contraindre à quelque rançon excessive et impossible, tenus cependant en condition et en lieu où ils n'ont moyen quelconque d'expression et signification de leurs pensées et de leur misère.

^ALes poètes ont feint quelques dieux favorables à la délivrance de ceux qui traînaient ainsi une mort languissante:

---

⁷ Ovid, *Tristia*, I, iii, 12.

make certain movements of the body, we seem to see signs that they still have some consciousness left; but I have always thought, I say, that their soul and body were buried in sleep.

᳇He lives, and is unconscious of his life.⁷

ᴬAnd I could not believe that with so great a paralysis of the limbs, and so great a failing of the senses, the soul could maintain any force within by which to be conscious of itself; and so I believed that they had no reflections to torment them, nothing able to make them judge and feel the misery of their condition, and that consequently they were not much to be pitied.

ᴮI can imagine no state so horrible and unbearable for me as to have my soul alive and afflicted, without means to express itself. I should say the same of those who are sent to execution with their tongue cut out, were it not that in this sort of death the most silent seems to be the most becoming, if it goes with a firm, grave countenance; and the same of those miserable prisoners who fall into the hands of the villainous murdering soldiers of these days, who torture them with every kind of cruel treatment to force them to pay some excessive and impossible ransom, keeping them meanwhile in a condition and in a place where they have no means whatever of expressing or signifying their thoughts and their misery.

ᴬThe poets have portrayed some gods as favorable to the deliverance of those who thus drag out a lingering death:

[II:6] *Of Practice*

> hunc ego Diti
> Sacrum jussa fero, teque isto corpore solvo.[8]

Et les voix et réponses courtes et décousues qu'on leur arrache à force de crier autour de leurs oreilles et de les tempêter, ou des mouvements qui semblent avoir quelque consentement à ce qu'on leur demande, ce n'est pas témoignage qu'ils vivent pourtant, au moins d'une vie entière. Il nous advient ainsi sur le bégayement du sommeil, avant qu'il nous ait du tout saisis, de sentir comme en songe ce qui se fait autour de nous, et suivre les voix d'une ouïe trouble et incertaine qui semble ne donner qu'aux bords de l'âme; et faisons des réponses, à la suite des dernières paroles qu'on nous a dites, qui ont plus de fortune que de sens.

Or, à présent que je l'ai essayé par effet, je ne fais nul doute que je n'en aie bien jugé jusqu'à cette heure. Car, premièrement, étant tout évanoui, je me travaillais d'entr'-ouvrir mon pourpoint à belles ongles (car j'étais désarmé), et si sais que je ne sentais en l'imagination rien qui me blessât: car il y a plusieurs mouvements en nous qui ne partent pas de notre ordonnance:

> [B]Semianimesque micant digiti ferrumque retractant.[9]

[A]Ceux qui tombent élancent ainsi les bras au-devant de leur chute, par une naturelle impulsion qui fait que nos membres se prêtent des offices [B]et ont des agitations à part de notre discours:

---

[8] Virgil, *Aeneid*, IV, 702-3.

I bear to Pluto, by decree,
This lock of hair, and from your body set you free.[8]

Nonetheless, the short and incoherent words and replies
that are extorted from them by dint of shouting about
their ears and storming at them, or the movements that
seem to have some connection with what is asked them,
are not evidence that they are alive, at least fully alive. So
it happens to us in the early stages of sleep, before it has
seized us completely, to sense as in a dream what is happening around us, and to follow voices with a blurred and
uncertain hearing which seems to touch on only the edges
of the soul; and following the last words spoken to us, we
make answers that are more random than sensible.

Now I have no doubt, now that I have tried this out by
experience, that I judged this matter rightly all along. For
from the first, while wholly unconscious, I was laboring to
rip open my doublet with my nails (for I was not in
armor); and yet I know that I felt nothing in my imagination that hurt me; for there are many movements of ours
that do not come from our will:

BAnd half-dead fingers writhe and seize the sword again.[9]

AThus those who are falling throw out their arms in front
of them, by a natural impulse which makes our limbs lend
each other their services Band have stirrings apart from our
reason:

---

[9] Virgil, *Aeneid*, x, 396.

Falciferos memorant currus abscindere membra,
Ut tremere in terra videatur ab artubus id quod
Decidit abscissum, cum mens tamen atque hominis vis
Mobilitate mali non quit sentire dolorem.[10]

^AJ'avais mon estomac pressé de ce sang caillé, mes mains y couraient d'elles-mêmes, comme elles font souvent où il nous démange, contre l'avis de notre volonté. Il y a plusieurs animaux, et des hommes mêmes, après qu'ils sont trépassés, auxquels on voit resserrer et remuer des muscles. Chacun sait par expérience qu'il y a des parties qui se branlent, dressent et couchent souvent sans son congé. Or ces passions qui ne nous touchent que par l'écorce ne se peuvent dire nôtres. Pour les faire nôtres il faut que l'homme y soit engagé tout entier; et les douleurs que le pied ou la main sentent pendant que nous dormons ne sont pas à nous.

Comme j'approchai de chez moi, où l'alarme de ma chute avait déjà couru, et que ceux de ma famille m'eurent rencontré avec les cris accoutumés en telles choses, non seulement je répondais quelque mot à ce qu'on me demandait, mais encore ils disent que je m'avisai de commander qu'on donnât un cheval à ma femme, que je voyais s'empêtrer et se tracasser dans le chemin, qui est montueux et malaisé. Il semble que cette considération dût partir d'une âme éveillée; si est-ce que je n'y étais aucunement: c'étaient des pensements vains, en nue, qui étaient émus par les sens des yeux et des oreilles; ils ne venaient pas de chez moi. Je ne savais pourtant ni d'où je venais, ni où j'allais;

---

[10] Lucretius, *De Rerum Natura*, iii, 642–5.

They say that chariots bearing scythes will cut so fast
That severed limbs are writhing on the ground below
Before the victim's soul and strength can ever know
Or even feel the pain, so swift has been the hurt.[10]

ᴬMy stomach was oppressed with the clotted blood; my
hands flew to it of their own accord, as they often do
where we itch, against the intention of our will.

There are many animals, and even men, whose muscles
we can see contract and move after they are dead. Every
man knows by experience that there are parts that often
move, stand up, and lie down, without his leave. Now
these passions which touch only the rind of us cannot be
called ours. To make them ours, the whole man must be
involved; and the pains which the foot or the hand feel
while we are asleep are not ours.

As I approached my house, where the alarm of my fall
had already come, and the members of my family had met
me with the outcries customary in such cases, not only did
I make some sort of answer to what was asked me, but also
(they say) I thought of ordering them to give a horse to
my wife, whom I saw stumbling and having trouble on the
road, which is steep and rugged. It would seem that this
consideration must have proceeded from a wide-awake
soul; yet the fact is that I was not there at all. These were
idle thoughts, in the clouds, set in motion by the sensations
of the eyes and ears; they did not come from within me. I
did not know, for all that, where I was coming from or
where I was going, nor could I weigh and consider what I

[II:6] *Of Practice*

ni ne pouvais peser et considérer ce qu'on me demandait: ce sont des légers effets que les sens produisaient d'eux-mêmes, comme d'un usage; ce que l'âme y prêtait, c'était en songe, touchée bien légèrement, et comme léchée seulement et arrosée par la molle impression des sens. Cependant mon assiette était à la vérité très douce et paisible; je n'avais affliction ni pour autrui ni pour moi: c'était une langueur et une extrême faiblesse sans aucune douleur. Je vis ma maison sans la reconnaître.

Quand on m'eut couché, je sentis une infinie douceur à ce repos, car j'avais été vilainement tirassé par ces pauvres gens, qui avaient pris la peine de me porter sur leurs bras par un long et très mauvais chemin, et s'y étaient lassés deux ou trois fois les uns après les autres. On me présenta force remèdes, de quoi je n'en reçus aucun, tenant pour certain que j'étais blessé à mort par la tête. C'eût été sans mentir une mort bien heureuse: car la faiblesse de mon discours me gardait d'en rien juger, et celle du corps d'en rien sentir. Je me laissais couler si doucement et d'une façon si douce et si aisée que je ne sens guère autre action moins pesante que celle-là était. Quand je vins à revivre et à reprendre mes forces,

^BUt tandem sensus convaluere mei,[11]

^Aqui fut deux ou trois heures après, je me sentis tout d'un train rengager aux douleurs, ayant les membres tous moulus et froissés de ma chute; et en fus si mal deux ou trois nuits après que j'en cuidai remourir encore un coup,

---

[11] Ovid, *Tristia*, I, iii, 14.

was asked. These are slight effects which the senses produce of themselves, as if by habit; what the soul contributed was in a dream, touched very lightly, and merely licked and sprinkled, as it were, by the soft impression of the senses.

Meanwhile my condition was, in truth, very pleasant and peaceful; I felt no affliction either for others or for myself; it was a languor and an extreme weakness, without any pain. I saw my house without recognizing it. When they had put me to bed, I felt infinite sweetness in this repose, for I had been villainously yanked about by those poor fellows, who had taken the pains to carry me in their arms over a long and very bad road, and had tired themselves out two or three times in relays. They offered me many remedies, of which I accepted none, holding it for certain that I was mortally wounded in the head. It would, in truth, have been a very happy death; for the weakness of my understanding kept me from having any judgment of it, and that of my body from having any feeling of it. I was letting myself slip away so gently, so gradually and easily, that I hardly ever did anything with less of a feeling of effort.

When I came back to life and regained my powers,

ᴮWhen my senses at last regained their strength.¹¹

ᴬwhich was two or three hours later, I felt myself all of a sudden caught up again in the pains, my limbs being all battered and bruised by my fall; and I felt so bad two or three nights after that I thought I was going to die all over

mais d'une mort plus vive; et me sens encore de la secousse de cette froissure.

Je ne veux pas oublier ceci, que la dernière chose en quoi je me pus remettre, ce fut la souvenance de cet accident; et me fis redire plusieurs fois où j'allais, d'où je venais, à quelle heure cela m'était advenu, avant que de le pouvoir concevoir. Quant à la façon de ma chute, on me la cachait en faveur de celui qui en avait été cause, et m'en forgeait-on d'autres. Mais longtemps après, et le lendemain, quand ma mémoire vint à s'entr'ouvrir et me représenter l'état où je m'étais trouvé en l'instant que j'avais aperçu ce cheval fondant sur moi (car je l'avais vu à mes talons et me tins pour mort, mais ce pensement avait été si soudain que la peur n'eut pas loisir de s'y engendrer), il me sembla que c'était un éclair qui me frappait l'âme de secousse et que je revenais de l'autre monde.

Ce conte d'un événement si léger est assez vain, n'était l'instruction que j'en ai tirée pour moi: car à la vérité, pour s'apprivoiser à la mort, je trouve qu'il n'y a que de s'en avoisiner. Or, comme dit Pline, chacun est à soi-même une très bonne discipline, pourvu qu'il ait la suffisance de s'épier de près. Ce n'est pas ici ma doctrine, c'est mon étude; et n'est pas la leçon d'autrui, c'est la mienne.

ᶜEt ne me doit-on savoir mauvais gré pourtant, si je la communique. Ce qui me sert peut aussi par accident servir à un autre. Au demeurant, je ne gâte rien, je n'use que du mien. Et si je fais le fou, c'est à mes dépens et sans l'intérêt de personne. Car c'est en folie qui meurt en moi, qui n'a point de suite. Nous n'avons nouvelles que de

again, but by a more painful death; and I still feel the effect of the shock of that collision.

I do not want to forget this, that the last thing I was able to recover was the memory of this accident; I had people repeat to me several times where I was going, where I was coming from, at what time it had happened to me, before I could take it in. As for the manner of my fall, they concealed it from me and made up other versions for the sake of the man who had been the cause of it. But a long time after, and the next day, when my memory came to open up and picture to me the state I had been in at the instant I had perceived that horse bearing down on me (for I had seen him at my heels and thought I was a dead man, but that thought had been so sudden that I had no time to be afraid), it seemed to me that a flash of lightning was striking my soul with a violent shock, and that I was coming back from the other world.

This account of so trivial an event would be rather pointless, were it not for the instruction that I have derived from it for myself; for in truth, in order to get used to the idea of death, I find there is nothing like coming close to it. Now as Pliny says, each man is a good education to himself, provided he has the capacity to spy on himself from close up. What I write here is not my teaching, but my study; it is not a lesson for others, but for me.

cAnd yet it should not be held against me if I publish what I write. What is useful to me may also by accident be useful to another. Moreover, I am not spoiling anything, I am using only what is mine. And if I play the fool, it is at my expense and without harm to anyone. For it is a folly that will die with me, and will have no conse-

deux ou trois anciens qui aient battu ce chemin; et si ne pouvons dire si c'est du tout en pareille manière à celle-ci, n'en connaissant que les noms. Nul depuis ne s'est jeté sur leur trace. C'est une épineuse entreprise, et plus qu'il ne semble, de suivre une allure si vagabonde que celle de notre esprit; de pénétrer les profondeurs opaques de ses replis internes; de choisir et arrêter tant de menus airs de ses agitations. Et est un amusement nouveau et extraordinaire, qui nous retire des occupations communes du monde, oui, et des plus recommandées.

Il y a plusieurs années que je n'ai que moi pour visée à mes pensées, que je ne contrôle et étudie que moi; et si j'étudie autre chose, c'est pour soudain le coucher sur moi, ou en moi, pour mieux dire. Et ne me semble point faillir si, comme il se fait des autres sciences, sans comparaison moins utiles, je fais part de ce que j'ai appris en celle-ci; quoique je ne me contente guère du progrès que j'y ai fait. Il n'est description pareille en difficulté à la description de soi-même, ni certes en utilité. Encore se faut-il testonner, encore se faut-il ordonner et ranger pour sortir en place. Or je me pare sans cesse, car je me décris sans cesse.

La coutume a fait le parler de soi vicieux, et le prohibe obstinément en haine de la vantance qui semble toujours être attachée aux propres témoignages. Au lieu qu'on doit moucher l'enfant, cela s'appelle l'ennaser.

quences. We have heard of only two or three three ancients who opened up this road, and even of them we cannot say whether their manner in the least resembled mine, since we know only their names. No one since has followed their lead. It is a thorny undertaking, and more so than it seems, to follow a movement so wandering as that of our mind, to penetrate the opaque depths of its innermost folds, to pick out and immobilize the innumerable flutterings that agitate it. And it is a new and extraordinary amusement, which withdraws us from the ordinary occupations of the world, yes, even from those most recommended.

It is many years now that I have had only myself as object of my thoughts, that I have been examining and studying only myself; and if I study anything else, it is in order promptly to apply it to myself, or rather within myself. And it does not seem to me that I am making a mistake if—as is done in the other sciences, which are incomparably less useful—I impart what I have learned in this one, though I am hardly satisfied with the progress I have made in it. There is no description equal in difficulty, or certainly in usefulness, to the description of oneself. Even so one must spruce up, even so one must present oneself in an orderly arrangement, if one would go out in public. Now, I am constantly adorning myself, for I am constantly describing myself.

Custom has made speaking of oneself a vice, and obstinately forbids it out of hatred for the boasting that seems always to accompany it. Instead of blowing the child's nose, as we should, this amounts to pulling it off.

[II:6] *Of Practice*

In vitium ducit culpæ fuga.[12]

Je trouve plus de mal que de bien à ce remède.

Mais quand il serait vrai que ce fût nécessairement présomption d'entretenir le peuple de soi, je ne dois pas, suivant mon général dessein, refuser une action qui publie cette maladive qualité, puisqu'elle est en moi; et ne dois cacher cette faute que j'ai non seulement en usage, mais en profession. Toutefois, à dire ce que j'en crois, cette coutume a tort de condamner le vin parce que plusieurs s'y enivrent. On ne peut abuser que des choses qui sont bonnes. Et crois de cette règle qu'elle ne regarde que la populaire défaillance. Ce sont brides à veaux, desquelles ni les saints, que nous oyons si hautement parler d'eux, ni les philosophes, ni les théologiens ne se brident. Ne fais-je, moi, quoique je sois aussi peu l'un que l'autre. S'ils n'en écrivent à point nommé, au moins quand l'occasion les y porte ne feignent-ils pas de se jeter bien avant sur le trottoir. De quoi traite Socratès plus largement que de soi? A quoi achemine-t-il plus souvent les propos de ses disciples, qu'à parler d'eux, non pas de la leçon de leur livre, mais de l'être et branle de leur âme? Nous nous disons religieusement à Dieu, et à notre confesseur, comme nos voisins [13] à tout le peuple. Mais nous n'en disons, me répondra-t-on, que les accusations. Nous disons donc tout: car notre vertu même est fautière et repentable.

Mon métier et mon art, c'est vivre. Qui me défend d'en

---

[12] Horace, *Ars Poetica*, 31.

Flight from a fault will lead us into crime.[12]

I find more harm than good in this remedy.

But even if it were true that it is presumptuous, no matter what the circumstances, to talk to the public about oneself, I still must not, according to my general plan, refrain from an action that openly displays this morbid quality, since it is in me; nor may I conceal this fault, which I not only practice but profess. However, to say what I think about it, custom is wrong to condemn wine because many get drunk on it. We can misuse only things which are good. And I believe that the rule against speaking of oneself applies only to the vulgar form of this failing. Such rules are bridles for calves, with which neither the saints, whom we hear speaking so boldly about themselves, nor the philosophers, nor the theologians curb themselves. Nor do I, though I am none of these. If they do not write about themselves expressly, at least when the occasion leads them to it they do not hesitate to put themselves prominently on display. What does Socrates treat of more fully than himself? To what does he lead his disciples' conversation more often than to talk about themselves, not about the lesson of their book, but about the essence and movement of their soul? We speak our thoughts religiously to God, and to our confessor, as our neighbors [13] do to the whole people. But, someone will answer, we speak only our self-accusations. Then we speak everything: for our very virtue is faulty and fit for repentance.

My trade and my art is living. He who forbids me to

---

[13] The Protestants.

[II:6] *Of Practice*

parler selon mon sens, expérience et usage, qu'il ordonne à l'architecte de parler des bâtiments non selon soi, mais selon son voisin; selon la science d'un autre, non selon la sienne. Si c'est gloire de soi-même publier ses valeurs, que ne met Cicéron en avant l'éloquence de Hortance, Hortance celle de Cicéron?[14]

A l'aventure entendent-ils que je témoigne de moi par ouvrages et effets, non nuement par des paroles. Je peins principalement mes cogitations, sujet informe, qui ne peut tomber en production ouvragère. A toute peine le puis-je coucher en ce corps aéré de la voix. Des plus sages hommes et des plus dévots ont vécu fuyant tous apparents effets. Les effets diraient plus de la fortune que de moi. Ils témoignent leur rôle, non pas le mien, si ce n'est conjecturalement et incertainement: échantillons d'une montre particulière. Je m'étale entier: c'est un *skeletos* où, d'une vue, les veines, les muscles, les tendons paraissent, chaque pièce en son siège. L'effet de la toux en produisit une partie; l'effet de la pâleur ou battement de cœur, une autre, et douteusement. Ce ne sont mes gestes que j'écris, c'est moi, c'est mon essence.

Je tiens qu'il faut être prudent à estimer de soi, et pareillement consciencieux à en témoigner, soit bas, soit haut, indifféremment. Si je me semblais bon et sage ou près de là, je l'entonnerais à pleine tête. De dire moins de soi qu'il n'y en a, c'est sottise, non modestie. Se payer de moins qu'on ne vaut, c'est lâcheté et pusillanimité, selon

---

[14] Hortensius was a rival orator whom Cicero praised in his *Brutus,* while still seeming to set himself higher.

speak about it according to my sense, experience, and practice, let him order the architect to speak of buildings not according to himself but according to his neighbor; according to another man's knowledge, not according to his own. If it is vainglory for a man himself to publish his own merits, why doesn't Cicero proclaim the eloquence of Hortensius, Hortensius that of Cicero? [14]

Perhaps they mean that I should testify about myself by works and deeds, not by bare words. What I chiefly portray is my cogitations, a shapeless subject that does not lend itself to expression in actions. It is all I can do to couch my thoughts in this airy medium of words. Some of the wisest and most devout men have lived avoiding all noticeable actions. My actions would tell more about fortune than about me. They bear witness to their own part, not to mine, unless it be by conjecture and without certainty: they are samples which display only details. I expose myself entire: my portrait is a cadaver on which the veins, the muscles, and the tendons appear at a glance, each part in its place. One part of what I am was produced by a cough, another by a pallor or a palpitation of the heart—in any case dubiously. It is not my deeds that I write down; it is myself, it is my essence.

I hold that a man should be cautious in making an estimate of himself, and equally conscientious in testifying about himself—whether he rates himself high or low makes no difference. If I seemed to myself good and wise or nearly so, I would shout it out at the top of my voice. To say less of yourself than is true is stupidity, not modesty. To pay yourself less than you are worth is cowardice and pusillanimity, according to Aristotle. No vir-

[II:6] *Of Practice*

Aristote. Nulle vertu ne s'aide de la fausseté; et la vérité n'est jamais matière d'erreur. De dire de soi plus qu'il n'y en a, ce n'est pas toujours présomption, c'est encore souvent sottise. Se complaire outre mesure de ce qu'on est, en tomber en amour de soi indiscrète, est, à mon avis, la substance de ce vice. Le suprême remède à le guérir c'est faire tout le rebours de ce que ceux-ci ordonnent, qui en défendant le parler de soi défendent par conséquent encore plus de penser à soi. L'orgueil gît en la pensée. La langue n'y peut avoir qu'une bien légère part.

De s'amuser à soi, il leur semble que c'est se plaire en soi; de se hanter et pratiquer, que c'est se trop chérir. Il peut être. Mais cet excès naît seulement en ceux qui ne se tâtent que superficiellement, qui se voient après leurs affaires, qui appellent rêverie et oisiveté s'entretenir de soi; et s'étoffer et bâtir, faire des châteaux en Espagne: s'estimant chose tierce et étrangère à eux-mêmes.

Si quelqu'un s'enivre de sa science, regardant sous soi, qu'il tourne les yeux au-dessus vers les siècles passés; il baissera les cornes, y trouvant tant de milliers d'esprits qui le foulent aux pieds. S'il entre en quelque flatteuse présomption de sa vaillance, qu'il se ramentoive les vies des deux Scipions, de tant d'armées, de tant de peuples, qui le laissent si loin derrière eux. Nulle particulière qualité n'enorgueillira celui qui mettra quand et quand en compte tant d'imparfaites et faibles qualités autres qui sont en lui, et, au bout, la nihilité de l'humaine condition.

tue is helped by falsehood, and truth is never subject to error. To say more of yourself than is true is not always presumption; it too is often stupidity. To be immoderately pleased with what you are, to fall therefore into an undiscerning self-love, is in my opinion the substance of this vice. The supreme remedy to cure it is to do just the opposite of what those people prescribe who, by prohibiting talking about oneself, even more strongly prohibit thinking about oneself. The pride lies in the thought; the tongue can have only a very slight share in it.

It seems to them that to be occupied with oneself means to be pleased with oneself, that to frequent and associate with oneself means to cherish oneself too much. That may be. But this excess arises only in those who touch themselves no more than superficially; who observe themselves only after taking care of their business; who call it daydreaming and idleness to be concerned with oneself, and making castles in Spain to furnish and build oneself; who think themselves something alien and foreign to themselves.

If anyone gets intoxicated with his knowledge when he looks beneath him, let him turn his eyes upward toward past ages, and he will lower his horns, finding there so many thousands of minds that trample him underfoot. If he gets into some flattering presumption about his valor, let him remember the lives of the two Scipios, so many armies, so many nations, all of whom leave him so far behind them. No particular quality will make a man proud who balances it against the many weaknesses and imperfections that are also in him, and, in the end, against the nullity of man's estate.

Parce que Socratès avait seul mordu à certes au précepte de son Dieu, de se connaître, et par cet étude était arrivé à se mépriser, il fut estimé seul digne du surnom de sage. Qui se connaîtra ainsi, qu'il se donne hardiment à connaître par sa bouche.

Because Socrates alone had seriously digested the precept of his god—to know himself—and because by that study he had come to despise himself, he alone was deemed worthy of the name *wise*. Whoever knows himself thus, let him boldly make himself known by his own mouth.

Editor's Note

[This chapter, far the longest of the *Essays*, has been the most influential and remains one of the most perplexing. The extreme skepticism of the famous *Que sçay-je?* (What do I know?) was accepted for centuries as Montaigne's central position, though recent scholarship sees it rather as a step toward the convictions of Book Three.

It perplexes us mainly by its title and apparent aim. Sebond, whose *Natural Theology* Montaigne had translated at his father's behest, had argued that man could learn all about Christianity in the book of God's creation, the world. Montaigne's complete disagreement shows here as it had in his translation of Sebond's Prologue (see below, pp. 464–67). He is the most apologetic of apologists. In the page or two that he devotes to defense, he can say little more than that Sebond means well and that his faith gives his book some merit and value, since Christianity is now in such bad state that few Frenchmen seem able to receive it for the right reasons and in the right way. Less than one-tenth of the chapter deals with Sebond at all. Most of it is a long demonstration of the impotence of unaided human reason, here set in the form of a counterattack against one group of objectors to Sebond and his book.

The main divisions and their proportions are shown, with the pagination of the newer (1950) Pléiade edition, in the following table, which also shows the pages of the excerpts included in this text:

Keynote: Knowledge is useful but overrated	481	(198–9)
Introduction: The two objections to Sebond, and Montaigne's defense	481–94	(198–219)
Counterattack against the second objection: The vanity of man and man's knowledge without God	494–683	(218–53)
1. Man is no better or wiser than the animals	494–537	(218–25)
2. Man's knowledge (if any) makes him neither happy nor good	537–56	(224–25)
3. Man has no knowledge	556–626	(226–31)
4. Warning: what follows is a last resort	626–28	(230–33)
5. Man is incapable of true knowledge	628–82	(232–51)
6. Conclusion: Man can rise above humanity only by the grace of God	682–83	(250–53)

Many interpreters have argued that Montaigne merely forgot Sebond; some, that he betrayed him and Christianity as well. The present editor prefers the theory that most of the chapter was already written by around 1576, with no thought of Sebond, as an assault on human reason and presumption, when the princess to whom Montaigne addressed his warning, almost certainly Margaret of Valois, asked him to defend the author he had translated; and that he then built upon this assault a superstructure designed to make of it the best apology he could honestly make for his author.]

ᴬC'est, à la vérité, une très utile et grande partie que la science; ceux qui la méprisent témoignent assez leur bêtise. Mais je n'estime pas pourtant sa valeur jusqu'à cette mesure extrême qu'aucuns lui attribuent, comme Hérillus le philosophe, qui logeait en elle le souverain bien et tenait qu'il fut en elle de nous rendre sages et contents: ce que je ne crois pas, ni ce que d'autres ont dit, que la science est mère de toute vertu et que tout vice est produit par l'ignorance. Si cela est vrai, il est sujet à une longue interprétation.

Ma maison a été de longtemps ouverte aux gens de savoir, et en est fort connue; car mon père, qui l'a commandée cinquante ans et plus, échauffé de cette ardeur nouvelle de quoi le roi François Premier embrassa les lettres et les mit en crédit, rechercha avec grand soin et dépense l'accointance des hommes doctes, les recevant chez lui comme personnes saintes et ayant quelque particulière inspiration de sagesse divine, recueillant leurs sentences et leurs discours comme des oracles, et avec d'autant plus de révérence et de religion qu'il avait moins de loi d'en juger; car il n'avait aucune connaissance des lettres, non plus que ses prédécesseurs. Moi je les aime bien, mais je ne les adore pas.

Entre autres, Pierre Bunel, homme de grande réputation de savoir en son temps, ayant arrêté quelques jours à Montaigne en la compagnie de mon père avec d'autres hommes de sa sorte, lui fit présent au déloger d'un livre qui s'intitule *Theologia naturalis sive liber creaturarum*

^AIn truth, knowledge is a great and very useful quality; those who despise it give evidence enough of their stupidity. But yet I do not set its value at that extreme measure that some attribute to it, like Herillus the philosopher, who placed in it the sovereign good, and held that it was in its power to make us wise and content. That I do not believe, nor what others have said, that knowledge is the mother of all virtue, and that all vice is produced by ignorance. If that is true, it is subject to a long interpretation.

My house has long been open to men of learning, and is well known to them. For my father, who ruled it for fifty years and more, inflamed with that new ardor with which King Francis I embraced letters and brought them into credit, sought with great diligence and expense the acquaintance of learned men, receiving them at his house like holy persons having some particular inspiration of divine wisdom, collecting their sayings and discourses like oracles, and with all the more reverence and religion as he was less qualified to judge them; for he had no knowledge of letters, any more than his predecessors. Myself, I like them well enough, but I do not worship them.

Among others, Pierre Bunel, a man of great reputation for learning in his time, after staying a few days at Montaigne in the company of my father with other men of his sort, made him a present, on his departure, of a book entitled *Natural Theology, or Book of Creatures, by Master*

magistri Raymondi de Sabonde.[1] Et parce que la langue italienne et espagnole étaient familières à mon père, et que ce livre est bâti d'un espagnol baragouiné en terminaisons latines, il espérait qu'avec un bien peu d'aide il en pourrait faire son profit, et le lui recommanda comme livre très utile et propre à la saison en laquelle il le lui donna: ce fut lorsque les nouveautés de Luther commençaient d'entrer en crédit et ébranler en beaucoup de lieux notre ancienne croyance. En quoi il avait un très bon avis, prévoyant bien, par discours de raison, que ce commencement de maladie déclinerait aisément en un exécrable athéisme. Car le vulgaire, n'ayant pas la faculté de juger des choses par elles-mêmes, se laissant emporter à la fortune et aux apparences, après qu'on lui a mis en main la hardiesse de mépriser et contrôler les opinions qu'il avait eues en extrême révérence, comme sont celles où il va de son salut, et qu'on a mis aucuns articles de sa religion en doute et à la balance: il jette tantôt après aisément en pareille incertitude toutes les autres pièces de sa croyance, qui n'avaient pas chez lui plus d'autorité ni de fondement que celles qu'on lui a ébranlées, et secoue comme un joug tyrannique toutes les impressions qu'il avait reçues par l'autorité des lois ou révérence de l'ancien usage:

ᴮNam cupide conculcatur nimis ante metutum; [2]

---

[1] Raymond de Sebonde, Sebond, Sabaude, Sebeyde, Sabonde, etc., as his name is variously spelled, was a professor of medicine, theology, and philosophy at Toulouse around 1430. His *Natural The-*

Raymond de Sabonde.[1] And because the Italian and Spanish languages were familiar to my father, and this book was composed in a Spanish scrambled up with Latin endings, Bunel hoped that with a very little help he could make his profit of it, and recommended it to him as a very useful book and suited to the time in which he gave it to him; this was when the innovations of Luther were beginning to gain favor and to shake our old belief in many places.

In this he was very well advised, rightly foreseeing by rational inference that this incipient malady would easily degenerate into an execrable atheism. For the common herd, not having the faculty of judging things in themselves, let themselves be carried away by chance and by appearances, when once they have been given the temerity to despise and judge the opinions that they had held in extreme reverence, such as are those in which their salvation is concerned. And when some articles of their religion have been set in doubt and upon the balance, they will soon after cast easily into like uncertainty all the other parts of their belief, which had no more authority or foundation in them than those that have been shaken; and they shake off as a tyrannical yoke all the impressions they had once received from the authority of the laws or the reverence of ancient usage—

^BFor eagerly is trampled what once was too much feared [2]

---

ology was published in 1484.
[2] Lucretius, *De Rerum Natura*, v, 1140.

[II:12] *Apology for Raymond Sebond*

ᴬentreprenant dès lors en avant de ne recevoir rien à quoi il n'ait interposé son décret et prêté particulier consentement.

Or, quelques jours avant sa mort, mon père, ayant de fortune rencontré ce livre sous un tas d'autres papiers abandonnés, me commanda de le lui mettre en français. Il fait bon traduire les auteurs comme celui-là, où il n'y a guère que la matière à représenter; mais ceux qui ont donné beaucoup à la grâce et à l'élégance du langage, ils sont dangereux à entreprendre, ᶜnommément pour les rapporter à un idiome plus faible.³ ᴬC'était une occupation bien étrange et nouvelle pour moi; mais étant de fortune pour lors de loisir et ne pouvant rien refuser au commandement du meilleur père qui fut onques, j'en vins à bout comme je pus: à quoi il prit un singulier plaisir, et donna charge qu'on le fît imprimer, ce qui fut exécuté après sa mort.

Je trouvai belles les imaginations de cet auteur, la contexture de son ouvrage bien suivie, et son dessein plein de piété. Parce que beaucoup de gens s'amusent à le lire, et notamment les dames, à qui nous devons plus de service, je me suis trouvé souvent à même de les secourir, pour décharger leur livre de deux principales objections qu'on lui fait. Sa fin est hardie et courageuse, car il entreprend, par raisons humaines et naturelles, établir et vérifier contre les athéistes tous les articles de la religion chrétienne: en quoi, à dire la vérité, je le trouve si ferme et si heureux que je ne pense point qu'il soit possible de mieux faire en cet argument-là, et crois que nul ne l'a égalé. . . .

La première répréhension qu'on fait de son ouvrage,

---

³ French, which was still considered weaker than Latin.

—^Adetermined from then on to accept nothing to which they have not applied their judgment and granted their personal consent.

Now some days before his death, my father, having by chance come across this book under a pile of other abandoned papers, commanded me to put it into French for him. It is nice to translate authors like this one, where there is hardly anything but the matter to reproduce; but those who have given much care to grace and elegance of language are dangerous to undertake, ^Cespecially to render them into a weaker idiom.[3] ^AIt was a very strange and a new occupation for me; but being by chance at leisure at the time, and being unable to disobey any command of the best father there ever was, I got through it as best I could; at which he was singularly pleased, and ordered it to be printed; and this was done after his death.

I found the ideas of this author fine, the arrangement and sequence of his work good, and his plan full of piety. Because many people are busy reading it, and especially the ladies, to whom we owe additional help, I have often found myself in a position to help them by clearing their book of two principal objections that are made against it. His purpose is bold and courageous, for he undertakes by human and natural reasons to establish and prove against the atheists all the articles of the Christian religion; wherein, to tell the truth, I find him so firm and felicitous that I do not think it is possible to do better in that argument, and I think that no one has equaled him. . . .

The first criticism that they make of his work is that

c'est que les Chrétiens se font tort de vouloir appuyer leur croyance par des raisons humaines, qui ne se conçoit que par foi et par une inspiration particulière de la grâce divine. En cette objection il semble qu'il y ait quelque zèle de piété, et à cette cause nous faut-il avec autant plus de douceur et de respect essayer de satisfaire à ceux qui la mettent en avant. Ce serait mieux la charge d'un homme versé en la théologie que de moi qui n'y sais rien.

Toutefois je juge ainsi, qu'à une chose si divine et si hautaine et surpassant de si loin l'humaine intelligence comme est cette vérité de laquelle il a plu à la bonté de Dieu nous éclairer, il est bien besoin qu'il nous prête encore son secours, d'une faveur extraordinaire et privilégiée, pour la pouvoir concevoir et loger en nous; et ne crois pas que les moyens purement humains en soient aucunement capables; et s'ils l'étaient, tant d'âmes rares et excellentes et si abondamment garnies de forces naturelles ès siècles anciens n'eussent pas failli par leur discours d'arriver à cette connaissance. C'est la foi seule qui embrasse vivement et certainement les hauts mystères de notre religion.

Mais ce n'est pas à dire que ce ne soit une très belle et très louable entreprise d'accommoder encore au service de notre foi les outils naturels et humains que Dieu nous a donnés. Il ne faut pas douter que ce ne soit l'usage le plus honorable que nous leur saurions donner, et qu'il n'est occupation ni dessein plus digne d'un homme chrétien que de viser par tous ses études et pensements à embellir, étendre et amplifier la vérité de sa croyance. Nous ne nous contentons point de servir Dieu d'esprit et d'âme; nous lui devons encore et rendons une révérence

Christians do themselves harm in trying to support their belief by human reasons, since it is conceived only by faith and by a particular inspiration of divine grace. In this objection there seems to be a certain pious zeal, and for this reason we must try with all the more mildness and respect to satisfy those who advance it. This would be rather the task for a man versed in theology than for myself, who know nothing about it.

However, I think thus, that in a thing so divine and so lofty, and so far surpassing human intelligence, as is this truth with which it has pleased the goodness of God to enlighten us, it is very necessary that he still lend us his help, by extraordinary and privileged favor, so that we may conceive it and lodge it in us. And I do not think that purely human means are at all capable of this; if they were, so many rare and excellent souls, so abundantly furnished with natural powers, in ancient times, would not have failed to arrive at this knowledge through their reason. It is faith alone that embraces vividly and surely the high mysteries of our religion.

But this is not to say that it is not a very fine and very laudable enterprise to accommodate also to the service of our faith the natural and human tools that God has given us. There can be no doubt that this is the most honorable use that we could put them to, and that there is no occupation or design more worthy of a Christian man than to aim, by all his studies and thoughts, to embellish, extend, and amplify the truth of his belief. We do not content ourselves with serving God with mind and soul, we also owe and render him a bodily reverence; we apply even our

corporelle; nous appliquons nos membres mêmes et nos mouvements et les choses externes à l'honorer. Il en faut faire de même, et accompagner notre foi de toute la raison qui est en nous, mais toujours avec cette réservation de n'estimer pas que ce soit de nous qu'elle dépende, ni que nos efforts et arguments puissent atteindre à une si surnaturelle et divine science. Si elle n'entre chez nous par une infusion extraordinaire; si elle y entre non seulement par discours, mais encore par moyens humains, elle n'y est pas en sa dignité ni en sa splendeur.

Et certes je crains pourtant que nous ne la jouissions que par cette voie. Si nous tenions à Dieu par l'entremise d'une foi vive; si nous tenions à Dieu par lui, non par nous; si nous avions un pied et un fondement divin, les occasions humaines n'auraient pas le pouvoir de nous ébranler, comme elles ont; notre fort ne serait pas pour se rendre à une si faible batterie. L'amour de la nouveauté, la contrainte des princes, la bonne fortune d'un parti, le changement téméraire et fortuit de nos opinions, n'auraient pas la force de secouer et altérer notre croyance; nous ne la laisserions pas troubler à la merci d'un nouvel argument et à la persuasion, non pas de toute la rhétorique qui fût onques; nous soutiendrions ces flots d'une fermeté inflexible et immobile,

Illisos fluctus rupes ut vasta refundit,
Et varias circum latrantes dissipat undas
Mole sua.[4]

---

[4] Anonymous verses in praise of Ronsard, imitated from Virgil, *Aeneid*, VII, 587–9.

limbs and movements and external things to honor him. We must do the same here, and accompany our faith with all the reason that is in us, but always with this reservation, not to think that it is on us that faith depends, or that our efforts and arguments can attain a knowledge so supernatural and divine.

If it does not enter into us by an extraordinary infusion; if it enters, I will not say only by reason, but by human means of any sort, it is not in us in its dignity or in its splendor. And yet I am afraid that we enjoy it only in this way. If we held to God by the mediation of a living faith, if we held to God through him and not through ourselves, if we had a divine foothold and foundation, human accidents would not have the power to shake us as they do. Our fort would not be prone to surrender to so weak a battery; the love of novelty, the constraint of princes, the good fortune of one party, a heedless and accidental change in our opinions, would not have the power to shake and alter our belief; we would not allow it to be troubled by every new argument or by persuasion, not even by all the rhetoric there ever was; we should withstand those waves with inflexible and immobile firmness,

As a vast rock repels the dashing seas
And sprays the roaring waves into the breeze
With its great bulk.[4]

Si ce rayon de la divinité nous touchait aucunement, il y paraîtrait partout: non seulement nos paroles, mais encore nos opérations en porteraient la lueur et le lustre. Tout ce qui partirait de nous, on le verrait illuminé de cette noble clarté. Nous devrions avoir honte qu'ès sectes humaines il ne fût jamais partisan, quelque difficulté et étrangeté que maintînt sa doctrine, qui n'y conformât aucunement ses déportements et sa vie; et une si divine et céleste institution ne marque les Chrétiens que par la langue.

ᴮVoulez-vous voir cela? Comparez nos mœurs à un mahométan, à un païen; vous demeurez toujours au-dessous, là où, au regard de l'avantage de notre religion, nous devrions luire en excellence, d'une extrême et incomparable distance, et devrait-on dire: "Sont-ils si justes, si charitables, si bons? Ils sont donc Chrétiens." . . .

ᶜVoyez l'horrible impudence de quoi nous pelotons les raisons divines, et combien irréligieusement nous les avons et rejetées et reprises selon que la fortune nous a changé de place en ces orages publics. Cette proposition si solemne, S'il est permis au sujet de se rebeller et armer contre son prince pour la défense de la religion: souvienne-vous en quelles bouches, cette année passée, l'affirmative d'icelle était l'arc-boutant d'un parti; la négative, de quel autre parti c'était l'arc-boutant. Et oyez à présent de quel quartier vient la voix et instruction de l'une et de l'autre, et si les armes bruissent moins pour cette cause que pour celle-là.⁵ Et nous brûlons les gens qui disent

---

⁵ Before the death of the Catholic king Henry III, assassinated in 1589, the Protestants claimed the right to revolt, and the Cath-

If this ray of divinity touched us at all, it would appear all over: not only our words, but also our works would bear its light and luster. Everything that came from us would be seen to be illuminated by this noble brightness. We ought to be ashamed that in human sects there never was a partisan, whatever difficult and strange thing his doctrine maintained, who did not to some extent conform his conduct and his life to it; and so divine and celestial a teaching as ours marks Christians only by their words.

ᴮDo you want to see this? Compare our morals with a Mohammedan's, or a pagan's; we always fall short of them. Whereas, in view of the advantage of our religion, we should shine with excellence at an extreme and incomparable distance, and people ought to say: "Are they so just, so charitable, so good? Then they are Christians." . . .

ᶜSee the horrible impudence with which we bandy divine reasons about, and how irreligiously we have both rejected them and taken them again, according as fortune has changed our place in these public storms. This proposition, so solemn, whether it is lawful for a subject to rebel and take arms against his prince in defense of religion— remember in whose mouths, this year just past, the affirmative of this was the buttress of one party, the negative was the buttress of what other party; and hear now from what quarter comes the voice and the instruction of both sides, and whether the weapons make less din for this cause than for that.⁵ And we burn the people who say that

---

olics denied it. When the Protestant king Henry ɪᴠ succeeded Henry ɪɪɪ, both parties did an about-face.

qu'il faut faire souffrir à la vérité le joug de notre besoin: et de combien fait la France pis que de le dire!

^AConfessons la vérité: qui trierait de l'armée, même légitime et moyenne, ceux qui y marchent par le seul zèle d'une affection religieuse, et encore ceux qui regardent seulement la protection des lois de leur pays ou service du prince, il n'en saurait bâtir une compagnie de gendarmes complète. D'où vient cela, qu'il s'en trouve si peu qui aient maintenu même volonté et même progrès en nos mouvements publics, et que nous les voyons tantôt n'aller que le pas, tantôt y courir à bride avalée? et mêmes hommes tantôt gâter nos affaires par leur violence et âpreté, tantôt par leur froideur, mollesse et pesanteur? si ce n'est qu'ils y sont poussés par des considérations particulières ^Cet casuelles, ^Aselon la diversité desquelles ils se remuent.

^CJe vois cela évidemment, que nous ne prêtons volontiers à la dévotion que les offices qui flattent nos passions. Il n'est point d'hostilité excellente comme la chrétienne. Notre zèle fait merveilles quand il va secondant notre pente vers la haine, la cruauté, l'ambition, l'avarice, la détraction, la rébellion. A contre-poil, vers la bonté, la bénignité, la tempérance, si comme par miracle quelque rare complexion ne l'y porte, il ne va ni de pied ni d'aile.

Notre religion est faite pour extirper les vices; elle les couvre, les nourrit, les incite.

^AIl ne faut point faire barbe de foarre à Dieu, comme on dit. Si nous le croyions, je ne dis pas par foi, mais d'une simple croyance, voire (et je le dis à notre grande confusion) si nous le croyions et connaissions comme une autre histoire, comme l'un de nos compagnons, nous

truth must be made to endure the yoke of our need. And how much worse France does than say it!

ᴬLet us confess the truth: if anyone should sift out of the army, even the average loyalist army, those who march in it from the pure zeal of affection for religion, and also those who consider only the protection of the laws of their country or the service of their prince, he could not make up one complete company of men-at-arms out of them. Whence comes this, that there are so few who have maintained the same will and the same pace in our public movements, and that we see them now going only at a walk, now riding with free rein, and the same men now spoiling our affairs by their violence and asperity, now by their coolness, sluggishness, and heaviness, if it is not that they are driven to it by private ᶜand accidental ᴬconsiderations according to whose diversity they are stirred?

ᶜI see this evident, that we willingly accord to piety only the services that flatter our passions. There is no hostility that excels Christian hostility. Our zeal does wonders when it is seconding our leaning toward hatred, cruelty, ambition, avarice, detraction, rebellion. Against the grain, toward goodness, benignity, moderation, unless as by a miracle some rare nature bears it, it will neither walk nor fly.

Our religion is made to extirpate vices; it covers them, fosters them, incites them.

ᴬWe must not give God chaff for wheat, as they say. If we believed in him, I do not say by faith, but with a simple belief; in fact (and I say it to our great confusion), if we believed in him just as in any other history, if we knew him like one of our comrades, we would love him above all

l'aimerions au-dessus de toutes autres choses, pour l'infinie bonté et beauté qui reluit en lui. Au moins marcherait-il en même rang de notre affection que les richesses, les plaisirs, la gloire et nos amis.

ᶜLe meilleur de nous ne craint pas de l'outrager comme il craint d'outrager son voisin, son parent, son maître. Est-il si simple entendement lequel, ayant d'un côté l'objet d'un de nos vicieux plaisirs et de l'autre en pareille connaissance et persuasion l'état d'une gloire immortelle, entrât en troque de l'un pour l'autre? Et si, nous y renonçons souvent de pur mépris: car quel goût nous attire au blasphémer, sinon à l'aventure le goût même de l'offense? . . .

ᴬTout cela, c'est un signe très évident que nous ne recevons notre religion qu'à notre façon et par nos mains, et non autrement que comme les autres religions se reçoivent. Nous nous sommes rencontrés au pays où elle était en usage; ou nous regardons son ancienneté ou l'autorité des hommes qui l'ont maintenue; ou craignons les menaces qu'elle attache aux mécréants; ou suivons ses promesses. Ces considérations-là doivent être employées à notre croyance, mais comme subsidiaires: ce sont liaisons humaines. Une autre région, d'autres témoins, pareilles promesses et menaces nous pourraient imprimer par même voie une croyance contraire.

ᴮNous sommes Chrétiens à même titre que nous sommes ou Périgourdins ou Allemands. . . .

ᴬOr nos raisons et nos discours humains, c'est comme la matière lourde et stérile: la grâce de Dieu en est la forme; c'est elle qui y donne la façon et le prix. . . . La

other things, for the infinite goodness and beauty that shines in him. At least he would march in the same rank in our affection as riches, pleasures, glory, and our friends.

ᶜThe best of us does not fear to outrage him as he fears to outrage his neighbor, his kinsman, his master. Is there any mind so simple that, having on one side the object of one of our vicious pleasures and on the other in equal knowledge and conviction the state of immortal glory, he would trade the one for the other? And yet we often renounce immortal glory out of pure disdain; for what taste leads us to blaspheme, unless perhaps the very taste of the offense? . . .

ᴬAll this is a very evident sign that we receive our religion only in our own way and with our own hands, and not otherwise than as other religions are received. We happen to have been born in a country where it was in practice; or we regard its antiquity or the authority of the men who have maintained it; or we fear the threats it fastens upon unbelievers, or pursue its promises. Those considerations should be employed in our belief, but as subsidiaries; they are human ties. Another region, other witnesses, similar promises and threats, might imprint upon us in the same way a contrary belief.

ᴮWe are Christians by the same title that we are Perigordians or Germans. . . .

ᴬNow our human reasons and arguments are as it were the heavy and barren matter; the grace of God is their form; it is that which gives them shape and value. . . .

[II:12] *Apology for Raymond Sebond*

foi venant à teindre et illustrer les arguments de Sebond, elle les rend fermes et solides: ils sont capables de servir d'acheminement et de premier guide à un apprenti pour le mettre à la voie de cette connaissance; ils le façonnent aucunement et rendent capable de la grâce de Dieu, par le moyen de laquelle se parfournit et se parfait après notre croyance. . . . Et, quand on les dépouillera de cet ornement et du secours et approbation de la foi, et qu'on les prendra pour fantaisies pures humaines, pour en combattre ceux qui sont précipités aux épouvantables et horribles ténèbres de l'irréligion, ils se trouveront encore lors aussi solides et autant fermes que nuls autres de même condition qu'on leur puisse opposer. . . .

Je me suis, sans y penser, à demi déjà engagé dans la seconde objection à laquelle j'avais proposé de· répondre pour Sebond.

Aucuns disent que ses arguments sont faibles et ineptes à vérifier ce qu'il veut, et entreprennent de les choquer aisément. Il faut secouer ceux-ci un peu plus rudement, car ils sont plus dangereux et plus malicieux que les premiers. ^cOn couche volontiers le sens des écrits d'autrui à la faveur des opinions qu'on a préjugées en soi; et un athéiste se flatte à ramener tous auteurs à l'athéisme, infectant de son propre venin la matière innocente. ^aCeux-ci ont quelque préoccupation de jugement qui leur rend le goût fade aux raisons de Sebond. Au demeurant, il leur semble qu'on leur donne beau jeu de les mettre en liberté de combattre notre religion par des armes pures humaines, laquelle ils n'oseraient attaquer en sa majesté pleine d'autorité et de commandement.

Le moyen que je prends pour rabattre cette frénésie et

Faith, coming to color and illumine Sebond's arguments, makes them firm and solid; they are capable of serving as a start and a first guide to an apprentice to set him on the road to this knowledge; they fashion him to some extent and make him capable of the grace of God, by means of which our belief is afterward completed and perfected. . . . And even if we strip them of this ornament and of the help and approbation of faith, and take them as purely human fancies, to combat those who are precipitated into the frightful and horrible darkness of irreligion, they will still be found as solid and as firm as any others of the same type that may be opposed to them. . . .

I have already, without thinking about it, half involved myself in the second objection which I had proposed to answer for Sebond.

Some say that his arguments are weak and unfit to prove what he proposes, and undertake to shatter them with ease. These must be shaken up a little more roughly, for they are more dangerous and malicious than the others. ᶜPeople are prone to apply the meaning of other men's writings to suit opinions that they have previously determined in their minds; and an atheist flatters himself by reducing all authors to atheism, infecting innocent matter with his own venom. ᴬThese men have some prepossession in judgment that makes their taste jaded for Sebond's reasons. Furthermore, it seems to them that they are given an easy game when set at liberty to combat our religion by purely human weapons, which they would not dare attack in its authoritative and commanding majesty.

The means I take to beat down this frenzy, and which

qui me semble le plus propre, c'est de froisser et fouler aux pieds l'orgueil et humaine fierté; leur faire sentir l'inanité, la vanité et dénéantise de l'homme; leur arracher des poings les chétives armes de leur raison; leur faire baisser la tête et mordre la terre sous l'autorité et révérence de la majesté divine. C'est à elle seule qu'appartient la science et la sapience; elle seule qui peut estimer de soi quelque chose, et à qui nous dérobons ce que nous nous comptons et ce que nous nous prisons:

Οὐ γὰρ ἐᾶ φρονέιν ὁ Θεὸς μέγα ἄλλον ἢ ἑωυτον.[6]

CAbattons ce cuider, premier fondement de la tyrannie du malin Esprit: *Deus superbis resistit; humilibus autem dat gratiam.*[7] L'intelligence est en tous les dieux, dit Platon, et en fort peu d'hommes.

AOr c'est cependant beaucoup de consolation à l'homme chrétien de voir nos outils mortels et caducs si proprement assortis à notre foi sainte et divine que lorsqu'on les emploie aux sujets de leur nature mortels et caducs ils n'y soient pas appropriés plus uniment ni avec plus de force. Voyons donc si l'homme a en sa puissance d'autres raisons plus fortes que celles de Sebond, voire s'il est en lui d'arriver à aucune certitude par argument et par discours. . . .

Que nous prêche la vérité quand elle nous prêche de fuir la mondaine philosophie, quand elle nous inculque si souvent que notre sagesse n'est que folie devant Dieu; que de toutes les vanités, la plus vaine c'est l'homme; que

---

[6] Herodotus, *History*, VII, x.

seems fittest to me, is to crush and trample underfoot human arrogance and pride; to make them feel the inanity, the vanity and nothingness, of man; to wrest from their hands the puny weapons of their reason; to make them bow their heads and bite the ground beneath the authority and reverence of divine majesty. It is to this alone that knowledge and wisdom belong; it alone that can have some self-esteem, and from which we steal what we account and prize ourselves for:

For God allows great thoughts to no one else.[6]

cLet us beat down this presumption, the first foundation of the tyranny of the evil spirit. *For God resisteth the proud, and giveth grace to the humble.*[7] Intelligence is in all gods, says Plato, and in very few men.

ANow it is nevertheless a great consolation to the Christian to see our frail mortal tools so properly suited to our holy and divine faith, that when they are used on subjects that are by their nature frail and mortal, they are no more completely and powerfully appropriate. Let us see then if man has within his power other reasons more powerful than those of Sebond, or indeed if it is in him to arrive at any certainty by argument and reason. . . .

What does truth preach to us, when she exhorts us to flee worldly philosophy, when she so often inculcates in us that our wisdom is but folly before God; that of all vanities the vainest is man; that the man who is presumptu-

---

[7] I Peter 5:5, via St. Augustine, *City of God*, xvii, iv.

l'homme qui présume de son savoir ne sait pas encore que c'est que savoir; et que l'homme, qui n'est rien, s'il pense être quelque chose, se séduit soi-même et se trompe? Ces sentences du Saint-Esprit expriment si clairement et si vivement ce que je veux maintenir qu'il ne me faudrait aucune autre preuve contre des gens qui se rendraient avec toute soumission et obéissance à son autorité. Mais ceux-ci veulent être fouettés à leurs propres dépens, et ne veulent souffrir qu'on combatte leur raison que par elle-même.

Considérons donc pour cette heure l'homme seul, sans secours étranger, armé seulement de ses armes, et dépourvu de la grâce et connaissance divine, qui est tout son honneur, sa force et le fondement de son être. Voyons combien il a de tenue en ce bel équipage. . . .

La présomption est notre maladie naturelle et originelle. La plus calamiteuse et frêle de toutes les créatures c'est l'homme, et quand et quand la plus orgueilleuse. Elle se sent et se voit logée ici, parmi la bourbe et la fiente du monde, attachée et clouée à la pire, plus morte et croupie partie de l'univers, au dernier étage du logis et le plus éloigné de la voûte céleste, avec les animaux de la pire condition des trois; [8] et se va plantant par imagination au-dessus du cercle de la lune et ramenant le ciel sous ses pieds. C'est par la vanité de cette même imagination qu'il s'égale à Dieu, qu'il s'attribue les conditions divines, qu'il se trie soi-même et sépare de la presse des autres créatures, taille les parts aux animaux ses confrères et compagnons,

---

[8] Those that walk, those that fly, those that swim.

ous of his knowledge does not yet know what knowledge is; and that man, who is nothing, if he thinks he is something, seduces and deceives himself? These statements of the Holy Spirit express so clearly and so vividly what I wish to maintain, that no other proof would be needed against men who would surrender with all submission and obedience to its authority. But these men insist on being whipped to their own cost and will not allow us to combat their reason except by itself.

Let us then consider for the moment man alone, without outside assistance, armed solely with his own weapons, and deprived of divine grace and knowledge, which is his whole honor, his strength, and the foundation of his being. Let us see how much presence he has in this fine array. . . .

Presumption is our natural and original malady. The most vulnerable and frail of all creatures is man, and at the same time the most arrogant. He feels and sees himself lodged here, amid the mire and dung of the world, nailed and riveted to the worst, the deadest, and the most stagnant part of the universe, on the lowest story of the house and the farthest from the vault of heaven, with the animals of the worst condition of the three; [8] and in his imagination he goes planting himself above the circle of the moon, and bringing the sky down beneath his feet. It is by the vanity of this same imagination that he equals himself to God, attributes to himself divine characteristics, picks himself out and separates himself from the horde of other creatures, carves out their shares to his

et leur distribue telle portion de facultés et de forces que bon lui semble. Comment connaît-il, par l'effort de son intelligence, les branles internes et secrets des animaux? par quelle comparaison d'eux à nous conclut-il la bêtise qu'il leur attribue?

^CQuand je me joue à ma chatte, qui sait si elle passe son temps de moi plus que je ne fais d'elle? . . .[9]

^AJ'ai dit tout ceci pour maintenir cette ressemblance qu'il y a aux choses humaines, et pour nous ramener et joindre au nombre. Nous ne sommes ni au-dessus ni au-dessous du reste: tout ce qui est sous le Ciel, dit le sage,[10] court une loi et fortune pareille:

> ^BIndupedita suis fatalibus omnia vinclis.[11]

^AIl y a quelque différence, il y a des ordres et des degrés; mais c'est sous le visage d'une même nature:

> ^Bres quæque suo ritu procedit, et omnes
> Fœdere naturæ certo discrimina servant.[12]

^AIl faut contraindre l'homme et le ranger dans les barrières de cette police. Le misérable n'a garde d'enjamber par effet au delà; il est entravé et engagé, il est assujetti de pareille obligation que les autres créatures de son ordre,

---

[9] The 1595 edition adds: "Nous nous entretenons de singeries réciproques. Si j'ai mon heure de commencer ou de refuser, aussi a-t-elle la sienne."—"We entertain each other with reciprocal monkey tricks. If I have my time to begin or to refuse, so has she hers." Montaigne goes on to state in general one of the main theses of the "Apologie": that fundamentally man is very much like the

fellows and companions the animals, and distributes among them such portions of faculties and powers as he sees fit. How does he know, by the force of his intelligence, the secret internal stirrings of animals? By what comparison between them and us does he infer the stupidity that he attributes to them?

^CWhen I play with my cat, who knows if I am not a pastime to her more than she is to me? . . .⁹

^AI have said all this to maintain this resemblance that exists to human things, and to bring us back and join us to the majority. We are neither above nor below the rest: all that is under heaven, says the sage,¹⁰ incurs the same law and the same fortune,

^BAll things are bound by their own chains of fate.¹¹

^AThere is some difference, there are orders and degrees; but it is under the aspect of one and the same nature:

^BAnd all things go their own way, nor forget
Distinctions by the law of nature set.¹²

^AMan must be constrained and forced into line inside the barriers of this order. The poor wretch is in no position really to step outside them; he is fettered and bound, he is subjected to the same obligation as the other creatures of his class, and in a very ordinary condition, without any

---

animals; that every clear distinction in faculties that man attributes to himself is refuted by examples of animal behavior.

¹⁰ Compare Ecclesiastes 2:14, 9:2–3. This sentence is inscribed on one of the beams in Montaigne's library.

¹¹ Lucretius, *De Rerum Natura*, v, 876.

¹² Lucretius, *De Rerum Natura*, v, 923–4.

et d'une condition fort moyenne, sans aucune prérogative, préexcellence vraie et essentielle. Celle qu'il se donne par opinion et par fantaisie n'a ni corps ni goût. Et s'il est ainsi que lui seul de tous les animaux ait cette liberté de l'imagination et ce dérèglement de pensées, lui représentant ce qui est, ce qui n'est pas, et ce qu'il veut, le faux et le véritable, c'est un avantage qui lui est bien cher vendu et duquel il a bien peu à se glorifier; car de là naît la source principale des maux qui le pressent: péché, maladie, irrésolution, trouble, désespoir.

Je dis donc, pour revenir à mon propos, qu'il n'y a point d'apparence d'estimer que les bêtes fassent par inclination naturelle et forcée les mêmes choses que nous faisons par notre choix et industrie. Nous devons conclure, de pareils effets, pareilles facultés; et confesser par conséquent que ce même discours, cette même voie, que nous tenons à ouvrer, c'est aussi celle des animaux. . . .

Par ainsi le renard, de quoi se servent les habitants de la Thrace quand ils veulent entreprendre de passer pardessus la glace quelque rivière gelée, et le lâchent devant eux pour cet effet—quand nous le verrions au bord de l'eau approcher son oreille bien près de la glace, pour sentir s'il orra d'une longue ou d'une voisine distance bruire l'eau courant au-dessous; et selon qu'il trouve par là qu'il y a plus ou moins d'épaisseur en la glace, se reculer ou s'avancer; n'aurions-nous pas raison de juger qu'il lui passe par la tête ce même discours qu'il ferait en la nôtre, et que c'est une ratiocination et conséquence tirée du sens naturel: Ce qui fait bruit, se remue; ce qui se remue n'est pas gelé; ce qui n'est pas gelé est liquide; et ce qui est liquide plie sous le faix? Car d'attribuer cela seulement

real and essential prerogative or pre-eminence. That which he accords himself in his mind and in his fancy has neither body nor taste. And if it is true that he alone of all the animals has this freedom of imagination and this unruliness in thought that represents to him what is, what is not, what he wants, the false and the true, it is an advantage that is sold him very dear, and in which he has little cause to glory, for from it springs the principal source of the ills that oppress him: sin, disease, irresolution, confusion, despair.

So I say, to return to my subject, that there is no apparent reason to judge that the beasts do by natural and obligatory instinct the same things that we do by our choice and cleverness. We must infer from like results like faculties, and consequently confess that this same reason, this same method that we have for working, is also that of the animals. . . .

Take for example the fox, whom the inhabitants of Thrace use when they want to undertake to cross some frozen stream over the ice, turning him loose ahead of them for this reason. If we saw him at the edge of the water bring his ear very near the ice, to hear whether the water running beneath sounds near or far away, and draw back or advance according as he finds the ice too thin or thick enough, would we not have reason to suppose that there passes through his head the same reasoning that would pass through ours, and that it is a ratiocination and conclusion drawn from natural common sense: "What makes a noise, moves; what moves is not frozen; what is not frozen is liquid; and what is liquid gives way under a weight"? For to attribute this simply to a keenness of

à une vivacité du sens de l'ouïe, sans discours et sans conséquence, c'est une chimère, et ne peut entrer en notre imagination. De même faut-il estimer de tant de sortes de ruses et d'inventions de quoi les bêtes se couvrent des entreprises que nous faisons sur elles. . . .[13]

La participation que nous avons à la connaissance de la vérité, quelle qu'elle soit, ce n'est pas par nos propres forces que nous l'avons acquise. Dieu nous a assez appris cela par les témoins qu'il a choisis du vulgaire, simples et ignorants, pour nous instruire de ses admirables secrets: notre foi ce n'est pas notre acquêt, c'est un pur présent de la libéralité d'autrui. Ce n'est pas par discours ou par notre entendement que nous avons reçu notre religion, c'est par autorité et par commandement étranger. La faiblesse de notre jugement nous y aide plus que la force, et notre aveuglement plus que notre clairvoyance. C'est par l'entremise de notre ignorance plus que de notre science que nous sommes savants de ce divin savoir. Ce n'est pas merveille si nos moyens naturels et terrestres ne peuvent concevoir cette connaissance surnaturelle et céleste. Apportons-y seulement, du nôtre, l'obéissance et la subjection. Car, comme il est écrit: "Je détruirai la sapience des sages, et abattrai la prudence des prudents. Où est le sage? où est l'écrivain? où est le disputateur de ce siècle? Dieu n'a-t-il pas abêti la sapience de ce monde? Car puisque le monde n'a point connu Dieu par sapience, il lui a plu, par la vanité de la prédication, sauver les croyants." [14]

---

[13] There follows a long though generally amusing series of animal stories, taken mostly from Plutarch and Pliny, designed to show two things: first that man has indeed no faculty, not even knowledge, which sets him above the other animals; and second that even if

the sense of hearing, without reasoning or inference, is a chimera, and cannot enter our imagination. We must make the same supposition about the many sorts of ruses and tricks by which the animals protect themselves from the attacks we make upon them. . . .[13]

The participation that we have in the knowledge of truth, whatever it may be, has not been acquired by our own powers. God has taught us that clearly enough by the witnesses that he has chosen from the common people, simple and ignorant, to instruct us in his admirable secrets. Our faith is not of our own acquiring, it is a pure present of another's liberality. It is not by reasoning or by our understanding that we have received our religion; it is by external authority and command. The weakness of our judgment helps us more in this than its strength, and our blindness more than our clear-sightedness. It is by the mediation of our ignorance more than of our knowledge that we are learned with that divine learning. It is no wonder if our natural and earthly powers cannot conceive that supernatural and heavenly knowledge; let us bring to it nothing of our own but obedience and submission. For, as it is written, "I will destroy the wisdom of the wise, and will bring to nothing the understanding of the prudent. Where is the wise? where is the scribe? where is the disputer of this world? hath not God made foolish the wisdom of this world? For after that the world by wisdom knew not God, it pleased God by the foolishness of preaching to save them that believe." [14]

---

he does have a greater share of knowledge and imagination, this serves to make him neither happy nor good—if anything, the contrary.

[14] I Corinthians 1:19–21.

Si me faut-il voir enfin s'il est en la puissance de l'homme de trouver ce qu'il cherche, et si cette quête qu'il y a employée depuis tant de siècles l'a enrichi de quelque nouvelle force et de quelque vérité solide.

Je crois qu'il me confessera, s'il parle en conscience, que tout l'acquêt qu'il a retiré d'une si longue poursuite, c'est d'avoir appris à reconnaître sa faiblesse. L'ignorance qui était naturellement en nous, nous l'avons par longue étude confirmée et avérée. Il est advenu aux gens véritablement savants ce qui advient aux épis de blé: ils vont s'élevant et haussant, la tête droite et fière, tant qu'ils sont vides; mais quand ils sont pleins et grossis de grain en leur maturité, ils commencent à s'humilier et à baisser les cornes. Pareillement, les hommes ayant tout essayé et tout sondé, n'ayant trouvé en cet amas de science et provision de tant de choses diverses rien de massif et ferme, et rien que vanité, ils ont renoncé à leur présomption et reconnu leur condition naturelle. . . .[15]

Notre parler a ses faiblesses et ses défauts, comme tout le reste. La plupart des occasions des troubles du monde sont grammairiennes. Nos procès ne naissent que du débat de l'interprétation des lois; et la plupart des

---

[15] Leaving aside for the time the first part of the inquiry that he has just announced (whether man by his own unaided powers can know anything), Montaigne proceeds with the second part: whether man does know anything. Confining himself to the philosophers as the most learned class, he divides them into three groups: those who claim that they have found the truth, those who claim that it cannot be found, and those who merely state that they

Yet must I see at last whether it is in the power of man to find what he seeks, and whether that quest that he has been making for so many centuries has enriched him with any new power and any solid truth.

I think he will confess to me, if he speaks in all conscience, that all the profit he has gained from so long a pursuit is to have learned to acknowledge his weakness. The ignorance that was naturally in us we have by long study confirmed and verified.

To really learned men has happened what happens to ears of wheat: they rise high and lofty, heads erect and proud, as long as they are empty; but when they are full and swollen with grain in their ripeness, they begin to grow humble and lower their horns. Similarly, men who have tried everything and sounded everything, having found in that pile of knowledge and store of so many various things nothing solid and firm, and nothing but vanity, have renounced their presumption and recognized their natural condition. . . .[15]

Our speech has its weaknesses and its defects, like all the rest. Most of the occasions for the troubles of the world are grammatical. Our lawsuits spring only from debate over the interpretation of the laws, and most of our

---

have not found it. The Pyrrhonists—followers of Pyrrho of Elis (c. 360–275 B.C.), whose skeptical system Montaigne read about and admired in the *Outlines of Pyrrhonism* of Sextus Empiricus (c. 160–210 A.D.)—who are the leading examples of the last class, are the wisest and best of philosophers; but their position is hard to express.

[II:12] *Apology for Raymond Sebond*

guerres, de cette impuissance de n'avoir su clairement exprimer les conventions et traités d'accord des princes. Combien de querelles et combien importantes a produites au monde le doute du sens de cette syllabe, *Hoc!* [16]

^BPrenons la clause que la logique même nous présentera pour la plus claire. Si vous dites "Il fait beau temps," et que vous disiez vérité, il fait donc beau temps. Voilà pas une forme de parler certaine? Encore nous trompera-t-elle. Qu'il soit ainsi, suivons l'exemple. Si vous dites "Je mens," et que vous disiez vrai, vous mentez donc. L'art, la raison, la force de la conclusion de celle-ci sont pareilles à l'autre; toutefois nous voilà embourbés.

^AJe vois les philosophes pyrrhoniens qui ne peuvent exprimer leur générale conception en aucune manière de parler: car il leur faudrait un nouveau langage. Le nôtre est tout formé de propositions affirmatives, qui leur sont du tout ennemies: de façon que quand ils disent "Je doute," on les tient incontinent à la gorge pour leur faire avouer qu'au moins assurent et savent-ils cela, qu'ils doutent. Ainsi on les a contraints de se sauver dans cette comparaison de la médecine, sans laquelle leur humeur serait inexplicable: quand ils prononcent "J'ignore" ou "Je doute," ils disent que cette proposition s'emporte elle-même, quand et quand le reste, ni plus ni moins que la rhubarbe, qui pousse hors les mauvaises humeurs et s'emporte hors quand et quand elle-même.

^BCette fantaisie est plus sûrement conçue par inter-

---

[16] Many Catholic-Protestant quarrels over transubstantiation centered on the interpretation of *hoc* in the phrase of the Eucharist

wars from the inability to express clearly the conventions and treaties of agreement of princes. How many quarrels, and how important, have been produced in the world by doubt of the meaning of that syllable *Hoc!* [16]

^BLet us take the sentence that logic itself offers us as the clearest. If you say "It is fine weather," and if you are speaking the truth, then it is fine weather. Isn't that a sure way of speaking? Still it will deceive us. To show this let us continue the example. If you say "I lie," and if you are speaking the truth, then you lie. The art, the reason, the force, of the conclusion of this one are the same as in the other; yet there we are stuck in the mud.

^AI can see why the Pyrrhonian philosophers cannot express their general conception in any manner of speaking; for they would need a new language. Ours is wholly formed of affirmative propositions, which to them are utterly repugnant; so that when they say "I doubt," immediately you have them by the throat to make them admit that at least they know and are sure of this fact, that they doubt. Thus they have been constrained to take refuge in this comparison from medicine, without which their attitude would be inexplicable: when they declare "I do not know" or "I doubt," they say that this proposition carries itself away with the rest, no more nor less than rhubarb, which expels evil humors and carries itself off with them.

^BThis idea is more firmly grasped in the form of inter-

_____

(Matthew 26:26): "Hoc est corpus meum" (King James version: "This is my body").

rogation: "Que sais-je?" [17] comme je la porte à la devise d'une balance. . . . [18]

[A]Vous,[19] pour qui j'ai pris la peine d'étendre un si long corps contre ma coutume, ne refuirez point de maintenir votre Sebond par la forme ordinaire d'argumenter de quoi vous êtes tous les jours instruite, et exercerez en cela votre esprit et votre étude: car ce dernier tour d'escrime-ci, il ne le faut employer que comme un extrême remède. C'est un coup désespéré, auquel il faut abandonner vos armes pour faire perdre à votre adversaire les siennes; et un tour secret, duquel il se faut servir rarement et réservément. C'est grande témérité de vous perdre vous-même pour perdre un autre. . . .

Nous secouons ici les limites et dernières clôtures des sciences, auxquelles l'extrémité est vicieuse, comme en la vertu. Tenez-vous dans la route commune; il ne fait mie bon être si subtil et si fin. Souvienne-vous de ce que dit le proverbe toscan: *Chi troppo s'assottiglia si scavezza.* [20]

Je vous conseille, en vos opinions et en vos discours autant qu'en vos mœurs et en toute autre chose, la modération et l'attrempance et la fuite de la nouveauté et de l'étrangeté. Toutes les voies extravagantes me fâchent. Vous qui par l'autorité que votre grandeur vous apporte, et encore plus par les avantages que vous donnent

---

[17] Montaigne's most famous and most influential remark, long considered his final word.

[18] Montaigne had a medal struck in 1576 bearing a similar motto —ἐπέχω (I abstain)—and a pair of scales evenly balanced to indicate perfect suspension of judgment.

Montaigne goes on to argue that man's self-made notions about God, his own soul, and his own body are ridiculous, conflicting, and utterly chaotic. God is the most important thing for man to know,

rogation: "What do I know?" [17]—the words I bear as a motto, inscribed over a pair of scales. . . .[18]

^AYou,[19] for whom I have taken the pains to extend so long a work contrary to my custom, will not shrink from upholding your Sebond by the ordinary form of argument in which you are instructed every day, and in that you will exercise your mind and your learning. For this final fencer's trick must not be employed except as an extreme remedy. It is a desperate stroke, in which you must abandon your weapons to make your adversary lose his, and a secret trick that must be used rarely and reservedly. It is great rashness to ruin yourself in order to ruin another. . . .

Here we are shaking the barriers and last fences of knowledge, in which extremity is a vice, as in virtue. Stay on the highroad; it is no good to be so subtle and clever. Remember what the Tuscan proverb says: *He who grows too keen cuts himself.*[20]

In your opinions and remarks, as well as in your conduct and everything else, I advise moderation and temperance, and avoidance of novelty and strangeness. All eccentric ways irritate me. You who, by the authority that your greatness brings you, and still more by the advantages which the qualities that are more your own give you,

---

man himself the easiest thing. Since—as Montaigne shows at length —man knows neither. we can only conclude that by his own efforts he has learned nothing, he knows nothing.

[19] The lady he addresses is almost certainly Margaret of Valois (1553–1615), sister of Henry III and wife of Henry of Navarre, friend of Montaigne and reader of Sebond's book, presumably in Montaigne's translation.

[20] Petrarch, *Canzoniere,* XXII, x, 48.

les qualités plus vôtres, pouvez d'un clin d'œil commander à qui il vous plaît, deviez donner cette charge à quelqu'un qui fît profession des lettres, qui vous eût bien autrement appuyé et enrichi cette fantaisie. Toutefois en voici assez pour ce que vous en avez à faire.

. . . Notre esprit est un outil vagabond, dangereux et téméraire; il est malaisé d'y joindre l'ordre et la mesure. Et de mon temps ceux qui ont quelque rare excellence au-dessus des autres et quelque vivacité extraordinaire, nous les voyons quasi tous débordés en licence d'opinions et de mœurs. C'est miracle s'il s'en rencontre un rassis et sociable.

On a raison de donner à l'esprit humain les barrières les plus contraintes qu'on peut. . . . Par quoi il vous siéra mieux de vous resserrer dans le train accoutumé, quel qu'il soit, que de jeter votre vol à cette licence effrénée. Mais si quelqu'un de ces nouveaux docteurs [21] entreprend de faire l'ingénieux en votre présence, aux dépens de son salut et du vôtre: pour vous défaire de cette dangereuse peste qui se répand tous les jours en vos cours, ce préservatif, à l'extrême nécessité, empêchera que la contagion de ce venin n'offensera ni vous ni votre assistance. . . . [22]

. . . Combien diversement jugeons-nous des choses! combien de fois changeons-nous nos fantaisies! Ce que je tiens aujourd'hui et ce que je crois, je le tiens et le crois de toute ma croyance; tous mes outils et tous mes ressorts empoignent cette opinion et m'en répondent sur tout ce

---

[21] Presumably Protestants.

[22] Having given this warning, Montaigne is free to move on to the climax of his attack on human knowledge and reason, the proof

can by the flicker of an eye command whomever you please, should have given this assignment to some professional man of letters, who would have supported and enriched this theme for you in quite another way. However, here is enough for your needs.

. . . Our mind is an erratic, dangerous, and heedless tool; it is hard to impose order and moderation upon it. And in my time those who have some rare excellence beyond the others, and some extraordinary quickness, are nearly all, we see, incontinent in the license of their opinions and conduct. It is a miracle if you find a sedate and sociable one.

People are right to give the tightest possible barriers to the human mind. . . . Wherefore it will become you better to confine yourself to the accustomed routine, whatever it is, than to fly headlong into this unbridled license. But if one of these new doctors [21] tries to show off his ingenuity in your presence, at the risk of his salvation and yours; to rid yourself of this dangerous pestilence that spreads day by day in your courts, this preservative, in case of extreme necessity, will keep the contagion of that poison from harming either you or the others present. . . .[22]

. . . How diversely we judge things! How many times we change our notions! What I hold today and what I believe, I hold and believe it with all my belief; all my tools and all my springs of action grip this opinion and sponsor it for me in every way they can. I could not embrace or

---

that we can know nothing. One proof of this is our utter variability —from which, however, by self-study, we can at least learn to become wise at our own expense.

[II:12] *Apology for Raymond Sebond*

qu'ils peuvent. Je ne saurais embrasser aucune vérité ni conserver avec plus de force que je fais celle-ci. J'y suis tout entier, j'y suis voirement; mais ne m'est-il pas advenu, non une fois, mais cent, mais mille, et tous les jours, d'avoir embrassé quelque autre chose à tout ces mêmes instruments, en cette même condition, que depuis j'aie jugée fausse?

Au moins faut-il devenir sage à ses propres dépens. Si je me suis trouvé souvent trahi sous cette couleur, si ma touche se trouve ordinairement fausse et ma balance inégale et injuste, quelle assurance en puis-je prendre à cette fois plus qu'aux autres? N'est-ce pas sottise de me laisser tant de fois piper à un guide?

Toutefois, que la fortune nous remue cinq cents fois de place, qu'elle ne fasse que vider et remplir sans cesse, comme dans un vaisseau, dans notre croyance autres et autres opinions, toujours la présente et dernière c'est la certaine et l'infaillible. Pour celle-ci il faut abandonner les biens, l'honneur, la vie et le salut, et tout:

> posterior res illa reperta,
> Perdit, et immutat sensus ad pristina quæque.[23]

ᴮQuoi qu'on nous prêche, quoi que nous apprenons, il faudrait toujours se souvenir que c'est l'homme qui donne et l'homme qui reçoit; c'est une mortelle main qui nous le présente, c'est une mortelle main qui l'accepte. Les choses qui nous viennent du ciel ont seules droit et autorité de persuasion; seules, marque de vérité; laquelle aussi ne voyons-nous pas de nos yeux ni ne la recevons

---

[23] Lucretius, *De Rerum Natura*, v, 1414-5.

preserve any truth with more strength than this one. I belong to it entirely, I belong to it truly. But has it not happened to me, not once, but a hundred times, a thousand times, and every day, to have embraced with these same instruments, in this same condition, something else that I have since judged false?

At least we must become wise at our own expense. If I have often found myself betrayed under just these colors, if my touchstone is found to be ordinarily false, and my scales uneven and incorrect, what assurance can I have in them this time more than at other times? Is it not stupidity to let myself be fooled so many times by one guide?

Nevertheless, whether fortune moves us five hundred times from our position, whether it does nothing but empty and pour back incessantly into our belief, as into a vessel, more and more different opinions, always the present and the latest one is the certain and infallible one. For this one we must abandon possessions, honor, life and salvation, and everything:

> The latest find
> Kills prior things and spoils them in our mind.[23]

^BWhatever they preach to us, whatever we learn, we should always remember that it is man that gives and man that receives; it is a mortal hand that presents it to us, a mortal hand that accepts it. The things that come to us from heaven have alone the right and authority for persuasion, alone the stamp of truth; which also we do not see with our own eyes, or receive by our own means. This

par nos moyens. Cette sainte et grande image ne pourrait pas en un si chétif domicile, si Dieu ne le réforme et fortifie par sa grâce et faveur particulière et surnaturelle. . . .

ᴬMoi qui m'épie de plus près, qui ai les yeux incessamment tendus sur moi, comme celui qui n'ai pas fort à faire ailleurs,

> quis sub Arcto
> Rex gelidæ metuatur oræ,
> Quid Tyridatem terreat, unice
> Securus,[24]

à peine oserais-je dire la vanité et la faiblesse que je trouve chez moi. J'ai le pied si instable et si mal assis, je le trouve si aisé à crouler et si prêt au branle, et ma vue si déréglée, qu'à jeun je me sens autre qu'après le repas. Si ma santé me rit et la clarté d'un beau jour, me voilà honnête homme; si j'ai un cor qui me presse l'orteil, me voilà renfrogné, malplaisant et inaccessible. ᴮUn même pas de cheval me semble tantôt rude, tantôt aisé, et même chemin à cette heure plus court, une autre fois plus long; et une même forme ores plus, ores moins agréable. ᴬMaintenant je suis à tout faire, maintenant à rien faire; ce qui m'est plaisir à cette heure me sera quelquefois peine. Il se fait mille agitations indiscrètes et casuelles chez moi. Ou l'humeur mélancolique me tient, ou la colérique; et de son autorité privée, à cette heure le chagrin prédomine en moi, à cette heure l'allégresse. Quand je

---

[24] Horace, *Odes*, i, xxvi, 3–6.

great and holy image could not be in so mean a domicile, unless God prepares it for that purpose, unless God reforms and fortifies it by his particular and supernatural grace and favor. . . .

^AI who spy on myself more closely, who have my eyes unceasingly intent on myself, as one who has not much business elsewhere—

> Quite without care
> What king, in frigid lands beneath the Bear,
> Is feared, or what makes Tiridates quake [24]

—I would hardly dare tell of the vanity and weakness that I find in myself. My footing is so unsteady and so insecure, I find it so vacillating and ready to slip, and my sight is so unreliable, that on an empty stomach I feel myself another man than after a meal. If my health smiles upon me, and the brightness of a beautiful day, I am a fine fellow; if I have a corn bothering my toe, I am surly, unpleasant, and unapproachable. ^BOne and the same pace of a horse seems to me now rough, now easy, and the same road at one time shorter, another time longer, and one and the same shape now more, now less agreeable. ^ANow I am ready to do anything, now to do nothing; what is a pleasure to me at this moment will some time be a trouble. A thousand unconsidered and accidental impulses arise in me. Either the melancholic humor grips me, or the choleric; and at this moment sadness predominates in me by its own private authority, at that moment good cheer.

prends des livres, j'aurai aperçu en tel passage des grâces excellentes et qui auront féru mon âme; qu'une autre fois j'y retombe, j'ai beau le tourner et virer, j'ai beau le plier et le manier, c'est une masse inconnue et informe pour moi.

^BEn mes écrits mêmes je ne retrouve pas toujours l'air de ma première imagination: je ne sais ce que j'ai voulu dire, et m'échaude souvent à corriger et y mettre un nouveau sens, pour avoir perdu le premier, qui valait mieux.

Je ne fais qu'aller et venir: mon jugement ne tire pas toujours en avant; il flotte, il vague:

> velut minuta magno
> Deprensa navis in mari vesaniente vento.[25]

Maintes fois (comme il m'advient de faire volontiers) ayant pris pour exercice et pour ébat à maintenir une contraire opinion à la mienne, mon esprit, s'appliquant et tournant de ce côté-là, m'y attache si bien que je ne trouve plus la raison de mon premier avis, et m'en dépars. Je m'entraîne quasi où je penche, comment que ce soit, et m'emporte de mon poids.

Chacun à peu près en dirait autant de soi, s'il se regardait comme moi. Les prêcheurs savent que l'émotion qui leur vient en parlant les anime vers la croyance; et qu'en colère nous nous adonnons plus à la défense de notre proposition, l'imprimons en nous et l'embrassons avec plus de véhémence et d'approbation que nous ne faisons étant en notre sens froid et reposé.

---

[25] Catullus, *Poems*, xxv, 12–3.

When I pick up books, I will have perceived in such-and-such a passage surpassing charms which will have struck my soul; let me come upon it another time, in vain I turn it over and over, in vain I twist it and manipulate it, to me it is a shapeless and unrecognizable mass.

^BEven in my own writings I do not always find again the sense of my first thought; I do not know what I meant to say, and often I get burned by correcting and putting in a new meaning, because I have lost the first one, which was better.

I do nothing but come and go. My judgment does not always go forward; it floats, it strays,

> Like a tiny boat,
> Caught by a raging wind on the vast sea.[26]

Many times (as I sometimes do deliberately), having undertaken as exercise and sport to maintain an opinion contrary to my own, my mind, applying itself and turning in that direction, attaches me to it so firmly that I can no longer find the reason for my former opinion, and I abandon it. I draw myself along in almost any direction I lean, whatever it may be, and carry myself away by my own weight.

Nearly every man would say as much of himself, if he considered himself as I do. Preachers know that the emotion that comes to them as they talk incites them toward belief; and that in anger we give ourselves up more completely to the defense of our proposition, imprint it on ourselves, and embrace it with more vehemence and approval than we do in our cool and sedate mood.

Vous récitez simplement une cause à l'avocat, il vous y répond chancelant et douteux, vous sentez qu'il lui est indifférent de prendre à soutenir l'un ou l'autre parti. L'avez-vous bien payé pour y mordre et pour s'en formaliser, commence-t-il d'en être intéressé, y a-t-il échauffé sa volonté? sa raison et sa science s'y échauffent quand et quand; voilà une apparente et indubitable vérité qui se présente à son entendement; il y découvre une toute nouvelle lumière, et le croit à bon escient, et se le persuade ainsi.

ᴬ. . . De croire toutes les apparences desquelles nous ne pouvons nous défaire, c'est une grande simplesse. Il en adviendrait par là que tout le vulgaire, ᶜet nous sommes tous du vulgaire, ᴬaurait sa croyance contournable comme une girouette: car leur âme, étant molle et sans résistance, serait forcée de recevoir sans cesse autres et autres impressions, la dernière effaçant toujours la trace de la précédente. Celui qui se trouve faible, il doit répondre, suivant la pratique, qu'il en parlera à son conseil, ou s'en rapporter aux plus sages, desquels il a reçu son apprentissage.

Combien y a-t-il que la médecine est au monde? On dit qu'un nouveau venu, qu'on nomme Paracelse,[26] change et renverse tout l'ordre des règles anciennes, et maintient que jusqu'à cette heure elle n'a servi qu'à faire mourir les hommes. Je crois qu'il vérifiera aisément cela; mais de mettre ma vie à la preuve de sa nouvelle expérience, je trouve que ce ne serait pas grande sagesse.

---

[26] Paracelsus (1493–1541), Swiss physician and alchemist, whose works were just beginning to be published (1578–89).

You recite a case simply to a lawyer, he answers you wavering and doubtful, you feel that it is a matter of indifference to him whether he undertakes to support one party or the other. Have you paid him well to get his teeth into it and get excited about it, is he beginning to be involved in it, has he got his will warmed up about it? His reason and his knowledge are warmed up at the same time. Behold an evident and indubitable truth that appears to his intelligence. He discovers a wholly new light on your case, and believes it in all conscience, and persuades himself that it is so.

ᴬ. . . To believe all likelihoods that we cannot shake off is great simplicity. The result of that would be that all the common herd—ᶜand we are all of the common herd—ᴬwould have its belief as easy to turn as a weathercock; for their soul, being soft and without resistance, would be forced to receive incessantly more and more different impressions, the last one always effacing the traces of the preceding one. He who finds himself weak should answer, following legal practice, that he will discuss it with his counsel, or refer to wiser men, from whom he received his teaching.

How long is it that medicine has been in the world? They say that a newcomer, whom they call Paracelsus,²⁶ is changing and overthrowing the whole order of the ancient rules, and maintaining that up to this moment it has been good for nothing but killing men. I think he will easily prove that; but as for putting my life to the test of his new experience, I think that would not be great wisdom.

Il ne faut pas croire à chacun, dit le précepte, parce que chacun peut dire toutes choses.

Un homme de cette profession de nouveautés et de réformations physiques me disait, il n'y a pas longtemps, que tous les anciens s'étaient évidemment mécomptés en la nature et mouvements des vents, ce qu'il me ferait très évidemment toucher à la main, si je voulais l'entendre. Après que j'eus eu un peu de patience à ouïr ses arguments, qui avaient tout plein de vérisimilitude: "Comment donc," lui fis-je, "ceux qui navigaient sous les lois de Théophraste allaient-ils en occident quand ils tiraient en levant? allaient-ils à côté, ou à reculons?" — "C'est la fortune," me répondit-il; "tant y a qu'ils se mécomptaient." Je lui répliquai lors que j'aimais mieux suivre les effets que la raison. Or ce sont choses qui se choquent souvent. . . .

ᶜEt chez nous ici j'ai vu telle chose qui nous était capitale devenir légitime; et nous qui en tenons d'autres sommes à même, selon l'incertitude de la fortune guerrière, d'être un jour criminels de lèse-majesté humaine et divine, notre justice tombant à la merci de l'injustice et, en l'espace de peu d'années de possession, prenant une essence contraire.

Comment pouvait ce Dieu ancien [27] plus clairement accuser en l'humaine connaissance l'ignorance de l'être divin, et apprendre aux hommes que la religion n'était qu'une pièce de leur invention, propre à lier leur société, qu'en déclarant, comme il fit, à ceux qui en recherchaient l'instruction de son trépied, que le vrai culte à chacun

---

[27] Apollo (see Xenophon, *Memorabilia*, i, iii, 1).

We must not believe every man, says the maxim, because any man may say anything.

A man of that profession of novelties and of reforms in physics was saying to me not long ago that all the ancients had evidently been mistaken about the nature and movements of the winds, which fact he would make so palpable that I could touch it, if I would hear him out. After I had taken some patience to listen to his arguments, which were full of likelihood: "What?" I said to him. "Then did those who navigated under the laws of Theophrastus go west when they headed east? Did they go sideways, or backward?" "That was luck," he replied; "at all events they miscalculated." I then replied to him that I would rather follow facts than reason. Now these are things that often clash. . . .

^CAnd here at home I have seen things which were capital offenses among us become legitimate; and we who consider other things legitimate are liable, according to the uncertainty of the fortunes of war, to be one day guilty of human and divine high treason, when our justice falls into the mercy of injustice, and, after a few years of captivity, assumes a contrary character.

How could that ancient god [27] more clearly accuse human knowledge of ignorance of the divine being, and teach men that religion was only a creature of their own invention, suitable to bind their society together, than by declaring, as he did, to those who sought instruction therein at his tripod, that the true cult for each man was

était celui qu'il trouvait observé par l'usage du lieu où il était?

Ô Dieu! quelle obligation n'avons-nous à la bénignité de notre souverain créateur pour avoir déniaisé notre croyance de ces vagabondes et arbitraires dévotions et l'avoir logée sur l'éternelle base de sa sainte parole!

ᴬQue nous dira donc en cette nécessité la philosophie? Que nous suivons les lois de notre pays? c'est-à-dire cette mer flottante des opinions d'un peuple ou d'un prince, qui me peindront la justice d'autant de couleurs, et la réformeront en autant de visages, qu'il y aura en eux de changements de passion? Je ne puis pas avoir le jugement si flexible. Quelle bonté est-ce que je voyais hier en crédit, et demain plus, ᶜet que le trajet d'une rivière fait crime? Quelle vérité que ces montagnes bornent, qui est mensonge au monde qui se tient au delà? . . .²⁸

ᴬOr, notre état accommodant les choses à soi et les transformant selon soi, nous ne savons plus quelles sont les choses en vérité; car rien ne vient à nous que falsifié et altéré par nos sens. Où le compas, l'équerre et la règle sont gauches, toutes les proportions qui s'en tirent, tous les bâtiments qui se dressent à leur mesure, sont aussi nécessairement manques et défaillants. L'incertitude de

---

²⁸ From the variability of the individual Montaigne now has moved to that of mankind, both in time and in place. The best products of man's wit and wisdom, he shows, are ever changing; and consequently not true—or if so, only for a moment which we cannot know as such. Worse yet, the mechanism of our knowledge is faulty. The senses are deficient; we probably should have eight

that which he found observed according to the practice of the place he was in?

O God, what an obligation do we not have to the benignity of our sovereign creator for having freed our belief from the folly of those vagabond and arbitrary devotions, and having based it on the eternal foundation of his holy word?

ᴬWhat then will philosophy tell us in this our need? To follow the laws of our country—that is to say, the undulating sea of the opinions of a people or a prince, which will paint me justice in as many colors, and refashion it into as many faces, as there are changes of passion in those men? I cannot have my judgment so flexible.

What goodness is this that I saw in credit yesterday, that will be no longer so tomorrow, ᶜand that becomes a crime on the other side of the river? What truth that is bounded by these mountains and is falsehood to the world that lives beyond? . . .²⁸

ᴬNow, since our condition accommodates things to itself and transforms them according to itself, we no longer know what things are in truth; for nothing comes to us except falsified and altered by our senses. When the compass, the square, and the ruler are off, all the proportions drawn from them, all the buildings erected by their measure, are also necessarily imperfect and defective. The un-

---

or ten instead of five in order to know the truth. They deceive the soul, which knows only the impressions of things that they report to it. And the soul in turn deceives them, coloring their reports by its own passions. This accumulation of unreliabilities makes perfect knowledge impossible, or if by any chance possible then unrecognizable, to man.

nos sens rend incertain tout ce qu'ils produisent. . . .

Au demeurant, qui sera propre à juger de ces différences? . . . S'il est vieux, il ne peut juger du sentiment de la vieillesse, étant lui-même partie en ce débat; s'il est jeune, de même; sain, de même; de même, malade, dormant et veillant. Il nous faudrait quelqu'un exempt de toutes ces qualités, afin que, sans préoccupation de jugement, il jugeât de ces propositions comme à lui indifférentes; et à ce compte il nous faudrait un juge qui ne fut pas.

Pour juger des apparences que nous recevons des sujets, il nous faudrait un instrument judicatoire; pour vérifier cet instrument, il nous y faut de la démonstration; pour vérifier la démonstration, un instrument: nous voilà au rouet.

Puisque les sens ne peuvent arrêter notre dispute, étant pleins eux-mêmes d'incertitude, il faut que ce soit la raison; aucune raison ne s'établira sans une autre raison: nous voilà à reculons jusqu'à l'infini.

Notre fantaisie ne s'applique pas aux choses étrangères, ains elle est conçue par l'entremise des sens; et les sens ne comprennent pas le sujet, ains seulement leurs propres passions; et par ainsi la fantaisie et apparence n'est pas du sujet, ains seulement de la passion et souffrance du sens, laquelle passion et sujet sont choses diverses: par quoi qui juge par les apparences, juge par chose autre que le sujet.

Et de dire que les passions des sens rapportent à l'âme la qualité des sujets étrangers par ressemblance, comment se peut l'âme et l'entendement assurer de cette ressemblance,

certainty of our senses makes everything they produce uncertain. . . . Furthermore, who shall be fit to judge these differences? . . . If he is old, he cannot judge the sense perception of old age, being himself a party in this dispute; if he is young, likewise; healthy, likewise; likewise sick, asleep, or awake. We would need someone exempt from all these qualities, so that with an unprejudiced judgment he might judge of these propositions as of things indifferent to him; and by that score we would need a judge that never was.

To judge the appearances that we receive of objects, we would need a judicatory instrument; to verify this instrument, we need a demonstration; to verify the demonstration, an instrument: there we are in a circle.

Since the senses cannot decide our dispute, being themselves full of uncertainty, it must be reason that does so. No reason can be established without another reason: there we go retreating back to infinity.

Our conception is not itself applied to foreign objects, but is conceived through the mediation of the senses; and the senses do not comprehend the foreign object, but only their own impressions. And thus the conception and semblance we form is not of the object, but only of the impression and effect made on the sense; which impression and the object are different things. Wherefore whoever judges by appearances judges by something other than the object.

And as for saying that the impressions of the senses convey to the soul the quality of the foreign objects by resemblance, how can the soul and understanding make

n'ayant de soi nul commerce avec les sujets étrangers? Tout ainsi comme qui ne connaît pas Socratès, voyant son portrait, ne peut dire qu'il lui ressemble.

Or qui voudrait toutefois juger par les apparences: si c'est par toutes, il est impossible, car elles s'entr'empêchent par leurs contrariétés et discrépances, comme nous voyons par expérience. Sera-ce qu'aucunes apparences choisies règlent les autres? Il faudra vérifier cette choisie par une autre choisie, la seconde par la tierce; et par ainsi ce ne sera jamais fait.

Finalement, il n'y a aucune constante existence, ni de notre être, ni de celui des objets. Et nous et notre jugement et toutes choses mortelles vont coulant et roulant sans cesse. Ainsi il ne se peut établir rien de certain de l'un à l'autre, et le jugeant et le jugé étant en continuelle mutation et branle.

Nous n'avons aucune communication à l'être,[29] parce que toute humaine nature est toujours au milieu entre le naître et le mourir, ne baillant de soi qu'une obscure apparence et ombre, et une incertaine et débile opinion. . . . La fleur d'âge se meurt et passe quand la vieillesse survient, et la jeunesse se termine en fleur d'âge d'homme fait, l'enfance en la jeunesse, et le premier âge meurt en l'enfance; et le jour d'hier meurt en celui du jourd'hui, et le jourd'hui mourra en celui de demain; et n'y a rien qui demeure ni qui soit toujours un.

Car, qu'il soit ainsi, si nous demeurons toujours mêmes et uns, comment est-ce que nous nous éjouissons main-

---

[29] The three paragraphs that follow, down to "sans commencement et sans fin"—"without beginning and without end," are taken

sure of this resemblance, having of itself no communication with foreign objects? Just as a man who does not know Socrates, seeing his portrait, cannot say that it resembles him.

Now if anyone should want to judge by appearances anyway, to judge by all appearances is impossible, for they clash with one another by their contradictions and discrepancies, as we see by experience. Shall some selected appearances rule the others? We shall have to verify this selection by another selection, the second by a third; and thus it will never be finished.

Finally, there is no existence that is constant, either of our being or of that of objects. And we, and our judgment, and all mortal things go on flowing and rolling unceasingly. Thus nothing certain can be established about one thing by another, both the judging and the judged being in continual change and motion.

We have no communication with being,[29] because every human nature is always midway between birth and death, offering only a dim semblance and shadow of itself, and an uncertain and feeble opinion. . . . Our prime dies and passes when old age comes along, and youth ends in the prime of the grown man, childhood in youth, and infancy in childhood. And yesterday dies in today, and today will die in tomorrow; and there is nothing that abides and is always the same.

For, to prove that this is so, if we always remain one and the same, how is it that we rejoice now in one thing, and

---

almost word for word from Plutarch's *Moralia*, "Que signifiait εἲ" ("On the Meaning of εἲ"), in Jacques Amyot's translation.

[II:12] *Apology for Raymond Sebond*

tenant d'une chose, et maintenant d'une autre? . . . Car il n'est pas vraisemblable que sans mutation nous prenions autres passions; et ce qui souffre mutation ne demeure pas un même, et, s'il n'est pas un même, il n'*est* donc pas aussi. Ains quand et *l'être tout un,* change aussi *l'être* simplement, devenant toujours autre d'un autre. Et par conséquent se trompent et mentent les sens de nature, prenant ce qui apparaît pour ce qui est, à faute de bien savoir que c'est qui *est.*

Mais qu'est-ce donc qui *est* véritablement? Ce qui est éternel, c'est-à-dire qui n'a jamais eu de naissance ni n'aura jamais fin; à qui le temps n'apporte jamais aucune mutation. . . . Autant en advient-il à la nature qui est mesurée comme au temps qui la mesure. Car il n'y a non plus en elle rien qui demeure, ni qui soit subsistant; ains y sont toutes choses ou nées, ou naissantes, ou mourantes. Au moyen de quoi ce serait péché de dire de Dieu, qui est le seul qui *est,* qu'il *fut* ou il *sera.* Car ces termes-là sont déclinaisons, passages ou vicissitudes de ce qui ne peut durer ni demeurer en être. Par quoi il faut conclure que Dieu seul *est,* non point selon aucune mesure du temps, mais selon une éternité immuable et immobile, non mesurée par temps, ni sujette à aucune déclinaison; devant lequel rien n'est, ni ne sera après, ni plus nouveau ni plus récent; ains un réellement étant, qui par un seul *maintenant* emplit le *toujours;* et n'y a rien qui véritablement *soit* que lui seul, sans qu'on puisse dire "Il a été" ou "Il sera"; sans commencement et sans fin.

A cette conclusion si religieuse d'un homme païen je veux joindre seulement ce mot d'un témoin de même

now in another? . . . For it is not plausible that we take up different passions without changing; and what suffers change does not remain one and the same, and if it is not one and the same, it also *is* not; but together with its *being the same*, it also changes its simple *being*, from one thing always becoming another. And consequently the senses of nature are mistaken and lie, taking what appears for what is, for want of really knowing what it is that *is*.

But then what really *is*? That which is eternal: that is to say, what never had birth, nor will ever have an end; to which time never brings any change. . . . The same thing happens to nature that is measured, as to time that measures it. For there is nothing in it either that abides or is stable; but all things in it are either born, or being born, or dying. For which reason it would be a sin to say of God, who is the only one that *is*, that he *was* or *will be*. For those terms represent declinings, transitions, or vicissitudes of what cannot endure or remain in being. Wherefore we must conclude that God alone *is*—not at all according to any measure of time, but according to an eternity immutable and immobile, not measured by time or subject to any decline; before whom there is nothing, nor will there be after, nor is there anything more new or more recent; but one who really is—who by one single *now* fills the *ever*; and there is nothing that really is but he alone—nor can we say "He has been," or "He will be"— without beginning and without end.

To this most religious conclusion of a pagan I want to

condition,[30] pour la fin de ce long et ennuyeux discours qui me fournirait de matière sans fin: Ô la vile chose," dit-il, "et abjecte, que l'homme, s'il ne s'élève au-dessus de l'humanité!"

ᶜVoilà un bon mot et un utile désir, mais pareillement absurde. Car ᴬde faire la poignée plus grande que le poing, la brassée plus grande que le bras, et d'espérer enjamber plus que de l'étendue de nos jambes, cela est impossible et monstrueux. Ni que l'homme se monte au-dessus de soi et de l'humanité; car il ne peut voir que de ses yeux, ni saisir que de ses prises.

Il s'élèvera, si Dieu lui prête extraordinairement la main; il s'élèvera, abandonnant et renonçant à ses propres moyens, et se laissant hausser et soulever par les moyens purement célestes.

ᶜC'est à notre foi chrétienne, non à sa vertu stoïque, de prétendre à cette divine et miraculeuse métamorphose.[31]

---

30 Seneca (*Natural Questions*, Book I, Preface).

31 In the 1580–88 editions Montaigne's conclusion was less clear and strong. After "au-dessus de l'humanité!" ("above humanity!") it read as follows: "Il n'est nul mot en toute sa secte Stoïque plus véritable que celui-là: mais de faire la poignée plus grande que le poing, la brassée plus grande que le bras, et d'espérer enjamber plus que de l'étendue de nos jambes, cela est impossible et monstrueux. Ni que l'homme se monte au-dessus de soi et de l'humanité: car il ne peut voir que de ses yeux, ni saisir que de ses prises. Il s'élèvera, si Dieu lui prête la main; il s'élèvera, abandonnant et renonçant à ses propres moyens, et se laissant hausser et soulever par la grâce divine: mais

add only this remark of a witness of the same condition,[30] for an ending to this long and boring discourse, which would give me material without end: "O what a vile and abject thing is man," he says, "if he does not raise himself above humanity!"

ᶜThat is a good statement and a useful desire, but equally absurd. For ᴬto make the handful bigger than the hand, the armful bigger than the arm, and to hope to straddle more than the reach of our legs, is impossible and unnatural. Nor can man raise himself above himself and humanity; for he can see only with his own eyes, and seize only with his own grasp.

He will rise, if God by exception lends him a hand; he will rise by abandoning and renouncing his own means, and letting himself be raised and uplifted by purely celestial means.

ᶜIt is for our Christian faith, not for his Stoical virtue, to aspire to that divine and miraculous metamorphosis.[31]

---

non autrement."—"There is no truer saying in all his Stoic school than that one. But to make the handful bigger than the hand, the armful bigger than the arm, and to hope to straddle more than the reach of our legs, is impossible and unnatural. Nor can man raise himself above himself and humanity; for he can see only with his own eyes, and seize only with his own grasp. He will rise, if God lends him his hand; he will rise by abandoning and renouncing his own means, and letting himself be raised and uplifted by divine grace; but not otherwise."

The manuscript variations of the final lines show how anxious Montaigne was to make his meaning here clear and exact.

[A]Il y a une autre sorte de gloire,[2] qui est une trop bonne opinion que nous concevons de notre valeur. C'est une affection inconsidérée, de quoi nous nous chérissons, qui nous représente à nous-mêmes autres que nous ne sommes. . . .

Je ne veux pas que, de peur de faillir de ce côté-là, un homme se méconnaisse pourtant, ni qu'il pense être moins que ce qu'il est. Le jugement doit tout partout maintenir son droit: c'est raison qu'il voie en ce sujet, comme ailleurs, ce que la vérité lui présente. Si c'est Cæsar, qu'il se trouve hardiment le plus grand capitaine du monde.

Nous ne sommes que cérémonie: la cérémonie nous emporte, et laissons la substance des choses; nous nous tenons aux branches et abandonnons le tronc et le corps. Nous avons appris aux dames de rougir oyant seulement nommer ce qu'elles ne craignent aucunement à faire; nous n'osons appeler à droit nos membres, et ne craignons pas de les employer à toute sorte de débauche. La cérémonie nous défend d'exprimer par paroles les choses licites et naturelles, et nous l'en croyons; la raison nous défend de n'en faire point d'illicites et mauvaises, et personne ne l'en croit. Je me trouve ici empêtré ès lois de la cérémonie, car elle ne permet ni qu'on parle bien de soi, ni qu'on en parle mal. Nous la laisserons là pour ce coup.

---

[1] This chapter, composed in 1579–80, is Montaigne's first full self-portrait.

17 Of Presumption [1]

^AThere is another kind of vainglory,[2] which is an over-good opinion we form of our own worth. It is an unreasoning affection, by which we cherish ourselves, which represents us to ourselves as other than we are. . . .

However, I do not want a man to misjudge himself, for fear of erring in that direction, or to think himself less than he is. Judgment must maintain its rights in all matters; it is right that it should see, in this subject as elsewhere, what truth sets before it. If he is Caesar, let him boldly judge himself the greatest captain in the world.

We are nothing but ceremony; ceremony carries us away, and we leave the substance of things; we hang on to the branches and abandon the trunk and body. We have taught the ladies to blush at the mere mention of what they are not at all afraid to do; we dare not call our members by their right names, and we are not afraid to employ them in every kind of debauchery. Ceremony forbids our expressing in words things that are permissible and natural, and we obey it; reason forbids our doing things that are illicit and wicked, and no one obeys it. I find myself here entangled in the laws of ceremony, for she does not allow a man either to speak well of himself, or to speak ill. We shall let her alone for the moment.

---

[2] A reference to the preceding chapter, "De la gloire" ("Of Glory").

Ceux que la fortune (bonne ou mauvaise qu'on la doive appeler) a fait passer la vie en quelque éminent degré, ils peuvent par leurs actions publiques témoigner quels ils sont. Mais ceux qu'elle n'a employés qu'en foule, [c]et de qui personne ne parlera si eux-mêmes n'en parlent, [A]ils sont excusables s'ils prennent la hardiesse de parler d'eux-mêmes envers ceux qui ont intérêt de les connaître. . . .

Il y a deux parties en cette gloire: savoir est, de s'estimer trop, et n'estimer pas assez autrui. Quant à l'une, . . . [c]je me sens pressé d'une erreur d'âme qui me déplaît, et comme inique, et encore plus comme importune. J'essaie à la corriger; mais l'arracher, je ne puis. C'est que je diminue du juste prix les choses que je possède, de ce que je les possède; et hausse le prix aux choses d'autant qu'elles sont étrangères, absentes et non miennes. Cette humeur s'épand bien loin. . . . Les polices, les mœurs lointaines me flattent, et les langues; et m'aperçois que le latin me pipe à sa faveur par sa dignité au delà de ce qui lui appartient, comme aux enfants et au vulgaire. L'économie, la maison, le cheval de mon voisin, en égale valeur, vaut mieux que le mien, de ce qu'il n'est pas mien. . . .

Pareillement [A]j'ai en général ceci, que de toutes les opinions que l'ancienneté a eues de l'homme [c]en gros, [A]celles que j'embrasse plus volontiers et auxquelles je m'attache le plus ce sont celles qui nous méprisent, avilissent et anéantissent le plus. La philosophie ne me semble jamais avoir si beau jeu que quand elle combat notre présomption et vanité, quand elle reconnaît de bonne foi son irrésolution, sa faiblesse et son ignorance. Il me semble que la mère nourrice des plus fausses opinions et publiques et particulières, c'est la trop bonne opinion que

Those whom Fortune (whether we should call her good or bad) has caused to spend their lives in some eminent station, can testify to what they are by their public actions. But those whom she has employed only in a mass, ᶜand of whom no one will speak unless they do so themselves, ᴬmay be excused if they have the temerity to speak of themselves to those who have an interest in knowing them. . . .

There are two parts in this vainglory, namely, to esteem ourselves too highly, and not to esteem others highly enough. As for the first, . . . ᶜI feel myself oppressed by an error of my soul which I dislike, both as unjust and, even more, as troublesome. I try to correct it, but uproot it I cannot. It is that I lower the value of the things I possess, because I possess them, and raise the value of things when they are foreign, absent, and not mine. This humor spreads very far. . . . Far-off governments, customs, and languages delight me; and I realize that Latin, by its dignity, beguiles me more than it should, as it does children and common people. The housekeeping, the house, the horse of my neighbor, if equal in value, seem better than my own, because they are not mine. . . .

Likewise ᴬthis is generally true of me, that of all the opinions antiquity has held of man ᶜas a whole, ᴬthe ones I embrace most willingly and adhere to most firmly are those that despise, humiliate, and nullify us most. Philosophy seems to me never to have such an easy game as when she combats our presumption and vanity, when she honestly admits her uncertainty, weakness, and ignorance. It seems to me that the nursing mother of the falsest opinions, public and private, is the over-good opinion man has of himself.

[II:17] *Of Presumption*

l'homme a de soi. Ces gens qui se perchent à chevauchons sur l'épicycle de Mercure, ^cqui voient si avant dans le ciel, ^Ails m'arrachent les dents. Car en l'étude que je fais, duquel le sujet c'est l'homme, trouvant une si extrême variété de jugements, un si profond labyrinthe de difficultés les unes sur les autres, tant de diversité et incertitude en l'école même de la sapience, vous pouvez penser—puisque ces gens-là n'ont pu se résoudre de la connaissance d'eux-mêmes et de leur propre condition, qui est continuellement présente à leurs yeux, qui est dans eux; puisqu'ils ne savent comment branle ce qu'eux-mêmes font branler, ni comment nous peindre et déchiffrer les ressorts qu'ils tiennent et manient eux-mêmes—comment je les croirais de la cause du flux et reflux de la rivière du Nil. La curiosité de connaître les choses a été donnée aux hommes pour fléau, dit la sainte parole.

Mais, pour venir à mon particulier, il est bien difficile, ce me semble, qu'aucun autre s'estime moins, voire qu'aucun autre m'estime moins, que ce que je m'estime.

^cJe me tiens de la commune sorte, sauf en ce que je m'en tiens: coupable des défectuosités plus basses et populaires, mais non désavouées, non excusées; et ne me prise seulement que de ce que je sais mon prix.

S'il y a de la gloire, elle est infuse en moi superficiellement par la trahison de ma complexion, et n'a point de corps qui comparaisse à la vue de mon jugement. J'en suis arrosé, mais non pas teint.

^ACar à la vérité, quant aux effets de l'esprit, en quelque façon que ce soit, il n'est jamais parti de moi chose qui me remplît; et l'approbation d'autrui ne me paye

These people who perch astride the epicycle of Mercury, ^Cwho see so far into the heavens, ^Ayank out my teeth. For in the study I am making, the subject of which is man, when I find such an extreme variety of judgments, so deep a labyrinth of difficulties one on top of the other, so much diversity and uncertainty in the very school of wisdom, you may well wonder—since these people have not been able to come to an agreement in the knowledge of themselves and their own state, which is ever present before their eyes, which is in them; since they do not know the motion of what they move themselves, or how to depict and decipher to us the springs that they hold and manage themselves—how I should believe them about the cause of the ebb and flow of the river Nile. The curiosity to know things was given to men as a scourge, says the Holy Scripture.

But to come to my own particular case, it would be very difficult, it seems to me, for anyone else to esteem himself less, or indeed for anyone else to esteem me less, than I esteem myself.

^CI consider myself one of the common sort, except in that I consider myself so; guilty of the commoner and humbler faults, but not of faults disavowed or excused; and I value myself only for knowing my value.

If there is vainglory in me, it is infused in me superficially by the treachery of my nature, and has no body of its own to appear before my judgment. I am sprinkled with it, but not dyed.

^AFor in truth, as regards any kind of products of the mind, I have never brought forth anything that satisfied me; and the approbation of others does not repay me. . . .

pas. . . . J'ai la vue assez claire et réglée; mais à l'ouvrer, elle se trouble: comme j'essaie plus évidemment en la poésie. Je l'aime infiniment; je me connais assez aux ouvrages d'autrui; mais je fais, à la vérité, l'enfant quand j'y veux mettre la main; je ne me puis souffrir. On peut faire le sot partout ailleurs, mais non en la poésie. . . .

J'ai au demeurant la taille forte et ramassée; le visage non pas gras, mais plein; la complexion [B]entre le jovial et le mélancolique, moyennement [A]sanguine et chaude—

Unde rigent setis mihi crura, et pectora villis; [3]

la santé forte et allègre, jusque bien avant en mon âge [B]rarement troublée par les maladies. [A]J'étais tel, car je ne me considère pas à cette heure que je suis engagé dans les avenues de la vieillesse, ayant piéça franchi les quarante ans. . . .

D'adresse et de disposition, je n'en ai point eu. . . . De la musique, ni pour la voix que j'ai très inepte, ni pour les instruments, on ne m'y a jamais su rien apprendre. A la danse, à la paume, à la lutte, je n'ai pu acquérir qu'une bien fort légère et vulgaire suffisance; à nager, à escrimer, à voltiger et à sauter, nulle du tout. Les mains, je les ai si gourdes que je ne sais pas écrire seulement pour moi: de façon que ce que j'ai barbouillé, j'aime mieux le refaire que de me donner la peine de le démêler; [C]et ne lis guère mieux. Je me sens peser aux écoutants. Autrement, bon clerc.[4] [A]Je ne sais pas clore à droit une lettre, ni ne sus

---

[3] Martial, *Epigrams*, II, xxxvi, 5.
[4] A possible reminiscence of Clément Marot's well-known line, "Au demeurant, le meilleur fils du monde" ("For the rest, the best

My sight is clear and controlled enough; but when I put it to work, it grows blurred, as I find most evidently in poetry. I love it infinitely; I am a pretty good judge of other men's works; but in truth, I play the child when I try to set my hand to it; I cannot endure myself. A man may play the fool anywhere else, but not in poetry. . . .

For the rest, I have a strong, thick-set body, a face not fat but full, a temperament Bbetween the jovial and the melancholy, moderately Asanguine and warm—

My legs are stiff with bristles, my chest with shaggy hair [3]

—sound and sprightly health, Brarely troubled by illnesses, Auntil I was well along in years. Such I was, for I am not considering myself at this moment, when I am well on the road to old age, having long since passed forty. . . .

Adroitness and agility I have never had. . . . Of music, either vocal, for which my voice is very inept, or instrumental, they never succeeded in teaching me anything. At dancing, tennis, wrestling, I have never been able to acquire any but very slight and ordinary ability; at swimming, fencing, vaulting, and jumping, none at all. My hands are so clumsy that I cannot even write so I can read it; so that I would rather do over what I have scribbled than give myself the trouble of unscrambling it. CAnd I read hardly any better. I feel that I weigh upon my listeners. Otherwise, a good scholar.[4] AI cannot close

---

lad in the world"), which follows an impressive enumeration of his valet's vices.

jamais tailler plume ni trancher à table qui vaille; ^cni équiper un cheval de son harnais, ni porter à point un oiseau et le lâcher, ni parler aux chiens, aux oiseaux, aux chevaux.

^AMes conditions corporelles sont en somme très bien accordantes à celles de l'âme. Il n'y a rien d'allègre; il y a seulement une vigueur pleine et ferme. Je dure bien à la peine; mais j'y dure si je m'y porte moi-même, et autant que mon désir m'y conduit,

> Molliter austerum studio fallente laborem.[5]

Autrement, si je n'y suis alléché par quelque plaisir, et si j'ai autre guide que ma pure et libre volonté, je n'y vaux rien. Car j'en suis là, que sauf la santé et la vie, il n'est chose ^cpour quoi je veuille ronger mes ongles, et ^Aque je veuille acheter au prix du tourment d'esprit et de la contrainte:

> ^Btanti mihi non sit opaci
> Omnis arena Tagi, quodque in mare volvitur aurum: [6]

^Cextrêmement oisif, extrêmement libre, et par nature et par art. Je prêterais aussi volontiers mon sang que mon soin.

^AJ'ai une âme toute sienne, accoutumée à se conduire à sa mode. N'ayant eu jusqu'à cette heure ni commandant ni maître forcé, j'ai marché aussi avant et le pas qu'il m'a plu. Cela m'a amolli et rendu inutile au service d'autrui, et ne m'a fait bon qu'à moi. Et pour moi il n'a-été besoin

---

⁵ Horace, *Satires*, II, ii, 12.

a letter the right way, nor could I ever cut a pen, or carve at table worth a rap, ^Cor saddle a horse, or properly carry a bird and release it, or talk to dogs, birds, or horses.

^AMy bodily qualities, in short, are very well matched with those of my soul. There is no liveliness; there is only a full, firm vigor. I stand up well under hard work; but I do so only if I go to it of my own will, and as much as my desire leads me to it,

When gently zest beguiles the rigors of the toil.⁵

Otherwise, if I am not lured to it by some pleasure, and if I have any other guide than my own pure free will, I am good for nothing. For I have come to the point where except for health and life, there is nothing ^Cfor which I am willing to bite my nails, nothing ^Athat I am willing to buy at the price of mental torment and constraint:

^BI would not buy at such a fee
All Tagus' sands, and all the gold it rolls to sea.⁶

^CExtremely idle, extremely independent, both by nature and by art. I would as soon lend my blood as my pains.

^AI have a soul all its own, accustomed to conducting itself in its own way. Having had neither governor nor master forced on me to this day, I have gone just so far as I pleased, and at my own pace. This has made me soft and useless for serving others, and no good to anyone but my-

---

⁶ Juvenal, *Satires*, III, 54–5.

[II:17] *Of Presumption*

de forcer ce naturel pesant, paresseux et fainéant. Car m'étant trouvé en tel degré de fortune dès ma naissance que j'ai eu occasion de m'y arrêter, ᶜet en tel degré de sens que j'ai senti en avoir occasion, ᴬje n'ai rien cherché et n'ai aussi rien pris. . . . . Je n'ai eu besoin que de la suffisance de me contenter, . . . que de jouir doucement des biens que Dieu par sa libéralité m'avait mis entre mains. Je n'ai goûté aucune sorte de travail ennuyeux. Je n'ai eu guère en maniement que mes affaires; ᶜou, si j'en ai eu, ç'a été en condition de les manier à mon heure et à ma façon, commis par gens qui s'en fiaient à moi et qui ne me pressaient pas et me connaissaient. . . .[7]

ᴮA un danger, je ne songe pas tant comment j'en échapperai que combien peu il importe que j'en échappe. Quand j'y demeurerais, que serait-ce? Ne pouvant régler les événements, je me règle moi-même; et m'applique à eux, s'ils ne s'appliquent à moi. . . . L'horreur de la chute me donne plus de fièvre que le coup. Le jeu ne vaut pas la chandelle. L'avaricieux a plus mauvais compte de sa passion que n'a le pauvre, et le jaloux que le cocu. Et y a moins de mal souvent à perdre sa vigne qu'à la plaider. La plus basse marche est la plus ferme. C'est le siège de la constance. Vous n'y avez besoin que de vous. Elle se fonde là et appuie toute en soi.

Cet exemple d'un gentilhomme que plusieurs ont connu, a-t-il pas quelque air philosophique? Il se maria bien

---

[7] This addition, of course, comes after Montaigne's two terms as mayor of Bordeaux.

self. And for my own sake there was no need to force that heavy, lazy, and do-nothing nature. For having found myself from birth in such a degree of fortune that I had reason to be content with it, ^Cand having as much sense as I felt I had occasion for, ^AI have sought nothing, and have also acquired nothing . . . The only ability I have needed is the ability to content myself with my lot, . . . to enjoy pleasantly the good things that God in his liberality had placed in my hands. I have never tasted of any sort of tedious work. I have had hardly anything to manage but my own affairs; ^Cor, if I have, it has been on condition of managing them at my own times and in my own way, commissioned by people who trusted me and knew me, and did not hustle me. . . .[7]

^BWhen in danger, I do not think so much how I shall escape, as how little it matters that I escape. Even if I should fall, what would it matter? Not being able to rule events, I rule myself, and adapt myself to them if they do not adapt themselves to me. . . . The dread of falling gives me a greater fever than the fall. The game is not worth the candle. The miser is worse off for his passion than the poor man, and the jealous man than the cuckold. And often it is not as bad to lose your vineyard as to go to court for it. The lowest step is the firmest. It is the seat of constancy. There you need nothing but yourself. Constancy is founded there and leans only upon itself.

Is there not a certain philosophical air about the case of a gentleman known to many? He married well along in

avant en l'âge, ayant passé en bon compagnon sa jeunesse: grand diseur, grand gaudisseur. Se souvenant combien la matière de cornardise lui avait donné de quoi parler et se moquer des autres, pour se mettre à couvert, il épousa une femme qu'il prit au lieu où chacun en trouve pour son argent, et dressa avec elle ses alliances: "Bonjour, putain." — "Bonjour, cocu!" Et n'est chose de quoi plus souvent et ouvertement il entretînt chez lui les survenants que de ce sien dessein; par où il bridait les occultes caquets des moqueurs et émoussait la pointe de ce reproche.

ᴬQuant à l'ambition, qui est voisine de la présomption, ou fille plutôt, il eût fallu, pour m'avancer, que la fortune me fût venu quérir par le poing. . . .

Les qualités mêmes qui sont en moi non reprochables, je les trouvais inutiles en ce siècle. La facilité de mes mœurs, on l'eût nommée lâcheté et faiblesse; la foi et la conscience s'y fussent trouvées scrupuleuses et superstitieuses; la franchise et la liberté, importune, inconsidérée et téméraire.

A quelque chose sert le malheur. Il fait bon naître en un siècle fort dépravé; car par comparaison d'autrui vous êtes estimé vertueux à bon marché. Qui n'est que parricide en nos jours, et sacrilège, il est homme de bien et d'honneur. . . .

ᴮEt ne fut jamais temps et lieu où il y eût pour les princes loyer plus certain et plus grand proposé à la bonté et à la justice. Le premier qui s'avisera de se pousser en faveur et en crédit par cette voie-là, je suis bien déçu si à bon compte il ne devance ses compagnons. La force, la

years, having spent his youth in gay company, a great storyteller, a merry lad. Remembering how the subject of cuckoldry had given him material for talking and jesting about others, to take cover he married a woman whom he picked up in the place where each man can find one for his money, and made a compact with her that they would use these greetings: "Good morning, whore." "Good morning, cuckold." And there was nothing about which he talked more often and openly to visitors at his home than this arrangement of his; by which he checked the secret gossip of mockers, and blunted the point of this reproach.

ᴬAs for ambition, which is neighbor to presumption, or rather daughter, it would have been necessary, to advance me, for Fortune to come and take me by the hand. . . .

Even the qualities that are not reproachable in me, I have found useless in this age. My easygoing ways would have been called cowardice and weakness; fidelity and conscience would have been thought squeamish and superstitious; frankness and independence, troublesome, thoughtless, and rash.

Misfortune has its uses. It is good to be born in a very depraved time; for by comparison with others, you are considered virtuous for a cheap price. Anyone who is only a parricide and sacrilegious in our days is a good and honorable man. . . .

ᴮAnd there was never time and place where a surer and greater reward was offered to princes for goodness and justice. The first man who thinks to push himself into favor and credit by that path, I am much mistaken if he will not outstrip his fellows without much effort. Force and

violence peuvent quelque chose, mais non pas toujours tout.

ᴬ. . . Quant à cette nouvelle vertu de feintise et de dissimulation qui est à cette heure si fort en crédit, je la hais capitalement; et de tous les vices, je n'en trouve aucun qui témoigne tant de lâcheté et bassesse de cœur. C'est une humeur couarde et servile de s'aller déguiser et cacher sous un masque et de n'oser se faire voir tel qu'on est. Par là nos hommes se dressent à la perfidie. . . . Un cœur généreux ne doit point démentir ses pensées; il se veut faire voir jusqu'au dedans. ᶜOu tout y est bon, ou au moins tout y est humain. . . .

ᴬApollonius disait que c'était aux serfs de mentir, et aux libres de dire vérité.

ᶜC'est la première et fondamentale partie de la vertu. Il la faut aimer pour elle-même. . . . ᴬIl ne faut pas toujours dire tout, car ce serait sottise; mais ce qu'on dit, il faut qu'il soit tel qu'on le pense, autrement c'est méchanceté. . . .

C'est un outil de merveilleux service que la mémoire, et sans lequel le jugement fait bien à peine son office: elle me manque du tout. . . . ᶜPour apprendre trois vers, il me faut trois heures; et puis, en un mien ouvrage, la liberté et autorité de remuer l'ordre, de changer un mot, variant sans cesse la matière, la rend plus malaisée à concevoir.

ᴬOr plus je m'en défie, plus elle se trouble; elle me sert mieux par rencontre; il faut que je la sollicite nonchalamment: car si je la presse, elle s'étonne; et depuis qu'elle a commencé à chanceler, plus je la sonde, plus elle s'empêtre et embarrasse; elle me sert à son heure, non pas à la mienne.

violence can do something, but not always everything.

ᴬ . . . As for this new-fangled virtue of hypocrisy and dis-simulation, which is so highly honored at present, I mor-tally hate it; and of all vices, I know none that testifies to so much cowardice and baseness of heart. It is a craven and servile idea to disguise ourselves and hide under a mask, and not to dare to show ourselves as we are. In that way our men train for perfidy. . . . A generous heart should not belie its thoughts; it wants to reveal itself even to its inmost depths. ᶜThere everything is good, or at least everything is human. . . .

ᴬApollonius said that it was for slaves to lie, and for free men to speak truth.

ᶜTruth is the first and fundamental part of virtue. We must love it for itself. . . . ᴬWe must not always say everything, for that would be folly; but what we say must be what we think; otherwise it is wickedness. . . .

Memory is a wonderfully useful tool, and without it judgment does its work with difficulty; it is entirely lacking in me. . . . ᶜTo learn three lines of poetry I need three hours. And then, in a work of my own, the freedom and authority to change the order and alter a word, ever vary-ing the material, makes it harder to keep in mind.

ᴬNow, the more I distrust my memory, the more con-fused it becomes. It serves me better by chance encounter; I have to solicit it nonchalantly. For if I press it, it is stunned; and once it has begun to totter, the more I probe it, the more it gets mixed up and embarrassed. It serves me at its own time, not at mine.

Ceci [8] que je sens en la mémoire, je le sens en plusieurs autres parties. Je fuis le commandement, l'obligation et la contrainte. Ce que je fais aisément et naturellement, si je m'ordonne de le faire par une expresse et prescrite ordonnance, je ne le sais plus faire. Au corps même, les membres qui ont quelque liberté et juridiction plus particulière sur eux me refusent parfois leur obéissance quand je les destine et attache à certain point et heure de service nécessaire. . . .

Par ces traits de ma confession, on en peut imaginer d'autres à mes dépens. Mais quel que je me fasse connaître, pourvu que je me fasse connaître tel que je suis, je fais mon effet. Et si ne m'excuse pas d'oser mettre par écrit des propos si bas et frivoles que ceux-ci. La bassesse du sujet m'y contraint. ᶜQu'on accuse, si on veut, mon projet; mais mon progrès, non. ᴬTant y a que, sans l'avertissement d'autrui, je vois assez ce peu que tout ceci vaut et pèse, et la folie de mon dessein. C'est prou que mon jugement ne se déferre point, duquel ce sont ici les essais. . . . Je ne suis pas obligé à ne dire point de sottises, pourvu que je ne me trompe pas à les connaître. Et de faillir à mon escient, cela m'est si ordinaire que je ne faux guère d'autre façon: je ne faux jamais fortuitement. . . .

Je vis un jour à Bar-le-Duc qu'on présentait au roi François Second, pour la recommandation de la mémoire de René, roi de Sicile, un portrait qu'il avait lui-même fait de soi. Pourquoi n'est-il loisible de même à un chacun de se peindre de la plume comme il se peignait d'un crayon?

---

[8] The passage from "Ceci" ("This thing") to the end of the paragraph is an addition of 1582.

This thing [8] that I feel in my memory, I feel in several other parts. I flee command, obligation, and constraint. What I do easily and naturally, I can no longer do if I order myself to do it by strict and express command. Even as regards my body, the parts that have some particular freedom and jurisdiction over themselves sometimes refuse to obey me when I destine and bind them to a certain time and place for compulsory service. . . .

From these lines of my confession you can imagine others at my expense. But whatever I make myself known to be, provided I make myself known such as I am, I am carrying out my plan. And so I make no excuse for daring to put into writing such mean and trivial remarks as these. The meanness of my subject forces me to do so. ^CBlame my project if you will, but not my procedure. ^AAt all events, I see well enough, without others telling me, how little value and weight all this has, and the folly of my plan. It is enough that my judgment is not unshod, of which these are the essays. . . . I am not obliged not to say stupid things, provided I do not fool myself and that I recognize them as such. And to slip up knowingly is so common for me that I scarcely ever slip up in any other way; I never slip up accidentally. . . .

One day at Bar-le-Duc I saw King Francis II presented, in remembrance of René, king of Sicily, with a portrait that this king had made of himself. Why is it not permissible in the same way for each man to portray himself with the pen, as he portrayed himself with a pencil?

[II:17] Of *Presumption*

Je ne veux donc pas oublier encore cette cicatrice, bien malpropre à produire en public: c'est l'irrésolution, défaut très incommode à la négociation des affaires du monde. Je ne sais pas prendre parti ès entreprises douteuses. . . . ^BJe sais bien soutenir une opinion, mais non pas la choisir. . . .

^ASomme, pour revenir à moi, ce seul par où je m'estime quelque chose, c'est ce en quoi jamais homme ne s'estima défaillant: ma recommandation est vulgaire, commune et populaire, car qui a jamais cuidé avoir faute de sens? Ce serait une proposition qui impliquerait en soi de la contradiction: ^Cc'est une maladie qui n'est jamais où elle se voit; elle est bien tenace et forte, mais laquelle pourtant le premier rayon de la vue du patient perce et dissipe, comme le regard du soleil un brouillard opaque; ^As'accuser serait s'excuser en ce sujet-là; et se condamner, ce serait s'absoudre. Il ne fut jamais crocheteur ni femmelette qui ne pensât avoir assez de sens pour sa provision. Nous reconnaissons aisément ès autres l'avantage du courage, de la force corporelle, de l'expérience, de la disposition, de la beauté; mais l'avantage du jugement, nous ne le cédons à personne: et les raisons qui partent du simple discours naturel en autrui, il nous semble qu'il n'a tenu qu'à regarder de ce côté-là, que nous les ayons trouvées. . . .

Or mes opinions, je les trouve infiniment hardies et constantes à condamner mon insuffisance. De vrai, c'est aussi un sujet auquel j'exerce mon jugement autant qu'à nul autre. Le monde regarde toujours vis-à-vis; moi, je replie ma vue au dedans, je la plante, je l'amuse là. Chacun regarde devant soi; moi je regarde dedans moi: je n'ai

So I do not want to forget this further scar, very unfit to produce in public: irresolution, a most harmful failing in negotiating worldly affairs. I do not know which side to take in doubtful enterprises. . . . ^BI can easily maintain an opinion, but not choose one. . . .

^AAll in all, to return to myself, the only thing that makes me think something of myself is the thing in which no man ever thought himself deficient: my recommendation is vulgar, common, and popular, for who ever thought he lacked sense? That would be a proposition implying its own contradiction. ^CIt is a disease that is never where it is perceived; it is indeed tenacious and strong, but it is pierced and dispersed by the first glance from the patient's eye, like a dense fog by a glance from the sun. ^ATo accuse oneself would be to excuse oneself in that subject, and to condemn oneself would be to absolve oneself. There never was a porter or a silly woman who did not think they had enough sense to take care of themselves. We readily acknowledge in others an advantage in courage, in bodily strength, in experience, in agility, in beauty; but an advantage in judgment we yield to no one. And the arguments that come from simple natural reasoning in others, we think we would have found if we had merely glanced in that direction. . . .

Now I find my opinions infinitely bold and constant in condemning my inadequacy. In truth, this too is a subject on which I exercise my judgment as much as on any other. The world always looks straight ahead; as for me, I turn my gaze inward, I fix it there and keep it busy. Everyone looks in front of him; as for me, I look inside of me; I

affaire qu'à moi, je me considère sans cesse, je me contrôle, je me goûte. Les autres vont toujours ailleurs, s'ils y pensent bien; ils vont toujours avant;

nemo in sese tentat descendere; [9]

moi je me roule en moi-même.

Cette capacité de trier le vrai, quelle qu'elle soit en moi, et cette humeur libre de n'assujettir aisément ma croyance, je la dois principalement à moi: car les plus fermes imaginations que j'aie, et générales, sont celles qui par manière de dire naquirent avec moi. [B]Elles sont naturelles et toutes miennes. [A]Je les produisis crues et simples, d'une production hardie et forte, mais un peu trouble et imparfaite. Depuis je les ai établies et fortifiées par l'autorité d'autrui, et par les sains discours des anciens, auxquels je me suis rencontré conforme en jugement: ceux-là m'en ont assuré la prise et m'en ont donné la jouissance et possession plus entière. . . .

18 Du démentir [1]

[A]Voire, mais on me dira que ce dessein de se servir de soi pour sujet à écrire serait excusable à des hommes rares et fameux qui, par leur réputation, auraient donné quelque

---

[9] Persius, *Satires*, iv, 23.

have no business but with myself; I continually observe myself, I take stock of myself, I taste myself. Others always go elsewhere, if they stop to think about it; they always go forward;

No man tries to descend into himself; [9]

as for me, I roll about in myself.

This capacity for sifting truth, whatever it may amount to in me, and this free will not to enslave my belief easily, I owe principally to myself. For the firmest and most general ideas I have are those which, in a manner of speaking, were born with me. [B]They are natural and all mine. [A]I produced them crude and simple, with a conception bold and strong, but a little confused and imperfect. Since then I have established and fortified them by the authority of others and the sound arguments of the ancients, with whom I found my judgment in agreement. These men have given me a firmer grip on my ideas and a more complete enjoyment and possession of them. . . .

18   Of Giving the Lie [1]

[A]Yes, but someone will tell me that this plan of using oneself as a subject to write about would be excusable in rare and famous men who by their reputation had aroused

---

[1] As the first phrase suggests, this chapter seems to have been written immediately after the preceding one, that is, in 1579–80.

désir de leur connaissance. Il est certain; je l'avoue; et sais bien que pour voir un homme de la commune façon, à peine qu'un artisan lève les yeux de sa besogne, là où pour voir un personnage grand et signalé arriver en une ville, les ouvroirs et les boutiques s'abandonnent. Il messied à tout autre de se faire connaître, qu'à celui qui a de quoi se faire imiter, et duquel la vie et les opinions peuvent servir de patron. Cæsar et Xénophon ont eu de quoi fonder et fermir leur narration en la grandeur de leurs faits comme en une base juste et solide. Ainsi sont à souhaiter les papiers journaux du grand Alexandre, les commentaires qu'Auguste, ᶜCaton, ᴬSylla, Brutus et autres avaient laissés de leurs gestes. De telles gens on aime et étudie les figures, en cuivre même et en pierre.

Cette remontrance est très vraie, mais elle ne me touche que bien peu:

> Non recito cuiquam, nisi amicis, idque rogatus,
> Non ubivis, coramve quibuslibet. In medio qui
> Scripta foro recitent sunt multi, quique lavantes.[2]

Je ne dresse pas ici une statue à planter au carrefour d'une ville, ou dans une église ou place publique:

> ᴮNon equidem hoc studeo, bullatis ut mihi nugis
> Pagina turgescat . . .
> Secreti loquimur.[3]

ᴬC'est pour le coin d'une librairie, et pour en amuser un voisin, un parent, un ami, qui aura plaisir à me racointer et repratiquer en cette image. Les autres ont pris cœur de

_____.

[2] Horace, *Satires*, I, iv, 73–5.

some desire to know them. That is certain; I admit it; and I know full well that to see a man of the common sort, an artisan will hardly raise his eyes from his work, whereas to see a great and prominent personage arrive in a city, men leave workshops and stores empty. It ill befits anyone to make himself known save him who has qualities to be imitated, and whose life and opinions may serve as a model. In the greatness of their deeds Caesar and Xenophon had something to found and establish their narrative upon, as on a just and solid base. Desirable therefore would be the journals of Alexander the Great, and the commentaries that Augustus, ^CCato, ^ASulla, Brutus and others left about their deeds. People love and study the figures of such men, even in bronze and stone.

This remonstrance is very true, but it concerns me only very little:

> Only to friends do I recite, and on request,
> Not to all men, or everywhere. Some will not rest,
> And keep reciting in the Forum or the baths.[2]

I am not building here a statue to erect at the town crossroads, or in a church or a public square:

> ^BI do not aim to swell my page full-blown
> With windy trifles. . . .
> We two talk alone.[3]

^AThis is for a nook in a library, and to amuse a neighbor, a relative, a friend, who may take pleasure in associating and conversing with me again in this image. Others have

---

[3] Persius, *Satires*, v, 19–21.

[II:18] *Of Giving the Lie*

parler d'eux pour y avoir trouvé le sujet digne et riche; moi, au rebours, pour l'avoir trouvé si stérile et si maigre qu'il n'y peut échoir soupçon d'ostentation.

ᶜJe juge volontiers des actions d'autrui; des miennes, je donne peu à juger à cause de leur nihilité. ᴮJe ne trouve pas tant de bien en moi que je ne le puisse dire sans rougir.

ᴬQuel contentement me serait-ce d'ouïr ainsi quelqu'un qui me récitât les mœurs, le visage, la contenance, les paroles communes et les fortunes de mes ancêtres! Combien j'y serais attentif! Vraiment cela partirait d'une mauvaise nature d'avoir à mépris les portraits mêmes de nos amis et prédécesseurs, ᶜla forme de leurs vêtements et de leurs armes. J'en conserve l'écriture, le seing, des heures et une épée péculière qui leur a servi, et n'ai point chassé de mon cabinet des longues gaules que mon père portait ordinairement en la main. *Paterna vestis et annulus tanto charior est posteris, quanto erga parentes major affectus.*[4]

ᴬSi toutefois ma postérité est d'autre appétit, j'aurai bien de quoi me revancher: car ils ne sauraient faire moins de compte de moi que j'en ferai d'eux en ce temps-là. Tout le commerce que j'ai en ceci avec le public, c'est que j'emprunte les outils de son écriture, plus soudaine et plus aisée. En récompense, ᶜj'empêcherai peut-être que quelque coin de beurre ne se fonde au marché.

ᴬNe toga cordyllis, ne penula desit olivis;[5]
ᴮEt laxas scombris sæpe dabo tunicas.[6]

---

[4] St. Augustine, *City of God*, I, xiii.
[5] Martial, *Epigrams*, XIII, i, 1.

taken courage to speak of themselves because they found the subject worthy and rich; I, on the contrary, because I have found mine so barren and so meager that no suspicion of ostentation can fall upon my plan.

^CI willingly judge the actions of others; I give little chance to judge mine because of their nullity. ^BI do not find so much good in myself that I cannot tell it without blushing.

^AWhat a satisfaction it would be to me to hear someone tell me, in this way, of the habits, the face, the expression, the favorite remarks, and the fortunes of my ancestors! How attentive I would be! Truly it would spring from a bad nature to be scornful of even the portraits of our friends and predecessors, ^Cthe form of their clothes and their armor. I keep their handwriting, their seal, the breviary and a peculiar sword that they used, and I have not banished from my study some long sticks that my father ordinarily carried in his hand. *A father's coat and his ring are the more dear to his children the more they loved him.*[4]

^AHowever, if my descendants have other tastes, I shall have ample means for revenge: for they could not possibly have less concern about me than I shall have about them by that time. All the contact I have with the public in this book is that I borrow their tools of printing, as being swifter and easier. In recompense, ^Cperhaps I shall keep some pat of butter from melting in the market place.

^ALest tunny-fish and olives lack a robe.[5]
^BTo mackerel I'll often give a shirt.[6]

---

6 Catullus, *Poems*, xcv, 8.

^cEt quand personne ne me lira, ai-je perdu mon temps de m'être entretenu tant d'heures oisives à pensements si utiles et agréables? Moulant sur moi cette figure, il m'a fallu si souvent dresser et composer pour m'extraire, que le patron s'en est fermi et aucunement formé soi-même. Me peignant pour autrui, je me suis peint en moi de couleurs plus nettes que n'étaient les miennes premières. Je n'ai pas plus fait mon livre que mon livre m'a fait; livre consubstantiel à son auteur, d'une occupation propre, membre de ma vie; non d'une occupation et fin tierce et étrangère comme tous autres livres. Ai-je perdu mon temps de m'être rendu compte de moi si continuellement, si curieusement? Car ceux qui se repassent par fantaisie seulement et par langue quelque heure ne s'examinent pas si primement, ni ne se pénètrent, comme celui qui en fait son étude, son ouvrage et son métier, qui s'engage à un registre de durée, de toute sa foi, de toute sa force.

Les plus délicieux plaisirs, si se digèrent-ils au dedans, fuient à laisser trace de soi, et fuient la vue non seulement du peuple, mais d'un autre.

Combien de fois m'a cette besogne diverti de cogitations ennuyeuses! et doivent être comptées pour ennuyeuses toutes les frivoles. Nature nous a étrennés d'une large faculté à nous entretenir à part, et nous y appelle souvent pour nous apprendre que nous nous devons en partie à la société, mais en la meilleure partie à nous. Aux fins de ranger ma fantaisie à rêver même par quelque ordre et projet, et la garder de se perdre et extravaguer au vent, il n'est que de donner corps et mettre en registre tant de menues pensées qui se présentent à elle. J'écoute à mes rêveries parce que j'ai à les enrôler. Quant de fois, étant

^cAnd if no one reads me, have I wasted my time, entertaining myself for so many idle hours with such useful and agreeable thoughts? In modeling this figure upon myself, I have had to fashion and compose myself so often to bring myself out, that the model itself has to some extent grown firm and taken shape. Painting myself for others, I have painted my inward self with colors clearer than my original ones. I have no more made my book than my book has made me—a book consubstantial with its author, concerned with my own self, an integral part of my life; not concerned with some third-hand, extraneous purpose, like all other books. Have I wasted my time by taking stock of myself so continually, so carefully? For those who go over themselves only in their minds and occasionally in speech do not penetrate to essentials in their examination as does a man who makes that his study, his work, and his trade, who binds himself to keep an enduring account, with all his faith, with all his strength.

Indeed, the most delightful pleasures are digested inwardly, avoid leaving any traces, and avoid the sight not only of the public but of any other person.

How many times has this task diverted me from annoying cogitations! And all frivolous ones should be counted as annoying. Nature has made us a present of a broad capacity for entertaining ourselves apart, and often calls us to do so, to teach us that we owe ourselves in part to society, but in the best part to ourselves. In order to train my fancy even to dream with some order and purpose, and in order to keep it from losing its way and roving with the wind, there is nothing like embodying and registering all the little thoughts that come to it. I listen to my reveries

marri de quelque action que la civilité et la raison me prohibaient de reprendre à découvert, m'en suis-je ici dégorgé, non sans dessein de publique instruction! Et si ces verges poétiques—

> Zon dessus l'œil, zon sur le groin,
> Zon sur le dos du Sagouin! [7]

—s'impriment encore mieux en papier qu'en la chair vive. Quoi si je prête un peu plus attentivement l'oreille aux livres depuis que je guette si j'en pourrai friponner quelque chose de quoi émailler ou étayer le mien?

Je n'ai aucunement étudié pour faire un livre; mais j'ai aucunement étudié pour ce que je l'avais fait; si c'est aucunement étudier qu'effleurer et pincer par la tête ou par les pieds tantôt un auteur, tantôt un autre; nullement pour former mes opinions, oui pour les assister piéça formées, seconder et servir.

ᴬMais à qui croirons-nous parlant de soi en une saison si gâtée? vu qu'il en est peu ou point à qui nous puissions croire parlant d'autrui, où il y a moins d'intérêt à mentir. Le premier trait de la corruption des mœurs c'est le bannissement de la vérité: car comme disait Pindare, l'être véritable est le commencement d'une grande vertu, ᶜet le premier article que Platon demande au gouverneur de sa république. ᴬNotre vérité de maintenant ce n'est pas ce qui est, mais ce qui se persuade à autrui: comme nous appelons monnaie non celle qui est loyale seulement, mais la

---

[7] Marot, "Epître de Fripelipes, valet de Marot, à Sagon," 211–2. Sagon was a hostile versifier; *sagouin* is a kind of monkey. Marot does not pass up this chance.

because I have to record them. How many times, irritated by some action that civility and reason kept me from reproving openly, have I disgorged it here, not without ideas of instructing the public! And indeed, these poetic lashes—

> Bang in the eye, bang on the snout,
> Bang on the back of the apish lout! [7]

—imprint themselves even better on paper than on living flesh. What if I lend a slightly more attentive ear to books, since I have been lying in wait to pilfer something from them to adorn or support my own?

I have not studied one bit to make a book; but I have studied a bit because I had made it, if it is studying a bit to skim over and pinch, by his head or his feet, now one author, now another; not at all to form my opinions, but certainly to assist, second, and serve those which I formed long ago.

ᴬBut whom shall we believe when he talks about himself, in so corrupt an age, seeing that there are few or none whom we can believe when they speak of others, where there is less incentive for lying? The first stage in the corruption of morals is the banishment of truth; for, as Pindar said, to be truthful is the beginning of a great virtue, ᶜand is the first article that Plato requires in the governor of his Republic. ᴬOur truth of nowadays is not what is, but what others can be convinced of; just as we call "money" not only that which is legal, but also any counterfeit that will

[II:18] *Of Giving the Lie*

fausse aussi qui a mise. Notre nation est de longtemps reprochée de ce vice: car Salvianus Massiliensis, qui était du temps de Valentinian l'Empereur, dit qu'aux Français le mentir et se parjurer n'est pas vice, mais une façon de parler. Qui voudrait enchérir sur ce témoignage, il pourrait dire que ce leur est à présent vertu. On s'y forme, on s'y façonne, comme à un exercice d'honneur; car la dissimulation est des plus notables qualités de ce siècle.

Ainsi, j'ai souvent considéré d'où pouvait naître cette coutume que nous observons si religieusement, de nous sentir plus aigrement offensés du reproche de ce vice, qui nous est si ordinaire, que de nul autre; et que ce soit l'extrême injure qu'on nous puisse faire de parole, que de nous reprocher la mensonge. Sur cela je trouve qu'il est naturel de se défendre le plus des défauts de quoi nous sommes le plus entachés. Il semble qu'en nous ressentant de l'accusation et nous en émouvant, nous nous déchargeons aucunement de la coulpe; si nous l'avons par effet, au moins nous la condamnons par apparence.

ᴮSerait-ce pas aussi que ce reproche semble envelopper la couardise et lâcheté de cœur? En est-il de plus expresse que se dédire de sa parole? quoi, se dédire de sa propre science?

ᴬC'est un vilain vice que le mentir, et qu'un ancien peint bien honteusement quand il dit que c'est donner témoignage de mépriser Dieu, et quand et quand de craindre les hommes.[8] Il n'est pas possible d'en représenter plus richement l'horreur, la vileté et le dérèglement. Car que peut-on imaginer plus vilain que d'être couard à

---

[8] Plutarch, *Lives*, "Lysander."

pass. Our nation has long been reproached for this vice; for Salvianus of Massilia, who lived in the time of the Emperor Valentinian, says that to the French lying and perjury are not a vice but a manner of speaking. If a man wanted to go this testimony one better, he could say that it is now a virtue to them. Men form and fashion themselves for it as for an honorable practice; for dissimulation is among the most notable qualities of this century.

Thus I have often considered what could be the source of that custom, which we observe so religiously, of feeling more bitterly offended when reproached with this vice, which is so common among us, than with any other; and that it should be the worst insult that can be given us in words, to reproach us with lying. On that, I find that it is natural to defend ourselves most for the defects with which we are most besmirched. It seems that in resenting the accusation and growing excited about it, we unburden ourselves to some extent of the guilt; if we have it in fact, at least we condemn it in appearance.

ᴮWould it not also be that this reproach seems to involve cowardice and lack of courage? Is there any more obvious cowardice than to deny our own word? Worse yet, to deny what we know?

ᴬLying is an ugly vice, which an ancient paints in most shameful colors when he says that it is giving evidence of contempt for God, and at the same time of fear of men.⁸ It is not possible to represent more vividly the horror, the vileness, and the profligacy of it. For what can you imagine uglier than being a coward toward men and bold to-

l'endroit des hommes et brave à l'endroit de Dieu? Notre intelligence se conduisant par la seule voie de la parole, celui qui la fausse trahit la société publique. C'est le seul outil par le moyen duquel se communiquent nos volontés et nos pensées, c'est le truchement de notre âme: s'il nous faut, nous ne nous tenons plus, nous ne nous entreconnaissons plus. S'il nous trompe, il rompt tout notre commerce et dissout toutes les liaisons de notre police.

^BCertaines nations des nouvelles Indes (on n'a que faire d'en remarquer les noms, ils ne sont plus; car jusqu'à l'entier abolissement des noms et ancienne connaissance des lieux s'est étendue la désolation de cette conquête, d'un merveilleux exemple et inouï) offraient à leurs dieux du sang humain, mais non autre que tiré de leur langue et oreilles, pour expiation du péché de la mensonge, tant ouïe que prononcée.

^ACe bon compagnon de Grèce [9] disait que les enfants s'amusent par les osselets, les hommes par les paroles.

Quant aux divers usages de nos démentirs, et les lois de notre honneur en cela, et les changements qu'elles ont reçus, je remets à une autre fois d'en dire ce que j'en sais; et apprendrai cependant, si je puis, en quel temps prit commencement cette coutume de si exactement peser et mesurer les paroles et d'y attacher notre honneur. Car il est aisé à juger qu'elle n'était pas anciennement entre les Romains et les Grecs. Et m'a semblé souvent nouveau et étrange de les voir se démentir et s'injurier sans entrer pourtant en querelle. Les lois de leur devoir prenaient quelque autre voie que les nôtres. On appelle Cæsar tan-

---

[9] Lysander (in Plutarch's *Lives*).

ward God? Since mutual understanding is brought about solely by way of words, he who breaks his word betrays human society. It is the only instrument by means of which our wills and thoughts communicate, it is the interpreter of our soul. If it fails us, we have no more hold on each other, no more knowledge of each other. If it deceives us, it breaks up all our relations and dissolves all the bonds of our society.

ᴮCertain nations of the new Indies (there is no use mentioning their names, which are no more; for the desolation of their conquest—a monstrous and unheard-of case—has extended even to the entire abolition of the names and former knowledge of the places) offered to their gods human blood, but only such as was drawn from their tongue and ears, in expiation of the sin of falsehood, heard as well as uttered.

ᴬThat worthy fellow from Greece [9] used to say that children play with knucklebones, men with words.

As for the varied etiquette of giving the lie, and our laws of honor in that matter, and the changes they have undergone, I shall put off till another time telling what I know about that, and shall meanwhile learn, if I can, at what time the custom began of weighing and measuring words so exactly, and attaching our honor to them. For it is easy to see that it did not exist in olden times among the Romans and the Greeks. And it has often seemed to me novel and strange to see them giving each other the lie and insulting each other, without having a quarrel over it. The laws of their duty took some other path than ours.

tôt voleur, tantôt ivrogne, à sa barbe. Nous voyons la liberté des invectives qu'ils font les uns contre les autres, je dis les plus grands chefs de guerre de l'une et l'autre nation, où les paroles se revanchent seulement par les paroles et ne se tirent à autre conséquence.

37   De la ressemblance des enfants aux pères [1]

ᴬCe fagotage de tant de diverses pièces se fait en cette condition, que je n'y mets la main que lorsqu'une trop lâche oisiveté me presse, et non ailleurs que chez moi. Ainsi il s'est bâti à diverses poses et intervalles, comme les occasions me détiennent ailleurs parfois plusieurs mois. Au demeurant, je ne corrige point mes premières imaginations par les secondes; ᶜoui à l'aventure quelque mot, mais pour diversifier, non pour ôter. ᴬJe veux représenter le progrès de mes humeurs, et qu'on voie chaque pièce en sa naissance. Je prendrais plaisir d'avoir commencé plus tôt et à reconnaître le train de mes mutations. Un valet qui me servait à les écrire sous moi pensa faire un grand butin de m'en dérober plusieurs pièces choisies à sa poste. Cela me console qu'il n'y fera pas plus de gain que j'y ai fait de perte.

Je me suis envieilli de sept ou huit ans depuis que je commençai: ce n'a pas été sans quelque nouvel acquêt.

---

[1] Several statements of Montaigne's date this essay in 1579–80, probably during that winter.

Caesar is called now a robber, now a drunkard, to his face. We see how free are the invectives they use against each other, I mean the greatest warlords of both nations, where words are avenged merely by words, and do not lead to other consequences.

37   Of the Resemblance of Children to Fathers[1]

ᴬThis bundle of so many disparate pieces is being composed in this manner: I set my hand to it only when pressed by too unnerving an idleness, and nowhere but at home. Thus it has built itself up with diverse interruptions and intervals, as occasions sometimes detain me elsewhere for several months. Moreover, I do not correct my first imaginings by my second—ᶜwell, yes, perhaps a word or so, but only to vary, not to delete. ᴬI want to represent the course of my humors, and I want people to see each part at its birth. It would give me pleasure to have begun earlier, and to be able to trace the course of my mutations. A valet who served me by writing at my dictation thought he had made a rich booty by stealing from me several pieces chosen to his taste. It consoles me that he will gain no more by it than I have lost.

I have grown seven or eight years older since I began: not without some new acquisition. I have in that time be-

J'y ai pratiqué la colique par la libéralité des ans. Leur commerce et longue conversation ne se passe aisément sans quelque tel fruit. Je voudrais bien, de plusieurs autres présents qu'ils ont à faire à ceux qui les hantent longtemps, qu'ils en eussent choisi quelqu'un qui m'eût été plus acceptable: car ils ne m'en eussent su faire que j'eusse en plus grande horreur, dès mon enfance; c'était à point nommé, de tous les accidents de la vieillesse, celui que je craignais le plus. J'avais pensé maintes fois à part moi que j'allais trop avant et qu'à faire un si long chemin je ne faudrais pas de m'engager enfin en quelque malplaisant rencontre. Je sentais et protestais assez qu'il était heure de partir, et qu'il fallait trancher la vie dans le vif et dans le sein, suivant la règle des chirurgiens quand ils ont à couper quelque membre; ᶜqu'à celui qui ne la rendait à temps, nature avait accoutumé faire payer de bien rudes usures. ᴬMais c'étaient vaines propositions. Il s'en fallait tant que j'en fusse prêt lors, qu'en dix-huit mois ou environ qu'il y a que je suis en ce malplaisant état, j'ai déjà appris à m'y accommoder. J'entre déjà en composition de ce vivre coliqueux; j'y trouve de quoi me consoler et de quoi espérer. Tant les hommes sont acoquinés à leur être misérable, qu'il n'est si rude condition qu'ils n'acceptent pour s'y conserver! . . .

Les souffrances qui nous touchent simplement par l'âme m'affligent beaucoup moins qu'elles ne font la plupart des autres hommes: partie par jugement (car le monde estime plusieurs choses horribles, ou évitables au prix de la vie, qui me sont à peu près indifférentes), partie par une complexion stupide et insensible que j'ai aux

come acquainted with the kidney stone through the liberality of the years. Familiarity and long acquaintance with
them do not readily pass without some such fruit. I could
wish that, out of many other presents that they reserve for
those who frequent them long, they had chosen one that
would have been more acceptable to me. For they could
not have given me one that I had had in greater horror
since my childhood. It was precisely, of all the accidents of
old age, the one I feared the most. I had thought to myself many times that I was going forward too far, and that
in making such a long journey I would not fail to get involved at last in some unpleasant encounter. I felt and
protested enough that it was time to leave, that I should
cut off life in the quick and in the breast, following the
rule of the surgeons when they have to cut off some limb;
^cthat from the man who did not pay back on time, nature
was accustomed to exact a very stiff usury. ^ABut those
were vain propositions. I was so far from being ready to
do that then, that in the eighteen months or thereabouts
that I have been in this unpleasant state, I have already
learned to adapt myself to it. I am already growing reconciled to this colicky life; I find in it food for consolation
and hope. So enthralled are men by their wretched existence, that there is no condition so harsh that they will not
accept it to keep alive. . . .

The sufferings that affect us simply through the soul
afflict me much less than they do most other men. Partly
through judgment; for the world considers many things
horrible or to be avoided at the cost of life, which are almost indifferent to me. Partly through a stupid and insensible disposition that I have toward accidents that do

accidents qui ne donnent à moi de droit fil; laquelle complexion j'estime l'une des meilleures pièces de ma naturelle condition. Mais les souffrances vraiment essentielles et corporelles, je les goûte bien vivement. Si est-ce pourtant que, les prévoyant autrefois d'une vue faible, délicate et amollie par la jouissance de cette longue et heureuse santé et repos que Dieu m'a prêté la meilleure part de mon âge, je les avais conçues par imagination si insupportables qu'à la vérité j'en avais plus de peur que je n'y ai trouvé de mal: par où j'augmente toujours cette croyance que la plupart des facultés de notre âme, ᶜcomme nous les employons, ᴬtroublent plus le repos de la vie qu'elles n'y servent.

Je suis aux prises avec la pire de toutes les maladies,[2] la plus soudaine, la plus douloureuse, la plus mortelle et la plus irrémédiable. J'en ai déjà essayé cinq ou six bien longs accès et pénibles; toutefois ou je me flatte, ou encore y a-t-il en cet état de quoi se soutenir, à qui a l'âme déchargée de la crainte de la mort et déchargée des menaces, conclusions et conséquences de quoi la médecine nous entête. Mais l'effet même de la douleur n'a pas cette aigreur si âpre et si poignante qu'un homme rassis en doive entrer en rage et en désespoir. J'ai au moins ce profit de la colique que ce que je n'avais encore pu sur moi pour me concilier du tout et m'accointer à la mort, elle le parfera; car d'autant plus elle me pressera et importunera, d'autant moins me sera la mort à craindre. J'avais déjà gagné cela, de ne tenir à la vie que par la vie seulement. Elle dénouera

---

[2] In an early essay not given here, "Coutume de l'île de Céa" ("A Custom of the Island of Cea": ii:3), Montaigne had quoted Pliny

not come to me head-on—which disposition I consider one of the best parts of my natural condition. But the really essential and bodily sufferings I feel very keenly. And yet for all that, foreseeing them in other days with a feeble, delicate vision that was softened by the enjoyment of that long and happy health and repose that God lent me for the better part of my life, I had conceived them in imagination so unendurable that in truth I had more fear of them than I have found pain in them. Wherefore I continue to confirm this belief, that most of the faculties of our soul, ᶜas we employ them, ᴬtrouble the repose of life more than they serve it.

I am at grips with the worst of all maladies,[2] the most sudden, the most painful, the most mortal, and the most irremediable. I have already experienced five or six very long and painful bouts of it. However, either I flatter myself or else there is even in this condition enough to bear up a man whose soul is unburdened of the fear of death and unburdened of the threats, sentences, and consequences which medicine dins into our ears. But the very impact of the pain has not such sharp and piercing bitterness as to drive a well-poised man to madness or despair. I have at least this profit from the stone, that it will complete what I have still not been able to accomplish in myself and reconcile and familiarize me completely with death: for the more my illness oppresses and bothers me, the less will death be something for me to fear. I had already accomplished this: to hold to life only by life alone.

---

as saying that there were three illnesses so painful as to justify suicide, and that the worst of these was the kidney stone.

[II:37] *Children and Fathers*

encore cette intelligence; et Dieu veuille qu'enfin, si son
âpreté vient à surmonter mes forces, elle ne me rejette à
l'autre extrémité, non moins vicieuse, d'aimer et désirer à
mourir!

Summum nec metuas diem, nec optes.[3]

Ce sont deux passions à craindre, mais l'une a son remède
bien plus prêt que l'autre.

Au demeurant, j'ai toujours trouvé ce précepte céré-
monieux, qui ordonne ^csi rigoureusement et exactement
^Ade tenir bonne contenance et un maintien dédaigneux et
posé à la tolérance des maux. Pourquoi la philosophie, qui
ne regarde que le vif et les effets, se va-t-elle amusant à
ces apparences externes? ^CQu'elle laisse ce soin aux farceurs
et maîtres de rhétorique qui font tant d'état de nos gestes.
Qu'elle condone hardiment au mal cette lâcheté voyelle,
si elle n'est ni cordiale ni stomacale; et prête ces plaintes
volontaires au genre des soupirs, sanglots, palpitations,
pâlissements que nature a mis hors de notre puissance.
Pourvu que le courage soit sans effroi, les paroles sans
désespoir, qu'elle se contente! Qu'importe que nous tordons
les bras, pourvu que nous ne tordons nos pensées! Elle
nous dresse pour nous, non pour autrui; pour être, non
pour sembler. ^AQu'elle s'arrête à gouverner notre entendement qu'elle a pris à instruire; qu'aux efforts de la colique,
elle maintienne l'âme capable de se reconnaître, de suivre

---

[3] Martial, *Epigrams*, x, xlvii, 13.

My illness will undo even this bond; and God grant that in the end, if its sharpness comes to surpass my powers, it may not throw me back to the other extreme, which is no less a vice, of loving and desiring to die.

Fear not the final day, nor wish for it.[3]

Those are two passions to fear, but one has its remedy much more ready than the other.

Moreover, I have always considered that precept formalistic which ᶜso rigorously and precisely ᴬorders us to maintain a good countenance and a disdainful and composed bearing in the endurance of pain. Why does philosophy, which has regard only for real substance and actions, go playing around with these external appearances? ᶜLet her leave this care to the actors and the teachers of rhetoric who set so much store by our gestures. Let her boldly grant to pain this cowardice in the voice, provided it is neither in the heart nor in the stomach, and let her assign these voluntary complaints to the category of the sighs, sobs, palpitations, and pallors that nature has put out of our control. Provided the heart is without fear, the words without despair, let her be content! What matter if we twist our arms, provided we do not twist our thoughts? Philosophy trains us for ourselves, not for others; for being, not for seeming. ᴬLet her confine herself to governing our understanding, which she has taken upon herself to instruct. In the attacks of the stone, let her preserve the soul's capacity for knowing itself, for following its accus-

son train accoutumé; combattant la douleur et la soutenant, non se prosternant honteusement à ses pieds; émue et échauffée du combat, non abattue et renversée; ^ccapable de commerce, capable d'entretien jusqu'à certaine mesure.

^AEn accidents si extrêmes c'est cruauté de requérir de nous une démarche si composée. Si nous avons beau jeu, c'est peu que nous ayons mauvaise mine. Si le corps se soulage en se plaignant, qu'il le fasse; si l'agitation lui plaît, qu'il se tourneboule et tracasse à sa fantaisie; s'il lui semble que le mal s'évapore aucunement (comme aucuns médecins disent que cela aide à la délivrance des femmes enceintes) pour pousser hors la voix avec plus grande violence, ou s'il en amuse son tourment, qu'il crie tout à fait. . . . Nous avons assez de travail du mal sans nous travailler à ces règles superflues.

Ce que je dis pour excuser ceux qu'on voit ordinairement se tempêter aux secousses et assauts de cette maladie. Car pour moi, je l'ai passée jusqu'à cette heure avec un peu meilleure contenance. Non pourtant que je me mette en peine pour maintenir cette décence extérieure, car je fais peu de compte d'un tel avantage, je prête en cela au mal autant qu'il veut; mais ou mes douleurs ne sont pas si excessives, ou j'y apporte plus de fermeté que le commun. Je me plains, je me dépite quand les aigres pointures me pressent, mais je n'en viens pas à me perdre. . . .

^cJe me tâte au plus épais du mal et ai toujours trouvé que j'étais capable de dire, de penser, de répondre aussi sainement qu'en une autre heure; mais non si constamment, la douleur me troublant et détournant. Quand on

tomed course, combating the pain and enduring it, not prostrating itself shamefully at its feet; stirred and heated by the combat, not beaten down and overthrown; ᶜcapable of communication and conversation to a certain degree.

ᴬIn such extreme accidents it is cruelty to require of us so composed a bearing. If we play a good game, it is a small matter that we make a bad face. If the body finds relief in complaining, let it do so. If it likes agitation, let it tumble and toss at its pleasure. If it thinks that the pain evaporates somewhat (as some doctors say that it helps the delivery of women with child) for crying out more violently, or if that distracts its torment, let it shout right out. . . . We have enough labor with the pain without laboring over these superfluous rules.

I say this to excuse those whom we see ordinarily crying out and storming in the shocks and attacks of this sickness. As for me, I have passed through it until now with a little better countenance. Not that I give myself trouble, however, to maintain this external decorum; for I take little account of such an advantage. In this respect I lend the pain as much as it likes. But either my pains are not so excessive, or I bring to them more firmness than most people. I complain, I fret when the sharp pains afflict me, but I do not come to the point of letting go of myself. . . .

ᶜI test myself in the thickest of the pain, and have always found that I was capable of speaking, thinking, and answering as sanely as at any other time, but not as steadily, being troubled and distracted by the pain. When I

me tient le plus atterré et que les assistants m'épargnent, j'essaie souvent mes forces et entame moi-même des propos les plus éloignés de mon état. Je puis tout par un soudain effort; mais ôtez-en la durée.

Ô que n'ai-je la faculté de ce songeur de Cicéron [4] qui, songeant embrasser une garce, trouva qu'il s'était déchargé de sa pierre emmi ses draps! Les miennes me dégarcent étrangement!

[A]Aux intervalles de cette douleur excessive, [c]que mes uretères languissent sans me poindre si fort, [A]je me remets soudain en ma forme ordinaire, d'autant que mon âme ne prend autre alarme que la sensible et corporelle; ce que je dois certainement au soin que j'ai eu à me préparer par discours à tels accidents. . . .

Je suis essayé pourtant un peu bien rudement pour un apprenti, et d'un changement bien soudain et bien rude, étant chu tout à coup d'une très douce condition de vie et très heureuse à la plus douloureuse et pénible qui se puisse imaginer: car outre que c'est une maladie bien fort à craindre d'elle-même, elle fait en moi ses commencements beaucoup plus âpres et difficiles qu'elle n'a accoutumé. Les accès me reprennent si souvent que je ne sens quasi plus d'entière santé. Je maintiens toutefois jusqu'à cette heure mon esprit en telle assiette que pourvu que j'y puisse apporter de la constance, je me trouve en assez meilleure condition de vie que mille autres qui n'ont ni fièvre ni mal que celui qu'ils se donnent eux-mêmes par la faute de leur discours. . . .

---

4 *De Divinatione,* II, lxix.

am thought to be the most stricken and those present are sparing me, I often test my powers, and myself broach subjects as remote as possible from my condition. I can do anything by a sudden effort; but don't make it last long.

Oh, why have I not the faculty of that dreamer in Cicero⁴ who, dreaming he was embracing a wench, found that he had discharged his stone in the sheets! Mine extraordinarily diswench me.

ᴬIn the intervals of this excessive pain, ᶜwhen my ureters are languid without stinging me so much, ᴬI promptly return to my natural condition, since my soul takes no other alarm than that which comes from the senses and the body; which I certainly owe to the care I have taken to prepare myself by reason for such accidents. . . .

I am tested, however, pretty roughly for a beginner, and by a very sudden and very rough change, having fallen all at once from a very gentle and very happy condition of life to the most painful and grievous that can be imagined. For besides its being a disease very much to be feared in itself, it is making its beginnings in me much sharper and harder than is customary. The attacks seize me so often that I hardly feel perfect health any more. Yet I have kept my mind, up to now, in such a state that, provided I can hold fast, I find myself in a considerably better condition of life than a thousand others, who have no fever or illness but what they give themselves by the fault of their reasoning. . . .

[II:37] *Children and Fathers*

Il est à croire que je dois à mon père cette qualité pierreuse, car il mourut merveilleusement affligé d'une grosse pierre qu'il avait en la vessie. Il ne s'aperçut de son mal que le soixante-septième an de son âge, et avant cela il n'en avait eu aucune menace ou ressentiment aux reins, aux côtes, ni ailleurs; et avait vécu jusque lors en une heureuse santé et bien peu sujette à maladies; et dura encore sept ans en ce mal, traînant une fin de vie bien douloureuse. J'étais né vingt-cinq ans et plus avant sa maladie, et durant le cours de son meilleur état, ^Ble troisième de ses enfants en rang de naissance.

^AOù se couvait tant de temps la propension à ce défaut? Et lorsqu'il était si loin du mal, cette légère pièce de sa substance de quoi il me bâtit, comment en portait-elle pour sa part une si grande impression? Et comment encore si couverte, que quarante-cinq ans après j'aie commencé à m'en ressentir, ^Bseul jusqu'à cette heure entre tant de frères et de sœurs, et tous d'une mère? ^AQui m'éclaircira de ce progrès, je le croirai d'autant d'autres miracles qu'il voudra; pourvu que, comme ils font, il ne me donne pas en payement une doctrine beaucoup plus difficile et fantastique que n'est la chose même.

Que les médecins excusent un peu ma liberté; car par cette même infusion et insinuation fatale j'ai reçu la haine et le mépris de leur doctrine: cette antipathie que j'ai à leur art m'est héréditaire. Mon père a vécu soixante et quatorze ans, mon aïeul soixante et neuf, mon bisaïeul près de quatre-vingts, sans avoir goûté aucune sorte de médecine; et entre eux tout ce qui n'était de l'usage ordinaire tenait lieu de drogue. La médecine se forme par exemples

It is probable that I owe this stony propensity to my father, for he died extraordinarily afflicted with a large stone he had in his bladder. He did not perceive his disease until his sixty-seventh year, and before that he had had no threat or symptom of it, in his loins, his sides, or elsewhere. And he had lived until then in a happy state of health, and very little subject to diseases; and he lasted seven years more with this ailment, painfully dragging out the last years of his life. I was born twenty-five years and more before his illness, at a time when he enjoyed his best health, Bthe third of his children in order of birth.

AWhere was the propensity to this infirmity hatching all this time? And when he was so far from the ailment, how did this slight bit of his substance, with which he made me, bear so great an impression of it for its share? And moreover, how did it remain so concealed that I began to feel it forty-five years later, Bthe only one to this hour out of so many brothers and sisters, and all of the same mother? AIf anyone will enlighten me about this process, I will believe him about as many other miracles as he wants; provided he does not palm off on me some explanation much more difficult and fantastic than the thing itself.

Let the doctors excuse my liberty a bit, for by this same fatal infusion and insinuation I have received my hatred and contempt for their teachings. The antipathy I have for their art is hereditary with me. My father lived seventy-four years, my grandfather sixty-nine, my great-grandfather nearly eighty, without having tasted any sort of medicine; and as far as they were concerned, whatever was not in ordinary use passed as a drug. Medicine is based

[II:37] *Children and Fathers*

et expérience; aussi fait mon opinion. Voilà pas une bien expresse expérience et bien avantageuse? . . .

Il est possible que j'ai reçu d'eux cette dyspathie naturelle à la médecine; mais s'il n'y eût eu que cette considération, j'eusse essayé de la forcer. Car toutes ces conditions qui naissent en nous sans raison, elles sont vicieuses; c'est une espèce de maladie qu'il faut combattre. Il peut être que j'y avais cette propension, mais je l'ai appuyée et fortifiée par les discours qui m'en ont établi l'opinion que j'en ai. . . .

cComme nous appelons justice le pâtissage des premières lois qui nous tombent en main et leur dispensation et pratique, souvent très inepte et très inique; et comme ceux qui s'en moquent et qui l'accusent n'entendent pas pourtant injurier cette noble vertu, ains condamner seulement l'abus et profanation de ce sacré titre; de même en la médecine, j'honore bien ce glorieux nom, sa proposition, sa promesse si utile au genre humain; mais ce qu'il désigne entre nous, je ne l'honore ni l'estime.

AEn premier lieu, l'expérience me le fait craindre; car de ce que j'ai de connaissance, je ne vois nulle race de gens si tôt malade et si tard guérie que celle qui est sous la juridiction de la médecine. . . .

Les promesses mêmes de la médecine sont incroyables: car ayant à pourvoir à divers accidents et contraires, qui nous pressent souvent ensemble et qui ont une relation quasi nécessaire, comme la chaleur du foie et froideur de l'estomac, ils nous vont persuadant que, de leurs ingrédients, celui-ci échauffera l'estomac, cet autre rafraîchira le foie; l'un a la charge d'aller droit aux reins, voire jusqu'à

on examples and experience; so is my opinion. Isn't that a very clear-cut and very advantageous experience? . . .

It is possible that I received from them this natural antipathy to medicine; but had there been only this consideration, I would have tried to overcome it. For all those predispositions that are born in us without reason are bad; they are a kind of disease that we must combat. It may be that I had this propensity, but I have supported and fortified it by arguments which have confirmed me in my opinion. . . .

^cAs we call "justice" the hodgepodge of the first laws that fall into our hands, and their application and practice, often very inept and very iniquitous; and as those who ridicule it and accuse it do not thereby intend to malign that noble virtue, but only to condemn the abuse and profanation of that sacred title; so in medicine I do indeed honor that glorious name, its purpose, its promise, so useful to the human race; but what it designates among us I neither honor nor esteem.

^AIn the first place, experience makes me fear it; for as far as my knowledge goes, I see no group of people so soon sick and so late cured as those who are under the jurisdiction of medicine. . . .

The very promises of medicine are incredible. For, having to provide against different and contrary accidents, which often afflict us at the same time and have an almost necessary relation, like heat in the liver and cold in the stomach, they try to persuade us that of their ingredients this one will warm the stomach, that other one will cool the liver. One has its commission to go straight to the kidneys, indeed even to the bladder, without dispersing its

la vessie, sans étaler ailleurs ses opérations, et conservant ses forces et sa vertu en ce long chemin et plein de destorbiers, jusqu'au lieu au service duquel il est destiné par sa propriété occulte; l'autre asséchera le cerveau; celui-là humectera le poumon.

De tout cet amas ayant fait une mixtion de breuvage, n'est-ce pas quelque espèce de rêverie d'espérer que ces vertus s'aillent divisant et triant de cette confusion et mélange pour courir à charges si diverses? Je craindrais infiniment qu'elles perdissent ou échangeassent leurs étiquettes et troublassent leurs quartiers. Et qui pourrait imaginer que, en cette confusion liquide, ces facultés ne se corrompent, confondent et altèrent l'une l'autre? Quoi, que l'exécution de cette ordonnance dépend d'un autre officier, à la foi et merci duquel nous abandonnons encore un coup notre vie? . . .

Au demeurant, j'honore les médecins, non pas, suivant le précepte,[5] pour la nécessité . . . mais pour l'amour d'eux-mêmes, en ayant vu beaucoup d'honnêtes hommes et dignes d'être aimés. Ce n'est pas à eux que j'en veux, c'est à leur art; et ne leur donne pas grand blâme de faire leur profit de notre sottise, car la plupart du monde fait ainsi.

. . . J'imagine l'homme regardant autour de lui le nombre infini des choses: plantes, animaux, métaux.[6] Je ne sais par où lui faire commencer son essai; et quand la première fantaisie se jettera sur la corne d'un élan, à quoi

---

[5] *Honora medicum propter necessitatem* (Ecclesiasticus 38:1), which the Authorized Version renders: "Honour a physician with the honour due unto him for the uses which ye may have of him . . ."

operations elsewhere, and conserving its powers and its virtue in that long road full of disturbances, right to the spot to whose service it is destined by its occult property. Another will dry the brain, still another will moisten the lungs.

Once a potion has been concocted out of all this pile, is it not a sort of daydream to hope that these virtues will separate and sort themselves out of this mixture and confusion to go running on such different errands? I would be infinitely afraid that they might lose or exchange their tags and get their quarters mixed up. And who could suppose that in this liquid confusion these faculties would not corrupt, confuse, and alter one another? What of the fact that the carrying out of this prescription depends on another practitioner, to whose good faith and mercy we again abandon our lives? . . .

For the rest, I honor doctors, not, according to the precept,[5] out of necessity . . . but for love of themselves, having known many decent and lovable men among them. My quarrel is not with them but with their art, and I do not greatly blame them for making their profit of our stupidity, for most people do so.

. . . I imagine a man looking around him at the infinite number of things: plants, animals, metals.[6] I do not know where to have him begin his experiment; and even if his fancy lights first upon an elk's horn, which requires a very pliant and easy faith, he still finds himself just as perplexed

---

[6] Montaigne is here setting up an imaginary case of a patient (an elderly Frenchman of a melancholy temperament) looking for a cure for epilepsy.

[II:37] *Children and Fathers*

il faut prêter une croyance bien molle et aisée, il se trouve encore autant empêché en sa seconde opération. Il lui est proposé tant de maladies et tant de circonstances qu'avant qu'il soit venu à la certitude de ce point où doit joindre la perfection de son expérience, le sens humain y perd son latin. Et avant qu'il ait trouvé, parmi cette infinité de choses, que c'est cette corne; parmi cette infinité de maladies, l'épilepsie; tant de complexions, au mélancolique; tant de saisons, en hiver; tant de nations, au Français; tant d'âges, en la vieillesse; tant de mutations célestes, en la conjonction de Vénus et de Saturne; tant de parties du corps, au doigt: à tout cela n'étant guidé ni d'argument, ni de conjecture, ni d'exemple, ni d'inspiration divine, ains du seul mouvement de la fortune, il faudrait que ce fût par une fortune parfaitement artificielle, réglée et méthodique. Et puis quand la guérison fut faite, comment se peut-il assurer que ce ne fût que le mal fut arrivé à sa période, ou un effet du hasard, ou l'opération de quelque autre chose qu'il eût ou mangé, ou bu, ou touché ce jour-là, ou le mérite des prières de sa mère grand? Davantage, quand cette preuve aurait été parfaite, combien de fois fut-elle réitérée? et cette longue cordée de fortunes et de rencontres renfilée, pour en conclure une règle?

ᴮQuand elle sera conclue, par qui est-ce? De tant de millions il n'y a que trois hommes ⁷ qui se mêlent d'enregistrer leurs expériences. Le sort aura-t-il rencontré à point nommé l'un de ceux-ci? Quoi si un autre et si cent autres ont fait des expériences contraires? A l'aventure verrions-

---

⁷ Just what three Montaigne had in mind is not known.

about the next thing to do. He is faced with so many maladies and so many circumstances that before he has attained certainty about the point that the successful completion of his experiment should reach, human wit is wasting its ingenuity. And for him to find, among that infinite number of things, that the right one is this horn; among this infinite number of diseases, epilepsy; among so many constitutions, the melancholic; so many seasons, in winter; so many nations, the French; so many times of life, old age; so many celestial mutations, at the conjunction of Venus and Saturn; so many parts of the body, the finger—since he is guided in all this neither by theory, nor by conjecture, nor by example, nor by divine inspiration, but by the sole movement of fortune—he would have to be guided by a perfectly workmanlike, regular, and methodical fortune. And then, even if the cure should be performed, how can he be sure that this was not because the illness had reached its term, or a result of chance, or the effect of something else he had eaten or drunk or touched that day, or the merit of his grandmother's prayers? Moreover, even if this proof had been perfect, how many times was the experiment repeated? How many times was that long string of chances and coincidences strung again for a rule to be derived from it?

ᴮWhen the rule is derived, then by whom? Out of so many millions there are only three men ⁷ who have undertaken to record their experiences. Will chance have lighted precisely on one of these? What if another man, and a hundred others, have had contrary experiences? Perhaps

nous quelque lumière si tous les jugements et raisonnements des hommes nous étaient connus. Mais que trois témoins et trois docteurs régentent l'humain genre, ce n'est pas la raison: il faudrait que l'humaine nature les eût députés et choisis, et qu'ils fussent déclarés nos syndics ^Cpar expresse procuration. . . .

^AJ'ai pris la peine de plaider cette cause, que j'entends assez mal, pour appuyer un peu et conforter la propension naturelle contre les drogues et pratique de notre médecine, qui s'est dérivée en moi par mes ancêtres, afin que ce ne fût pas seulement une inclination stupide et téméraire, et qu'elle eût un peu plus de forme; et aussi que ceux qui me voient si ferme contre les enhortements et menaces qu'on me fait quand mes maladies me pressent ne pensent pas que ce soit simple opiniâtreté, ou qu'il y ait quelqu'un si fâcheux qui juge encore que ce soit quelque aiguillon de gloire: qui serait un désir bien asséné, de vouloir tirer honneur d'une action qui m'est commune avec mon jardinier et mon muletier. Certes je n'ai point le cœur si enflé ni si venteux qu'un plaisir solide, charnu et moelleux comme la santé, je l'allasse échanger pour un plaisir imaginaire, spirituel et aéré. La gloire, voire celle des quatre fils Aymon,[8] est trop cher achetée à un homme de mon humeur si elle lui coûte trois bons accès de colique. La santé, de par Dieu!

Ceux qui aiment notre médecine peuvent avoir aussi leurs considérations bonnes, grandes et fortes: je ne hais point les fantaisies contraires aux miennes. Il s'en faut

---

[8] The four sons of Aymon are the heroes of *Renaud de Montauban*, a twelfth-century *chanson de geste* named for one of the four.

we would see some light if all the judgments and reasonings of men were known to us. But that three witnesses, and they three physicians, should lay down the law to mankind is not reasonable, unless human nature had deputed and chosen them and declared them to be our arbiters ᶜby express power of attorney. . . .

ᴬI have taken the trouble to plead this cause, which I understand rather poorly, to support a little and strengthen the natural aversion to drugs and to the practice of our medicine which I have derived from my ancestors, so that it should not be merely a stupid and thoughtless inclination and should have a little more form; and also so that those who see me so firm against the exhortations and menaces that are made to me when my sickness afflicts me may not think that I am acting out of plain stubbornness; or in case there should be anyone so unpleasant as to judge that I am spurred by vainglory. That would be a well-aimed ambition, to want to derive honor from conduct that I have in common with my gardener and my muleteer! Surely my heart is not so inflated or windy that I would choose to exchange a solid, meaty, and marrowy pleasure like health for an imaginary, immaterial, and airy pleasure. Glory, even that of the four sons of Aymon,⁸ is bought too dear by a man of my humor if it costs him three good attacks of colic. Health, in God's name!

Those who love our medicine may also have their own good, great, and strong considerations. I do not at all hate opinions contrary to mine. I am so far from being vexed to

tant que je m'effarouche de voir de la discordance de mes jugements à ceux d'autrui et que je me rende incompatible à la société des hommes pour être d'autre sens et parti que le mien, qu'au rebours, comme c'est la plus générale façon que nature ait suivie que la variété, ^cet plus aux esprits qu'aux corps, d'autant qu'ils sont de substance plus souple et susceptible de plus de formes, ^Aje trouve bien plus rare de voir convenir nos humeurs et nos desseins. Et ne fut jamais au monde deux opinions pareilles, non plus que deux poils ou deux grains. Leur plus universelle qualité, c'est la diversité.

see discord between my judgments and others', and from making myself incompatible with the society of men because they are of a different sentiment and party from mine, that on the contrary, since variety is the most general fashion that nature has followed, ^cand more in minds than bodies, inasmuch as minds are of a substance suppler and susceptible of more forms, ^AI find it much rarer to see our humors and plans agree. And there were never in the world two opinions alike, any more than two hairs or two grains. Their most universal quality is diversity.

Livre Troisième

2   Du repentir [1]

^BLes autres forment l'homme; je le récite, et en représente un particulier bien mal formé et lequel, si j'avais à façonner de nouveau, je ferais vraiment bien autre qu'il n'est. Meshui c'est fait.

Or les traits de ma peinture ne fourvoient point, quoiqu'ils se changent et diversifient. Le monde n'est qu'une branloire pérenne. Toutes choses y branlent sans cesse: la terre, les rochers du Caucase, les pyramides d'Égypte, et du branle public et du leur. La constance même n'est autre chose qu'un branle plus languissant.

Je ne puis assurer mon objet. Il va trouble et chancelant, d'une ivresse naturelle. Je le prends en ce point, comme il est en l'instant que je m'amuse à lui. Je ne peins pas l'être. Je peins le passage: non un passage d'âge en autre, ou comme dit le peuple de sept en sept ans, mais de jour en jour, de minute en minute. Il faut accommoder mon histoire à l'heure. Je pourrai tantôt changer, non de fortune seulement, mais aussi d'intention. C'est un contrôle

---

[1] This chapter probably dates from 1585–88.

Book Three

2 *Of Repentance* [1]

[B]Others form man; I tell of him, and portray a particular one, very ill-formed, whom I should really make very different from what he is if I had to fashion him over again. But now it is done.

Now the lines of my painting do not go astray, though they change and vary. The world is but a perennial movement. All things in it are in constant motion—the earth, the rocks of the Caucasus, the pyramids of Egypt—both with the common motion and with their own. Stability itself is nothing but a more languid motion.

I cannot keep my subject still. It goes along befuddled and staggering, with a natural drunkenness. I take it in this condition, just as it is at the moment I give my attention to it. I do not portray being: I portray passing. Not the passing from one age to another, or, as the people say, from seven years to seven years, but from day to day, from minute to minute. My history needs to be adapted to the moment. I may presently change, not only by chance, but also by intention. This is a record of various and change-

de divers et muables accidents et d'imaginations irrésolues, et quand il y échoit, contraires: soit que je sois autre moi-même, soit que je saisisse les sujets par autres circonstances et considérations. Tant y a que je me contredis bien à l'aventure; mais la vérité, comme disait Démadès,[2] je ne la contredis point. Si mon âme pouvait prendre pied je ne m'essaierais pas, je me résoudrais: elle est toujours en apprentissage et en épreuve.

Je propose une vie basse et sans lustre, c'est tout un. On attache aussi bien toute la philosophie morale à une vie populaire et privée qu'à une vie de plus riche étoffe: chaque homme porte la forme entière de l'humaine condition.

^CLes auteurs se communiquent au peuple par quelque marque particulière et étrangère; moi le premier par mon être universel, comme Michel de Montaigne, non comme grammairien ou poète ou jurisconsulte. Si le monde se plaint de quoi je parle trop de moi, je me plains de quoi il ne pense seulement pas à soi.

^BMais est-ce raison que, si particulier en usage, je prétende me rendre public en connaissance? Est-il aussi raison que je produise au monde, où la façon et l'art ont tant de crédit et de commandement, des effets de nature crus et simples, et d'une nature encore bien faiblette? Est-ce pas faire une muraille sans pierre, ou chose semblable, que de bâtir des livres sans science et sans art? Les fantaisies de la musique sont conduites par art, les miennes par sort.

Au moins j'ai ceci selon la discipline, que jamais hom-

---

[2] Adapted from Plutarch, *Lives*, "Demosthenes."

able occurrences, and of irresolute and, when it so befalls, contradictory ideas: whether I am different myself, or whether I take hold of my subjects in different circumstances and aspects. So, all in all, I may indeed contradict myself now and then; but truth, as Demades [a] said, I do not contradict. If my mind could gain a firm footing, I would not make essays, I would make decisions; but it is always in apprenticeship and on trial.

I set forth a humble and inglorious life; that does not matter. You can tie up all moral philosophy with a common and private life just as well as with a life of richer stuff. Each man bears the entire form of man's estate.

cAuthors communicate with the people by some special extrinsic mark; I am the first to do so by my entire being, as Michel de Montaigne, not as a grammarian or a poet or a jurist. If the world complains that I speak too much of myself, I complain that it does not even think of itself.

BBut is it reasonable that I, so fond of privacy in actual life, should aspire to publicity in the knowledge of me? Is it reasonable too that I should set forth to the world, where fashioning and art have so much credit and authority, some crude and simple products of nature, and of a very feeble nature at that? Is it not making a wall without stone, or something like that, to construct books without knowledge and without art? Musical fancies are guided by art, mine by chance.

At least I have one thing according to the rules: that no

me ne traita sujet qu'il entendît ni connût mieux que je fais celui que j'ai entrepris, et qu'en celui-là je suis le plus savant homme qui vive; secondement, que jamais aucun [c]ne pénétra en sa matière plus avant, ni en éplucha plus particulièrement les membres et suites; et [B]n'arriva plus exactement et pleinement à la fin qu'il s'était proposé à sa besogne. Pour la parfaire, je n'ai besoin d'y apporter que la fidélité: celle-là y est, la plus sincère et pure qui se trouve. Je dis vrai, non pas tout mon soûl, mais autant que je l'ose dire; et l'ose un peu plus en vieillissant, car il semble que la coutume concède à cet âge plus de liberté de bavasser et d'indiscrétion à parler de soi. Il ne peut advenir ici ce que je vois advenir souvent, que l'artisan et sa besogne se contrarient: un homme de si honnête conversation a-t-il fait un si sot écrit? ou, des écrits si savants sont-ils partis d'un homme de si faible conversation?

[C]Qui a un entretien commun et ses écrits rares, c'est-à-dire que sa capacité est en lieu d'où il l'emprunte et non en lui. Un personnage savant n'est pas savant partout; mais le suffisant est partout suffisant, et à ignorer même.

[B]Ici nous allons conformément tout d'un train, mon livre et moi. Ailleurs on peut recommander et accuser l'ouvrage à part de l'ouvrier, ici non: qui touche l'un touche l'autre. Celui qui en jugera sans le connaître se fera plus de tort qu'à moi; celui qui l'aura connu m'a du tout satisfait. Heureux outre mon mérite si j'ai seulement cette part à l'approbation publique, que je fasse sentir aux gens d'entendement que j'étais capable de faire mon profit de la science si j'en eusse eu, et que je méritais que la mémoire me secourût mieux.

man ever treated a subject he knew and understood better than I do the subject I have undertaken; and that in this I am the most learned man alive. Secondly, that no man ever ᶜpenetrated more deeply into his material, or plucked its limbs and consequences cleaner, or ᴮreached more accurately and fully the goal he had set for his work. To accomplish it, I need only bring it to fidelity; and that is in it, as sincere and pure as can be found. I speak the truth, not my fill of it, but as much as I dare speak; and I dare to do so a little more as I grow old, for it seems that custom allows old age more freedom to prate and more indiscretion in talking about oneself. It cannot happen here as I see it happening often, that the craftsman and his work contradict each other: "Has a man whose conversation is so good written such a stupid book?" or "Have such learned writings come from a man whose conversation is so feeble?"

ᶜIf a man is commonplace in conversation and rare in writing, that means that his capacity is in the place from which he borrows it, and not in himself. A learned man is not learned in all matters; but the capable man is capable in all matters, even in ignorance.

ᴮIn this case we go hand in hand and at the same pace, my book and I. In other cases one may commend or blame the work apart from the workman; not so here; he who touches the one, touches the other. He who judges it without knowing it will injure himself more than me; he who has known it will completely satisfy me. Happy beyond my deserts if I have just this share of public approval, that I make men of understanding feel that I was capable of profiting by knowledge, if I had had any, and that I deserved better assistance from my memory.

Excusons ici ce que je dis souvent, que je me repens rarement ^Cet que ma conscience se contente de soi, non comme de la conscience d'un ange ou d'un cheval, mais comme de la conscience d'un homme; ^Bajoutant toujours ce refrain, non un refrain de cérémonie, mais de naïve et essentielle soumission: que je parle enquérant et ignorant, me rapportant de la résolution purement et simplement aux croyances communes et légitimes. Je n'enseigne point, je raconte.

Il n'est vice véritablement vice qui n'offense, et qu'un jugement entier n'accuse: car il a de la laideur et incommodité si apparente qu'à l'aventure ceux-là ont raison qui disent qu'il est principalement produit par bêtise et ignorance. Tant est-il malaisé d'imaginer qu'on le connaisse sans le haïr.

^CLa malice hume la plupart de son propre venin et s'en empoisonne. ^BLe vice laisse, comme un ulcère en la chair, une repentance en l'âme, qui toujours s'égratigne et s'ensanglante elle-même. Car la raison efface les autres tristesses et douleurs, mais elle engendre celle de la repentance, qui est plus griève, d'autant qu'elle naît au dedans; comme le froid et le chaud des fièvres est plus poignant que celui qui vient du dehors. Je tiens pour vices (mais chacun selon sa mesure) non seulement ceux que la raison et la nature condamnent, mais ceux aussi que l'opinion des hommes a forgés, voire fausse et erronée, si les lois et l'usage l'autorise.

Il n'est pareillement bonté qui ne réjouisse une nature bien née. Il y a certes je ne sais quelle congratulation de bien faire qui nous réjouit en nous-mêmes, et une fierté généreuse qui accompagne la bonne conscience. Une âme

Let me here excuse what I often say, that I rarely repent ^Cand that my conscience is content with itself—not as the conscience of an angel or a horse, but as the conscience of a man; ^Balways adding this refrain, not perfunctorily but in sincere and complete submission: that I speak as an ignorant inquirer, referring the decision purely and simply to the common and authorized beliefs. I do not teach, I tell.

There is no vice truly a vice which is not offensive, and which a sound judgment does not condemn; for its ugliness and painfulness is so apparent that perhaps the people are right who say it is chiefly produced by stupidity and ignorance. So hard it is to imagine anyone knowing it without hating it.

^CMalice sucks up the greater part of its own venom, and poisons itself with it. ^BVice leaves repentance in the soul, like an ulcer in the flesh, which is always scratching itself and drawing blood. For reason effaces other griefs and sorrows; but it engenders that of repentance, which is all the more grievous because it springs from within, as the cold and heat of fevers is sharper than that which comes from outside. I consider as vices (but each one according to its measure) not only those that reason and nature condemn, but also those that man's opinion has created, even false and erroneous opinion, if it is authorized by laws and customs.

There is likewise no good deed that does not rejoice a wellborn nature. Indeed there is a sort of gratification in doing good which makes us rejoice in ourselves, and a generous pride that accompanies a good conscience. A boldly

courageusement vicieuse se peut à l'aventure garnir de sécurité; mais de cette complaisance et satisfaction elle ne s'en peut fournir. Ce n'est pas un léger plaisir de se sentir préservé de la contagion d'un siècle si gâté, et de dire en soi: "Qui me verrait jusque dans l'âme, encore ne me trouverait-il coupable ni de l'affliction et ruine de personne, ni de vengeance ou d'envie, ni d'offense publique des lois, ni de nouveauté et de trouble, ni de faute à ma parole; et quoi que la licence du temps permît et apprît à chacun, si n'ai-je mis la main ni ès biens ni en la bourse d'homme français, et n'ai vécu que sur la mienne, non plus en guerre qu'en paix; ni ne me suis servi du travail de personne sans loyer." Ces témoignages de la conscience plaisent; et nous est grand bénéfice que cette éjouissance naturelle, et le seul payement qui jamais ne nous manque.

De fonder la récompense des actions vertueuses sur l'approbation d'autrui, c'est prendre un trop incertain et trouble fondement. °Signamment en un siècle corrompu et ignorant comme celui-ci, la bonne estime du peuple est injurieuse. A qui vous fiez-vous de voir ce qui est louable? Dieu me garde d'être homme de bien selon la description que je vois faire tous les jours par honneur à chacun de soi. *Quæ fuerant vitia, mores sunt.*[3]

Tels de mes amis ont parfois entrepris de me chapitrer et mercurialiser à cœur ouvert, ou de leur propre mouvement, ou semons par moi, comme d'un office qui, à une âme bien faite, non en utilité seulement mais en douceur aussi, surpasse tous les offices de l'amitié. Je l'ai tou-

---

[3] Seneca, *Epistles,* xxxix, 6.

vicious soul may perhaps arm itself with security, but with this complacency and satisfaction it cannot provide itself. It is no slight pleasure to feel oneself preserved from the contagion of so depraved an age, and to say to oneself: "If anyone should see right into my soul, still he would not find me guilty either of anyone's affliction or ruin, or of vengeance or envy, or of public offense against the laws, or of innovation and disturbance, or of failing in my word; and in spite of what the license of the times allows and teaches each man, still I have not put my hand either upon the property or into the purse of any Frenchman, and have lived only on my own, both in war and in peace; nor have I used any man's work without paying his wages." These testimonies of conscience give us pleasure; and this natural rejoicing is a great boon to us, and the only payment that never fails us.

To found the reward for virtuous actions on the approval of others is to choose too uncertain and shaky a foundation. ᶜEspecially in an age as corrupt and ignorant as this, the good opinion of the people is a dishonor. Whom can you trust to see what is praiseworthy? God keep me from being a worthy man according to the descriptions I see people every day giving of themselves in their own honor. *What were vices now are moral acts.*[3]

Certain of my friends have sometimes undertaken to call me on the carpet and lecture me unreservedly, either of their own accord or at my invitation, as a service which, to a well-formed soul, surpasses all the services of friendship, not only in usefulness, but also in pleasantness. I

jours accueilli des bras de la courtoisie et reconnaissance les plus ouverts. Mais, à en parler à cette heure en conscience, j'ai souvent trouvé en leurs reproches et louanges tant de fausse mesure que je n'eusse guère failli, de faillir, plutôt que de bien faire à leur mode.

ᴮNous autres principalement, qui vivons une vie privée qui n'est en montre qu'à nous, devons avoir établi un patron au dedans auquel toucher nos actions, et selon icelui nous caresser tantôt, tantôt nous châtier. J'ai mes lois et ma cour pour juger de moi, et m'y adresse plus qu'ailleurs. Je restreins bien selon autrui mes actions, mais je ne les étends que selon moi. Il n'y a que vous qui sache si vous êtes lâche et cruel, ou loyal et dévotieux; les autres ne vous voient point, ils vous devinent par conjectures incertaines; ils voient non tant votre nature que votre art. Par ainsi ne vous tenez pas à leur sentence; tenez-vous à la vôtre. ᶜTuo tibi judicio est utendum. . . .⁴ Virtutis et vitiorum grave ipsius conscientiæ pondus est: qua sublata, jacent omnia.⁵

ᴮMais ce qu'on dit, que la repentance suit de près le péché, ne semble pas regarder le péché qui est en son haut appareil, qui loge en nous comme en son propre domicile. On peut désavouer et dédire les vices qui nous surprennent et vers lesquels les passions nous emportent; mais ceux qui par longue habitude sont enracinés et ancrés en une volonté forte et vigoureuse ne sont sujets à contradiction. Le repentir n'est qu'une dédite de notre volonté

---

⁴ Cicero, *Tusculans*, ɪɪ, xxvi.

have always welcomed it with the wide-open arms of courtesy and gratitude. But to speak of it now in all conscience, I have often found in their reproach or praise such false measure that I would hardly have erred to err rather than to do good in their fashion.

ᴮThose of us especially who live a private life that is on display only to ourselves must have a pattern established within us by which to test our actions, and, according to this pattern, now pat ourselves on the back, now punish ourselves. I have my own laws and court to judge me, and I address myself to them more than anywhere else. To be sure, I restrain my actions according to others, but I extend them only according to myself. There is no one but yourself who knows whether you are cowardly and cruel, or loyal and devout. Others do not see you, they guess at you by uncertain conjectures; they see not so much your nature as your art. Therefore do not cling to their judgment; cling to your own. ᶜ*You must use your own judgment.* . . .⁴ *With regard to virtues and vices, your own conscience has great weight: take that away, and everything falls.*⁵

ᴮBut the saying that repentance follows close upon sin does not seem to consider the sin that is in robes of state, that dwells in us as in its own home. We can disown and retract the vices that take us by surprise, and toward which we are swept by passion; but those which by long habit are rooted and anchored in a strong and vigorous will cannot be denied. Repentance is nothing but a disavowal of our will and an opposition to our fancies, which

---

⁵ Cicero, *De Natura Deorum*, III, xxxv.

[III:2] *Of Repentance*

et opposition de nos fantaisies, qui nous promène à tous sens. Il fait désavouer à celui-là sa vertu passée et sa continence:

Quæ mens est hodie, cur eadem non puero fuit?
Vel cur his animis incolumes non redeunt genæ? [6]

C'est une vie exquise, celle qui se maintient en ordre jusqu'en son privé. Chacun peut avoir part au batelage et représenter un honnête personnage en l'échafaud; mais au dedans et en sa poitrine, où tout nous est loisible, où tout est caché—d'y être réglé, c'est le point. Le voisin degré, c'est de l'être en sa maison, en ses actions ordinaires, desquelles nous n'avons à rendre raison à personne; où il n'y a point d'étude, point d'artifice. Et pourtant Bias, peignant un excellent état de famille: "De laquelle," dit-il, "le maître soit tel au dedans, par lui-même, comme il est au dehors par la crainte de la loi et du dire des hommes." Et fut une digne parole de Julius Drusus aux ouvriers qui lui offraient pour trois mille écus mettre sa maison en tel point que ses voisins n'y auraient plus la vue qu'ils y avaient: "Je vous en donnerai," dit-il, "six mille, et faites que chacun y voie de toutes parts." On remarque avec honneur l'usage d'Agésilas, de prendre en voyageant son logis dans les églises, afin que le peuple et les dieux mêmes vissent dans ses actions privées. Tel a été miraculeux au monde, auquel sa femme et son valet n'ont rien vu seulement de remarquable. Peu d'hommes ont été admirés par leurs domestiques.

---

[6] Horace, *Odes*, IV, x, 7–8.

leads us about in all directions. It makes this man disown
his past virtue and his continence:

Why had I not in youth the mind I have today?
Or why, with old desires, have red cheeks flown away? [8]

It is a rare life that remains well ordered even in private.
Any man can play his part in the side show and represent
a worthy man on the boards; but to be disciplined within,
in his own bosom, where all is permissible, where all is
concealed—that's the point. The next step to that is to be
so in our own house, in our ordinary actions, for which we
need render account to no one, where nothing is studied or
artificial. And therefore Bias, depicting an excellent state
of family life, says it is one in which the master is the
same within, by his own volition, as he is outside for fear
of the law and of what people will say. And it was a
worthy remark of Julius Drusus to the workmen who offered, for three thousand crowns, to arrange his house so
that his neighbors would no longer be able to look into it
as they could before. "I will give you six thousand," he
said; "make it so that everyone can see in from all sides."
The practice of Agesilaus is noted with honor, of taking
lodging in the churches when traveling, so that the people and the gods themselves might see into his private actions. Men have seemed miraculous to the world, in whom
their wives and valets have never seen anything even
worth noticing. Few men have been admired by their own
households.

ᶜNul n'a été prophète non seulement en sa maison mais en son pays, dit l'expérience des histoires. De même aux choses de néant. Et en ce bas exemple se voit l'image des grands. En mon climat de Gascogne on tient pour drôlerie de me voir imprimé. D'autant que la connaissance qu'on prend de moi s'éloigne de mon gîte, j'en vaux d'autant mieux. J'achète les imprimeurs en Guyenne, ailleurs ils m'achètent. Sur cet accident se fondent ceux qui se cachent, vivants et présents, pour se mettre en crédit trépassés et absents. J'aime mieux en avoir moins. Et ne me jette au monde que pour la part que j'en tire. Au partir de là, je l'en quitte.

ᴮLe peuple reconvoie celui-là d'un acte public, avec étonnement, jusqu'à sa porte: il laisse avec sa robe ce rôle, il en retombe d'autant plus bas qu'il s'était plus haut monté; au dedans, chez lui, tout est tumultuaire et vil. Quand le règlement s'y trouverait, il faut un jugement vif et bien trié pour l'apercevoir en ces actions basses et privées. Joint que l'ordre est une vertu morne et sombre. Gagner une brèche, conduire une ambassade, régir un peuple, ce sont actions éclatantes. Tancer, rire, vendre, payer, aimer, haïr, et converser avec les siens et avec soi-même doucement et justement, ne relâcher point, ne se démentir point, c'est chose plus rare, plus difficile et moins remarquable.

Les vies retirées soutiennent par là, quoi qu'on dise, des devoirs autant ou plus âpres et tendus que ne font les autres vies. ᶜEt les privés, dit Aristote,⁷ servent la vertu plus difficilement et hautement que ne font ceux qui sont

---

⁷ *Nicomachean Ethics*, x, vii.

^CNo man has been a prophet, not merely in his own house, but in his own country, says the experience of history. Likewise in things of no importance. And in this humble example you may see an image of greater ones. In my region of Gascony they think it a joke to see me in print. The farther from my lair the knowledge of me spreads, the more I am valued. I buy printers in Guienne, elsewhere they buy me. On this phenomenon those people base their hopes who hide themselves while alive and present, to gain favor when dead and gone. I would rather have less of it. And I cast myself on the world only for the share of favor I get now. When I leave it, I shall hold it quits.

^BThe people escort this man back to his door, with awe, from a public function. He drops his part with his gown; the higher he has hoisted himself, the lower he falls back; inside, in his home, everything is tumultuous and vile. Even if there is order there, it takes a keen and select judgment to perceive it in these humble private actions. Besides, order is a dull and somber virtue. To win through a breach, to conduct an embassy, to govern a people, these are dazzling actions. To scold, to laugh, to sell, to pay, to love, to hate, and to deal pleasantly and justly with our household and ourselves, not to let ourselves go, not to be false to ourselves, that is a rarer matter, more difficult and less noticeable.

Therefore retired lives, whatever people may say, accomplish duties as harsh and strenuous as other lives, or more so. ^CAnd private persons, says Aristotle,[7] render higher and more difficult service to virtue than those who are in au-

en magistrats. ᴮNous nous préparons aux occasions éminentes plus par gloire que par conscience. ᶜLa plus courte façon d'arriver à la gloire, ce serait faire par conscience ce que nous faisons pour la gloire. ᴮEt la vertu d'Alexandre me semble représenter assez moins de vigueur en son théâtre que ne fait celle de Socratès en cette exercitation basse et obscure. Je conçois aisément Socratès en la place d'Alexandre; Alexandre en celle de Socratès, je ne puis. Qui demandera à celui-là ce qu'il sait faire, il répondra "Subjuguer le monde"; qui le demandera à celui-ci, il dira "Mener l'humaine vie conformément à sa naturelle condition": science bien plus générale, plus pesante et plus légitime.

Le prix de l'âme ne consiste pas à aller haut, mais ordonnément. ᶜSa grandeur ne s'exerce pas en la grandeur, c'est en la médiocrité. Ainsi que ceux qui nous jugent et touchent au dedans ne font pas grande recette de la lueur de nos actions publiques et voient que ce ne sont que filets et pointes d'eau fine rejaillies d'un fond au demeurant limoneux et pesant; en pareil cas, ceux qui nous jugent par cette brave apparence concluent de même de notre constitution interne, et ne peuvent accoupler des facultés populaires et pareilles aux leurs à ces autres facultés qui les étonnent, si loin de leur visée. Ainsi donnons-nous aux démons des formes sauvages. Et qui non à Tamburlan des sourcils élevés, des naseaux ouverts, un visage affreux et une taille démesurée, comme est la taille de l'imagination qu'il en a conçue par le bruit de son nom? Qui m'eût fait voir Érasme ⁸ autrefois, il eût été malaisé

---

⁸ The Latin *Adages* of Erasmus (1466–1536) were extremely popular in the sixteenth century and a favorite work of Montaigne.

328

thority. ᴮWe prepare ourselves for eminent occasions more for glory than for conscience. ᶜThe shortest way to attain glory would be to do for conscience what we do for glory. ᴮAnd Alexander's virtue seems to me to represent much less vigor in his theater than does that of Socrates in his lowly and obscure activity. I can easily imagine Socrates in Alexander's place; Alexander in that of Socrates, I cannot. If you ask the former what he knows how to do, he will answer, "Subdue the world"; if you ask the latter, he will say, "Lead the life of man in conformity with its natural condition"; a knowledge much more general, more weighty, and more legitimate.

The value of the soul consists not in flying high, but in an orderly pace. ᶜIts greatness is exercised not in greatness, but in mediocrity. As those who judge and touch us inwardly make little account of the brilliance of our public acts, and see that these are only thin streams and jets of water spurting from a bottom otherwise muddy and thick; so likewise those who judge us by this brave outward appearance draw similar conclusions about our inner constitution, and cannot associate common faculties, just like their own, with these other faculties that astonish them and are so far beyond their scope. So we give demons wild shapes. And who does not give Tamerlane raised eyebrows, open nostrils, a dreadful face, and immense size, like the size of the imaginary picture of him we have formed from the renown of his name? If I had been able to see Erasmus ⁸ in other days, it would have been hard

[III:2] *Of Repentance*

que je n'eusse pris pour adages et apophtegmes tout ce qu'il eût dit à son valet et à son hôtesse. Nous imaginons bien plus sortablement un artisan sur sa garde-robe ou sur sa femme qu'un grand président, vénérable par son maintien et suffisance. Il nous semble que de ces hauts trônes ils ne s'abaissent pas jusqu'à vivre.

ᴮComme les âmes vicieuses sont incitées souvent à bien faire par quelque impulsion étrangère, aussi sont les vertueuses à faire mal. Il les faut donc juger par leur état rassis, quand elles sont chez elles, si quelquefois elles y sont; ou au moins quand elles sont plus voisines du repos et de leur naïve assiette. Les inclinations naturelles s'aident et fortifient par institution; mais elles ne se changent guère et surmontent. Mille natures, de mon temps, ont échappé vers la vertu ou vers le vice au travers d'une discipline contraire:

> Sic ubi desuetæ silvis in carcere clausæ
> Mansuevere feræ, et vultus posuere minaces,
> Atque hominem didicere pati, si torrida parvus
> Venit in ora cruor, redeunt rabiesque furorque,
> Admonitæque tument gustato sanguine fauces;
> Fervet, et a trepido vix abstinet ira magistro.⁹

On n'extirpe pas ces qualités originelles, on les couvre, on les cache. Le langage latin m'est comme naturel, je l'entends mieux que le français, mais il y a quarante ans que je ne m'en suis du tout point servi à parler ni à écrire: si est-ce qu'à des extrêmes et soudaines émotions où je suis tombé deux ou trois fois en ma vie,—et l'une,

---

⁹ Lucan, *Pharsalia*, ɪᴠ, 237–42.

for me not to take for adages and apophthegms everything he said to his valet and his hostess. We imagine much more appropriately an artisan on the toilet seat or on his wife than a great president, venerable by his demeanor and his ability. It seems to us that they do not stoop from their lofty thrones even to live.

[B]As vicious souls are often incited to do good by some extraneous impulse, so are virtuous souls to do evil. Thus we must judge them by their settled state, when they are at home, if ever they are; or at least when they are closest to repose and their natural position.

Natural inclinations gain assistance and strength from education; but they are scarcely to be changed and overcome. A thousand natures, in my time, have escaped toward virtue or toward vice through the lines of a contrary training:

> As when wild beasts grow tame, shut in a cage,
> Forget the woods, and lose their look of rage,
> And learn to suffer man; but if they taste
> Hot blood, their rage and fury is replaced,
> Their reminiscent jaws distend, they burn,
> And for their trembling keeper's blood they yearn.[9]

We do not root out these original qualities, we cover them up, we conceal them. Latin is like a native tongue to me; I understand it better than French; but for forty years I have not used it at all for speaking or writing. Yet in sudden and extreme emotions, into which I have fallen two or three times in my life—one of them when I saw my

voyant mon père tout sain se renverser sur moi, pâmé,—
j'ai toujours élancé du fond de mes entrailles les premières
paroles latines: ^cnature se sourdant et s'exprimant à force,
à l'encontre d'un long usage. ^BEt cet exemple se dit d'assez
d'autres.

Ceux qui ont essayé de raviser les mœurs du monde, de
mon temps, par nouvelles opinions, réforment les vices
de l'apparence; ceux de l'essence, ils les laissent là, s'ils ne
les augmentent: et l'augmentation y est à craindre. On se
séjourne volontiers de tout autre bien faire sur ces réformations externes arbitraires, de moindre coût et de plus
grand mérite; et satisfait-on par là à bon marché les autres
vices naturels consubstantiels et intestins.

Regardez un peu comment s'en porte notre expérience:
il n'est personne, s'il s'écoute, qui ne découvre en soi une
forme sienne, une forme maîtresse, qui lutte contre l'institution et contre la tempête des passions qui lui sont contraires. De moi, je ne me sens guère agiter par secousse,
je me trouve quasi toujours en ma place, comme sont
les corps lourds et pesants. Si je ne suis chez moi, j'en
suis toujours bien près. Mes débauches ne m'emportent
pas fort loin. Il n'y a rien d'extrême et d'étrange; et si ai
des ravisements sains et vigoureux.

La vraie condamnation et qui touche la commune façon
de nos hommes, c'est que leur retraite même est pleine de
corruption et d'ordure; l'idée de leur amendement, chaf-
fourée; leur pénitence, malade et en coulpe, autant à
peu près que leur péché. Aucuns, ou pour être collés au
vice d'une attache naturelle, ou par longue accoutumance,
n'en trouvent plus la laideur. A d'autres (duquel régiment
je suis) le vice pèse, mais ils le contre-balancent avec le

father, in perfect health, fall back into my arms in a faint—I have always poured out my first words from the depths of my entrails in Latin; ᶜNature surging forth and expressing herself by force, in the face of long habit. ᴮAnd this experience is told of many others.

Those who in my time have tried to correct the world's morals by new ideas, reform the superficial vices; the essential ones they leave as they were, if they do not increase them; and increase is to be feared. People are likely to rest from all other well-doing on the strength of these external, arbitrary reforms, which cost us less and bring greater acclaim; and thereby they satisfy at little expense the other natural, consubstantial, and internal vices.

Just consider the evidence of this in our own experience. There is no one who, if he listens to himself, does not discover in himself a pattern all his own, a ruling pattern, which struggles against education and against the tempest of the passions that oppose it. For my part, I do not feel much sudden agitation; I am nearly always in place, like heavy and inert bodies. If I am not at home, I am always very near it. My excesses do not carry me very far away. There is nothing extreme or strange about them. And besides I have periods of vigorous and healthy reaction.

The real condemnation, which applies to the common run of men of today, is that even their retirement is full of corruption and filth; their idea of reformation, blurred; their penitence, diseased and guilty, almost as much as their sin. Some, either from being glued to vice by a natural attachment, or from long habit, no longer recognize its ugliness. On others (in whose regiment I belong) vice weighs heavily, but they counterbalance it with pleasure

plaisir ou autre occasion et le souffrent et s'y prêtent à certain prix: vicieusement pourtant et lâchement. Si se [10] pourrait-il à l'aventure imaginer si éloignée disproportion de mesure où avec justice le plaisir excuserait le péché, comme nous disons de l'utilité; non seulement s'il était accidentel et hors du péché, comme au larcin, mais en l'exercice même d'icelui, comme en l'accointance des femmes, où l'incitation est violente et, dit-on, parfois invincible.

En la terre d'un mien parent, l'autre jour que j'étais en Armagnac, je vis un paysan que chacun surnomme le larron. Il faisait ainsi le conte de sa vie: Qu'étant né mendiant et trouvant qu'à gagner son pain au travail de ses mains il n'arriverait jamais à se fortifier assez contre l'indigence, il s'avisa de se faire larron; et avait employé à ce métier toute sa jeunesse en sûreté par le moyen de sa force corporelle. Car il moissonnait et vendangeait des terres d'autrui, mais c'était au loin et à si gros monceaux qu'il était inimaginable qu'un homme en eût tant rapporté en une nuit sur ses épaules; et avait soin outre cela d'égaler et disperser le dommage qu'il faisait, si que la foule était moins importable à chaque particulier. Il se trouve à cette heure, en sa vieillesse, riche pour un homme de sa condition, merci à ce trafic, de quoi il se confesse ouvertement; et pour s'accommoder avec Dieu de ses acquêts, il dit être tous les jours après à satisfaire par bienfaits aux successeurs de ceux qu'il a dérobés; et s'il n'achève (car d'y pourvoir tout à la fois il ne peut), qu'il en chargera ses héritiers, à la raison de la science qu'il a lui seul du mal qu'il a fait à chacun.

---

[10] The text reads *ce*, which does not seem to make sense.

or some other consideration, and endure it and lend themselves to it for a certain price; viciously, however, and basely. Yet it might be possible [10] to imagine a disproportion so extreme that the pleasure might justly excuse the sin, as we say utility does; not only if the pleasure was incidental and not a part of the sin, as in theft, but if it was in the very exercise of the sin, as in intercourse with women, where the impulse is violent, and, they say, sometimes invincible.

The other day when I was at Armagnac, on the estate of a kinsman of mine, I saw a country fellow whom everyone nicknames the Thief. He gave this account of his life: that born a beggar, and finding that by earning his bread by the toil of his hands he would never protect himself enough against want, he had decided to become a thief; and he had spent all his youth at this trade in security, by virtue of his bodily strength. For he reaped his harvest and vintage from other people's lands, but so far away and in such great loads that it was inconceivable that one man could have carried off so much on his shoulders in one night. And he was careful besides to equalize and spread out the damage he did, so that the loss was less insupportable for each individual. He is now, in his old age, rich for a man in his station, thanks to this traffic, which he openly confesses. And to make his peace with God for his acquisitions, he says that he spends his days compensating, by good deeds, the successors of the people he robbed; and that if he does not finish this task (for he cannot do it all at once), he will charge his heirs with it, according to the knowledge, which he alone has, of the amount of wrong he did to each.

[III:2] Of Repentance

Par cette description, soit vraie ou fausse, celui-ci regarde le larcin comme action déshonnête et le hait, mais moins que l'indigence; s'en repent bien simplement, mais en tant qu'elle était ainsi contre-balancée et compensée il ne s'en repent pas. Cela, ce n'est pas cette habitude qui nous incorpore au vice et y conforme notre entendement même; ni n'est ce vent impétueux qui va troublant et aveuglant à secousses notre âme et nous précipite pour l'heure, jugement et tout, en la puissance du vice.

Je fais coutumièrement entier ce que je fais, et marche tout d'une pièce; je n'ai guère de mouvement qui se cache et dérobe à ma raison et qui ne se conduise à peu près par le consentement de toutes mes parties, sans division, sans sédition intestine. Mon jugement en a la coulpe ou la louange entière; et la coulpe qu'il a une fois, il l'a toujours, car quasi dès sa naissance il est un: même inclination, même route, même force. Et en matière d'opinions universelles, dès l'enfance je me logeai au point où j'avais à me tenir.

Il y a des péchés impétueux, prompts et subits: laissons-les à part. Mais en ces autres péchés à tant de fois repris, délibérés et consultés, ou péchés de complexion, ᶜvoire péchés de profession et de vacation, ᴮje ne puis pas concevoir qu'ils soient plantés si longtemps en un même courage sans que la raison et la conscience de celui qui les possède le veuille constamment et l'entende ainsi; et le repentir qu'il se vante lui en venir à certain instant prescrit m'est un peu dur à imaginer et former.

Judging by this description, whether it is true or false, this man regards theft as a dishonorable action and hates it, but hates it less than poverty; he indeed repents of it in itself, but in so far as it was thus counterbalanced and compensated, he does not repent of it. This is not that habit that incorporates us with vice and brings even our understanding into conformity with it; nor is it that impetuous wind that comes in gusts to confuse and blind our soul, and hurls us for the moment headlong, judgment and all, into the power of vice.

I customarily do wholeheartedly whatever I do, and go my way all in one piece. I scarcely make a motion that is hidden and out of sight of my reason, and that is not guided by the consent of nearly all parts of me, without division, without internal sedition. My judgment takes all the blame or all the praise for it; and the blame it once takes, it always keeps, for virtually since its birth it has been one; the same inclination, the same road, the same strength. And in the matter of general opinions, in childhood I established myself in the position where I was to remain.

There are some impetuous, prompt, and sudden sins: let us leave them aside. But as for these other sins so many times repeated, planned, and premeditated, constitutional sins, ᶜor even professional or vocational sins, ᴮI cannot imagine that they can be implanted so long in one and the same heart, without the reason and conscience of their possessor constantly willing and intending it to be so. And the repentance which he claims comes to him at a certain prescribed moment is a little hard for me to imagine and conceive.

[III:2] *Of Repentance*

^CJe ne suis pas la secte de Pythagoras, que les hommes prennent une âme nouvelle quand ils approchent les simulacres des dieux pour recueillir leurs oracles. Sinon qu'il voulût dire cela même, qu'il faut bien qu'elle soit étrangère, nouvelle et prêtée pour le temps: la leur montrant si peu de signe de purification et netteté condigne à cet office.

^BIls font tout à l'opposite des préceptes stoïques, qui nous ordonnent bien de corriger les imperfections et vices que nous reconnaissons en nous, mais nous défendent d'en être marris et déplaisants. Ceux-ci nous font accroire qu'ils en ont grand regret et remords au dedans. Mais d'amendement et correction, ^Cni d'interruption, ^Bils ne nous en font rien apparaître. Si n'est-ce pas guérison si on ne se décharge du mal. Si la repentance pesait sur le plat de la balance, elle emporterait le péché. Je ne trouve aucune qualité si aisée à contrefaire que la dévotion, si on n'y conforme les mœurs et la vie. Son essence est abstruse et occulte, les apparences faciles et pompeuses.

Quant à moi, je puis désirer en général être autre; je puis condamner et me déplaire de ma forme universelle, et supplier Dieu pour mon entière réformation et pour l'excuse de ma faiblesse naturelle. Mais cela, je ne le dois nommer repentir, ce me semble, non plus que le déplaisir de n'être ni ange ni Caton. Mes actions sont réglées et conformes à ce que je suis et à ma condition. Je ne puis faire mieux. Et le repentir ne touche pas proprement les choses qui ne sont pas en notre force, oui bien le regretter. J'imagine infinies natures plus hautes et plus réglées que la mienne; je n'amende pourtant mes facultés: comme ni mon bras ni mon esprit ne deviennent plus vigoureux

^CI do not follow the belief of the sect of Pythagoras, that men take on a new soul when they approach the images of the gods to receive their oracles. Unless he meant just this, that the soul must indeed be foreign, new, and loaned for the occasion, since their own showed so little sign of any purification and cleanness worthy of this office.

^BThey do just the opposite of the Stoic precepts, which indeed order us to correct the imperfections and vices that we recognize in us, but forbid us to be repentant and glum about them. These men make us believe that they feel great regret and remorse within; but of amendment and correction, ^Cor interruption, ^Bthey show us no sign. Yet it is no cure if the disease is not thrown off. If repentance were weighing in the scale of the balance, it would outweigh the sin. I know of no quality so easy to counterfeit as piety, if conduct and life are not made to conform with it. Its essence is abstruse and occult; its semblance, easy and showy.

As for me, I may desire in a general way to be different; I may condemn and dislike my nature as a whole, and implore God to reform me completely and to pardon my natural weakness. But this I ought not to call repentance, it seems to me, any more than my displeasure at being neither an angel nor Cato. My actions are in order and conformity with what I am and with my condition. I can do no better. And repentance does not properly apply to the things that are not in our power; rather does regret. I imagine numberless natures loftier and better regulated than mine, but for all that, I do not amend my faculties; just as neither my arm nor my mind becomes more vigor-

[III:2] *Of Repentance*

pour en concevoir un autre qui le soit. Si d'imaginer et désirer un agir plus noble que le nôtre produisait la repentance du nôtre, nous aurions à nous repentir de nos opérations plus innocentes; d'autant que nous jugeons bien qu'en la nature plus excellente elles auraient été conduites d'une plus grande perfection et dignité, et voudrions faire de même.

Lorsque je consulte des déportements de ma jeunesse avec ma vieillesse, je trouve que je les ai communément conduits avec ordre, selon moi; c'est tout ce que peut ma résistance. Je ne me flatte pas: à circonstances pareilles, je serais toujours tel. Ce n'est pas mâchure, c'est plutôt une teinture universelle qui me tache. Je ne connais pas de repentance superficielle, moyenne et de cérémonie. Il faut qu'elle me touche de toutes parts avant que je la nomme ainsi, et qu'elle pince mes entrailles et les afflige autant profondément que Dieu me voit, et autant universellement.

Quant aux négoces, il m'est échappé plusieurs bonnes aventures à faute d'heureuse conduite. Mes conseils ont pourtant bien choisi selon les occurrences qu'on leur présentait; leur façon est de prendre toujours le plus facile et sûr parti. Je trouve qu'en mes délibérations passées j'ai, selon ma règle, sagement procédé pour l'état du sujet qu'on me proposait; et en ferais autant d'ici à mille ans en pareilles occasions. Je ne regarde pas quel il est à cette heure, mais quel il était quand j'en consultais.

ᶜLa force de tout conseil gît au temps; les occasions et les matières roulent et changent sans cesse. J'ai encouru quelques lourdes erreurs en ma vie et importantes, non

340

ous by imagining another that is so. If imagining and desiring a nobler conduct than ours produced repentance of our own, we should have to repent of our most innocent actions, inasmuch as we rightly judge that in a more excellent nature they would have been performed with greater perfection and dignity, and we should wish to do likewise.

When I consider the behavior of my youth in comparison with that of my old age, I find that I have generally conducted myself in orderly fashion, according to my lights; that is all my resistance can accomplish. I do not flatter myself; in similar circumstances I should always be the same. It is not a spot, it is rather a tincture with which I am stained all over. I know no superficial, halfway, and perfunctory repentance. It must affect me in every part before I will call it so, and must grip me by the vitals and afflict them as deeply and as completely as God sees into me.

In business matters, several good opportunities have escaped me for want of successful management. However, my counsels have been good, according to the circumstances they were faced with; their way is always to take the easiest and surest course. I find that in my past deliberations, according to my rule, I have proceeded wisely, considering the state of the matter proposed to me, and I should do the same a thousand years from now in similar situations. I am not considering what it is at this moment, but what it was when I was deliberating about it.

ᶜThe soundness of any plan depends on the time; circumstances and things roll about and change incessantly. I have fallen into some serious and important mistakes in

[III:2] *Of Repentance*

par faute de bon avis, mais par faute de bonheur. Il y a des parties secrètes aux objets qu'on manie et indivinables; signamment, en la nature des hommes, des conditions muettes, sans montre, inconnues parfois du possesseur même, qui se produisent et éveillent par des occasions survenantes. Si ma prudence ne les a pu pénétrer et prophétiser, je ne lui en sais nul mauvais gré; sa charge se contient en ses limites; l'événement me bat, et ^Bs'il favorise le parti que j'ai refusé, il n'y a remède; je ne m'en prends pas à moi; j'accuse ma fortune, non pas mon ouvrage: cela ne s'appelle pas repentir.

Phocion [11] avait donné aux Athéniens certain avis qui ne fut pas suivi. L'affaire pourtant se passant contre son opinion avec prospérité, quelqu'un lui dit: "Eh bien, Phocion, es-tu content que la chose aille si bien?" — "Bien suis-je content," fit-il, "qu'il soit advenu ceci, mais je ne me repens point d'avoir conseillé cela."

Quand mes amis s'adressent à moi pour être conseillés, je le fais librement et clairement, sans m'arrêter, comme fait quasi tout le monde, à ce que, la chose étant hasardeuse, il peut advenir au rebours de mon sens, par où ils aient à me faire reproche de mon conseil: de quoi il ne me chaut. Car ils auront tort, et je n'ai dû leur refuser cet office.
^CJe n'ai guère à me prendre de mes fautes ou infortunes à autre qu'à moi. Car en effet, je me sers rarement

---

[11] Plutarch, *Moralia,* "Notable Sayings of the Ancient Kings. . . ," "Phocion," 12.

my life, not for lack of good counsel but for lack of good luck. There are secret parts in the matters we handle which cannot be guessed, especially in human nature— mute factors that do not show, factors sometimes unknown to their possessor himself, which are brought forth and aroused by unexpected occasions. If my prudence has been unable to see into them and predict them, I bear it no ill will; its responsibility is restricted within its limitations. It is the outcome that beats me; and ᴮif it favors the course I have refused, there is no help for it; I do not blame myself; I accuse my luck, not my work. That is not to be called repentance.

Phocion [11] had given the Athenians some advice that was not followed. When, however, the affair came out prosperously against his opinion, someone said to him: "Well, Phocion, are you glad that the thing is going so well?" "Indeed I am glad," he said, "that it has turned out this way, but I do not repent of having advised that way."

When my friends apply to me for advice, I give it freely and clearly, and without hesitating as nearly everyone else does because, the affair being hazardous, it may come out contrary to my expectations, wherefore they may have cause to reproach me for my advice; that does not worry me. For they will be wrong, and I should not have refused them this service.

ᶜI have scarcely any occasion to blame my mistakes or mishaps on anyone but myself. For in practice I rarely ask

des avis d'autrui, si ce n'est par honneur de cérémonie, sauf où j'ai besoin d'instruction de science ou de la connaissance du fait. Mais ès choses où je n'ai à employer que le jugement, les raisons étrangères peuvent servir à m'appuyer, mais peu à me détourner. Je les écoute favorablement et décemment toutes; mais, qu'il m'en souvienne, je n'en ai cru jusqu'à cette heure que les miennes. Selon moi, ce ne sont que mouches et atomes qui promènent ma volonté. Je prise peu mes opinions, mais je prise aussi peu celles des autres. Fortune me paye dignement. Si je ne reçois pas de conseil, j'en donne encore moins. J'en suis fort peu enquis, mais j'en suis encore moins cru; et ne sache nulle entreprise publique ni privée que mon avis ait redressée et ramenée. Ceux mêmes que la fortune y avait aucunement attachés se sont laissé plus volontiers manier à toute autre cervelle. Comme celui qui suis bien autant jaloux des droits de mon repos que des droits de mon autorité, je l'aime mieux ainsi. Me laissant là, on fait selon ma profession, qui est de m'établir et contenir tout en moi; ce m'est plaisir d'être désintéressé des affaires d'autrui et dégagé de leur gariment.

^BEn tous affaires, quand ils sont passés, comment que ce soit, j'y ai peu de regret. Car cette imagination me met hors de peine, qu'ils devaient ainsi passer; les voilà dans le grand cours de l'univers et dans l'enchaînure des causes stoïques; votre fantaisie n'en peut, par souhait et imagination, remuer un point, que tout l'ordre des choses ne renverse, et le passé et l'avenir.

other people's advice, unless as a compliment and out of politeness, except when I need scientific information or knowledge of the facts. But in things where I have only my judgment to employ, other people's reasons can serve to support me, but seldom to change my course. I listen to them all favorably and decently; but so far as I can remember, I have never up to this moment followed any but my own. If you ask me, they are nothing but flies and atoms that distract my will. I set little value on my own opinions, but I set just as little on those of others. Fortune pays me properly. If I do not take advice, I give still less. Mine is seldom asked, but it is followed even less; and I know of no public or private enterprise that my advice restored to its feet and to the right path. Even the people whom fortune has made somewhat dependent on it have let themselves be managed more readily by anyone else's brains. Being a man who is quite as jealous of the rights of my repose as of the rights of my authority, I prefer it so; by leaving me alone, they treat me according to my professed principle, which is to be wholly contained and established within myself. To me it is a pleasure not to be concerned in other people's affairs and to be free of responsibility for them.

    ^BIn all affairs, when they are past, however they have turned out, I have little regret. For this idea takes away the pain: that they were bound to happen thus, and now they are in the great stream of the universe and in the chain of Stoical causes. Your fancy, by wish or imagination, cannot change a single point without overturning the whole order of things, and the past and the future.

[III:2] *Of Repentance*

Au demeurant, je hais cet accidentel repentir que l'âge apporte. Celui qui [12] disait anciennement être obligé aux années de quoi elles l'avaient défait de la volupté avait autre opinion que la mienne: je ne saurai jamais bon gré à l'impuissance de bien qu'elle me fasse. ᶜNec tam aversa unquam videbitur ab opere suo providentia, ut debilitas inter optima inventa sit.[13] ᴮNos appétits sont rares en la vieillesse, une profonde satiété nous saisit après: en cela je ne vois rien de conscience; le chagrin et la faiblesse nous impriment une vertu lâche et catarrheuse. Il ne nous faut pas laisser emporter si entiers aux altérations naturelles que d'en abâtardir notre jugement. La jeunesse et le plaisir n'ont pas fait autrefois que j'aie méconnu le visage du vice en la volupté; ni ne fait à cette heure le dégoût que les ans m'apportent, que je méconnaisse celui de la volupté au vice. Ores que je n'y suis plus, j'en juge comme si j'y étais.

ᶜMoi qui la secoue vivement et attentivement, trouve que ᴮma raison est celle même que j'avais en l'âge plus licencieux, sinon à l'aventure d'autant qu'elle s'est affaiblie et empirée en vieillissant; ᶜet trouve que ce qu'elle refuse de m'enfourner à ce plaisir en considération de l'intérêt de ma santé corporelle, elle ne le ferait non plus qu'autrefois pour la santé spirituelle. ᴮPour la voir hors de combat, je ne l'estime pas plus valeureuse. Mes tentations sont si cassées et mortifiées qu'elles ne valent pas qu'elle s'y oppose. Tendant seulement les mains au devant, je les conjure. Qu'on lui remette en présence cette ancienne

---

12 Sophocles, as quoted in Plato, Republic, I, 329, and mentioned in Plutarch, Moralia, "That We Cannot Live Happily by the Doc-

For the rest, I hate that accidental repentance that age brings. The man [12] who said of old that he was obliged to the years for having rid him of sensuality had a different viewpoint from mine; I shall never be grateful to impotence for any good it may do me. ^C*Nor will Providence ever be so hostile to her own work that debility should be ranked among the best things.*[13] ^BOur appetites are few in old age; a profound satiety seizes us after the act. In that I see nothing of conscience; sourness and weakness imprint on us a sluggish and rheumatic virtue. We must not let ourselves be so carried away by natural changes as to let our judgment degenerate. Youth and pleasure in other days did not make me fail to recognize the face of vice in voluptuousness; nor does the distaste that the years bring me make me fail to recognize the face of voluptuousness in vice. Now that I am no longer in that state, I judge it as though I were in it.

^CI who shake up my reason sharply and attentively, find that ^Bit is the very same I had in my more licentious years, except perhaps in so far as it has grown weaker and worse as it has grown old. ^CAnd I find that even if it refuses, out of consideration for the interests of my bodily health, to put me in the furnace of this pleasure, it would not refuse to do so, any more than formerly, for my spiritual health. ^BI do not consider it any more valiant for seeing it *hors de combat*. My temptations are so broken and mortified that they are not worth its opposition. By merely stretching out my hands to them, I exorcise them. If my reason were con-

---

trines of Epicurus," vii.
    [13] Quintilian, *Institutio Oratoria*, v, xii.

concupiscence, je crains qu'elle aurait moins de force à la soutenir qu'elle n'avait autrefois. Je ne lui vois rien juger à part soi, que lors elle ne jugeât; ni aucune nouvelle clarté. Par quoi s'il y a convalescence, c'est une convalescence maléficiée.

^cMisérable sorte de remède, devoir à la maladie sa santé! Ce n'est pas à notre malheur de faire cet office; c'est au bonheur de notre jugement. On ne me fait rien faire par les offenses et afflictions, que les maudire. C'est aux gens qui ne s'éveillent qu'à coups de fouet. Ma raison a bien son cours plus délivre en la prospérité. Elle est bien plus distraite et occupée à digérer les maux que les plaisirs. Je vois bien plus clair en temps serein. La santé m'avertit, comme plus allègrement, aussi plus utilement que la maladie. Je me suis avancé le plus que j'ai pu vers ma réparation et règlement lorsque j'avais à en jouir. Je serais honteux et envieux que la misère et défortune de ma décrépitude eût à se préférer à mes bonnes années saines, éveillées, vigoureuses; et qu'on eût à m'estimer non par où j'ai été mais par où j'ai cessé d'être.

A mon avis c'est le vivre heureusement, non, comme disait Antisthénès, le mourir heureusement qui fait l'humaine félicité. Je ne me suis pas attendu d'attacher monstrueusement la queue d'un philosophe à la tête et au corps d'un homme perdu; ni que ce chétif bout eût à désavouer et démentir la plus belle, entière et longue partie de ma vie. Je me veux présenter et faire voir partout uniformément. Si j'avais à revivre, je revivrais comme j'ai vécu; ni je ne plains le passé, ni je ne crains l'avenir. Et si je ne me déçois, il est allé du dedans environ comme du dehors.

fronted with my former lust, I fear that it would have less strength to resist than it used to have. I do not see that of itself it judges anything differently than it did then, nor that it has gained any new light. Wherefore, if there is any convalescence, it is a deformed convalescence.

CMiserable sort of remedy, to owe our health to disease! It is not for our misfortune to do us this service, it is for the good fortune of our judgment. You cannot make me do anything by ills and afflictions except curse them. They are for people who are only awakened by whipping. My reason runs a much freer course in prosperity. It is much more distracted and busy digesting pains than pleasures. I see much more clearly in fair weather. Health admonishes me more cheerfully and so more usefully than sickness. I advanced as far as I could toward reform and a regulated life when I had health to enjoy. I should be ashamed and resentful if the misery and misfortune of my decrepitude were to be thought better than my good, healthy, lively, vigorous years, and if people were to esteem me not for what I have been, but for ceasing to be that.

In my opinion it is living happily, not, as Antisthenes said, dying happily, that constitutes human felicity. I have made no effort to attach, monstrously, the tail of a philosopher to the head and body of a dissipated man; or that this sickly remainder of my life should disavow and belie its fairest, longest, and most complete part. I want to present and show myself uniformly throughout. If I had to live over again, I would live as I have lived. I have neither tears for the past nor fears for the future. And unless I am fooling myself, it has gone about the same way within

C'est une des principales obligations que j'aie à ma fortune, que le cours de mon état corporel ait été conduit chaque chose en sa saison. J'en ai vu l'herbe et les fleurs et le fruit; et en vois la sécheresse. Heureusement, puisque c'est naturellement. Je porte bien plus doucement les maux que j'ai d'autant qu'ils sont en leur point et qu'ils me font aussi plus favorablement souvenir de la longue félicité de ma vie passée.

Pareillement ma sagesse peut bien être de même taille en l'un et l'autre temps; mais elle était bien de plus d'exploit et de meilleure grâce, verte, gaie, naïve, qu'elle n'est à présent, croupie, grondeuse, laborieuse. Je renonce donc à ces réformations casuelles et douloureuses.

ᴮIl faut que Dieu nous touche le courage. Il faut que notre conscience s'amende d'elle-même par renforcement de notre raison, non par l'affaiblissement de nos appétits. La volupté n'en est en soi ni pâle ni décolorée pour être aperçue par des yeux chassieux et troubles. On doit aimer la tempérance par elle-même et pour le respect de Dieu, qui nous l'a ordonnée, et la chasteté; celle que les catarrhes nous prêtent et que je dois au bénéfice de ma colique, ce n'est ni chasteté ni tempérance. On ne peut se vanter de mépriser et combattre la volupté si on ne la voit, si on l'ignore, et ses grâces, et ses forces, et sa beauté plus attrayante.

Je connais l'une et l'autre, c'est à moi à le dire; mais il me semble qu'en la vieillesse nos âmes sont sujettes à des maladies et imperfections plus importunes qu'en la jeunesse. Je le disais étant jeune; lors on me donnait de mon menton par le nez.¹⁴ Je le dis encore à cette heure que mon

me as without. It is one of the chief obligations I have to my fortune that my bodily state has run its course with each thing in due season. I have seen the grass, the flower, and the fruit; now I see the dryness—happily, since it is naturally. I bear the ills I have much more easily because they are properly timed, and also because they make me remember more pleasantly the long felicity of my past life.

Likewise my wisdom may well have been of the same proportions in one age as in the other; but it was much more potent and graceful when green, gay, and natural, than it is now, being broken down, peevish, and labored. Therefore I renounce these casual and painful reformations.

^BGod must touch our hearts. Our conscience must reform by itself through the strengthening of our reason, not through the weakening of our appetites. Sensual pleasure is neither pale nor colorless in itself for being seen through dim and bleary eyes. We should love temperance for itself and out of reverence toward God, who has commanded it, and also chastity; what catarrh lends us, and what I owe to the favor of my colic, is neither chastity nor temperance. We cannot boast of despising and fighting sensual pleasure, if we do not see or know it, and its charms, its powers, and its most alluring beauty.

I know them both; I have a right to speak; but it seems to me that in old age our souls are subject to more troublesome ailments and imperfections than in our youth. I used to say so when I was young; then they taunted me with my beardless chin.[14] I still say so now that my ^Cgray

poil ^Cgris ^Bm'en donne le crédit. Nous appelons sagesse la difficulté de nos humeurs, le dégoût des choses présentes. Mais à la vérité nous ne quittons pas tant les vices comme nous les changeons, et à mon opinion en pis. Outre une sotte et caduque fierté, un babil ennuyeux, ces humeurs épineuses et inassociables, et la superstition, et un soin ridicule des richesses lorsque l'usage en est perdu, j'y trouve plus d'envie, d'injustice et de malignité. Elle nous attache plus de rides en l'esprit qu'au visage; et ne se voit point d'âmes, ou fort rares, qui en vieillissant ne sentent à l'aigre et au moisi. L'homme marche entier vers son croît et vers son décroît.

^CA voir la sagesse de Socratès et plusieurs circonstances de sa condamnation, j'oserais croire qu'il s'y prêta aucunement lui-même par prévarication, à dessein, ayant de si près, âgé de soixante et dix ans, à souffrir l'engourdissement des riches allures de son esprit et l'éblouissement de sa clarté accoutumée.

^BQuelles Métamorphoses[15] lui vois-je faire tous les jours en plusieurs de mes connaissants! C'est une puissante maladie, et qui se coule naturellement et imperceptiblement. Il y faut grande provision d'étude et grande précaution pour éviter les imperfections qu'elle nous charge, ou au moins affaiblir leur progrès. Je sens que nonobstant tous mes retranchements elle gagne pied à pied sur moi. Je soutiens tant que je puis. Mais je ne sais enfin où elle me mènera moi-même. A toutes aventures, je suis content qu'on sache d'où je serai tombé.

---

[14] More literally, "cast in my nose my (beardless) chin."

^Bhair gives me authority to speak. We call "wisdom" the difficulty of our humors, our distaste for present things. But in truth we do not so much abandon our vices as change them, and, in my opinion, for the worse. Besides a silly and decrepit pride, a tedious prattle, prickly and unsociable humors, superstition, and a ridiculous concern for riches when we have lost the use of them, I find there more envy, injustice, and malice. Old age puts more wrinkles in our minds than on our faces; and we never, or rarely, see a soul that in growing old does not come to smell sour and musty. Man grows and dwindles in his entirety.

^CSeeing the wisdom of Socrates and several circumstances of his condemnation, I should venture to believe that he lent himself to it to some extent, purposely, by prevarication, being seventy, and having so soon to suffer an increasing torpor of the rich activity of his mind, and the dimming of its accustomed brightness.

^BWhat Metamorphoses [15] I see old age producing every day in many of my acquaintances! It is a powerful malady, and it creeps up on us naturally and imperceptibly. We need a great provision of study, and great precaution, to avoid the imperfections it loads upon us, or at least to slow up their progress. I feel that, notwithstanding all my retrenchments, it gains on me foot by foot. I stand fast as well as I can. But I do not know where it will lead even me in the end. In any event, I am glad to have people know whence I shall have fallen.

---

[15] Montaigne capitalizes Metamorphoses presumably as an allusion to Ovid's work.

[III:2] Of Repentance

[B]Il n'en est à l'aventure aucune plus expresse que d'en écrire si vainement. Ce que la divinité nous en a si divinement exprimé [2] devrait être soigneusement et continuellement médité par les gens d'entendement.

Qui ne voit que j'ai pris une route par laquelle, sans cesse et sans travail, j'irai autant qu'il y aura d'encre et de papier au monde? Je ne puis tenir registre de ma vie par mes actions: fortune les met trop bas. Je le tiens par mes fantaisies. Si ai-je vu un gentilhomme qui ne communiquait sa vie que par les opérations de son ventre. Vous voyez chez lui, en montre, un ordre de bassins de sept ou huit jours; c'était son étude, ses discours; tout autre propos lui puait.

Ce sont ici, un peu plus civilement, des excréments d'un vieil esprit, dur tantôt, tantôt lâche, et toujours indigeste. . . .

Cette humeur avide des choses nouvelles et inconnues aide bien à nourrir en moi le désir de voyager, mais assez d'autres circonstances y confèrent. Je me détourne volontiers du gouvernement de ma maison. . . . Il y a toujours quelque pièce qui va de travers. Les négoces, tantôt d'une maison, tantôt d'une autre, vous tirassent. Vous éclairez toutes choses de trop près; votre perspicacité vous nuit ici, comme si fait-elle assez ailleurs. . . . [C]Les friponneries qu'on me cache le plus sont celles que je sais le mieux. Il

---

[1] Composed in 1586–88.

[B]There is perhaps no more obvious vanity than to write of it so vainly. What the Divinity has so divinely told us about it [2] ought to be carefully and continually meditated by people of understanding.

Who does not see that I have taken a road along which I shall go, without stopping and without effort, as long as there is ink and paper in the world? I cannot keep a record of my life by my actions; fortune places them too low. I keep it by my thoughts. Thus I knew a gentleman who gave knowledge of his life only by the workings of his belly; you would see on display at his home a row of chamber pots, seven or eight days' worth. That was his study, his conversation; all other talk stank in his nostrils.

Here you have, a little more decently, some excrements of an aged mind, now hard, now loose, and always undigested. . . .

This greedy appetite for new and unknown things indeed helps to foster in me the desire to travel, but enough other circumstances contribute to it. I gladly turn aside from governing my house. . . . There is always something that goes wrong. The affairs, now of one house, now of another, pester you. You pry into everything too closely; your perspicacity hurts you here, as indeed it does often enough elsewhere. . . . [C]The knaveries that they most hide from me are the ones I know best. There are

---

[2] "Vanity of vanities, saith the Preacher, vanity of vanities; all is vanity." (Ecclesiastes 1:2.)

en est que, pour faire moins mal, il faut aider soi-même à cacher. [B]Vaines pointures, [C]vaines parfois, [B]mais toujours pointures. Les plus menus et grêles empêchements sont les plus perçants. . . .

[C]Je ne suis pas philosophe: les maux me foulent selon qu'ils pèsent; et pèsent selon la forme comme selon la matière, et souvent plus. J'en ai plus de connaissance que le vulgaire; si j'ai plus de patience. Enfin, s'ils ne me blessent, ils m'offensent. [B]C'est chose tendre que la vie, et aisée à troubler. . . .

Mon père aimait à bâtir Montaigne, où il était né; et en toute cette police d'affaires domestiques, j'aime à me servir de son exemple et de ses règles, et y attacherai mes successeurs autant que je pourrai. Si je pouvais mieux pour lui, je le ferais. Je me glorifie que sa volonté s'exerce encore et agisse par moi. Jà, à Dieu ne plaise que je laisse faillir entre mes mains aucune image de vie que je puisse rendre à un si bon père. . . . Quant à mon application particulière, ni ce plaisir de bâtir qu'on dit être si attrayant, ni la chasse, ni les jardins, ni ces autres plaisirs de la vie retirée, ne me peuvent beaucoup amuser. C'est chose de quoi je me veux mal, comme de toutes autres opinions qui me sont incommodes. Je ne me soucie pas tant de les avoir vigoureuses et doctes comme je me soucie de les avoir aisées et commodes à la vie: [C]elles sont assez vraies et saines si elles sont utiles et agréables. . . .

[B]L'autre cause qui me convie à ces promenades, c'est la disconvenance aux mœurs présentes de notre état. Je me consolerais aisément de cette corruption pour le regard de l'intérêt public, . . . mais pour le mien, non. J'en suis en

some that we must ourselves help to conceal, so that they will hurt less. ᴮTrivial pinpricks: ᶜsometimes trivial, ᴮbut always pinpricks. The pettiest and slightest nuisances are the most acute. . . .

ᶜI am no philosopher. Evils crush me according to their weight; and their weight depends on their form as much as on their matter, and often more. I have more experience of them than the common people; so I have more patience. In short, if they do not wound me, they hurt me. ᴮLife is a tender thing and easy to disturb. . . .

My father loved to build up Montaigne, where he was born; and in all this administration of domestic affairs, I love to follow his example and his rules, and shall bind my successors to them as much as I can. If I could do better for him, I would. I glory in the fact that his will still operates and acts through me. God forbid that I should allow to fail in my hands any semblance of life that I could restore to so good a father. . . . As regards my own personal inclination, neither the pleasure of building, which is said to be so alluring, nor hunting, nor gardens, nor the other pleasures of a retired life, can amuse me very much. That is a thing for which I am annoyed with myself, as I am for all other notions that are a nuisance to me. I do not care so much that ideas be vigorous and learned, as I care that they be easy and suitable for life; ᶜthey are true and sound enough if they are useful and pleasing. . . .

ᴮThe other thing that invites me to these excursions is that the present moral state of our country does not suit me. I could easily console myself for this corruption as regards the public interest, . . . but with regard to my own.

particulier trop pressé. Car en mon voisinage nous sommes tantôt par la longue licence de ces guerres civiles envieillis en une forme d'état si débordée . . . qu'à la vérité c'est merveille qu'elle se puisse maintenir. . . . Enfin je vois par notre exemple que la société des hommes se tient et se coud à quelque prix que ce soit. En quelque assiette qu'on les couche, ils s'appilent et se rangent en se remuant et s'entassant, comme des corps mal unis qu'on empoche sans ordre trouvent d'eux-mêmes la façon de se joindre et s'emplacer les uns parmi les autres, souvent mieux que l'art ne les eût su disposer. Le roi Philippus fit un amas des plus méchants hommes et incorrigibles qu'il pût trouver et les logea tous en une ville qu'il leur fit bâtir, qui en portait le nom.[3] J'estime qu'ils dressèrent des vices mêmes une contexture politique entre eux et une commode et juste société.

Je vois non une action, ou trois, ou cent, mais des mœurs en usage commun et reçu si monstrueuses en inhumanité surtout et déloyauté, qui est pour moi la pire espèce des vices, que je n'ai point le courage de les concevoir sans horreur; et les admire quasi autant que je les déteste. . . .

Laisse, lecteur, courir encore ce coup d'essai et ce troisième allongeail du reste des pièces de ma peinture. J'ajoute, mais je ne corrige pas. Premièrement, parce que celui qui a hypothéqué au monde son ouvrage, je trouve apparence qu'il n'y ait plus de droit. . . .

ᶜMon livre est toujours un. Sauf qu'à mesure qu'on se

---

[3] Poneropolis (City of the Wicked). See Plutarch, *Moralia*, "Of Curiosity," x.

no. I in particular suffer from it too much. For in my neighborhood we have now grown old, through the long license of these civil wars, in so riotous a form of government . . . that in truth it is a marvel that it can subsist. . . . In fine, I see from our example that human society holds and is knit together at any cost whatever. Whatever position you set men in, they pile up and arrange themselves by moving and crowding together, just as ill-matched objects, put in a bag without order, find of themselves a way to unite and fall into place together, often better than they could have been arranged by art. King Philip collected the most wicked and incorrigible men he could find, and settled them all in a city he had built for them, which bore their name.³ I judge that from their very vices they set up a political system among themselves and a workable and just society.

I see not one action, or three, or a hundred, but morals in common and accepted practice, so monstrous, especially in inhumanity and treachery, that I have not the heart to think of them without horror; and I marvel at them almost as much as I detest them. . . .

Reader, let this essay of myself run on, and this third extension of the other parts of my painting. I add, but I do not correct. First, because when a man has mortgaged his work to the world, it seems to me that he has no further right to it. . . .

ᶜMy book is always one. Except that at each new edi-

met à le renouveler, afin que l'acheteur ne s'en aille les mains du tout vides, je me donne loi d'y attacher, comme ce n'est qu'une marqueterie mal jointe, quelque emblème surnuméraire. Ce ne sont que surpoids, qui ne condamnent point la première forme, mais donnent quelque prix particulier à chacune des suivantes par une petite subtilité ambitieuse. De là toutefois il adviendra facilement qu'il s'y mêle quelque transposition de chronologie, mes contes prenant place selon leur opportunité, non toujours selon leur âge.

[B]Secondement que, pour mon regard, je crains de perdre au change: mon entendement ne va pas toujours avant, il va à reculons aussi. Je ne me défie guère moins de mes fantaisies pour être secondes ou tierces que premières, ou présentes que passées. Nous nous corrigeons aussi sottement souvent comme nous corrigeons les autres. [C]Mes premières publications furent l'an 1580. Depuis, d'un long trait de temps je suis envieilli, mais assagi je ne le suis certes pas d'un pouce. Moi à cette heure et moi tantôt sommes bien deux; mais quand meilleur, je n'en puis rien dire. . . .

Je me connais bien. Mais il m'est malaisé d'imaginer nulle si pure libéralité de personne, nulle hospitalité si franche et gratuite, qui ne me semblât disgraciée, tyrannique et teinte de reproche, si la nécessité m'y avait enchevêtré. . . . Mes connaissants, et au-dessus et au-dessous de moi, savent s'ils en ont jamais vu de moins chargeant sur autrui. . . . Mes amis m'importunent étrangement quand ils me requièrent de requérir un tiers. . . .

[B]Je veux donc dire que s'il faut ainsi devoir quelque chose, ce doit être à plus légitime titre que celui de quoi je

tion, so that the buyer may not come off completely empty-handed, I allow myself to add, since it is only an ill-fitted patchwork, some extra ornaments. These are only overweights, which do not condemn the original form, but give some special value to each of the subsequent ones, by a bit of ambitious subtlety. Thence, however, it will easily happen that some transposition of chronology may slip in, for my stories take their place according to their timeliness, not always according to their age.

ᴮSecond, because, as far as I am concerned, I fear to lose by the change: my understanding does not always go forward, it goes backward too. I distrust my thoughts hardly any less for being second or third than for being first, or for being present than for being past. We often correct ourselves as stupidly as we correct others. ᶜMy first edition was in the year 1580. Since then I have grown older by a long stretch of time; but certainly I have not grown an inch wiser. Myself now and myself a while ago are indeed two; but when better, I simply cannot say. . . .

I know myself well; but it is hard for me to imagine anyone's liberality so pure, any hospitality so free and genuine, that it would not seem to me ill-favored, tyrannical, and tainted with reproach, if necessity had entangled me in it. . . . Those who know me, both above and below me, know whether they have ever seen a man less demanding of others. . . . My friends bother me greatly when they ask me to ask a favor of a third person. . . .

ᴮI mean to say, then, that if we must thus owe something, it should be by a more legitimate title than the one

parle, auquel la loi de cette misérable guerre m'engage, et non d'un si gros dette comme celui de ma totale conservation: il m'accable. Je me suis couché mille fois chez moi, imaginant qu'on me trahirait et assommerait cette nuit-là, composant avec la fortune que ce fût sans effroi et sans langueur. . . . Il m'advient souvent d'imaginer avec quelque plaisir les dangers mortels et les attendre: je me plonge la tête baissée stupidement dans la mort, sans la considérer et reconnaître, comme dans une profondeur muette et obscure qui m'engloutit d'un saut et accable en un instant d'un puissant sommeil plein d'insipidité et indolence. . . .

Non parce que Socratès l'a dit mais parce qu'en vérité c'est mon humeur, et à l'aventure non sans quelque excès, j'estime tous les hommes mes compatriotes, et embrasse un Polonais comme un Français, postposant cette liaison nationale à l'universelle et commune. Je ne suis guère féru de la douceur d'un air naturel. Les connaissances toutes neuves et toutes miennes me semblent bien valoir ces autres communes et fortuites connaissances du voisinage. Les amitiés pures de notre acquêt emportent ordinairement celles auxquelles la communication du climat ou du sang nous joignent. Nature nous a mis au monde libres et déliés; nous nous emprisonnons en certains détroits: comme les rois de Perse, qui s'obligeaient de ne boire jamais autre eau que celle du fleuve de Choaspès, renonçaient par sottise à leur droit d'usage en toutes les autres eaux, et asséchaient pour leur regard tout le reste du monde. . . .

Outre ces raisons, le voyager me semble un exercice profitable. L'âme y a une continuelle exercitation à re-

362

I am speaking of, to which the law of this miserable war binds me; and not with so great a debt as that of my total preservation: that overwhelms me. I have gone to bed a thousand times in my own home, imagining that someone would betray me and slaughter me that very night, arranging with fortune that it should be without fright and not lingering. . . . It often happens that I imagine and await mortal dangers with some pleasure: I plunge head down, stupidly, into death, without looking at it and recognizing it, as into a silent and dark abyss which swallows me up at one leap and overwhelms me in an instant with a heavy sleep free from feeling and pain. . . .

Not because Socrates said it, but because it is really my feeling, and perhaps excessively so, I consider all men my compatriots, and embrace a Pole as I do a Frenchman, setting this national bond after the universal and common one. I am scarcely infatuated with the sweetness of my native air. Brand-new acquaintances that are wholly of my own choice seem to me to be well worth those other common chance acquaintances of the neighborhood. Friendships purely of our own acquisition usually surpass those to which community of climate or of blood binds us. Nature has put us into the world free and unfettered; we imprison ourselves in certain narrow districts, like the kings of Persia, who bound themselves never to drink any other water than that of the river Choaspes, stupidly gave up their right to use any other waters, and dried up all the rest of the world as far as they were concerned. . . .

Besides these reasons, travel seems to me a profitable exercise. The mind is continually exercised in observing

marquer les choses inconnues et nouvelles; et je ne sache point meilleure école, comme j'ai dit souvent, à former la vie, que de lui proposer incessamment la diversité de tant d'autres vies, ᶜfantaisies et usances, ᴮet lui faire goûter une si perpétuelle variété de formes de notre nature. Le corps n'y est ni oisif ni travaillé, et cette modérée agitation le met en haleine. Je me tiens à cheval sans démonter, tout coliqueux que je suis, et sans m'ennuyer, huit et dix heures. . . .

Je ne suis point arrivé à cette vigueur dédaigneuse qui se fortifie en soi-même, que rien n'aide ni ne trouble; je suis d'un point plus bas. . . . Je me contente d'une mort recueillie en soi, quiète et solitaire, toute mienne, convenable à ma vie retirée et privée. . . . Cette partie n'est pas du rôle de la société: c'est l'acte à un seul personnage. Vivons et rions entre les nôtres, allons mourir et rechigner entre les inconnus. . . .

Je me défais tous les jours par discours de cette humeur puérile et inhumaine qui fait que nous désirons d'émouvoir par nos maux la compassion et le deuil en nos amis. . . . La fermeté que nous louons en chacun à soutenir sa mauvaise fortune, nous l'accusons et reprochons à nos proches quand c'est en la nôtre. . . . Il faut étendre la joie, mais retrancher autant qu'on peut la tristesse. . . .

Je sens ce profit inespéré de la publication de mes mœurs, qu'elle me sert aucunement de règle. Il me vient parfois quelque considération de ne trahir l'histoire de ma vie. Cette publique déclaration m'oblige de me tenir en ma route et à ne démentir l'image de mes conditions, communément moins défigurées et contredites que ne porte la malignité et maladie des jugements d'aujourd'hui.

new and unknown things; and I know no better school, as I have often said, for forming one's life, than to set before it constantly the diversity of so many other lives, ^cideas, and customs, ^Band to make it taste such a perpetual variety of forms of our nature. In it the body is neither idle nor overworked, and this moderate movement puts it in good condition. I stay on horseback, though I have the colic, without dismounting and without pain, for eight or ten hours. . . .

I have not attained that disdainful vigor which finds fortitude in itself, which nothing can either aid or disturb; I am a peg lower. . . . I am content with a collected, calm, and solitary death, all my own, in keeping with my retired and private life. . . . Dying is not a role for society; it is an act for one single character. Let us live and laugh among our friends, let us go die and look sour among strangers. . . .

Day by day I rid myself by reflection of that childish and inhuman humor that makes us want to arouse compassion and mourning in our friends by our misfortunes. . . . The firmness in supporting misfortune that we praise in all men, we blame and reproach in our friends when the misfortune is our own. . . . We should spread joy, but cut down sadness as much as we can. . . .

I feel this unexpected profit from the publication of my behavior, that to some extent it serves me as a rule. Sometimes there comes to me a feeling that I should not betray the story of my life. This public declaration obliges me to keep on my path, and not to give the lie to the picture of my qualities, which are normally less disfigured and distorted than might be expected from the malice and sick-

L'uniformité et simplesse de mes mœurs produit bien un visage d'aisée interprétation; mais parce que la façon en est un peu nouvelle et hors d'usage, elle donne trop beau jeu à la médisance. Si est-il qu'à qui me veut loyalement injurier il me semble fournir bien suffisamment où mordre en mes imperfections avouées et connues, sans s'escarmoucher au vent. . . .

Outre ce profit que je tire d'écrire de moi, j'en espère cet autre, que s'il advient que mes humeurs plaisent et accordent à quelque honnète homme avant que je meure, il recherchera de nous joindre. Je lui donne beaucoup de pays gagné, car tout ce qu'une longue connaissance et familiarité lui pourrait avoir acquis en plusieurs années, il le voit en trois jours en ce registre, et plus sûrement et exactement.

ᶜPlaisante fantaisie: plusieurs choses que je ne voudrais dire à personne, je les dis au peuple, et sur mes plus secrètes sciences ou pensées renvoie à une boutique de libraire mes amis plus féaux. . . . ᴮSi à bonnes enseignes je savais quelqu'un qui me fût propre, certes je l'irais trouver bien loin; car la douceur d'une sortable et agréable compagnie ne se peut assez acheter à mon gré. Ô un ami! Combien est vraie cette ancienne sentence, que l'usage en est plus nécessaire et plus doux que des éléments de l'eau et du feu![4] . . .

Je sais bien qu'à le prendre à la lettre, ce plaisir de voyager porte témoignage d'inquiétude et d'irrésolution. Aussi sont-ce nos maîtresses qualités, et prédominantes.

---

[4] Plutarch, *Moralia*, "Of Flatterers and Friends," v.

ness of the judgments of today. The uniformity and simplicity of my behavior indeed produces an appearance easy
to interpret, but, because the manner of it is a bit new and
unusual, it gives too fine a chance to calumny. Yet the fact
is, it seems to me, that to anyone who wants to abuse me
fairly I give plenty to bite on in my known and avowed
imperfections, and enough to gorge on, without skirmish-
ing with the wind. . . .

Besides this profit that I derive from writing about myself, I hope for this other advantage, that if my humors
happen to please and suit some worthy man before I die,
he will try to meet me. I give him a big advantage in
ground covered; for all that long acquaintance and familiarity could have gained for him in several years, he can
see in three days in this record, and more surely and exactly.

cAmusing notion: many things that I would not want
to tell anyone, I tell the public; and for my most secret
knowledge and thoughts I send my most faithful friends
to a bookseller's shop. . . . BIf by reliable signs I knew
of a man who was suited to me, truly I would go very far
to find him; for the sweetness of harmonious and agreeable company cannot be bought too dearly, in my opinion. Oh, a friend! How true is that old saying, that the
enjoyment of one is sweeter and more necessary than that
of the elements of water and fire! [4] . . .

I know well that if you take it literally, this pleasure in
traveling is a testimony of restlessness and irresolution.
And indeed these are our ruling and predominant qualities.

Oui, je le confesse, je ne vois rien, seulement en songe et par souhait, où je me puisse tenir; la seule variété me paye, et la possession de la diversité, au moins si aucune chose me paye. A voyager, cela même me nourrit que je me puis arrêter sans intérêts, et que j'ai où m'en divertir commodément.

J'aime la vie privée parce que c'est par mon choix que je l'aime, non par disconvenance à la vie publique, qui est à l'aventure autant selon ma complexion. J'en sers plus gaiement mon prince parce que c'est par libre élection de mon jugement et de ma raison, ^csans obligation particulière, ^Bet que je n'y suis pas rejeté ni contraint pour être irrecevable à tout autre parti et mal voulu. Ainsi du reste. Je hais les morceaux que la nécessité me taille. Toute commodité me tiendrait à la gorge, de laquelle seule j'aurais à dépendre:

Alter remus aquas, alter mihi radat arenas.[5]

Une seule corde ne m'arrête jamais assis.

—"Il y a de la vanité," dites-vous, "en cet amusement."

— Mais où non? Et ces beaux préceptes sont vanité, et vanité toute la sagesse. . . . Ces exquises subtilités ne sont propres qu'au prêche: ce sont discours qui nous veulent envoyer tous bâtés en l'autre monde. La vie est un mouvement matériel et corporel, action imparfaite de sa propre essence, et déréglée; je m'emploie à la servir selon elle. . . .

A quoi faire ces pointes élevées de la philosophie sur lesquelles aucun être humain ne se peut rasseoir, et ces

---

[5] Adapted from Propertius, *Elegies*, iii, iii, 23.

Yes, I confess, I see nothing, even in a dream or a wish, that I could hold myself to; variety alone satisfies me, and the enjoyment of diversity, at least if anything satisfies me. In traveling, I am encouraged by the very fact that I can stop without loss, and that I have a place where I can turn aside from it comfortably.

I love private life because it is by my own choice that I love it, not because of unfitness for public life, which is perhaps just as well suited to my nature. I serve my prince the more gaily because I do so by the free choice of my judgment and my reason, Cwithout personal obligation, Band because I am not thrown back on his service and constrained to it by being unacceptable and unwelcome to every other party. So with the rest. I hate the morsels that necessity carves for me. Any advantage on which I had to depend exclusively would have me by the throat.

Let one oar row in water, the other on the shore.[5]

A single cord never keeps me in place.

"There is vanity," you say, "in this amusement." But where is there not? And these fine precepts are vanity, and all wisdom is vanity. . . . These exquisite subtleties are only fit for preaching; they are arguments that would send us all saddled into the other world. Life is a material and corporeal movement, an action which by its very essence is imperfect and irregular; I apply myself to serving it in its own way. . . .

What is the use of these lofty points of philosophy on which no human being can settle, and these rules that ex-

règles qui excèdent notre usage et notre force? Je vois souvent qu'on nous propose des images de vie, lesquelles ni le proposant ni les auditeurs n'ont aucune espérance de suivre, ni, qui plus est, envie. . . .

Il serait à désirer qu'il y eût plus de proportion du commandement à l'obéissance; et semble la visée injuste, à laquelle on ne peut atteindre. Il n'est si homme de bien, qu'il mette à l'examen des lois toutes ses actions et pensées, qui ne soit pendable dix fois en sa vie, voire tel qu'il serait très grand dommage et très injuste de punir et de perdre. . . . Et tel pourrait n'offenser point les lois, qui n'en mériterait point la louange d'homme de vertu, ^Cet que la philosophie ferait très justement fouetter. ^BTant cette relation est trouble et inégale.

Nous n'avons garde d'être gens de bien selon Dieu; nous ne le saurions être selon nous. L'humaine sagesse n'arriva jamais aux devoirs qu'elle s'était elle-même prescrits, et si elle y était arrivée, elle s'en prescrirait d'autres au delà, où elle aspirât toujours et prétendît, tant notre état est ennemi de consistance. ^CL'homme s'ordonne à soi-même d'être nécessairement en faute. Il n'est guère fin de tailler son obligation à la raison d'un autre être que le sien. A qui prescrit-il ce qu'il s'attend que personne ne fasse? Lui est-il injuste de ne faire point ce qu'il lui est impossible à faire? Les lois qui nous condamnent à ne pouvoir pas nous accusent elles-mêmes de ne pouvoir pas. . . . ^BLa vertu de Caton était vigoureuse outre la me-

ceed our use and our strength? I often see people propose to us patterns of life which neither the proposer nor his hearers have any hope of following, or, what is more, any desire to follow. . . .

It would be desirable that there should be more proportion between the command and the obedience; and a goal that we cannot reach seems unjust. There is no man so good that if he placed all his actions and thoughts under the scrutiny of the laws, he would not deserve hanging ten times in his life—even such a man that it would be a very great loss and very unjust to punish and destroy him. . . . And one man might not offend the laws at all, who would not for all that deserve in any degree to be praised as a virtuous man, ^Cand whom philosophy would very justly cause to be whipped: ^Bso confused and uneven is this relationship.

There is no question of our being good men according to God; we cannot be so according to ourselves. Human wisdom has never yet come up to the duties that she has prescribed for herself; and if she ever did come up to them, she would prescribe herself others beyond, to which she would ever aim and aspire, so hostile to consistency is our condition. ^CMan ordains that he himself shall be necessarily at fault. He is not very clever to cut out his own duty by the pattern of a different nature than his own. To whom does he prescribe what he expects no one to do? Is it wrong of him not to do what it is impossible for him to do? The laws which condemn us not to be able, themselves accuse us for not being able.

. . . ^BThe virtue of Cato was vigorous beyond the

sure de son siècle; et à un homme qui se mêlait de gouverner les autres, destiné au service commun, il se pourrait dire que c'était une justice, sinon injuste, au moins vaine et hors de saison. . . .

La vertu assignée aux affaires du monde est une vertu à plusieurs plis, encoignures et coudes, pour s'appliquer et joindre à l'humaine faiblesse, mêlée et artificielle, non droite, nette, constante, ni purement innocente. . . . J'ai autrefois essayé d'employer au service des maniements publics les opinions et règles de vivre ainsi rudes, neuves, impolies ou impollues, comme je les ai nées chez moi ou rapportées de mon institution, et desquelles je me sers ᶜsinon ᴮcommodément ᶜau moins sûrement ᴮen particulier: une vertu scolastique et novice. Je les y ai trouvées ineptes et dangereuses. Celui qui va en la presse, il faut qu'il gauchisse, qu'il serre ses coudes, qu'il recule ou qu'il avance, voire qu'il quitte le droit chemin, selon ce qu'il rencontre; qu'il vive non tant selon soi que selon autrui, non selon ce qu'il se propose mais selon ce qu'on lui propose, selon le temps, selon les hommes, selon les affaires. . . .

Cette farcissure est un peu hors de mon thème. Je m'égare, mais plutôt par licence que par mégarde. Mes fantaisies se suivent, mais parfois c'est de loin; et se regardent, mais d'une vue oblique.

. . . J'aime l'allure poétique, à sauts et à gambades. . . . ᶜC'est l'indiligent lecteur qui perd mon sujet, non pas moi; il s'en trouvera toujours en un coin quelque mot qui ne laisse pas d'être bastant, quoiqu'il soit serré. ᴮJe vais au change, indiscrètement et tumultuairement. ᶜMon

measure of his time; and for a man who took a hand in governing others, a man dedicated to the public service, it might be said that his was a righteousness, if not un-righteous, at least vain and out of season. . . .

The virtue assigned to the affairs of the world is a virtue with many bends, angles, and elbows, so as to join and adapt itself to human weakness; mixed and artificial, not straight, clean, constant, or purely innocent. . . . I once tried to employ in the service of public dealings ideas and rules for living as crude, green, unpolished—or un-polluted—as they were born in me or derived from my education, and which I use, ^Cif not ^Bconveniently, ^Cat least surely, ^Bin private matters: a scholastic and novice virtue. I found them inept and dangerous for such matters. He who walks in the crowd must step aside, keep his elbows in, step back or advance, even leave the straight way, ac-cording to what he encounters. He must live not so much according to himself as according to others, not according to what he proposes to himself but according to what others propose to him, according to the time, according to the men, according to the business. . . .

This stuffing is a little out of my subject. I go out of my way, but rather by license than carelessness. My ideas fol-low one another, but sometimes it is from a distance, and look at each other, but with a sidelong glance. . . .

. . . I love the poetic gait, by leaps and gambols. . . . ^CIt is the inattentive reader who loses my subject, not I. Some word about it will always be found off in a corner, which will not fail to be sufficient, though it takes little room. ^BI seek out change indiscriminately and tumultu-

style et mon esprit vont vagabondant de même. ^B"Il faut avoir un peu de folie, qui ne veut avoir plus de sottise." . . .

J'entends que la matière se distingue soi-même. Elle montre assez où elle se change, où elle conclut, où elle commence, où elle se reprend, sans s'entrelacer de paroles, de liaison et de couture introduites pour le service des oreilles faibles ou nonchalantes, et sans me gloser moi-même. . . .

Puisque je ne puis arrêter l'attention du lecteur par le poids, *manco male* s'il advient que je l'arrête par mon embrouillure. — Voire, mais il se repentira par après de s'y être amusé. — C'est mon, mais il s'y sera toujours amusé. Et puis il est des humeurs comme cela, à qui l'intelligence porte dédain, qui m'en estimeront mieux de ce qu'ils ne sauront ce que je dis: ils concluront la profondeur de mon sens par l'obscurité; laquelle, à parler en bon escient, je hais bien fort, et l'éviterais si je me savais éviter. Aristote se vante en quelque lieu de l'affecter: vicieuse affectation.

^CParce que la coupure si fréquente des chapitres, de quoi j'usais au commencement, m'a semblé rompre l'attention avant qu'elle soit née, et la dissoudre, dédaignant s'y coucher pour si peu et se recueillir, je me suis mis à les faire plus longs, qui requièrent de la proposition et du loisir assigné. En telle occupation, à qui on ne veut donner une seule heure on ne veut rien donner. Et ne fait-on rien pour celui pour qui on ne fait qu'autre chose faisant. Joint qu'à l'aventure ai-je quelque obligation particulière à ne dire qu'à demi, à dire confusément, à dire discordamment.

ously. ᶜMy style and my mind alike go roaming. ᴮ"A man must be a little mad if he does not want to be even more stupid." . . .

I want the matter to make its own divisions. It shows well enough where it changes, where it concludes, where it begins, where it resumes, without my interlacing it with words, with links and seams introduced for the benefit of weak or heedless ears, and without writing glosses on myself. . . .

Since I cannot arrest the attention of the reader by weight, it is all to the good if I chance to arrest it by my embroilment.—True, but he will afterward repent of having wasted his time over it.—That may be, but still he will have wasted his time over it. And then there are natures like that, in whom understanding breeds disdain, who will think the better of me because they will not know what I mean. They will conclude that my meaning is profound from its obscurity, which, to speak in all earnest, I hate very strongly, and I would avoid it if I could avoid myself. Aristotle somewhere boasts of affecting it: blameworthy affectation!

ᶜBecause such frequent breaks into chapters as I used at the beginning seemed to me to disrupt and dissolve attention before it was aroused, making it disdain to settle and collect for so little, I have begun making them longer, requiring fixed purpose and assigned leisure. In such an occupation, if you will not give a man a single hour, you will not give him anything. And you do nothing for a man for whom you do nothing except while doing something else. Besides, perhaps I have some personal obligation to speak only by halves, to speak confusedly, to speak discordantly.

[III:9] *Of Vanity*

ᴮJ'avais à dire que je veux mal à cette raison trouble-fête, et que ces projets extravagants qui travaillent la vie, et ces opinions si fines, si elles ont de la vérité, je la trouve trop chère et incommode. Au rebours, je m'emploie à faire valoir la vanité même et l'ânerie si elle m'apporte du plaisir, et me laisse aller après mes inclinations naturelles sans les contrôler de si près. . . .

Cette opinion et usance commune de regarder ailleurs qu'à nous a bien pourvu à notre affaire. C'est un objet plein de mécontentement; nous n'y voyons que misère et vanité. Pour ne nous déconforter, nature a rejeté bien à propos l'action de notre vue au dehors. Nous allons en avant à-vau-l'eau, mais de rebrousser vers nous notre course c'est un mouvement pénible: la mer se brouille et s'empêche ainsi quand elle est repoussée à soi. Regardez, dit chacun, les branles du ciel, regardez au public, à la querelle de celui-là, au pouls d'un tel, au testament de cet autre; somme, regardez toujours haut ou bas, ou à côté, ou devant, ou derrière vous.

C'était un commandement paradoxe que nous faisait anciennement ce dieu à Delphes: [6] "Regardez dans vous, reconnaissez-vous, tenez-vous à vous; votre esprit et votre volonté, qui se consomme ailleurs, ramenez-la en soi; vous vous écoulez, vous vous répandez; appilez-vous, soutenez-vous; on vous trahit, on vous dissipe, on vous dérobe à vous. Vois-tu pas que ce monde tient toutes ses vues con-

---

[6] Apollo, on the gate of whose temple at Delphi was written the famous "γνῶθι σεαυτόν" (Know thyself).

[B]I was about to say that I am ill-disposed toward that kill-joy reason; and that if those extravagant projects that torment our lives, and those wondrously subtle ideas, have any truth in them, I consider it too expensive and inconvenient. On the contrary, I apply myself to make use of vanity itself, and asininity, if it brings me any pleasure, and let myself follow my natural inclinations without examining them too closely. . . .

This common attitude and habit of looking elsewhere than at ourselves has been very useful for our own business. We are an object that fills us with discontent; we see nothing in us but misery and vanity. In order not to dishearten us, Nature has very appropriately thrown the action of our vision outward. We go forward with the current, but to turn our course back toward ourselves is a painful movement: thus the sea grows troubled and turbulent when it is tossed back on itself. Look, says everyone, at the movement of the heavens, look at the public, look at that man's quarrel, at this man's pulse, at another man's will; in short, always look high or low, or to one side, or in front, or behind you.

It was a paradoxical command that was given us of old by that god at Delphi: [6] "Look into yourself, know yourself, keep to yourself; bring back your mind and your will, which are spending themselves elsewhere, into themselves; you are running out, you are scattering yourself; concentrate yourself, resist yourself; you are being betrayed, dispersed, and stolen away from yourself. Do you

traintes au dedans et ses yeux ouverts à se contempler soi-même? C'est toujours vanité pour toi, dedans et dehors, mais elle est moins vanité quand elle est moins étendue. Sauf toi, ô homme," disait ce dieu, "chaque chose s'étudie la première et a, selon son besoin, des limites à ses travaux et désirs. Il n'en est une seule si vide et nécessiteuse que toi, qui embrasses l'univers: tu es le scrutateur sans connaissance, le magistrat sans juridiction et après tout le badin de la farce."

10   De ménager sa volonté [1]

^BAu prix du commun des hommes, peu de choses me touchent, ou pour mieux dire, me tiennent; car c'est raison qu'elles touchent, pourvu qu'elles ne nous possèdent. J'ai grand soin d'augmenter par étude et par discours ce privilège d'insensibilité, qui est naturellement bien avancé en moi. J'épouse, et me passionne par conséquent de, peu de choses. J'ai la vue claire, mais je l'attache à peu d'objets; le sens, délicat et mou. Mais l'appréhension et l'application je l'ai dure et sourde: je m'engage difficilement. Autant que je puis, je m'emploie tout à moi; et en ce sujet même je briderais pourtant et soutiendrais volontiers mon affection qu'elle ne s'y plonge trop entière, puisque c'est un sujet que je possède à la merci d'autrui et

---

[1] Composed between 1585 and 1588.

not see that this world keeps its sight all concentrated inward and its eyes open to contemplate itself? It is always vanity for you, within and without; but it is less vanity when it is less extensive. Except for you, O man," said that god, "each thing studies itself first, and, according to its needs, has limits to its labors and desires. There is not a single thing as empty and needy as you, who embrace the universe: you are the investigator without knowledge, the magistrate without jurisdiction, and all in all, the fool of the farce."

10   Of Husbanding Your Will [1]

[B]In comparison with most men, few things touch me, or, to put it better, hold me; for it is right that things should touch us, provided they do not possess us. I take great care to augment by study and reasoning this privilege of insensibility, which is naturally well advanced in me. I espouse, and in consequence grow passionate about, few things. My sight is clear, but I fix it on few objects; my sensitivity is delicate and tender. But my perception and application are hard and deaf: I do not engage myself easily. As much as I can, I employ myself entirely upon myself; and even in that subject I would still fain bridle my affection and keep it from plunging in too entirely, since this is a subject that I possess at the mercy of others, and over which

sur lequel la fortune a plus de droit que je n'ai. De manière que jusqu'à la santé que j'estime tant, il me serait besoin de ne la pas désirer et m'y adonner si furieusement que j'en trouve les maladies importables. ᶜOn se doit modérer entre la haine de la douleur et l'amour de la volupté; et ordonne Platon une moyenne route de vie entre les deux.

ᴮMais aux affections qui me distraient de moi et attachent ailleurs, à celles-là certes m'opposé-je de toute ma force. Mon opinion est qu'il se faut prêter à autrui et ne se donner qu'à soi-même. Si ma volonté se trouvait aisée à s'hypothéquer et à s'appliquer, je n'y durerais pas: je suis trop tendre, et par nature et par usage,

> fugax rerum, securaque in otia natus.[2]

Les débats contestés et opiniâtrés qui donneraient enfin avantage à mon adversaire, l'issue qui rendrait honteuse ma chaude poursuite, me rongerait à l'aventure bien cruellement. Si je mordais à même, comme font les autres, mon âme n'aurait jamais la force de porter les alarmes et émotions qui suivent ceux qui embrassent tant; elle serait incontinent disloquée par cette agitation intestine. Si quelquefois on m'a poussé au maniement d'affaires étrangères, j'ai promis de les prendre en main, non pas au poumon et au foie; de m'en charger, non de les incorporer; de m'en soigner oui, de m'en passionner nullement. J'y regarde, mais je ne les couve point. J'ai assez à faire à disposer et ranger la presse domestique que j'ai dans mes entrailles

---

[2] Ovid, *Tristia*, iii, ii, 9.

fortune has more right than I have. So that even in regard to health, which I so esteem, I ought not to desire it and give myself to it so frantically as to find illnesses therefore unbearable. ᶜOne must moderate oneself between hatred of pain and love of pleasure; and Plato prescribes a middle way of life between the two.

ᴮBut the passions that distract me from myself and attach me elsewhere, those in truth I oppose with all my strength. My opinion is that we must lend ourselves to others and give ourselves only to ourselves. If my will happened to be prone to mortgage and attach itself, I would not last: I am too tender, both by nature and by practice,

> Fleeing affairs, and born in idle ease.[2]

To engage in contested disputes only to see my opponent get the better of me, or to have to turn back red-faced after giving hot pursuit, might well vex me cruelly. If I were to bite off as much as others do, my soul would never have the strength to bear the alarms and emotions that afflict those who embrace so much; it would be put out of joint from the start by this inner agitation.

If people have sometimes pushed me into the management of other men's affairs, I have promised to take them in hand, not in lungs and liver; to take them on my shoulders, not incorporate them into me; to be concerned over them, yes; to be impassioned over them, never. I look to them, but I do not brood over them. I have enough to do to order and arrange the domestic pressures that oppress

et dans mes veines sans y loger et me fouler d'une presse étrangère; et suis assez intéressé de mes affaires essentiels, propres et naturels, sans en convier d'autres forains.

Ceux qui savent combien ils se doivent et de combien d'offices ils sont obligés à eux trouvent que nature leur a donné cette commission pleine assez et nullement oisive. Tu as bien largement affaire chez toi, ne t'éloigne pas.

Les hommes se donnent à louage. Leurs facultés ne sont pas pour eux, elles sont pour ceux à qui ils s'asservissent; leurs locataires sont chez eux, ce ne sont pas eux. Cette humeur commune ne me plaît pas: il faut ménager la liberté de notre âme et ne l'hypothéquer qu'aux occasions justes, lesquelles sont en bien petit nombre, si nous jugeons sainement. Voyez les gens appris à se laisser emporter et saisir: ils le font partout, aux petites choses comme aux grandes, à ce qui ne les touche point comme à ce qui les touche; ils s'ingèrent indifféremment où il y a de la besogne ᶜet de l'obligation, ᴮet sont sans vie quand ils sont sans agitation tumultuaire. ᶜ*In negotiis sunt negotii causa.*³ Ils ne cherchent la besogne que pour l'embesognement.

Ce n'est pas qu'ils veuillent aller, tant comme c'est qu'ils ne se peuvent tenir: ni plus ni moins qu'une pierre ébranlée en sa chute, qui ne s'arrête jusqu'à tant qu'elle se couche. L'occupation est à certaine manière de gens marque de suffisance et de dignité. ᴮLeur esprit cherche son repos au branle, comme les enfants au berceau. Ils se

---

³ Seneca, *Epistles*, xxii, 8.

my entrails and veins, without giving myself the trouble of adding extraneous pressures to them; I am enough involved in my essential, proper, and natural affairs, without inviting in foreign ones.

Those who know how much they owe to themselves, and for how many duties they are obligated to themselves, find that nature has given them in this a commission full enough and not at all idle. You have quite enough to do at home; don't go away.

Men give themselves for hire. Their faculties are not for them, they are for those to whom they enslave themselves; their tenants are at home inside, not they. This common humor I do not like. We must husband the freedom of our soul and mortgage it only on the right occasions; which are in very small number, if we judge sanely. See the people who have been taught to let themselves be seized and carried away: they do so everywhere, in little things as in big, in what does not touch them as in what does; they push in indiscriminately wherever there is business ᶜand involvement, ᴮand are without life when they are without tumultuous agitation. ᶜ*They are in business for business' sake.*[3] They seek business only for busyness.

It is not that they want to be on the go, so much as that they cannot keep still; no more nor less than a stone that has started falling, and that does not stop until it comes to rest. Occupation is to a certain manner of people a mark of ability and dignity. ᴮTheir mind seeks its repose in movement, like children in the cradle. They may be said to

peuvent dire autant serviables à leurs amis comme importuns à eux-mêmes. Personne ne distribue son argent à autrui, chacun y distribue son temps et sa vie. Il n'est rien de quoi nous soyons si prodigues que de ces choses-là, desquelles seules l'avarice nous serait utile et louable.

Je prends une complexion toute diverse. Je me tiens sur moi, et communément désire mollement ce que je désire, et désire peu; m'occupe et embesogne de même, rarement et tranquillement. Tout ce qu'ils veulent et conduisent, ils le font de toute leur volonté et véhémence. Il y a tant de mauvais pas que, pour le plus sûr, il faut un peu légèrement et superficiellement couler ce monde. ᶜIl le faut glisser, non pas s'y enfoncer. ᴮLa volupté même est douloureuse en sa profondeur:

> incedis per ignes
> Suppositos cineri doloso.⁴

Messieurs de Bordeaux ⁵ m'élurent maire de leur ville, étant éloigné de France et encore plus éloigné d'un tel pensement. Je m'en excusai, mais on m'apprit que j'avais tort, le commandement du roi aussi s'y interposant. C'est une charge qui en doit sembler d'autant plus belle qu'elle n'a ni loyer ni gain autre que l'honneur de son exécution. Elle dure deux ans; mais elle peut être continuée par seconde élection, ce qui advient très rarement. Elle le fut à moi; et ne l'avait été que deux fois auparavant. . . .

A mon arrivée je me déchiffrai fidèlement et consciencieusement, tout tel que je me sens être: sans mémoire,

---

⁴ Horace, *Odes*, ii, i, 7–8.

be as serviceable to their friends as they are importunate to themselves. No one distributes his money to others, everyone distributes his time and his life on them. There is nothing of which we are so prodigal as of the only things in which avarice would be useful to us and laudable.

I take a wholly different attitude. I keep myself to myself, and commonly desire mildly what I desire, and desire little; occupy and busy myself likewise: rarely and tranquilly. Whatever they desire and take in hand, they do with all their will and vehemence. There are so many bad spots that, for greatest safety, we must slide over this world a bit lightly and on the surface. ^CWe must glide over it, not break through into it. ^BEven sensual pleasure is painful in its depth:

> Treacherous ashes hide
> The fires through which you stride.[4]

Messieurs of Bordeaux [5] elected me mayor of their city when I was far from France and still farther from such a thought. I excused myself, but I was informed that I was wrong, since the king's command also figured in the matter. It is an office that must appear all the handsomer for this, that it has no remuneration or gain other than the honor of its execution. The term is two years; but it can be extended by a second election, which happens very rarely. This was done in my case, and had been done only twice before. . . .

On my arrival I deciphered myself to them faithfully and conscientiously, exactly such as I feel myself to be:

---

⁵ The Jurats of Bordeaux, who formed a sort of municipal council.

sans vigilance, sans expérience et sans vigueur; sans haine aussi, sans ambition, sans avarice et sans violence; à ce qu'ils fussent informés et instruits de ce qu'ils avaient à attendre de mon service. Et parce que la connaissance de feu mon père les avait seule incités à cela, et l'honneur de sa mémoire,[6] je leur ajoutai bien clairement que je serais très marri que chose quelconque fît autant d'impression en ma volonté comme avaient fait autrefois en la sienne leurs affaires et leur ville, pendant qu'il l'avait en gouvernement, en ce même lieu où ils m'avaient appelé.

Il me souvenait de l'avoir vu vieil en mon enfance, l'âme cruellement agitée de cette tracasserie publique, oubliant le doux air de sa maison, où la faiblesse des ans l'avait attaché longtemps avant, et son ménage et sa santé; et, en méprisant certes sa vie qu'il y cuida perdre, engagé pour eux à de longs et pénibles voyages. Il était tel; et lui partait cette humeur d'une grande bonté de nature: il ne fut jamais âme plus charitable et populaire.

Ce train, que je loue en autrui, je n'aime point à le suivre, et ne suis pas sans excuse. Il avait ouï dire qu'il se fallait oublier pour le prochain, que le particulier ne venait en aucune considération au prix du général. . . .

J'estime qu'au temple de Pallas, comme nous voyons en toutes autres religions, il y avait des mystères apparents pour être montrés au peuple, et d'autres mystères plus

---

[6] Probably Montaigne sincerely believed this; but it now seems more likely that he was elected because he was the man most acceptable to all four royal personages concerned with the election:

without memory, without vigilance, without experience, and without vigor; also without hate, without ambition, without avarice, and without violence; so that they should be informed and instructed about what they were to expect of my service. And because their knowledge of my late father had alone incited them to this, and their honor for his memory,[6] I added very clearly that I should be very sorry if anything whatsoever were to weigh so heavily on my will as their affairs and their city had formerly done on his, while he was administering it in this same spot to which they had called me.

I remembered in my boyhood having seen him old, his soul cruelly agitated by this public turmoil, forgetting the sweet air of his home, to which the weakness of years had attached him long since, and his household and his health; and, truly heedless of his life, which he nearly lost in this, engaged for them in long and painful journeys. He was like that; and this disposition in him sprang from a great goodness of nature: there was never a more kindly and public-spirited soul.

This course, which I commend in others, I do not love to follow, and I am not without excuse. He had heard it said that we must forget ourselves for our neighbor, that the individual was not to be considered at all in comparison with the general. . . .

I think that in the temple of Pallas, as we see in all other religions, there were apparent mysteries to be shown to the people, and other mysteries, more secret and high,

Henry III, Catherine de' Medici, Henry of Navarre, and Margaret of Valois.

secrets et plus hauts pour être montrés seulement à ceux qui en étaient profès. Il est vraisemblable qu'en ceux-ci se trouve le vrai point de l'amitié que chacun se doit. Non une amitié ᶜfausse, qui nous fait embrasser la gloire, la science, la richesse et telles choses d'une affection principale et immodérée, comme membres de notre être, ni une amitié ᴮmolle et indiscrète, en laquelle il advient ce qui se voit au lierre, qu'il corrompt et ruine la paroi qu'il accole; mais une amitié salutaire et réglée, également utile et plaisante. Qui en sait les devoirs et les exerce, il est vraiment du cabinet des muses; il a atteint le sommet de la sagesse humaine et de notre bonheur. Celui-ci, sachant exactement ce qu'il se doit, trouve dans son rôle qu'il doit appliquer à soi l'usage des autres hommes et du monde, et, pour ce faire, contribuer à la société publique les devoirs et offices qui le touchent. ᶜQui ne vit aucunement à autrui ne vit guère à soi. *Qui sibi amicus est, scito hunc amicum omnibus esse.*[7] ᴮLa principale charge que nous ayons, c'est à chacun sa conduite; ᶜet est-ce pourquoi nous sommes ici. ᴮComme qui oublierait de bien et saintement vivre, et penserait être quitte de son devoir en y acheminant et dressant les autres, ce serait un sot; tout de même, qui abandonne en son propre le sainement et gaiement vivre pour en servir autrui, prend à mon gré un mauvais et dénaturé parti.

Je ne veux pas qu'on refuse aux charges qu'on prend l'attention, les pas, les paroles, et la sueur et le sang au besoin:

---

[7] Adapted from Seneca, *Epistles*, vi, 7.

to be shown only to those who were initiated. It is likely that among the latter is to be found the true point of the friendship that each man owes to himself. Not ^Ca false friendship, that makes us embrace glory, learning, riches, and such things with paramount and immoderate affection, as members of our being; nor ^Ban overindulgent and undiscriminating friendship, in which it happens as we see with ivy, that it decays and ruins the wall it clings to; but a salutary and well-regulated friendship, useful and pleasant alike. He who knows its duties and practices them, he is truly of the cabinet of the Muses; he has attained the summit of human wisdom and of our happiness. This man, knowing exactly what he owes to himself, finds it in his part that he is to apply to himself his experience of other men and of the world, and, in order to do so, contribute to public society the duties and services within his province. ^CHe who lives not at all unto others, hardly lives unto himself. *He who is a friend to himself, know that that man is a friend to all.*ⁱ ^BThe main responsibility of each of us is his own conduct; ^Cand that is what we are here for. ^BJust as anyone who should forget to live a good and saintly life, and think he was quit of his duty by guiding and training others to do so, would be a fool; even so he who abandons healthy and gay living of his own to serve others thereby, takes, to my taste, a bad and unnatural course.

I do not want a man to refuse, to the charges he takes on, attention, steps, words, and sweat and blood if need be:

> non ipse pro charis amicis
> Aut patria timidus perire.[8]

Mais c'est par emprunt et accidentellement, l'esprit se tenant toujours en repos et en santé, non pas sans action, mais sans vexation, sans passion. L'agir simplement lui coûte si peu, qu'en dormant même il agit. Mais il lui faut donner le branle avec discrétion. Car le corps reçoit les charges qu'on lui met sus, justement selon qu'elles sont; l'esprit les étend et les appesantit souvent à ses dépens, leur donnant la mesure que bon lui semble. On fait pareilles choses avec divers efforts et différente contention de volonté. L'un va bien sans l'autre.[9] Car combien de gens se hasardent tous les jours aux guerres, de quoi il ne leur chaut, et se pressent aux dangers des batailles, desquelles la perte ne leur troublera pas le voisin sommeil! Tel en sa maison, hors de ce danger qu'il n'oserait avoir regardé, est plus passionné de l'issue de cette guerre et en a l'âme plus travaillée que n'a le soldat qui y emploie son sang et sa vie.

J'ai pu me mêler des charges publiques sans me départir de moi de la largeur d'une ongle, ^Cet me donner à autrui sans m'ôter à moi. ^BCette âpreté et violence de désir empêche plus qu'elle ne sert à la conduite de ce qu'on entreprend, nous remplit d'impatience envers les événements ou contraires ou tardifs, et d'aigreur et de soupçon envers ceux avec qui nous négocions. Nous ne conduisons jamais bien la chose de laquelle nous sommes possédés et conduits. . . .

---

[8] Adapted from Horace, *Odes*, IV, ix, 51-2.

> To die for what is dear,
> Country or friends, I do not fear.[8]

But this is by way of loan and accidentally, the mind holding itself ever in repose and in health, not without action, but without vexation, without passion. Simply to act costs it so little that it is acting even in sleep. But it must be set in motion with discretion. For the body receives the loads that are placed on it exactly according as they are; the mind often extends them and makes them heavier to its cost, giving them the measurements it sees fit. We do like things with different degrees of effort and tension of the will. The one goes very well without the other.[9] For how many people risk themselves every day in the wars, which are no concern to them, and press forward to the dangers of battles, the loss of which will not trouble their next night's sleep! This man in his own house, outside of this danger which he would not have dared to face, is more passionate about the outcome of this war, and more worked up in his soul about it, than the soldier who is spending his blood and his life in it.

I have been able to take part in public office without departing one nail's breadth from myself, ᶜand to give myself to others without taking myself from myself. ᴮThis fierceness and violence of desire hinders more than it serves the performance of what we undertake, fills us with impatience toward things that come out contrary or late, and with bitterness and suspicion toward the people we deal with. We never conduct well the thing that possesses and conducts us. . . .

---

[9] Action without passion.

[III:10] *Of Husbanding Your Will*

La plupart de nos vacations sont farcesques. *Mundus universus exercet histrionam.*[10] Il faut jouer dûment notre rôle, mais comme rôle d'un personnage emprunté. Du masque et de l'apparence il n'en faut pas faire une essence réelle, ni de l'étranger le propre. Nous ne savons pas distinguer la peau de la chemise. ^CC'est assez de s'enfariner le visage, sans s'enfariner la poitrine. ^BJ'en vois qui . . . se prélatent jusqu'au foie et aux intestins, et entraînent leur office jusqu'en leur garde-robe. Je ne puis leur apprendre à distinguer les bonnetades qui les regardent de celles qui regardent leur commission, ou leur suite, ou leur mule. . . . Le Maire et Montaigne ont toujours été deux, d'une séparation bien claire.

. . . C'est agir pour sa réputation et profit particulier, non pour le bien, de remettre à faire en la place ce qu'on peut faire en la chambre du conseil, et en plein midi ce qu'on eût fait la nuit précédente, et d'être jaloux de faire soi-même ce que son compagnon fait aussi bien.

. . . Je n'ai point eu cette humeur inique et assez commune de désirer que le trouble et maladie des affaires de cette cité rehaussât et honorât mon gouvernement: j'ai prêté de bon cœur l'épaule à leur aisance et facilité. Qui ne me voudra savoir gré de l'ordre, de la douce et muette tranquillité qui a accompagné ma conduite, au moins ne peut-il me priver de la part qui m'en appartient par le titre de ma bonne fortune. Et je suis ainsi fait que j'aime autant être heureux que sage, et devoir mes succès purement à la grâce de Dieu qu'à l'entremise de mon opéra-

---

[10] Fragment from Petronius, quoted by Justus Lipsius, *De Constantia*, I, viii.

Most of our occupations are low comedy. *The whole world plays a part.*[10] We must play our part duly, but as the part of a borrowed character. Of the mask and appearance we must not make a real essence, nor of what is foreign what is our very own. We cannot distinguish the skin from the shirt. CIt is enough to make up our face, without making up our heart. BI see some who . . . are prelates to their very liver and intestines, and drag their position with them even into their privy. I cannot teach them to distinguish the tips of the hat that are for them from those that are for their office, or their retinue, or their mule. . . . The mayor and Montaigne have always been two, with a very clear separation.

. . . It is acting for our private reputation and profit, not for the good, to put off and do in the public square what we can do in the council chamber, and at high noon what we could have done the night before, and to be jealous to do ourselves what our colleague does as well.

. . . I have not had that iniquitous and rather common disposition of wanting the trouble and sickness of the affairs of this city to exalt and honor my government; I heartily lent a shoulder to make them easy and light. Anyone who will not be grateful to me for the order, the gentle and mute tranquillity, that accompanied my administration, at least cannot deprive me of the share of it that belongs to me by right of my good fortune. And I am so made that I like as well to be lucky as wise, and to owe my successes purely to the grace of God as to the effect

tion. . . . Je ne me suis en cette entremise non plus satisfait à moi-même, mais à peu près j'en suis arrivé à ce que je m'en étais promis, et ai de beaucoup surmonté ce que j'en avais promis à ceux à qui j'avais affaire: car je promets volontiers un peu moins de ce que je puis et de ce que j'espère tenir. . . .

12 De la physionomie [1]

. . . [B]Il ne nous faut guère de doctrine pour vivre à notre aise. Et Socratès nous apprend qu'elle est en nous, et la manière de l'y trouver et de s'en aider. Toute cette notre suffisance qui est au delà de la naturelle est [C]à peu près [B]vaine et superflue. C'est beaucoup si elle ne nous charge et trouble plus qu'elle ne nous sert. [C]*Paucis opus est litteris ad mentem bonam.*[2] [B]Ce sont des excès fiévreux de notre esprit, instrument brouillon et inquiet.

Recueillez-vous: vous trouverez en vous les arguments de la nature contre la mort, vrais, et les plus propres à vous servir à la nécessité; ce sont ceux qui font mourir un paysan et des peuples entiers aussi constamment qu'un philosophe. [C]Fussé-je mort moins allègrement avant qu'avoir vu les *Tusculanes*?[3] J'estime que non. . . .

[B]A quoi faire nous allons-nous gendarmant par ces efforts de la science? Regardons à terre les pauvres gens

---

[1] Composed in 1585–88.
[2] Seneca, *Epistles*, cvi, 12.

of my own action. . . . I did not satisfy myself either in this undertaking, but I accomplished about what I had promised myself, and far surpassed what I had promised those whom I had to deal with. For I am apt to promise a little less than what I can do and what I hope to deliver. . . .

12 Of Physiognomy [1]

. . . ᴮWe need hardly any learning to live at ease. And Socrates teaches us that it is in us, and the way to find it and help ourselves with it. All this ability of ours that is beyond the natural is ᶜas good as ᴮvain and superfluous. It is a lot if it does not load us down and bother us more than it serves us. ᶜ*Little learning is needed for a good mind.*[2] ᴮThese are feverish excesses of our mind, a meddlesome and restless instrument.

Collect yourself: you will find in yourself Nature's arguments against death, true ones, and the fittest to serve you in case of necessity; they are the ones that make a peasant, and whole nations, die as steadfastly as a philosopher. ᶜShould I have died less cheerfully before having read the *Tusculans?*[3] I think not. . . .

ᴮTo what end do we keep rousing ourselves with these efforts of learning? Let us look on the earth at the poor

_____
[3] Cicero's *Tusculan Disputations,* of which the first book deals with contempt of death.

que nous y voyons épandus, la tête penchante après leur besogne, qui ne savent ni Aristote ni Caton, ni exemple ni précepte: de ceux-là tire nature tous les jours des effets de constance et de patience plus purs et plus raides que ne sont ceux que nous étudions si curieusement en l'école. Combien en vois-je ordinairement qui méconnaissent la pauvreté? combien qui désirent la mort ou qui la passent sans alarme et sans affliction? Celui-là qui fouit mon jardin, il a ce matin enterré son père ou son fils. Les noms mêmes de quoi ils appellent les maladies en adoucissent et amollissent l'âpreté: la phtisie c'est la toux pour eux; la dysenterie, dévoiement d'estomac; une pleurésie, c'est un morfondement; et selon qu'ils les nomment doucement, ils les supportent aussi. Elles sont bien grièves quand elles rompent leur travail ordinaire; ils ne s'alitent que pour mourir. . . .

J'écrivais ceci environ le temps qu'une forte charge de nos troubles se croupit plusieurs mois, de tout son poids, droit sur moi. J'avais d'une part les ennemis à ma porte, d'autre part les picoreurs, pires ennemis. . . . Monstrueuse guerre: les autres agissent au dehors, celle-ci encore contre soi se ronge et se défait par son propre venin. . . . Elle vient guérir la sédition et en est pleine, veut châtier la désobéissance et en montre l'exemple; et employée à la défense des lois, fait sa part de rébellion à l'encontre des siennes propres. . . .

Outre cette secousse, j'en souffris d'autres. J'encourus les inconvénients que la modération apporte en telles maladies. Je fus pelaudé à toutes mains: au Gibelin j'étais Guelfe, au Guelfe Gibelin.[4] . . .

---

[4] The Ghibellines and Guelphs were rival parties in medieval Italy.

people we see scattered there, heads bowed over their toil, who know neither Aristotle nor Cato, neither example nor precept. From them Nature every day draws deeds of constancy and endurance purer and harder than those that we study with such care in school. How many of them I see all the time who ignore poverty! How many who desire death, or who meet it without alarm and without affliction! This man who is digging up my garden, this morning he buried his father or his son. The very names by which they call diseases relieve and soften their harshness: phthisis is the cough to them; dysentery, looseness of the bowels; pleurisy, a cold; and according as they name them mildly, so also they endure them. A disease must be very grave to interrupt their ordinary work; they take to their beds only to die. . . .

I was writing this about the time when a mighty load of our disturbances settled down for several months with all its weight right on me. I had on the one hand the enemy at my door, on the other hand the freebooters, worse enemies. . . . Monstrous war! Other wars act outward; this one acts also against itself, eats and destroys itself by its own venom. . . . It comes to cure sedition and is full of it, would chastise disobedience and sets the example of it; and employed in defense of the laws, plays the part of a rebel against its own laws. . . .

Besides this shock I suffered others. I incurred the disadvantages that moderation brings in such maladies. I was belabored from every quarter; to the Ghibelline I was a Guelph, to the Guelph a Ghibelline.[4] . . .

[III:12] *Of Physiognomy*

Voici un autre rengrègement de mal qui m'arriva à la suite du reste. Et dehors et dedans ma maison je fus accueilli d'une peste véhémente au prix de toute autre. . . .

Or lors, quel exemple de résolution ne vîmes-nous en la simplicité de tout ce peuple? Généralement chacun renonçait au soin de la vie. Les raisins demeurèrent suspendus aux vignes, le bien principal du pays, tous indifféremment se préparant et attendant la mort à ce soir ou au lendemain, d'un visage et d'une voix si peu effrayée qu'il semblait qu'ils eussent compromis à cette nécessité et que ce fût une condamnation universelle et inévitable. Elle est toujours telle. Mais à combien peu tient la résolution au mourir: la distance et différence de quelques heures, la seule considération de la compagnie, nous en rend l'appréhension diverse. Voyez ceux-ci: pour ce qu'ils meurent en même mois, enfants, jeunes, vieillards, ils ne s'étonnent plus, ils ne se pleurent plus. J'en vis qui craignaient de demeurer derrière, comme en une horrible solitude; et n'y connus communément autre soin que des sépultures: il leur fâchait de voir les corps épars emmi les champs, à la merci des bêtes, qui y peuplèrent incontinent. . . .

Tel, sain, faisait déjà sa fosse; d'autres s'y couchaient encore vivants. Et un manœuvre des miens à tout ses mains et ses pieds attira sur soi la terre en mourant: était-ce pas s'abriter pour s'endormir plus à son aise? . . . Somme, toute une nation fut incontinent, par usage, logée en une marche qui ne cède en raideur à aucune résolution étudiée et consultée.

Now a further increase of trouble came upon me following the others. Both outside and inside my house I was greeted by a plague of the utmost virulence. . . .

Now, what example of resoluteness did we not see then in the simplicity of this whole people? Each man universally gave up caring for his life. The grapes remained hanging on the vines, the principal produce of the country, as all prepared themselves indifferently, and awaited death that evening or the next day with face and voice so little frightened that it seemed that they had made their peace with this necessity and that they were under a universal and inevitable sentence of death. Death is always that. But on how little depends our resoluteness in the face of death! A few hours' difference in our distance from it, the mere consideration of having company, makes our apprehension of it different. See these people: because they are dying in the same month, children, young people, old people, they are no longer stunned, they no longer bewail one another. I saw some who feared to remain behind, as in a horrible solitude; and found them generally to be concerned only about their burial. It pained them to see the bodies scattered amid the fields, at the mercy of the animals that promptly appeared in swarms. . . .

Here a man, healthy, was already digging his grave; others lay down in them while still alive. And one of my laborers, with his hands and feet, pulled the earth over him as he was dying. Was that not taking shelter so as to go to sleep more comfortably? . . . In short, a whole nation was suddenly, by habit alone, placed on a level that concedes nothing in firmness to any studied and premeditated fortitude.

[III:12] *Of Physiognomy*

La plupart des instructions de la science à nous encourager ont plus de montre que de force, et plus d'ornement que de fruit. Nous avons abandonné nature et lui voulons apprendre sa leçon, elle qui nous menait si heureusement et si sûrement. Et cependant les traces de son instruction et ce peu qui par le bénéfice de l'ignorance reste de son image empreint en la vie de cette tourbe rustique d'hommes impolis, la science est contrainte de l'aller tous les jours empruntant pour en faire patron à ses disciples de constance, d'innocence et de tranquillité. Il fait beau voir que ceux-ci, pleins de tant de belle connaissance, aient à imiter cette sotte simplicité, et à l'imiter aux premières actions de la vertu; et que notre sapience apprenne des bêtes mêmes les plus utiles enseignements aux plus grandes et nécessaires parties de notre vie: comme il nous faut vivre et mourir, ménager nos biens, aimer et élever nos enfants, entretenir justice, singulier témoignage de l'humaine maladie; et que cette raison qui se manie à notre poste, trouvant toujours quelque diversité et nouveauté, ne laisse chez nous aucune trace apparente de la nature. Et en ont fait les hommes comme les parfumiers de l'huile: ils l'ont sophistiquée de tant d'argumentations et de discours appelés du dehors qu'elle en est devenue variable et particulière à chacun et a perdu son propre visage constant et universel; et nous faut en chercher témoignage des bêtes, non sujet à faveur, corruption, ni à diversité d'opinions. Car il est bien vrai qu'elles-mêmes ne vont pas toujours exactement dans la route de nature; mais ce qu'elles en dévoient, c'est si peu que vous en apercevez toujours l'ornière. . . .

A quoi nous sert cette curiosité de préoccuper tous les

Most of the instructions that learning uses to encourage us are more showy than powerful and more ornamental than effective. We have abandoned Nature and we want to teach her her lesson, she who used to guide us so happily and so surely. And yet the traces of her teaching and the little that remains of her image—imprinted, by the benefit of ignorance, on the life of that rustic, unpolished mob—learning is constrained every day to go and borrow, to give its disciples models of constancy, innocence, and tranquillity. It is fine to see these disciples, full of so much beautiful knowledge, obliged to imitate that stupid simplicity, and imitate it in the primary actions of virtue; and a fine thing that our sapience learns from the very animals the most useful teachings for the greatest and most necessary parts of our life: how we should live and die, husband our possessions, love and bring up our children, maintain justice—a singular testimony of human infirmity; and that this reason of ours that we handle as we will, always finding some diversity and novelty, leaves in us no apparent trace of Nature. And men have done with Nature as perfumers do with oil: they have sophisticated her with so many arguments and farfetched reasonings that she has become variable and particular for each man, and has lost her own constant and universal countenance; and we must seek in the animals evidence of her that is not subject to favor, corruption, or diversity of opinion. For it is indeed true that they themselves do not always go exactly in Nature's road; but they deviate from it so little that you can always perceive the ruts. . . .

Of what use to us is this curiosity to anticipate all the

[III:12] *Of Physiognomy*

inconvénients de l'humaine nature, et nous préparer avec tant de peine à l'encontre de ceux mêmes qui n'ont à l'aventure point à nous toucher? . . . ^Cet prendre votre robe fourrée dès la Saint-Jean parce que vous en aurez besoin à Noël? ^B"Jetez-vous en l'expérience des maux qui vous peuvent arriver, nommément des plus extrêmes: éprouvez-vous là," disent-ils, "assurez-vous là." Au rebours, le plus facile et plus naturel serait en décharger même sa pensée. Ils ne viendront pas assez tôt, leur vrai être ne nous dure pas assez: il faut que notre esprit les étende et allonge et qu'avant la main il les incorpore en soi et s'en entretienne, comme s'ils ne pesaient pas raisonnablement à nos sens. ^C"Ils pèseront assez quand ils y seront," dit un des maîtres,[5] non de quelque tendre secte mais de la plus dure. "Cependant favorise-toi; crois ce que tu aimes le mieux. Que te sert-il d'aller recueillant et prévenant ta male fortune, et de perdre le présent par la crainte du futur, et être à cette heure misérable parce que tu le dois être avec le temps?" Ce sont ses mots. ^BLa science nous fait volontiers un bon office de nous instruire bien exactement des dimensions des maux. . . . Ce serait dommage si partie de leur grandeur échappait à notre sentiment et connaissance.

Il est certain qu'à la plupart la préparation à la mort a donné plus de tourment que n'a fait la souffrance.

. . . Si vous ne savez pas mourir, ne vous chaille: nature vous en informera sur-le-champ, pleinement et suffisamment; elle fera exactement cette besogne pour vous; n'en empêchez votre soin. . . . Nous troublons la vie par le

---

⁵ Seneca (a Stoic), *Epistles*, xiii, 10; xxiv, 1.

ills of human nature, and prepare ourselves with so much trouble to encounter even those which are perhaps never to touch us? . . . ᶜand put on your furred gown on Midsummer Day because you will need it at Christmas? ᴮ"Hurry up and experience the evils that may befall you, especially the most extreme. Test yourself in them," they say, "make sure." On the contrary, the easiest and most natural thing would be to unburden even our thoughts of them. Apparently they will not come soon enough, their true being does not last us long enough; our mind must extend and prolong them, incorporate them into itself and dwell on them beforehand, as if they did not weigh reasonably upon our senses. ᶜ"They will weigh heavily enough when they are there," says one of the masters,[5] not of some tender sect, but of the hardest. "Meanwhile favor yourself; believe what you like best. What good does it do you to welcome and anticipate your bad fortune, to lose the present through fear of the future, and to be miserable now because you are to be so in time?" Those are his words. ᴮLearning doubtless does us a good service by instructing us very exactly about the dimensions of evils. . . . It would be a pity if part of their greatness escaped our feeling and knowledge.

It is certain that to most people preparation for death has given more torment than the dying.

. . . If you don't know how to die, don't worry; Nature will tell you what to do on the spot, fully and adequately. She will do this job perfectly for you; don't bother your head about it. . . . We trouble our life by concern about

soin de la mort, et la mort par le soin de la vie. . . . ^CMais il m'est avis que c'est bien le bout, non pourtant le but de la vie; c'est sa fin, son extrémité, non pourtant son objet. Elle doit être elle-même à soi sa visée, son dessein; son droit étude est se régler, se conduire, se souffrir. Au nombre de plusieurs autres offices que comprend ce général et principal chapitre de savoir vivre est cet article de savoir mourir; et des plus légers, si notre crainte ne lui donnait poids.

^BA les juger par l'utilité et par la vérité naïve, les leçons de la simplicité ne cèdent guère à celles que nous prêche la doctrine au contraire. . . . Je ne vis jamais paysan de mes voisins entrer en cogitation de quelle contenance et assurance il passerait cette heure dernière. Nature lui apprend à ne songer à la mort que quand il se meurt. Et lors il y a meilleure grâce qu'Aristote, lequel la mort presse doublement, et par elle, et par une si longue prévoyance. . . .

^CLe commun n'a besoin ni de remède ni de consolation qu'au coup, et n'en considère qu'autant justement qu'il en sent. ^BEst-ce pas ce que nous disons, que la stupidité et faute d'appréhension du vulgaire lui donne cette patience aux maux présents et cette profonde nonchalance des sinistres accidents futurs? ^Cque leur âme, pour être crasse et obtuse, est moins pénétrable et agitable? ^BPour Dieu, s'il est ainsi, tenons dorénavant école de bêtise. C'est l'extrême fruit que les sciences nous promettent, auquel celle-ci conduit si doucement ses disciples.

Nous n'aurons pas faute de bons régents, interprètes de la simplicité naturelle. Socratès en sera l'un. . . .

death, and death by concern about life. . . . ᶜBut it seems to me that death is indeed the end, but not therefore the goal, of life; it is its finish, its extremity, but not therefore its object. Life should be an aim unto itself, a purpose unto itself; its rightful study is to regulate, conduct, and suffer itself. Among the many other duties comprised in this general and principal chapter on knowing how to live is this article on knowing how to die; and it is one of the lightest, if our fear did not give it weight.

ᴮTo judge by utility and natural truth, the lessons of simplicity yield little to those which learning preaches to us to the contrary. . . . I never saw one of my peasant neighbors cogitating over the countenance and assurance with which he would pass this last hour. Nature teaches him not to think about death except when he is dying. And then he has better grace about it than Aristotle, whom death oppresses doubly, both by itself and by such a long foreknowledge. . . .

ᶜThe common people need neither remedy nor consolation except when the blow falls, and consider only precisely as much of it as they feel. ᴮIsn't that what we say, that the stupidity and lack of apprehension of the vulgar gives them this endurance of present troubles and this profound nonchalance about sinister accidents to come, ᶜthat their souls, because they are thick and obtuse, are less penetrable and unstable? ᴮFor Heaven's sake, if that is so, let us henceforth hold a school of stupidity. Learning promises us no greater boon than this, to which stupidity so gently leads its disciples.

We shall have no lack of good teachers, interpreters of the simplicity of nature. Socrates will be one. . . .

[III:12] *Of Physiognomy*

13 De l'expérience [1]

^BIl n'est désir plus naturel que le désir de connaissance. Nous essayons tous les moyens qui nous y peuvent mener. Quand la raison nous faut, nous y employons l'expérience . . . qui est un moyen plus faible et moins digne; mais la vérité est chose si grande que nous ne devons dédaigner aucune entremise qui nous y conduise. La raison a tant de formes que nous ne savons à laquelle nous prendre; l'expérience n'en a pas moins. La conséquence que nous voulons tirer de la ressemblance des événements est mal sûre, d'autant qu'ils sont toujours dissemblables: il n'est aucune qualité si universelle en cette image des choses que la diversité et variété. . . . La ressemblance ne fait pas tant un comme la dissemblance fait autre. ^CNature s'est obligée à ne rien faire autre qui ne fût dissemblable.

. . . ^BQu'ont gagné nos législateurs à choisir cent mille espèces et faits particuliers et y attacher cent mille lois? Ce nombre n'a aucune proportion avec l'infinie diversité des actions humaines. La multiplication de nos inventions n'arrivera pas à la variation des exemples. . . . Il y a peu de relation de nos actions, qui sont en perpétuelle mutation, avec les lois fixes et immobiles. Les plus désirables, ce sont les plus rares, plus simples et générales; et encore

---

[1] This final chapter of the *Essais*, written in 1587–88, is a real conclusion. Montaigne notes that experience is a surer though less glamorous guide to knowledge than reason. The essays are a record of his experience of himself, which is considerable in physical and medical matters where experience rules supreme. Therefore he gives a long account of his bodily ways and habits. His vexation with

[B]There is no desire more natural than the desire for knowledge. We try all the ways that can lead us to it. When reason fails us, we use experience . . . which is a weaker and less dignified means. But truth is so great a thing that we must not disdain any medium that will lead us to it. Reason has so many shapes that we know not which to lay hold of; experience has no fewer. The inference that we try to draw from the resemblance of events is uncertain, because they are always dissimilar: there is no quality so universal in this aspect of things as diversity and variety. . . . Resemblance does not make things so much alike as difference makes them unlike. [C]Nature has committed herself to make nothing separate that was not different.

. . . [B]What have our legislators gained by selecting a hundred thousand particular cases and actions, and applying a hundred thousand laws to them? This number bears no proportion to the infinite diversity of human actions. Multiplication of our imaginary cases will never equal the variety of the real examples. . . . There is little relation between our actions, which are in perpetual mutation, and fixed and immutable laws. The most desirable laws are

---

those who disdain the body leads him to his conclusion. God has made us of soul and body, and given each part many things to enjoy. To live as a man, to be not an angel or a beast but simply a man—this is not only the happiest life and the most appropriate, but the finest.

crois-je qu'il vaudrait mieux n'en avoir point du tout que
de les avoir en tel nombre que nous les avons.

. . . Jamais deux hommes ne jugèrent pareillement de
même chose, et est impossible de voir deux opinions semblables exactement, non seulement en divers hommes,
mais en même homme à diverses heures. Ordinairement
je trouve à douter en ce que le commentaire n'a daigné
toucher. Je bronche plus volontiers en pays plat, comme
certains chevaux que je connais qui choppent plus souvent en chemin uni.

Qui ne dirait que les gloses augmentent les doutes et
l'ignorance, puisqu'il ne se voit aucun livre, soit humain,
soit divin, auquel le monde s'embesogne, duquel l'interprétation fasse tarir la difficulté? Le centième commentaire le renvoie à son suivant, plus épineux et plus sca-
breux que le premier ne l'avait trouvé. Quand est-il
convenu entre nous: ce livre en a assez, il n'y a meshui
plus que dire? . . . Les hommes méconnaissent la maladie
naturelle de leur esprit: il ne fait que fureter et quêter, et
va sans cesse tournoyant, bâtissant et s'empêtrant en sa
besogne, comme nos vers de soie, et s'y étouffe.

. . . ^CNul esprit généreux ne s'arrête en soi: il pré-
tend toujours et va outre ses forces; il a des élans au delà
de ses effets; s'il ne s'avance et ne se presse et ne s'accule
et ne se choque, il n'est vif qu'à demi. . . . ^BC'est un
mouvement irrégulier, perpétuel, sans patron, et sans but.
Ses inventions s'échauffent, se suivent, et s'entreproduisent
l'une l'autre. . . .

Il y a plus à faire à interpréter les interprétations qu'à
interpréter les choses, et plus de livres sur les livres que

those that are rarest, simplest, and most general; and I even think that it would be better to have none at all than to have them in such numbers as we have. . . . Never did two men judge alike about the same thing, and it is impossible to find two opinions exactly alike, not only in different men, but in the same man at different times. Ordinarily I find subject for doubt in what the commentary has not deigned to touch on. I am more apt to trip on flat ground, like certain horses I know which stumble more often on a smooth road.

Who would not say that glosses increase doubts and ignorance, since there is no book to be found, whether human or divine, with which the world busies itself, whose difficulties are cleared up by interpretation? The hundredth commentator hands it on to his successor thornier and rougher than the first one had found it. When do we agree and say, "There has been enough about this book; henceforth there is nothing more to say about it"? . . . Men do not know the natural infirmity of their mind: it does nothing but ferret and quest, and keeps incessantly whirling around, building up and becoming entangled in its own work, like our silkworms, and is suffocated in it. . . . ᶜA spirited mind never stops within itself; it is always aspiring and going beyond its strength; it has impulses beyond its powers of achievement. If it does not advance and press forward and stand at bay and clash, it is only half alive. . . . ᴮIt is an irregular, perpetual motion, without model and without aim. Its inventions excite, pursue, and produce one another. . . .

It is more of a job to interpret the interpretations than to interpret the things, and there are more books about

sur autre sujet: nous ne faisons que nous entregloser. ^CTout fourmille de commentaires; d'auteurs, il en est grande cherté. . . .

^BJ'ai vu en Allemagne que Luther a laissé autant de divisions et d'altercations sur le doute de ses opinions, et plus, qu'il n'en émut sur les Écritures Saintes.

Notre contestation est verbale. Je demande que c'est que nature, volupté, cercle, et substitution. La question est de paroles et se paye de même. "Une pierre c'est un corps." Mais qui presserait: "Et ce corps, qu'est-ce?" — "Substance" — "Et substance quoi?" ainsi de suite, ac- culerait enfin le répondant au bout de son calepin. On échange un mot pour un autre mot, et souvent plus in- connu. Je sais mieux que c'est qu'homme que je ne sais que c'est animal, ou mortel, ou raisonnable. Pour satisfaire à un doute, ils m'en donnent trois: c'est la tête de Hydra. Socratès demandait à Memnon que c'était que vertu. "Il y a," fit Memnon, "vertu d'homme et de femme, de magistrat et d'homme privé, d'enfant et de vieillard." — "Voici qui va bien!" s'écria Socratès. "Nous étions en cherche d'une vertu, en voici un essaim." Nous com- muniquons une question, on nous en redonne une ruchée. Comme nul événement et nulle forme ressemble entière- ment à une autre, aussi ne diffère nulle de l'autre entière- ment. ^OIngénieux mélange de nature: si nos faces n'étaient semblables, on ne saurait discerner l'homme de la bête; si elles n'étaient dissemblables, on ne saurait discerner l'homme de l'homme. ^BToutes choses se tiennent par quelque similitude; tout exemple cloche; et la relation qui

books than about any other subject: we do nothing but write glosses about each other. ᶜThe world is swarming with commentaries; of authors there is a great scarcity. . . .

ᴮI have observed in Germany that Luther has left as many divisions and altercations over the uncertainty of his opinions, and more, as he raised about the Holy Scriptures.

Our disputes are purely verbal. I ask what is "nature," "pleasure," "circle," "substitution." The question is one of words, and is answered in the same way. "A stone is a body." But if you pressed on: "And what is a body?"— "Substance."—"And what is substance?" and so on, you would finally drive the respondent to the end of his lexicon. We exchange one word for another word, often more unknown. I know better what is man than I know what is animal, or mortal, or rational. To satisfy one doubt, they give me three; it is the Hydra's head.

Socrates asked Meno what virtue was. "There is," said Meno, "the virtue of a man and of a woman, of a magistrate and of a private individual, of a child and of an old man." "That's fine," exclaimed Socrates; "we were in search of one virtue, and here is a whole swarm of them." We put one question, they give us back a hive of them.

As no event and no shape is entirely like another, so none is entirely different from another. ᶜAn ingenious mixture on the part of nature. If our faces were not similar, we could not distinguish man from beast; if they were not dissimilar, we could not distinguish man from man. ᴮAll things hold together by some similarity; every example is lame, and the comparison that is drawn from ex-

[III:13] *Of Experience*

se tire de l'expérience est toujours défaillante et imparfaite; on joint toutefois les comparaisons par quelque coin. Ainsi servent les lois, et s'assortissent ainsi à chacun de nos affaires, par quelque interprétation détournée, contrainte et biaise.

Puisque les lois éthiques, qui regardent le devoir particulier de chacun en soi, sont si difficiles à dresser, comme nous voyons qu'elles sont, ce n'est pas merveille si celles qui gouvernent tant de particuliers le sont davantage. . . .

Or les lois se maintiennent en crédit, non parce qu'elles sont justes, mais parce qu'elles sont lois. C'est le fondement mystique de leur autorité; elles n'en ont point d'autre. ᶜQui bien leur sert. Elles sont souvent faites par des sots, plus souvent par des gens qui en haine d'égalité ont faute d'équité; mais toujours par des hommes, auteurs vains et irrésolus. Il n'est rien si lourdement et largement fautier que les lois, ni si ordinairement. ᴮQuiconque leur obéit parce qu'elles sont justes ne leur obéit pas justement par où il doit. . . .

Quel que soit donc le fruit que nous pouvons avoir de l'expérience, à peine servira beaucoup à notre institution celle que nous tirons des exemples étrangers, si nous faisons si mal notre profit de celle que nous avons de nous-même, qui nous est plus familière, et certes suffisante à nous instruire de ce qu'il nous faut.

Je m'étudie plus qu'autre sujet. C'est ma métaphysique, c'est ma physique. . . .

ᶜEn cette université je me laisse ignoramment et négligemment manier à loi générale du monde. Je la saurai assez quand je la sentirai. Ma science ne lui saurait faire changer de route; elle ne se diversifiera pas pour moi. . . .

perience is always faulty and imperfect; however, we fasten together our comparisons by some corner. Thus the laws serve, and thus adapt themselves to each of our affairs, by some roundabout, forced, and biased interpretation.

Since the ethical laws, which concern the individual duty of each man in himself, are so hard to frame, as we see they are, it is no wonder if those that govern so many individuals are more so. . . .

Now laws remain in credit not because they are just, but because they are laws. That is the mystic foundation of their authority; they have no other. ᶜAnd that is a good thing for them. They are often made by fools, more often by people who, in their hatred of equality, are wanting in equity; but always by men, vain and irresolute authors. There is nothing so grossly and widely and ordinarily faulty as the laws. ᴮWhoever obeys them because they are just, does not obey them for just the reason he should. . . .

Then whatever may be the fruit we can reap from experience, what we derive from foreign examples will hardly be much use for our education, if we make such little profit from the experience we have of ourselves, which is more familiar to us, and certainly sufficient to inform us of what we need.

I study myself more than any other subject. That is my metaphysics, that is my physics. . . .

ᶜIn this universe of things I ignorantly and negligently let myself be guided by the general law of the world. I shall know it well enough when I feel it. My knowledge could not make it change its path; it will not modify

[III:13] *Of Experience*

La bonté et capacité du gouverneur [2] nous doit à pur et à plein décharger du soin de son gouvernement.

Les inquisitions et contemplations philosophiques ne servent que d'aliment à notre curiosité. Les philosophes, avec grande raison, nous renvoient aux règles de nature; mais elles n'ont que faire de si sublime connaissance: ils les falsifient et nous présentent son visage peint trop haut en couleur et trop sophistiqué, d'où naissent tant de divers portraits d'un sujet si uniforme.

Comme elle nous a fourni de pieds à marcher, aussi a-t-elle de prudence à nous guider en la vie: prudence non tant ingénieuse, robuste et pompeuse comme celle de leur invention, mais à l'avenant facile et salutaire, et qui fait très bien ce que l'autre dit, en celui qui a l'heur de savoir s'employer naïvement et ordonnément, c'est-à-dire naturellement.

Le plus simplement se commettre à nature, c'est s'y commettre le plus sagement. Ô que c'est un doux et mol chevet, et sain, que l'ignorance et l'incuriosité, à reposer une tête bien faite!

[B]J'aimerais mieux m'entendre en moi qu'en [C]Cicéron.[3] [B]De l'expérience que j'ai de moi je trouve assez de quoi me faire sage, si j'étais bon écolier. Qui remet en sa mémoire l'excès de sa colère passée et jusqu'où cette fièvre l'emporta, voit la laideur de cette passion mieux que dans Aristote et en conçoit une haine plus juste. Qui se souvient des maux qu'il a courus, de ceux qui l'ont menacé,

---

[2] God.

itself for me. . . . The goodness and capacity of the governor [2] should free us absolutely and fully from worrying about his government.

Philosophical inquiries and meditations serve only as food for our curiosity. The philosophers with much reason refer us to the rules of Nature; but these have no concern with such sublime knowledge. The philosophers falsify them and show us the face of Nature painted in too high a color, and too sophisticated, whence spring so many varied portraits of so uniform a subject.

As she has furnished us with feet to walk with, so she has given us wisdom to guide us in life: a wisdom not so ingenious, robust, and pompous as that of their invention, but correspondingly easy and salutary, performing very well what the other talks about, in a man who has the good fortune to know how to occupy himself simply and in an orderly way, that is to say naturally.

The more simply we trust to Nature, the more wisely we trust to her. Oh, what a sweet and soft and healthy pillow is ignorance and incuriosity, to rest a well-made head!

^BI would rather be an authority on myself than on ^CCicero.[3] ^BIn the experience I have of myself I find enough to make me wise, if I were a good scholar. He who calls back to mind the excess of his past anger, and how far this fever carried him away, sees the ugliness of this passion better than in Aristotle, and conceives a more justified hatred for it. He who remembers the evils he

---

[3] The 1588 text read *Platon* (Plato) instead of *Cicéron*.

[III:13] *Of Experience*

des légères occasions qui l'ont remué d'un état à autre, se prépare par là aux mutations futures et à la reconnaissance de sa condition. La vie de Cæsar n'a point plus d'exemple que la nôtre pour nous: et emperière, et populaire, c'est toujours une vie que tous accidents humains regardent. Écoutons-y seulement: nous nous disons tout ce de quoi nous avons principalement besoin.

Qui se souvient de s'être tant et tant de fois mécompté de son propre jugement, est-il pas un sot de n'en entrer pour jamais en défiance? Quand je me trouve convaincu par la raison d'autrui d'une opinion fausse, je n'apprends pas tant ce qu'il m'a dit de nouveau et cette ignorance particulière (ce serait peu d'acquêt), comme en général j'apprends ma débilité et la trahison de mon entendement; d'où je tire la réformation de toute la masse. En toutes mes autres erreurs je fais de même, et sens de cette règle grande utilité à la vie. Je ne regarde pas l'espèce et l'individu, comme une pierre où j'aie bronché; j'apprends à craindre mon allure partout, et m'attends à la régler. ^CD'apprendre qu'on a dit ou fait une sottise, ce n'est rien que cela; il faut apprendre qu'on n'est qu'un sot, instruction bien plus ample et importante. . . .

^BLe jugement tient chez moi un siège magistral, au moins il s'en efforce soigneusement. Il laisse mes appétits aller leur train, et la haine et l'amitié, voire et celle que je me porte à moi-même, sans s'en altérer et corrompre. S'il ne peut réformer les autres parties selon soi, au moins ne se laisse-t-il pas difformer à elles: il fait son jeu à part.

has undergone, and those that have threatened him, and the slight causes that have changed him from one state to another, prepares himself in that way for future changes and for recognizing his condition. The life of Caesar has no more to show us than our own; an emperor's or an ordinary man's, it is still a life subject to all human accidents. Let us only listen: we tell ourselves all we most need.

He who remembers having been mistaken so many, many times in his own judgment, is he not a fool if he does not distrust it forever after? When I find myself convicted of a false opinion by another man's reasoning, I do not so much learn what new thing he has told me and this particular bit of ignorance—that would be small gain—as I learn my weakness in general, and the treachery of my understanding; whence I derive the reformation of the whole mass. With all my other errors I do the same, and I feel that this rule is very useful for my life. I do not regard the species and the individual, like a stone I have stumbled on; I learn to mistrust my gait throughout, and I strive to regulate it. ^CTo learn that we have said or done a foolish thing, that is nothing; we must learn that we are nothing but fools, a far broader and more important lesson. . . .

^BJudgment holds in me a magisterial seat, at least it carefully tries to. It lets my feelings go their way, both hatred and friendship, even the friendship I bear myself, without being changed and corrupted by them. If it cannot reform the other parts according to itself, at least it does not let itself be deformed to match them; it plays its game apart.

L'avertissement à chacun de se connaître doit être d'un important effet. . . . Moi qui ne fais autre profession, y trouve une profondeur et variété si infinie que mon apprentissage n'a autre fruit que de me faire sentir combien il me reste à apprendre. A ma faiblesse si souvent reconnue je dois l'inclination que j'ai à la modestie, à l'obéissance des croyances qui me sont prescrites, à une constante froideur et modération d'opinions, et la haine à cette arrogance importune et querelleuse, se croyant et fiant toute à soi, ennemie capitale de discipline et de vérité. Oyez-les régenter: les premières sottises qu'ils mettent en avant, c'est au style qu'on établit les religions et les lois. . . .

L'affirmation et l'opiniâtreté sont signes exprès de bêtise. Celui-ci aura donné du nez à terre cent fois pour un jour: le voilà sur ses ergots,[4] aussi résolu et entier que devant; vous diriez qu'on lui a infus depuis quelque nouvelle âme et vigueur d'entendement, et qu'il lui advient comme à cet ancien fils de la terre [5] qui reprenait nouvelle fermeté et se renforçait par sa chute. . . . Ce têtu indocile pense-t-il pas reprendre un nouvel esprit pour reprendre une nouvelle dispute?

C'est par mon expérience que j'accuse l'humaine ignorance, qui est à mon avis le plus sûr parti de l'école du monde. Ceux qui ne la veulent conclure en eux par un si vain exemple que le mien ou que le leur, qu'ils la reconnaissent par Socratès, ᶜle maître des maîtres. . . .

---

[4] Montaigne's word means the spurs or hackles of a gamecock. But it also may mean *ergos* or *ergotisms,* the quibbling use of Latin *ergo* (therefore) by a choplogic (see Rabelais, *Pantagruel,* ch. 10).

The advice to everyone to know himself must have an important effect. . . . I, who make no other profession, find in me such infinite depth and variety, that what I have learned bears no other fruit than to make me realize how much I still have to learn. To my weakness, so often recognized, I owe the inclination I have to modesty, obedience to the beliefs that are prescribed me, a constant coolness and moderation in my opinions, and my hatred for that aggressive and quarrelsome arrogance that believes and trusts wholly in itself, a mortal enemy of discipline and truth. Hear them laying down the law: the first stupidities that they advance are in the style in which men establish religions and laws. . . . Affirmation and opinionativeness are express signs of stupidity. This man must have fallen on his nose a hundred times in one day; there he stands on his "ergos,"[4] as positive and unshaken as before. You would think that someone had since infused in him some sort of new soul and intellectual vigor, and that he was like that ancient son of the earth,[5] who renewed his courage and strength by his fall. . . . Does not this headstrong incorrigible think that he picks up a new mind by picking up a new argument?

It is from my experience that I affirm human ignorance, which is, in my opinion, the most certain fact in the school of the world. Those who will not conclude their own ignorance from so vain an example as mine, or as theirs, let them recognize it through Socrates, ^cthe master of masters. . . .

---

[5] Antaeus, son of Ge (Mother Earth), in Greek mythology. When he fought with Hercules, each time he was thrown he regained strength from contact with Mother Earth until Hercules raised him in the air and crushed him to death.

[III:13] *Of Experience*

ᴮCette longue attention que j'emploie à me considérer me dresse à juger aussi passablement des autres; et est peu de choses de quoi je parle plus heureusement et excusablement. Il m'advient souvent de voir et distinguer plus exactement les conditions de mes amis qu'ils ne font eux-mêmes. J'en ai étonné quelqu'un par la pertinence de ma description, et l'ai averti de soi. Pour m'être dès mon enfance dressé à mirer ma vie dans celle d'autrui, j'ai acquis une complexion studieuse en cela; et quand j'y pense, je laisse échapper autour de moi peu de choses qui y servent: contenances, humeurs, discours. J'étudie tout: ce qu'il me faut fuir, ce qu'il me faut suivre. Ainsi à mes amis je découvre, par leurs productions, leurs inclinations internes; non pour ranger cette infinie variété d'actions, si diverses et si découpées, à certains genres et chapitres, et distribuer distinctement mes partages et divisions en classes et régions connues. . . . Je prononce ma sentence par articles décousus, ainsi que de chose qui ne se peut dire à la fois et en bloc. . . . Je laisse aux artistes, et ne sais s'ils en viennent à bout en chose si mêlée, si menue et fortuite, de ranger en bandes cette infinie diversité de visages, et arrêter notre inconstance et la mettre par ordre. Non seulement je trouve malaisé d'attacher nos actions les unes aux autres, mais chacune à part soi je trouve malaisé de la désigner proprement par quelque qualité principale, tant elles sont doubles et bigarrées à divers lustres. . . .

Quelquefois on me demandait à quoi j'eusse pensé être bon, qui se fût avisé de se servir de moi pendant que

^BThis long attention that I devote to studying myself trains me also to judge passably of others, and there are few things of which I speak more felicitously and excusably. It often happens that I see and distinguish the characters of my friends more exactly than they do themselves. I have astonished at least one by the pertinence of my description, and have given him information about himself. By training myself from my youth to see my own life mirrored in that of others, I have acquired a studious bent in that subject, and when I am thinking about it, I let few things around me which are useful for that purpose escape my notice: countenances, humors, statements. I study everything: what I must flee, what I must follow. So I reveal to my friends, by their outward manifestations, their inward inclinations. I do not attempt to arrange this infinite variety of actions, so diverse and so disconnected, into certain types and categories, and distribute my lots and divisions distinctly into recognized classes and sections. . . . I speak my meaning in disjointed parts, as something that cannot be said all at once and in a lump. . . . I leave it to artists, and I do not know if they will achieve it in a matter so complex, minute, and accidental, to arrange into bands this infinite diversity of aspects, to check our inconsistency and set it down in order. Not only do I find it hard to link our actions with one another, but each one separately I find hard to designate properly by some principal characteristic, so two-sided and motley do they seem in different lights. . . .

Sometimes people used to ask me what I would have thought myself good for, if anyone had thought of using

[III:13] *Of Experience*

j'en avais l'âge. . . . "A rien," fis-je. Et m'excuse volontiers de ne savoir faire chose qui m'esclave à autrui. Mais j'eusse dit ses vérités à mon maître, et eusse contrôlé ses mœurs, s'il eût voulu. Non en gros, par leçons scolastiques, que je ne sais point (et n'en vois naître aucune vraie réformation en ceux qui les savent), mais les observant pas à pas, à toute opportunité, et en jugeant à l'œil pièce à pièce, simplement et naturellement, lui faisant voir quel il est en l'opinion commune, m'opposant à ses flatteurs. Il n'y a nul de nous qui ne valût moins que les rois s'il était ainsi continuellement corrompu, comme ils sont, de cette canaille de gens. . . .

Enfin, toute cette fricassée que je barbouille ici n'est qu'un registre des essais de ma vie, qui est, pour l'interne santé, exemplaire assez, à prendre l'instruction à contrepoil. Mais quant à la santé corporelle, personne ne peut fournir d'expérience plus utile que moi, qui la présente pure, nullement corrompue et altérée par art et par opination. L'expérience est proprement sur son fumier [6] au sujet de la médecine, où la raison lui quitte toute la place. . . .

L'expérience m'a encore appris ceci, que nous nous perdons d'impatience. . . . Laissons faire un peu à nature: elle entend mieux ses affaires que nous. . . . J'ai laissé envieillir et mourir en moi de mort naturelle des rhumes, défluxions goutteuses, relaxation, battement de cœur, migraines, et autres accidents, que j'ai perdus quand je m'étais à demi formé à les nourrir. On les conjure mieux par courtoisie que par braverie. . . .

---

[6] (Like a lordly rooster.)

me while I was young enough. . . . "For nothing," I said. And I readily excuse myself for not knowing how to do anything that would enslave me to others. But I would have told my master home truths, and watched over his conduct, if he had been willing. Not in general, by schoolmasterly lessons, which I do not know—and I see no true reform spring from them in those who know them—but by observing his conduct step by step, at every opportunity, judging it with my own eyes, piece by piece, simply and naturally, making him see how he stands in public opinion, and opposing his flatterers. There is not one of us who would not be worse than the kings if he were as continually spoiled as they are by that rabble. . . .

In fine, all this fricassee that I am scribbling here is nothing but a record of the essays of my life, which, for spiritual health, is exemplary enough if you take its instruction in reverse. But as for bodily health, no one can furnish more useful experience than I, who present it pure, not at all corrupted or altered by art or theorizing. Experience is really on its own dunghill [6] in the subject of medicine, where reason yields it the whole field. . . .

Experience has further taught me this, that we ruin ourselves by impatience. . . . Let us give Nature a chance; she knows her business better than we do. . . . I have allowed colds, gouty discharges, looseness, palpitations of the heart, migraines, and other ailments to grow old and die a natural death within me; I lost them when I had half trained myself to harbor them. They are conjured better by courtesy than by defiance. . . .

[III:13] *Of Experience*

Il faut apprendre à souffrir ce qu'on ne péut éviter. Notre vie est composée, comme l'harmonie du monde, de choses contraires, aussi de divers tons: doux et âpres, aigus et plats, mous et graves. Le musicien qui n'en aimerait que les uns, que voudrait-il dire? Il faut qu'il s'en sache servir en commun et les mêler. Et nous aussi les biens et les maux, qui sont consubstantiels à notre vie. Notre être ne peut sans ce mélange; et y est l'une bande non moins nécessaire que l'autre. . . .

Or je traite mon imagination le plus doucement que je puis, et la déchargerais, si je pouvais, de toute peine et contestation. Il la faut secourir et flatter, et piper qui peut. Mon esprit est propre à ce service: il n'a point faute d'apparences partout; s'il persuadait comme il prêche, il me secourrait heureusement.

Vous en plaît-il un exemple? Il dit que c'est pour mon mieux que j'ai la gravelle; que les bâtiments de mon âge ont naturellement à souffrir quelque gouttière (il est temps qu'ils commencent à se lâcher et démentir; c'est une commune nécessité, et n'eût-on pas fait pour moi un nouveau miracle? je paye par là le loyer dû à la vieillesse, et ne saurais en avoir meilleur compte); que la compagnie me doit consoler, étant tombé en l'accident le plus ordinaire des hommes de mon temps (j'en vois partout d'affligés de même nature de mal, et m'en est la société honorable, d'autant qu'il se prend plus volontiers aux grands: son essence a de la noblesse et de la dignité); que des hommes qui en sont frappès il en est peu de quittes à meilleure raison: et si il leur coûte la peine d'un fâcheux régime et la prise ennuyeuse et quotidienne des drogues médicinales, là où je le dois purement à ma bonne fortune. . . .

We must learn to endure what we cannot avoid. Our life is composed, like the harmony of the world, of contrary things, also of different tones, sweet and harsh, sharp and flat, soft and loud. If a musician liked only one kind, what would he have to say? He must know how to use them together and blend them. And so must we do with good and evil, which are consubstantial with our life. Our existence is impossible without this mixture, and one element is no less necessary for it than the other. . . .

Now I treat my imagination as gently as I can, and would relieve it, if I could, of all trouble and conflict. We must help it and flatter it, and fool it if we can. My mind is suited to this service; it has no lack of plausible reasons for all things. If it could persuade as well as it preaches, it would help me out very happily.

Would you like an example? It tells me that it is for my own good that I have the stone; that buildings of my age must naturally suffer some leakage. It is time for them to begin to grow loose and give way. It is a common necessity—otherwise would it not have been a new miracle performed for me? Thereby I pay the tribute due to old age, and I could not get a better bargain.—That the company should console me, since I have fallen into the commonest ailment of men of my time of life. On all sides I see them afflicted with the same type of disease, and their society is honorable for me, since it preferably attacks the great; it is essentially noble and dignified.—That of the men who are stricken by it there are few that get off more cheaply; and at that, they pay the penalty of an unpleasant diet and daily doses of loathsome medicinal drugs, whereas I am indebted solely to my good fortune. . . .

"La crainte de ce mal," fait-il, "t'effrayait autrefois, quand il t'était inconnu: les cris et le désespoir de ceux qui l'aigrissent par leur impatience t'en engendraient l'horreur. C'est un mal qui te bat les membres par lesquels tu as le plus failli. Tu es homme de conscience:

Quæ venit indigne pœna, dolenda venit.[7]

Regarde ce châtiment: il est bien doux au prix d'autres, et d'une faveur paternelle. Regarde sa tardiveté: il n'incommode et occupe que la saison de ta vie qui, ainsi comme ainsi, est meshui perdue et stérile, ayant fait place à la licence et plaisirs de ta jeunesse, comme par composition.

"La crainte et pitié que le peuple a de ce mal te sert de matière de gloire—qualité de laquelle, si tu as le jugement purgé et en as guéri ton discours, tes amis pourtant en reconnaissent encore quelque teinture en ta complexion. Il y a plaisir à ouïr dire de soi: 'Voilà bien de la force, voilà bien de la patience.' On te voit suer d'ahan, pâlir, rougir, trembler, vomir jusqu'au sang, souffrir des contractions et convulsions étranges, dégoutter parfois de grosses larmes des yeux, rendre les urines épaisses, noires, et effroyables, ou les avoir arrêtées par quelque pierre épineuse et hérissée qui te point et écorche cruellement le col de la verge, entretenant cependant les assistants d'une contenance commune, bouffonnant à pauses avec tes gens, tenant ta partie en un discours tendu, excusant de parole ta douleur et rabattant de ta souffrance.

---

[7] Ovid, *Heroides*, v, 8.

"Fear of this disease," says my mind, "used to terrify you, when it was unknown to you; the cries and despair of those who make it worse by their lack of fortitude engendered in you a horror of it. It is an affliction that punishes those of your members by which you have most sinned. You are a man of conscience:

Punishment undeserved gives pain.[7]

Consider this chastisement; it is very gentle in comparison with others, and paternally tender. Consider its lateness; it bothers and occupies only the season of your life which in any case is henceforth wasted and barren, having given way, as if by agreement, to the licentiousness and pleasures of your youth.

"The fear and pity that people feel for this illness is a subject of vainglory for you; a quality of which, even if you have purged your judgment and cured your reason of it, your friends still recognize some tincture in your makeup. There is pleasure in hearing people say about you: 'There indeed is strength, there indeed is fortitude!' They see you sweat in agony, turn pale, turn red, tremble, vomit your very blood, suffer strange contractions and convulsions, sometimes shed great tears from your eyes, discharge thick, black, and frightful urine, or have it stopped up by some sharp rough stone that cruelly pricks and flays the neck of your penis; meanwhile keeping up conversation with your company with a normal countenance, jesting in the intervals with your servants, holding up your end in a sustained discussion, making excuses for your pain and minimizing your suffering.

"Te souvient-il de ces gens du temps passé qui recherchaient les maux avec si grande faim pour tenir leur vertu en haleine et en exercice? Mets le cas que nature te porte et pousse à cette glorieuse école, en laquelle tu ne fusses jamais entré de ton gré. Si tu me dis que c'est un mal dangereux et mortel, quels autres ne le sont? Car c'est une piperie médicinale d'en excepter aucuns, qu'ils disent n'aller point de droit fil à la mort. Qu'importe, s'ils y vont par accident, et s'ils glissent et gauchissent aisément vers la voie qui nous y mène?

ᶜ"Mais tu ne meurs pas de ce que tu es malade, tu meurs de ce que tu es vivant. La mort te tue bien sans le secours de la maladie. Et à d'aucuns les maladies ont éloigné la mort, qui ont plus vécu de ce qu'il leur semblait s'en aller mourants. Joint qu'il est, comme des plaies, aussi des maladies médicinales et salutaires.

ᴮ"La colique est souvent non moins vivace que vous; il se voit des hommes auxquels elle a continué depuis leur enfance jusqu'à leur extrême vieillesse, et, s'ils ne lui eussent failli de compagnie, elle était pour les assister plus outre. Vous la tuez plus souvent qu'elle ne vous tue; et quand elle te présenterait l'image de la mort voisine, serait-ce pas un bon office à un homme de tel âge de le ramener aux cogitations de sa fin?

ᶜ"Et qui pis est, tu n'as plus pour qui guérir. Ainsi comme ainsi, au premier jour la commune nécessité t'appelle. ᴮConsidère combien artificiellement et doucement elle te dégoûte de la vie et déprend du monde: non te forçant d'une subjection tyrannique, comme tant d'autres maux

"Do you remember those men of past times who sought out troubles with such great hunger, to keep their virtue in breath and in practice? Put the case this way, that nature is bearing and pushing you into that glorious school, which you would never have entered of your own free will. If you tell me that it is a dangerous and mortal disease, what others are not? For it is a doctor's trick to except some, which they say do not lead in a straight line to death. What does it matter if they go there by accident and slip and deviate easily toward the road that leads us there?

^c"But you do not die of being sick, you die of being alive. Death kills you well enough without the help of illness. And illnesses have put off death for some, who have lived longer for thinking that they were on their way out and dying. Furthermore, there are diseases, as there are wounds, that are medicinal and salutary.

^B"The stone is often no less fond of life than you. We see men in whom it has continued from their childhood up to their extreme old age; and if they had not deserted it, it was ready to accompany them still further. You kill it more often than it kills you; and even if it set before you the picture of imminent death, would it not be a kind service for a man of that age to bring him home to meditations upon his end?

^c"And what is worse, you have no reason left for being cured. In any case, the common fate will call you any day. ^BConsider how artfully and gently the stone weans you from life and detaches you from the world; not forcing you with tyrannical subjections, like so many other afflictions

que tu vois aux vieillards, qui les tiennent continuellement entravés, et sans relâche, de faiblesses et douleurs;
mais par avertissements et instructions reprises à intervalles, entremêlant des longues pauses de repos, comme
pour te donner moyen de méditer et répéter sa leçon à ton
aise. Pour te donner moyen de juger sainement et prendre
parti en homme de cœur, elle te présente l'état de ta condition, entière et en bien et en mal, et en même jour une vie
très allègre tantôt, tantôt insupportable. Si tu n'accoles la
mort, au moins tu lui touches en paume une fois le mois.
[c]Par où tu as de plus à espérer qu'elle t'attrapera un jour
sans menace, et que, étant si souvent conduit jusqu'au
port, te fiant d'être encore aux termes accoutumés, on
t'aura et ta fiance passé l'eau un matin inopinément. [B]On
n'a point à se plaindre des maladies qui partagent loyalement le temps avec la santé." . . .

Moi, qui ne manie que terre à terre, hais cette inhumaine sapience qui nous veut rendre dédaigneux et ennemis de la culture du corps. J'estime pareille injustice
prendre à contre-cœur les voluptés naturelles que de les
prendre trop à cœur. . . . Il ne les faut ni suivre ni fuir,
il les faut recevoir. Je les reçois un peu plus grassement et
gracieusement, et me laisse plus volontiers aller vers la
pente naturelle. [c]Nous n'avons que faire d'exagérer leur
inanité: elle se fait assez sentir et se produit assez.
Merci à notre esprit maladif, rabat-joie, qui nous dégoûte
d'elles comme de soi-même. Il traite et soi et tout ce qu'il
reçoit tantôt avant tantôt arrière, selon son être insatiable,
vagabond et versatile.

that you see in old people, which keep them continually hobbled and without relief from infirmities and pains, but by warnings and instructions repeated at intervals, intermingled with long pauses for rest, as if to give you a chance to meditate and repeat its lesson at your leisure. To give you a chance to form a sound judgment and make up your mind to it like a brave man, it sets before you the lot that is your condition, the good and also the bad, and a life that on the same day is now very joyous, now unbearable. If you do not embrace death, at least you shake hands with it once a month. ᶜWhereby you have the further hope that it will catch you some day without a threat, and that, being so often led to the port, confident that you are still within the accustomed limits, some morning you and your confidence will have crossed the water unawares. ᴮWe have no cause for complaint about illnesses that divide the time fairly with health." . . .

I, who operate only close to the ground, hate that inhuman wisdom that would make us disdainful enemies of the cultivation of the body. I consider it equal injustice to set our heart against natural pleasures and to set our heart too much on them. . . . We should neither pursue them nor flee them, we should accept them. I accept them with more gusto and with better grace than most, and more willingly let myself follow a natural inclination. ᶜWe have no need to exaggerate their inanity; it makes itself felt enough and evident enough. Much thanks to our sickly, kill-joy mind, which disgusts us with them as well as with itself. It treats both itself and all that it takes in, whether future or past, according to its insatiable, erratic, and versatile nature.

431   [III:13] *Of Experience*

Sincerum est nisi vas, quodcunque infundis, acescit.[8]

Moi qui me vante d'embrasser si curieusement les commodités de la vie, et si particulièrement, n'y trouve, quand j'y regarde ainsi finement, à peu près que du vent. Mais quoi, nous sommes partout vent. Et le vent encore, plus sagement que nous, s'aime à bruire, à s'agiter, et se contente en ses propres offices, sans désirer la stabilité, la solidité, qualités non siennes.

Les plaisirs purs de l'imagination, ainsi que les déplaisirs, disent aucuns, sont les plus grands, comme l'exprimait la balance de Critolaus.[9] Ce n'est pas merveille: elle les compose à sa poste et se les taille en plein drap. J'en vois tous les jours des exemples insignes et à l'aventure désirables. Mais moi, d'une condition mixte, grossier, ne puis mordre si à fait à ce seul objet; si simple que je me laisse tout lourdement aller aux plaisirs présents de la loi humaine et générale, intellectuellement sensibles, sensiblement intellectuels. . . .

[B]Il en est qui [C]d'une farouche stupidité, comme dit Aristote, [B]en sont dégoûtés. J'en connais qui par ambition le font; que ne renoncent-ils encore au respirer? que ne vivent-ils du leur, [C]et ne refusent la lumière, de ce qu'elle est gratuite et ne leur coûte ni invention ni vigueur? . . . Chercheront-ils pas la quadrature du cercle, juchés sur leurs femmes! [B]Je hais qu'on nous ordonne d'avoir l'esprit aux nues pendant que nous avons le corps à table. Je ne veux pas que l'esprit s'y cloue ni qu'il s'y vautre, mais je veux qu'il s'y applique: [C]qu'il y siée, non qu'il s'y couche. . . .

---

[8] Horace, *Epistles*, I, ii, 54.

Unless the vessel's pure, all you pour in turns sour.[8]

I, who boast of embracing the pleasures of life so as-
siduously and so particularly, find in them, when I look at
them thus minutely, virtually nothing but wind. But what
of it? We are all wind. And even the wind, more wisely
than we, loves to make a noise and move about, and is
content with its own functions, without wishing for stability and solidity, qualities that do not belong to it.

The pure pleasures of imagination, as well as the pains,
some say, are the greatest, as the scales of Critolaus [9] ex-
pressed it. No wonder; it composes them to its liking and
cuts them out of whole cloth. I see signal, and perhaps
desirable, examples of this every day. But I, being of a
mixed constitution, and coarse, am unable to cling so
completely to this single and simple object as to keep
myself from grossly pursuing the present pleasures of the
general human law—intellectually sensual, sensually intellectual. . . .

[B]There are some who [C]from savage stupidity, as Aristotle says, [B]are disgusted with them; I know some who act
that way from ambition. Why do they not also give up
breathing? Why do they not live on their own air, [C]and
refuse light, because it is free and costs them neither invention nor vigor? . . . Won't they try to square the
circle while perched on their wives! [B]I hate to have people
order us to keep our minds in the clouds while our bodies
are at table. I would not have the mind nailed down to it
nor wallowing at it, but attending to it; [C]sitting at it, not
lying down at it. . . .

---

[9] The scales of Critolaus, in which spiritual goods far outweigh
bodily goods, are described in Cicero, *Tusculans*, v, xvii.

[III:13] *Of Experience*

ᴮQuand je danse, je danse; quand je dors, je dors; voire et quand je me promène solitairement en un beau verger, si mes pensées se sont entretenues des occurrences étrangères quelque partie du temps, quelque autre partie je les ramène à la promenade, au verger, à la douceur de cette solitude et à moi. Nature a maternellement observé cela, que les actions qu'elle nous a enjointes pour notre besoin nous fussent aussi voluptueuses; et nous y convie non seulement par la raison mais aussi par l'appétit. C'est injustice de corrompre ses règles.

Quand je vois et Cæsar et Alexandre, au plus épais de sa grande besogne, jouir si pleinement des plaisirs ᶜnaturels et par conséquent nécessaires et justes, ᴮje ne dis pas que ce soit relâcher son âme, je dis que c'est la raidir, soumettant par vigueur de courage à l'usage de la vie ordinaire ces violentes occupations et laborieuses pensées. ᶜSages, s'ils eussent cru que c'était là leur ordinaire vacation, celle-ci l'extraordinaire.

Nous sommes de grands fous. "Il a passé sa vie en oisiveté," disons-nous; "je n'ai rien fait d'aujourd'hui." — Quoi, avez-vous pas vécu? C'est non seulement la fondamentale mais la plus illustre de vos occupations. — "Si on m'eût mis au propre des grands maniements, j'eusse montré ce que je savais faire." — Avez-vous su méditer et manier votre vie? vous avez fait la plus grande besogne de toutes. Pour se montrer et exploiter, nature n'a que faire de fortune: elle se montre également en tous étages, et derrière, comme sans, rideau. Composer nos mœurs est notre office, non pas composer des livres; et gagner non pas des batailles et provinces, mais l'ordre et tranquillité à notre conduite. Notre grand et glorieux chef-d'œuvre, c'est

434

ᴮWhen I dance, I dance; when I sleep, I sleep; yes, and when I walk alone in a beautiful orchard, if my thoughts have been dwelling on extraneous incidents for some part of the time, for some other part I bring them back to the walk, to the orchard, to the sweetness of this solitude, and to me. Nature has observed this principle like a mother, that the actions she has enjoined on us for our need should also give us pleasure; and she invites us to them not only through reason, but also through appetite. It is unjust to infringe her laws.

When I see both Caesar and Alexander, in the thick of their great tasks, so fully enjoying ᶜnatural and therefore necessary and just ᴮpleasures, I do not say that that is relaxing their souls, I say that it is toughening them, subordinating these violent occupations and laborious thoughts, by the vigor of their spirits, to the practice of everyday life: ᶜwise men, had they believed that this was their ordinary occupation, the other the extraordinary.

We are great fools. "He has spent his life in idleness," we say; "I have done nothing today." What, have you not lived? That is not only the fundamental but the most illustrious of your occupations. "If I had been placed in a position to manage great affairs, I would have shown what I could do." Have you been able to think out and manage your own life? You have done the greatest task of all. To show and exploit her resources Nature has no need of fortune; she shows herself equally on all levels and behind a curtain as well as without one. To compose our character is our duty, not to compose books, and to win, not battles and provinces, but order and tranquillity in our conduct. Our great and glorious masterpiece is to live appropri-

vivre à propos. Toutes autres choses, régner, thésauriser, bâtir, n'en sont qu'appendicules et adminicules, pour le plus.

^BJe prends plaisir de voir un général d'armée au pied d'une brèche qu'il veut tantôt attaquer, se prêtant tout entier et délivré à son dîner, ^Cà son devis, ^Bentre ses amis; ^Cet Brutus, ayant le ciel et la terre conspirés à l'encontre de lui et de la liberté romaine, dérober à ses rondes quelque heure de la nuit pour lire et breveter Polybe en toute sécurité. ^BC'est aux petites âmes, ensevelies du poids des affaires, de ne s'en savoir purement démêler, de ne les savoir et laisser et reprendre. . . .

Soit par gosserie, soit à certes, que le vin théologal et sorbonique est passé en proverbe, je trouve que c'est raison qu'ils en dînent d'autant plus commodément et plaisamment qu'ils ont utilement et sérieusement employé la matinée à l'exercice de leur école. La conscience d'avoir bien dispensé les autres heures est un juste et savoureux condiment des tables. Ainsi ont vécu les sages. Et cette inimitable contention à la vertu qui nous étonne en l'un et l'autre Caton, cette humeur sévère jusqu'à l'importunité, s'est ainsi mollement soumise et plue aux lois de l'humaine condition et de Vénus et de Bacchus; ^Csuivant les préceptes de leur secte, qui demandent le sage parfait autant expert et entendu à l'usage des voluptés naturelles qu'en tout autre devoir de la vie. *Cui cor sapiat, ei et sapiat palatus.*[10]

---

[10] Cicero, *De Finibus*, ii, viii.

ately. All other things, ruling, hoarding, building, are only little appendages and props, at most.

^BI take pleasure in seeing an army general, at the foot of a breach that he means to attack presently, lending himself wholly and freely to his dinner ^Cand his conversation, ^Bamong his friends; ^Cand Brutus, with heaven and earth conspiring against him and Roman liberty, stealing some hour of night from his rounds to read and annotate Polybius with complete assurance. ^BIt is for little souls, buried under the weight of business, to be unable to detach themselves cleanly from it or to leave it and pick it up again. . . .

Whether it is in jest or in earnest that the Sorbonne acquired its proverbial reputation for theological drinking and feasting, I think it right that the faculty should dine all the more comfortably and pleasantly for having used the morning profitably and seriously in the work of their school. The consciousness of having spent the other hours well is a proper and savory sauce for the dinner table. Thus did the sages live. And that inimitable straining for virtue that astounds us in both Catos, that disposition, severe to the point of being troublesome, submitted thus meekly and contentedly to the laws of human nature, and of Venus and Bacchus, ^Cin accordance with the precepts of their sect, which require the perfect sage to be as expert and versed in the enjoyment of the natural pleasures as in any other duty of life. *A wise palate should go with a wise heart.*[10]

ᴮLe relâchement et facilité honore, ce semble, à merveilles et sied mieux à une âme forte et généreuse. Épaminondas n'estimait pas que de se mêler à la danse des garçons de sa ville, ᶜde chanter, de sonner, ᴮet s'y embesogner avec attention, fût chose qui dérogeât à l'honneur de ses glorieuses victoires et à la parfaite réformation de mœurs qui était en lui. Et parmi tant d'admirables actions de Scipion ᶜl'aïeul, personnage digne de l'opinion d'une origine céleste,[11] ᴮil n'est rien qui lui donne plus de grâce que de le voir nonchalamment et puérilement baguenaudant à amasser et choisir des coquilles et jouer à cornichon va devant le long de la marine avec Lælius; et, s'il faisait mauvais temps, s'amusant et se chatouillant à représenter par écrit en comédies les plus populaires et basses actions des hommes; ᶜet, la tête pleine de cette merveilleuse entreprise d'Annibal et d'Afrique, visitant les écoles en Sicile, et se trouvant aux leçons de la philosophie jusqu'à en avoir armé les dents de l'aveugle envie de ses ennemis à Rome. ᴮNi chose plus remarquable en Socratès que ce que, tout vieux, il trouve le temps de se faire instruire à baller et jouer des instruments, et le tient pour bien employé.

Celui-ci s'est vu en extase, debout, un jour entier et une nuit, en présence de toute l'armée grecque, surpris et ravi par quelque profonde pensée. Il s'est vu, ᶜle premier parmi tant de vaillants hommes de l'armée, courir au secours d'Alcibiadès accablé des ennemis, le couvrir de son corps et le décharger de la presse à vive force d'armes;

---

[11] Instead of this phrase, Montaigne had written in 1588: "du jeune Scipion (tout compté, le premier homme des Romains)"

^BRelaxation and affability, it seems to me, are marvelously honorable and most becoming to a strong and generous soul. Epaminondas did not think that to mingle with the dance of the boys of his city, ^Cto sing, to play music, ^Band to concentrate attentively on these things, was at all derogatory to the honor of his glorious victories and the perfect purity of character that was his. And among so many admirable actions of Scipio ^Cthe grandfather, a personage worthy of the reputation of celestial descent,¹¹ ^Bthere is nothing that lends him more charm than to see him playing nonchalantly and childishly at picking up and selecting shells and running potato races by the sea with Laelius, and in bad weather amusing and tickling his fancy by writing comedies portraying the meanest and most vulgar actions of men; ^Cand, his head full of that wonderful campaign against Hannibal and Africa, visiting the schools in Sicily, and attending lectures on philosophy until he armed to the teeth the blind envy of his enemies in Rome. ^BNor is there anything more remarkable in Socrates than the fact that in his old age he finds time to take lessons in dancing and playing instruments, and considers it well spent.

The same man was once seen standing in a trance, an entire day and night, in the presence of the whole Greek army, overtaken and enraptured by some deep thought. He was seen, ^Cthe first among so many valiant men of the army, to run to the aid of Alcibiades, who was overwhelmed by enemies, to cover him with his body, and

---

—"of Scipio the Younger (everything considered, the first man of the Romans)." His first attribution was the correct one.

et le premier emmi tout le peuple d'Athènes, outré comme lui d'un si indigne spectacle, se présenter à recourir Théraménès que les trente tyrans faisaient mener à la mort par leurs satellites; et ne désista cette hardie entreprise qu'à la remontrance de Théraménès même, quoiqu'il ne fût suivi que de deux en tout. Il s'est vu, recherché par une beauté de laquelle il était épris,[12] maintenir au besoin une sévère abstinence. Il s'est vu, en la bataille délienne, relever et sauver Xénophon renversé de son cheval. Il s'est vu ^Bcontinuellement marcher à la guerre ^Cet fouler la glace ^Bles pieds nus, porter même robe en hiver et en été, surmonter tous ses compagnons en patience de travail, ne manger point autrement en festin qu'en son ordinaire.

^CIl s'est vu, vingt et sept ans, de pareil visage, porter la faim, la pauvreté, l'indocilité de ses enfants, les griffes de sa femme; et enfin la calomnie, la tyrannie, la prison, les fers et le venin. ^BMais cet homme-là était-il convié à boire à lutte par devoir de civilité, c'était aussi celui de l'armée à qui en demeurait l'avantage; et ne refusait ni à jouer aux noisettes avec les enfants, ni à courir avec eux sur un cheval de bois. Et y avait bonne grâce; car toutes actions, dit la philosophie, siéent également bien et honorent également le sage.

On a de quoi, et ne doit-on jamais se lasser de présenter l'image de ce personnage à tous patrons et formes de perfection. ^CIl est fort peu d'exemples de vie pleins et

---

12 The beauty was Alcibiades (see Plato's *Symposium*).

to extricate him from the melee by sheer force of arms; and the first among the people of Athens, all outraged like him at such a shameful spectacle, to come forward to rescue Theramenes, whom the Thirty Tyrants were having led to his death by their satellites; and he desisted from this bold undertaking only at the remonstrance of Theramenes himself, though he was followed by only two men in all. He was seen, when courted by a beauty with whom he was in love,[12] to maintain strict chastity when necessary. He was seen, in the battle of Delium, to pick up and save Xenophon, who had been thrown from his horse. He was ᴮconstantly ᶜseen ᴮto march to war ᶜand walk the ice ᴮbarefoot, to wear the same gown in winter and in summer, to surpass all his companions in enduring toil, to eat no differently at a feast than ordinarily.

ᶜHe was seen for twenty-seven years to endure with the same countenance hunger, poverty, the indocility of his children, the claws of his wife; and in the end calumny, tyranny, prison, irons, and poison. ᴮBut if that man was summoned to a drinking bout by the duty of civility, he was also the one who did the best in the whole army. And he never refused to play at cobnut with children, or to ride a hobbyhorse with them, and he did so gracefully; for all actions, says philosophy, are equally becoming and honorable in a wise man.

We have material enough, and we should never tire of presenting the picture of this man as a pattern and ideal of all sorts of perfection. ᶜThere are very few full and

purs, et fait-on tort à notre instruction de nous en proposer tous les jours d'imbéciles et manqués, à peine bons à un seul pli, qui nous tirent arrière plutôt, corrupteurs plutôt que correcteurs.

^BLe peuple se trompe: on va bien plus facilement par les bouts, où l'extrémité sert de borne d'arrêt et de guide, que par la voie du milieu, large et ouverte, et selon l'art que selon nature; mais bien moins noblement aussi et moins recommandablement. ^CLa grandeur de l'âme n'est pas tant tirer amont et tirer avant comme savoir se ranger et circonscrire. Elle tient pour grand tout ce qui est assez, et montre sa hauteur à aimer mieux les choses moyennes que les éminentes. ^BIl n'est rien si beau et légitime que de faire bien l'homme et dûment, ni science si ardue que de bien ^Cet naturellement ^Bsavoir vivre cette vie; et de nos maladies la plus sauvage c'est mépriser notre être.

Qui veut écarter son âme, le fasse hardiment, s'il peut, lorsque le corps se portera mal, pour la décharger de cette contagion; ailleurs, au contraire, qu'elle l'assiste et favorise et ne refuse point de participer à ses naturels plaisirs et de s'y complaire conjugalement, y apportant, si elle est plus sage, la modération, de peur que par indiscrétion ils ne se confondent avec le déplaisir. ^CL'intempérance est peste de la volupté; et la tempérance n'est pas son fléau, c'est son assaisonnement. Eudoxus, qui en établissait le souverain bien, et ses compagnons, qui la montèrent à si haut prix, la savourèrent en sa plus gracieuse douceur par le moyen de la tempérance, qui fut en eux singulière et exemplaire.

pure examples of life, and those who educate us are unfair when they set before us every day feeble and defective models, hardly good in a single vein, which rather pull us backward, corrupters rather than correctors.

^BPopular opinion is wrong: it is much easier to go along the sides, where the outer edge serves as a limit and a guide, than by the middle way, wide and open, and to go by art than by nature; but it is also much less noble and less commendable. ^CGreatness of soul is not so much pressing upward and forward as knowing how to set oneself in order and circumscribe oneself. It regards as great whatever is adequate, and shows its elevation by liking moderate things better than eminent ones. ^BThere is nothing so beautiful and legitimate as to play the man well and properly, no knowledge so hard to acquire as the knowledge of how to live this life well ^Cand naturally; ^Band the most barbarous of our maladies is to despise our being.

He who wants to detach his soul, let him do it boldly, if he can, when his body is ill, to free it from the contagion; at other times, on the contrary, let the soul assist and favor the body and not refuse to take part in its natural pleasures and enjoy them conjugally, bringing to them moderation, if it is the wiser of the two, for fear that through lack of discretion they may merge into pain. ^CIntemperance is the plague of sensual pleasure; and temperance is not its scourge, it is its seasoning. Eudoxus, who made pleasure the supreme good, and his fellows, who raised it to such high value, savored it in its most charming sweetness by means of temperance, which they possessed in singular and exemplary degree.

^BJ'ordonne à mon âme de regarder et la douleur et la volupté de vue pareillement ^Créglée (*eodem enim vitio est effusio animi in lætitia quo in dolore contractio*) [13] et pareillement ^Bferme, mais gaiement l'une, l'autre sévèrement, et, selon ce qu'elle y peut apporter, autant soigneuse d'en éteindre l'une que d'étendre l'autre. ^CLe voir sainement les biens tire après soi le voir sainement les maux. Et la douleur a quelque chose de non évitable en son tendre commencement, et la volupté quelque chose d'évitable en sa fin excessive. Platon les accouple, et veut que ce soit pareillement l'office de la fortitude combattre à l'encontre de la douleur et à l'encontre des immodérées et charmeresses blandices de la volupté. Ce sont deux fontaines auxquelles qui puise d'où, quand et combien il faut, soit cité, soit homme, soit bête, il est bienheureux. La première, il la faut prendre par médecine et par nécessité, plus écharsement; l'autre par soif, mais non jusqu'à l'ivresse. La douleur, la volupté, l'amour, la haine sont les premières choses que sent un enfant; si, la raison survenant, elles s'appliquent à elle, cela c'est vertu.

^BJ'ai un dictionnaire tout à part moi: je passe le temps quand il est mauvais et incommode; quand il est bon, je ne le veux pas passer, je le retâte, je m'y tiens. Il faut courir le mauvais et se rasseoir au bon. Cette phrase ordinaire de passe-temps et de passer le temps représente l'usage de ces prudentes gens qui ne pensent point avoir meilleur compte de leur vie que de la couler et échapper, de la passer, gauchir, et autant qu'il est en eux, ignorer et fuir, comme chose de qualité ennuyeuse et dédaignable.

---

[13] Cicero, *Tusculans*, IV, xxxi.

^BI order my soul to look upon both pain and pleasure with a gaze equally ^Cself-controlled—*for it is as wrong for the soul to overflow from joy as to contract in sorrow* [13]— and equally ^Bfirm, but gaily at the one, at the other severely, and, according to its ability, as anxious to extinguish the one as to extend the other. ^CViewing good things sanely implies viewing bad things sanely. And pain has something not to be avoided in its mild beginning, and pleasure something to be avoided in its excessive ending. Plato couples them together and claims that it is equally the function of fortitude to fight against pain and against the immoderate and bewitching blandishments of pleasure. They are two fountains: whoever draws the right amount from the right one at the right time, whether city, man, or beast, is blessed indeed. The first we must take as a necessary medicine, but more sparingly; the other for thirst, but not to the point of drunkenness. Pain, pleasure, love, hatred, are the first things a child feels; if when reason comes they cling to her, that is virtue.

^BI have a vocabulary all my own. I "pass the time," when it is rainy and disagreeable; when it is good, I do not want to pass it; I savor it, I cling to it. We must run through the bad and settle on the good. This ordinary expression "pastime" or "pass the time" represents the habit of those wise folk who think they can make no better use of their life than to let it slip by and escape it, pass it by, sidestep it, and, as far as in them lies, ignore it and run away from it, as something irksome and con-

Mais je la connais autre, et la trouve et prisable et commode, voire en son dernier décours, où je la tiens; et nous l'a nature mise en main garnie de telles circonstances et si favorables que nous n'avons à nous plaindre qu'à nous si elle nous presse et si elle nous échappe inutilement. *CStulti vita ingrata est, trepida est, tota in futurum fertur.*[14] BJe me compose pourtant à la perdre sans regret, mais comme perdable de sa condition, non comme moleste et importune. CAussi ne sied-il proprement bien de ne se déplaire à mourir qu'à ceux qui se plaisent à vivre. BIl y a du ménage à la jouir. Je la jouis au double des autres, car la mesure en la jouissance dépend du plus ou moins d'application que nous y prêtons. Principalement à cette heure que j'aperçois la mienne si brève en temps, je la veux étendre en poids; je veux arrêter la promptitude de sa fuite par la promptitude de ma saisie, et par la vigueur de l'usage compenser la hâtiveté de son écoulement. A mesure que la possession du vivre est plus courte, il me la faut rendre plus profonde et plus pleine.

Les autres sentent la douceur d'un contentement et de la prospérité; je la sens ainsi qu'eux, mais ce n'est pas en passant et glissant. Si la faut-il étudier, savourer et ruminer, pour en rendre grâces condignes à celui qui nous l'octroie. Ils jouissent les autres plaisirs comme ils font celui du sommeil, sans les connaître. A cette fin que le dormir même ne m'échappât ainsi stupidement, j'ai autrefois trouvé bon qu'on me le troublât pour que je l'entre-

---

[14] Seneca, *Epistles,* xv, 9.

temptible. But I know it to be otherwise and find it both agreeable and worth prizing, even in its last decline, in which I now possess it; and nature has placed it in our hands adorned with such favorable conditions that we have only ourselves to blame if it weighs on us and if it escapes us unprofitably. ^C*The life of the fool is joyless, full of trepidation, given over wholly to the future.*[14] ^BHowever, I am reconciling myself to the thought of losing it, without regret, but as something that by its nature must be lost; not as something annoying and troublesome. ^CThen too, not to dislike dying is properly becoming only to those who like living. ^BIt takes management to enjoy life. I enjoy it twice as much as others, for the measure of enjoyment depends on the greater or lesser attention that we lend it. Especially at this moment, when I perceive that mine is so brief in time, I try to increase it in weight; I try to arrest the speed of its flight by the speed with which I grasp it, and to compensate for the haste of its ebb by my vigor in using it. The shorter my possession of life, the deeper and fuller I must make it.

Others feel the sweetness of some satisfaction and of prosperity; I feel it as they do, but it is not in passing and slipping by. Instead we must study it, savor it, and ruminate it, to give proper thanks for it to him who grants it to us. They enjoy the other pleasures as they do that of sleep, without being conscious of them. To the end that sleep itself should not escape me thus stupidly, at one time I saw fit to have mine disturbed, so that I might gain a

[III:13] *Of Experience*

visse. Je consulte d'un contentement avec moi, je ne l'écume pas; je le sonde, et plie ma raison à le recueillir, devenue chagrine et dégoûtée. Me trouvé-je en quelque assiette tranquille? y a-t-il quelque volupté qui me chatouille? je ne la laisse pas friponner aux sens, j'y associe mon âme, non pas pour s'y engager mais pour s'y agréer, non pas pour s'y perdre mais pour s'y trouver; et l'emploie de sa part à se mirer dans ce prospère état, à en peser et estimer le bonheur, et amplifier. Elle mesure combien c'est qu'elle doit à Dieu d'être en repos de sa conscience et d'autres passions intestines, d'avoir le corps en sa disposition naturelle, jouissant ordonnément et compétemment des fonctions molles et flatteuses par lesquelles il lui plaît compenser de sa grâce les douleurs de quoi sa justice nous bat à son tour; combien lui vaut d'être logée en tel point que, où qu'elle jette sa vue, le ciel est calme autour d'elle: nul désir, nulle crainte ou doute qui lui trouble l'air, aucune difficulté ᶜpassée, présente, future, ᴮpar-dessus laquelle son imagination ne passe sans offense.

Cette considération prend grand lustre de la comparaison des conditions différentes. Ainsi je me propose, en mille visages, ceux que la fortune ou que leur propre erreur emporte et tempête, et encore ceux-ci, plus près de moi, qui reçoivent si lâchement et incurieusement leur bonne fortune. Ce sont gens qui passent voirement leur temps; ils outrepassent le présent et ce qu'ils possèdent, pour servir à l'espérance et pour des ombrages et vaines images que la fantaisie leur met au-devant—

glimpse of it. I meditate on any satisfaction; I do not skim over it, I sound it, and bend my reason, now grown peevish and hard to please, to welcome it. Do I find myself in some tranquil state? Is there some voluptuous pleasure that tickles me? I do not let my senses pilfer it, I bring my soul into it, not to implicate herself, but to enjoy herself, not to lose herself but to find herself. And I set her, for her part, to admire herself in this prosperous estate, to weigh and appreciate and amplify the happiness of it. She measures the extent of her debt to God for being at peace with her conscience and free from other inner passions, for having her body in its natural condition, enjoying controlledly and adequately the agreeable and pleasant functions with which he is pleased to compensate by his grace for the pains with which his justice chastises us in its turn; how much it is worth to her to be lodged at such a point that wherever she casts her eyes, the sky is calm around her: no desire, no fear or doubt to disturb the air for her, no difficulty, ᶜpast, present, or future, ᴮover which her imagination may not pass without hurt.

This consideration gains great luster by comparison between my condition and that of others. Thus I set before me in a thousand forms those who are carried away and tossed about by fortune or their own error, and also those, closer to my way, who accept their good fortune so languidly and indifferently. They are the people who really "pass their time"; they pass over the present and what they possess, to be the slaves of hope, and for shadows and vain images that fancy dangles before them—

Morte obita quales fama est volitare figuras,
Aut quæ sopitos deludunt somnia sensus,[15]

—lesquelles hâtent et allongent leur fuite à même qu'on les suit. Le fruit et but de leur poursuite c'est poursuivre, comme Alexandre disait que la fin de son travail c'était travailler,

Nil actum credens cum quid superesset agendum.[16]

Pour moi donc, j'aime la vie et la cultive telle qu'il a plu à Dieu nous l'octroyer. Je ne vais pas désirant qu'elle eût à dire la nécessité de boire et de manger, ^Cet me semblerait faillir non moins excusablement de désirer qu'elle l'eût double. *Sapiens divitiarum naturalium quæsitor acerrimus.*[17] Ni ^Bque nous nous sustentassions mettant seulement en la bouche un peu de cette drogue par laquelle Épiménidès se privait d'appétit et se maintenait; ni qu'on produisît stupidement des enfants par les doigts ou par les talons, ^Cains, parlant en révérence, plutôt qu'on les produise encore voluptueusement par les doigts et par les talons; ni ^Bque le corps fût sans désir et sans chatouillement. Ce sont plaintes ingrates ^Cet iniques. ^BJ'accepte de bon cœur, ^Cet reconnaissant, ^Bce que nature a fait pour moi, et m'en agrée et m'en loue. On fait tort à ce grand et tout-puissant donneur de refuser son don, l'annuler et défigurer. ^CTout bon, il a fait tout bon. *Omnia quæ secundum naturam sunt, æstimatione digna sunt.*[18]

^BDes opinions de la philosophie, j'embrasse plus vo-

---

[15] Virgil, *Aeneid*, x, 641–2.
[16] Lucan, *Pharsalia*, II, 657.

450

Like ghosts that after death are said to flit,
Or visions that delude the slumbering wit [15]

—which hasten and prolong their flight the more they are
pursued. The fruit and goal of their pursuit is to pursue,
as Alexander said that the purpose of his work was to work,

Believing nothing done while aught was left to do.[16]

As for me, then, I love life and cultivate it just as God
has been pleased to grant it to us. I do not go about wishing that it should lack the need to eat and drink, ^Cand it
would seem to me no less excusable a failing to wish that
need to be doubled. *The wise man is the keenest searcher
for natural treasures.*[17] Nor do I wish ^Bthat we should sustain ourselves by merely putting into our mouths a little
of that drug by which Epimenides took away his appetite
and kept himself alive; nor that we should beget children
insensibly with our fingers or our heels, ^Cbut rather, with
due respect, that we could also beget them voluptuously
with our fingers and heels; nor ^Bthat the body should be
without desire and without titillation. Those are ungrate-
ful ^Cand unfair ^Bcomplaints. I accept with all my heart
^Cand with gratitude ^Bwhat nature has done for me, and I
am pleased with myself and proud of myself that I do. We
wrong that great and all-powerful Giver by refusing his
gift, nullifying it, and disfiguring it. ^CHimself all good, he
has made all things good. *All things that are according to
nature are worthy of esteem.*[18]

^BOf the opinions of philosophy I most gladly embrace

---

[17] Seneca, *Epistles*, cxix, 5.
[18] Adapted from Cicero, *De Finibus*, III, vi.

lontiers celles qui sont les plus solides, c'est-à-dire les plus humaines et nôtres: mes discours sont, conformément à mes mœurs, bas et humbles. ^CElle fait bien l'enfant, à mon gré, quand elle se met sur ses ergots pour nous prêcher que c'est une farouche alliance de marier le divin avec le terrestre, le raisonnable avec le déraisonnable, le sévère à l'indulgent, l'honnête au déshonnête; que volupté est qualité brutale, indigne que le sage la goûte: le seul plaisir qu'il tire de la jouissance d'une belle jeune épouse c'est le plaisir de sa conscience de faire une action selon l'ordre, comme de chausser ses bottes pour une utile chevauchée. N'eussent ses suivants non plus de droit et de nerfs et de suc au dépucelage de leurs femmes qu'en a sa leçon!

Ce n'est pas ce que dit Socratès, son précepteur et le nôtre. Il prise comme il doit la volupté corporelle, mais il préfère celle de l'esprit comme ayant plus de force, de constance, de facilité, de variété, de dignité. Celle-ci va nullement seule selon lui (il n'est pas si fantastique), mais seulement première. Pour lui la tempérance est modératrice, non adversaire, des voluptés.

^BNature est un doux guide, mais non pas plus doux que prudent et juste. ^C*Intrandum est in rerum naturam et penitus quid ea postulet pervidendum.*[19] ^BJe quête partout sa piste. Nous l'avons confondue de traces artificielles; ^Cet ce souverain bien Académique et Péripatétique, qui est vivre selon icelle, devient à cette cause difficile à borner et exprimer; et celui des Stoïciens, voisin à celui-là, qui est consentir à nature.

---

[19] Cicero, *De Finibus*, v, xvi.

those that are most solid, that is to say, most human and most our own; my opinions, in conformity with my conduct, are low and humble. ^CPhilosophy is very childish, to my mind, when she gets up on her hind legs and preaches to us that it is a barbarous alliance to marry the divine with the earthly, the reasonable with the unreasonable, the severe with the indulgent, the honorable with the dishonorable; that sensual pleasure is a brutish thing unworthy of being enjoyed by the wise man; that the only pleasure he derives from the enjoyment of a beautiful young wife is the pleasure of his consciousness of doing the right thing, like putting on his boots for a useful ride. May her followers have no more right and sinews and sap in deflowering their wives than her lessons have!

That is not what Socrates says, her tutor and ours. He prizes bodily pleasure as he should, but he prefers that of the mind, as having more power, constancy, ease, variety, and dignity. The latter by no means goes alone, according to him—he is not so fanciful—but only comes first. For him temperance is the moderator, not the adversary, of pleasures.

^BNature is a gentle guide, but no more gentle than wise and just. ^C*We must penetrate into the nature of things and clearly see exactly what it demands.*[19] ^BI seek her footprints everywhere. We have confused them with artificial tracks, ^Cand for that reason the sovereign good of the Academics and the Peripatetics, which is "to live according to nature," becomes hard to limit and express; also that of the Stoics, a neighbor to the other, which is "to consent to nature."

[III:13] *Of Experience*

^BEst-ce pas erreur d'estimer aucunes actions moins dignes de ce qu'elles sont nécessaires? Si ne m'ôteront-ils pas de la tête que ce ne soit un très convenable mariage du plaisir avec la nécessité, ^Cavec laquelle, dit un ancien, les dieux complotent toujours. ^BA quoi faire démembrons-nous en divorce un bâtiment tissu d'une si jointe et fraternelle correspondance? Au rebours, renouons-le par mutuels offices. Que l'esprit éveille et vivifie la pesanteur du corps, le corps arrête la légèreté de l'esprit et la fixe. ^C*Qui velut summum bonum laudat animæ naturam, et tanquam malum naturam carnis accusat, profecto et animam carnaliter appetit et carnem carnaliter fugit, quoniam id vanitate sentit humana non veritate divina.*[20]

^BIl n'y a pièce indigne de notre soin en ce présent que Dieu nous a fait; nous en devons compte jusqu'à un poil. Et n'est pas une commission par acquit à l'homme de conduire l'homme selon sa condition: elle est expresse, naïve ^Cet très principale, ^Bet nous l'a le créateur donnée sérieusement et sévèrement. ^CL'autorité peut seule envers les communs entendements, et pèse plus en langage pérégrin. Rechargeons en ce lieu. *Stultitiæ proprium quis non dixerit, ignave et contumaciter facere quæ facienda sunt, et alio corpus impellere, alio animum, distrahique inter diversissimos motus.*[21]

^BOr sus, pour voir, faites-vous dire un jour les amusements et imaginations que celui-là met en sa tête et pour

---

[20] St. Augustine, *City of God*, xiv, v.

ᴮIs it not an error to consider some actions less worthy because they are necessary? No, they will not knock it out of my head that the marriage of pleasure with necessity, ᶜwith whom, says an ancient, the gods always conspire, ᴮis a very suitable one. To what purpose do we dismember by divorce a structure made up of such close and brotherly correspondence? On the contrary, let us bind it together again by mutual services. Let the mind arouse and quicken the heaviness of the body, and the body check and make fast the lightness of the mind. ᶜ*He who praises the nature of the soul as the sovereign good and condemns the nature of the flesh as evil, truly both carnally desires the soul and carnally shuns the flesh; for his feeling is inspired by human vanity, not by divine truth.*[20]

ᴮThere is no part unworthy of our care in this gift that God has given us; we are accountable for it even to a single hair. And it is not a perfunctory charge to man to guide man according to his nature; it is express, simple, ᶜand of prime importance, ᴮand the creator has given it to us seriously and sternly. ᶜAuthority alone has power over common intelligences, and has more weight in a foreign language. Let us renew the charge here. *Who would not say that it is the essence of folly to do lazily and rebelliously what has to be done, to impel the body one way and the soul another, to be split between the most conflicting motions?* [21]

ᴮCome on now, just to see, some day get some man to tell you the absorbing thoughts and fancies that he takes

---

²¹ Seneca, *Epistles,* lxxiv, 32.

　　　　　　　　[III:13] *Of Experience*

lesquelles il détourne sa pensée d'un bon repas et plaint l'heure qu'il emploie à se nourrir: vous trouverez qu'il n'y a rien si fade en tous les mets de votre table que ce bel entretien de son âme (le plus souvent il nous vaudrait mieux dormir tout à fait que de veiller à ce à quoi nous veillons), et trouverez que son discours et intentions ne valent pas votre capilotade. Quand ce seraient les ravissements d'Archimédès même, que serait-ce? Je ne touche pas ici et ne mêle point à cette marmaille d'hommes que nous sommes, et à cette vanité de désirs et cogitations qui nous divertissent, ces âmes vénérables, élevées par ardeur de dévotion et religion à une constante et consciencieuse méditation des choses divines; ^Clesquelles, préoccupant par l'effort d'une vive et véhémente espérance l'usage de la nourriture éternelle, but final et dernier arrêt des chrétiens désirs, seul plaisir constant, incorruptible, dédaignent de s'attendre à nos nécessiteuses commodités, fluides et ambiguës, et résignent facilement au corps le soin et l'usage de la pâture sensuelle et temporelle. ^BC'est un étude privilégié. ^CEntre nous, ce sont choses que j'ai toujours vues de singulier accord: les opinions supercélestes et les mœurs souterraines.

^BÉsope, ^Cce grand homme, ^Bvit son maître qui pissait en se promenant. "Quoi donc," fit-il, "nous faudra-t-il chier en courant?" Ménageons le temps; encore nous en reste-t-il beaucoup d'oisif et mal employé. Notre esprit n'a volontiers pas assez d'autres heures à faire ses besognes, sans se désassocier du corps en ce peu d'espace qu'il lui faut pour sa nécessité.

Ils veulent se mettre hors d'eux et échapper à l'homme.

into his head, and for the sake of which he turns his mind from a good meal and laments the time he spends on feeding himself. You will find there is nothing so insipid in all the dishes on your table as this fine entertainment of his mind (most of the time we should do better to go to sleep completely than to stay awake for what we do stay awake for); and you will find that his ideas and aspirations are not worth your stew. Even if they were the transports of Archimedes himself, what of it? I am not here touching on, or mixing up with that brattish rabble of men that we are, or with the vanity of the desires and musings that distract us, those venerable souls, exalted by ardent piety and religion to constant and conscientious meditation on divine things, ᶜwho, anticipating, by dint of keen and vehement hope, the enjoyment of eternal food, final goal and ultimate limit of Christian desires, sole constant and incorruptible pleasure, scorn to give their attention to our beggarly, watery, and ambiguous comforts, and readily resign to the body the concern and enjoyment of sensual and temporal fodder. ᴮThat is a privileged study. ᶜBetween ourselves, these are two things that I have always observed to be in singular accord: supercelestial thoughts and subterranean conduct.

ᴮAesop, ᶜthat great man, ᴮsaw his master pissing as he walked. "What next?" he said. "Shall we have to shit as we run?" Let us manage our time; we shall still have a lot left idle and ill spent. Our mind likes to think it has not enough leisure hours to do its own business unless it dissociates itself from the body for the little time that the body really needs it.

They want to get out of themselves and escape from the

C'est folie: au lieu de se transformer en anges, ils se transforment en bêtes; au lieu de se hausser, ils s'abattent. ᶜCes humeurs transcendantes m'effraient, comme les lieux hautains et inaccessibles; et rien ne m'est à digérer fâcheux en la vie de Socratès que ses extases et ses démoneries, rien si humain en Platon que ce pourquoi ils disent qu'on l'appelle divin. ᴮEt de nos sciences, celles-là me semblent plus terrestres et basses qui sont le plus haut montées. Et je ne trouve rien si humble et si mortel en la vie d'Alexandre que ses fantaisies autour de son immortalisation. Philotas le mordit plaisamment par sa réponse. Il s'était conjoui avec lui par lettre de l'oracle de Jupiter Ammon qui l'avait logé entre les dieux: "Pour ta considération j'en suis bien aise; mais il y a de quoi plaindre les hommes qui auront à vivre avec un homme et lui obéir, lequel outrepasse ᶜet ne se contente de ᴮla mesure d'un homme."

ᶜDiis te minorem quod geris, imperas.[22]

ᴮLa gentille inscription de quoi les Athéniens honorèrent la venue de Pompéius en leur ville se conforme à mon sens:

D'autant es-tu Dieu comme
Tu te reconnais homme.[23]

C'est une absolue perfection, et comme divine, de savoir jouir loyalement de son être. Nous cherchons d'autres conditions pour n'entendre l'usage des nôtres, et sortons

---

[22] Horace, *Odes*, III, vi, 5.

man. That is madness: instead of changing into angels, they change into beasts; instead of raising themselves, they lower themselves. ᶜThese transcendental humors frighten me, like lofty and inaccessible places; and nothing is so hard for me to stomach in the life of Socrates as his ecstasies and possessions by his daemon, nothing is so human in Plato as the qualities for which they say he is called divine. ᴮAnd of our sciences, those seem to me most terrestrial and low which have risen the highest. And I find nothing so humble and so mortal in the life of Alexander as his fancies about his immortalization. Philotas stung him wittily by his answer. He congratulated him by letter on the oracle of Jupiter Ammon which had lodged him among the gods: "As far as you are concerned, I am very glad of it; but there is reason to pity the men who will have to live with and obey a man who exceeds ᶜand is not content with ᴮa man's proportions."

ᶜSince you obey the gods, you rule the world.²²

ᴮThe nice inscription with which the Athenians honored the entry of Pompey into their city is in accord with my meaning.

You are as much a god as you will own
That you are nothing but a man alone.²³

It is an absolute perfection and virtually divine to know how to enjoy our being rightfully. We seek other conditions because we do not understand the use of our own,

---

²³ From Amyot's translation of Plutarch, *Lives*, "Pompey."

hors de nous pour ne savoir quel il y fait. ^CSi avons-nous beau monter sur des échasses, car sur des échasses encore faut-il marcher de nos jambes. Et au plus élevé trône du monde si ne sommes assis que sur notre cul.

^BLes plus belles vies sont, à mon gré, celles qui se rangent au modèle commun ^Cet humain, avec ordre, mais ^Bsans miracle et sans extravagance. Or la vieillesse a un peu besoin d'être traitée plus tendrement. Recommandons-la à ce dieu protecteur de santé et de sagesse, mais gaie et sociale:

> Frui paratis et valido mihi,
> Latoe, dones, et, precor, integra
> Cum mente, nec turpam senectam
> Degere, nec cythara carentem.[24]

---

[24] Horace, *Odes*, I, xxxi, 17–20. "Latona's son" is Apollo.

and go outside of ourselves because we do not know what it is like inside. ^CYet there is no use our mounting on stilts, for on stilts we must still walk on our own legs. And on the loftiest throne in the world we are still sitting only on our own rump.

^BThe most beautiful lives, to my mind, are those that conform to the common ^Chuman ^Bpattern, ^Cwith order, but ^Bwithout miracle and without eccentricity. Now old age needs to be treated a little more tenderly. Let us commend it to that god who is the protector of health and wisdom, but gay and sociable wisdom:

> Grant me but health, Latona's son,
> And to enjoy the wealth I've won,
> And honored age, with mind entire
> And not unsolaced by the lyre.[24]

Pages Choisies

Selected Writings

TRADUCTION DE LA THÉOLOGIE NATURELLE DE RAIMOND
SEBOND [1]

Préface de l'auteur [2]

A la louange et gloire de la très haute et très glorieuse
Trinité, de la Vierge Marie, et de toute la cour céleste; au
nom de notre Seigneur Jésus-Christ, au profit et salut de
tous les Chrétiens, s'ensuit la doctrine du livre des créatures ou livre de Nature: doctrine de l'homme, et à lui
propre en tant qu'il est homme; *doctrine convenable, naturelle et utile à tout homme;* [3] par laquelle il est illuminé à

---

[1] Montaigne's first published work, though only a translation,
sheds much light on his thought before the *Essays*. He undertook
the task at the behest of his father, who considered Sebond's Latin
book a good antidote to Lutheranism. Sebond seeks to demonstrate the existence and nature of God, and man's duties, by analogies drawn from the four main levels (inanimate, vegetable, animal, human) of the creation. His Prologue makes such extravagant
claims for the infallible powers of his doctrine that the entire book
was placed on the Index of Prohibited Books in 1558–59, and the
Prologue (but not the rest of the work) was retained on the re-
vised Index of 1564.
   Montaigne made a faithful translation of Sebond's text, but altered the Prologue in translation by drastically cutting down Sebond's sweeping claims, thus showing not only his own orthodoxy
but also the great reservations about Sebond that appear later in

Author's Preface [2]

To the praise and glory of the most lofty and most glorious Trinity, the Virgin Mary, and all the heavenly court;
in the name of our Lord Jesus Christ; to the profit and
salvation of all Christians; there follows the doctrine of
the book of creation, or book of Nature: a doctrine of
man, and appropriate to him in that he is man; *a doctrine suitable, natural, and useful to every man,* [3] by which

---

the longest of the *Essays,* "Apology for Raymond Sebond" (II: 12;
see above, pp. 196–253, especially pp. 198–203).

Sebond's book is entitled *Liber Creaturarum, sive Theologia Naturalis (Book of Creatures, or Natural Theology);* Montaigne uses both
titles (*Livre des créatures* and *Théologie naturelle*) but usually the
latter. His translation was published in 1569; a carefully corrected
second edition (1581) was several times reprinted. For further information on Sebond and the translation, see above, pp. 198–203.

In the extracts given here, the passages which Montaigne changed
substantially in translation are italicized and followed in the foot-
notes by Sebond's Latin text and its English translation.

[2] Sebond entitled this "Prologus" ("Prologue").

[3] "quæ est necessaria omni homini, et ei naturalis, et conveniens"
—"which is necessary to every man, and natural and suitable to
him."

se connaître soi-même, son créateur et *presque tout* [4] ce à
quoi il est tenu comme homme; doctrine contenant la
règle de Nature. . . .

En outre, cette doctrine apprend à tout homme de voir
à l'œil sans difficulté et sans peine *la vérité, autant qu'il
est possible à la raison naturelle,* [5] pour la connaissance de
Dieu et de soi-même, . . . *lui donne grand accès à l'intelligence de ce qui est prescrit et commandé aux Saintes
Écritures,* [6] et fait que l'entendement humain *est délivré
de plusieurs doutes,* [7] *et consent hardiment à ce qu'elles
contiennent concernant la connaissance de Dieu ou de soi-
même.* [8]

En ce livre se découvrent *les* [9] anciennes erreurs des
païens et philosophes infidèles, et par sa doctrine se maintient et se connaît *la foi catholique.* . . .[10] Les créatures
jointes ensemble et accouplées l'une à l'autre . . . contiennent la science qui nous est *nécessaire avant tout autre.* [11]

---

[4] "omne"—"everything."

[5] "omnem veritatem homini necessariam"—"all truth necessary
to man."

[6] "Et per istam scientiam homo cognoscit, sine difficultate et
realiter, quicquid in sacra scriptura continetur; et quicquid in sacra
scriptura dicitur et præcipitur, per istam scientiam cognoscitur infallibiliter, cum magna certitudine"—"And by this knowledge man
knows, without difficulty and in reality, whatever is contained in
the Holy Scripture; and whatever is said and prescribed in the Holy
Scripture, by this knowledge is known infallibly, with great certainty."

[7] "omni dubitatione postposita"—"all doubt removed."

he is enlightened to know himself, his Creator, and *almost everything* [4] for which he is responsible as a man; a doctrine containing the rule of Nature. . . .

Besides, this doctrine teaches every man to see with his own eyes, without difficulty or pains, *the truth, as far as this is possible to natural reason,* [5] for the knowledge of God and of himself, . . . *gives him great access to the understanding of what the Holy Scriptures prescribe for him and command him,* [6] and brings it about that human understanding *is delivered from several doubts,* [7] and *boldly consents to what the Scriptures contain concerning the knowledge of God or of oneself.* [8]

In this book are revealed *the* [9] ancient errors of the pagans and infidel philosophers, and by its teaching *the Catholic faith* [10] is maintained and known. . . . The creatures, joined together and coupled to one another, . . . contain the knowledge that is *necessary for us before any other.* [11]

---

[8] "toti sacræ scripturæ assentiat, et certificatur, ut non possit dubitare quæstionem in ista scientia. Et per istam scientiam potest solvi omnis quæstio quæ debet sciri tam de Deo quam de seipso, et hoc sine difficultate"—"assents to all the Holy Scripture, and is made certain, so that it cannot doubt about any question in this knowledge. And by this knowledge can be resolved every question that should be known both about God and about oneself, and this without difficulty."

[9] "omnes"—"all the."

[10] "tota fides catholica infallibiliter"—"all the Catholic faith, infallibly."

[11] "necessariam"—"necessary."

Natural Theology

An[no] Christi [1571] aet[ate] 38, pridie cal[endas] Mar-
t[ias], die suo natali, Mich[aelis] Montanus, servitii aulici
et munerum publicorum jamdudum pertæsus, dum se
integer in doctarum Virginum recessit sinus, ubi quietus
et omnium securus [quant]illum id tandem superabit de-
cursi multa jam plus parte spatii, si modo fata duint, exigat
istas sedes et dulces latebras avitasque libertati suæ tran-
quillitatique et otio consecravit.

---

[1] Montaigne had this inscription painted on the wall of the little
room next to his study, in the tower of his château.

In the year of Christ 1571, at the age of thirty-eight, on
the last day of February, anniversary of his birth, Michel
de Montaigne, long weary of the servitude of the Court
and of public employments, while still entire, retired to
the bosom of the learned Virgins [the Muses], where in
calm and freedom from all cares he will spend what little
remains of his life now more than half run out. If the
fates permit he will complete this abode, this sweet an-
cestral retreat; and he has consecrated it to his freedom,
tranquillity, and leisure.

AUGSBOURG [15–19 octobre, 1580]. . . . Quand il [2] passa par l'Église Notre-Dame, ayant un froid extrême . . . , il avait, sans y penser, le mouchoir au nez, estimant aussi qu'ainsi seul et très mal accommodé, nul ne se prendrait garde de lui. Quand ils furent plus apprivoisés avec lui, ils lui dirent que les gens de l'église avaient trouvé cette contenance étrange. Enfin il encourut le vice qu'il fuyait le plus, de se rendre remarquable par quelque façon ennemie du goût de ceux qui le voyaient. Car en tant qu'en lui est, il se conforme et range aux modes du lieu où il se trouve; et portait à Augsbourg un bonnet fourré par la ville. . . .

ROVERETO [29 octobre, 1580]. . . . Je crois à la vérité que s'il eût été seul avec les siens,[3] il fût allé plutôt à Cracovie ou vers la Grèce par terre, que de prendre le tour vers l'Italie. Mais le plaisir qu'il prenait à visiter les pays

---

[1] This diary of Montaigne's trip to Italy via Germany and Switzerland in 1580–81, which runs to a few hundred pages in most editions, was discovered and published in 1774. Written partly by a secretary, partly—in French and Italian—by Montaigne himself, it confirms his portrait in the *Essais* and brings out his love of travel,

AUGSBURG [October 15–19, 1580]. . . . When he [2] passed through the Church of Our Lady, being extremely cold . . . , he had, without thinking about it, his handkerchief to his nose, thinking that since he was thus alone and very plainly dressed, no one would pay attention to him. When they were better acquainted with him, they told him that the church people had found this bearing strange. At last he had fallen into the fault that he most avoided, that of making himself noticeable by some mannerism at variance with the taste of those who saw him; for as far as in him lies, he conforms and falls into line with the ways of the place where he happens to be, and in Augsburg he wore a fur cap around the town. . . .

ROVERETO [October 29, 1580]. . . . I truly believe that if he had been alone with his own attendants [3] he would rather have gone to Cracow or toward Greece by land than make the turn toward Italy; but the pleasure he took

___

his friendliness to other peoples and ways, and his strong interest in the ideas and practices of all religions.

[2] Montaigne. (The secretary is writing.)

[3] Again the secretary is writing about Montaigne. The party included four other noblemen and some servants.

inconnus, lequel il trouvait si doux que d'en oublier la faiblesse de son âge et de sa santé, il ne le pouvait imprimer à nul de la troupe, chacun ne demandant que la retraite. Là où il avait accoutumé de dire qu'après avoir passé une nuit inquiète, quand au matin il venait à se souvenir qu'il avait à voir ou une ville ou une nouvelle contrée, il se levait avec désir et allégresse. Je ne le vis jamais moins las ni moins se plaignant de ses douleurs, ayant l'esprit, et par chemin et en logis, si tendu à ce qu'il rencontrait, et recherchant toutes occasions d'entretenir les étrangers, que je crois que cela amusait son mal.

Quand on se plaignait à lui de ce qu'il conduisait souvent la troupe par chemins divers et contrées, revenant souvent bien près d'où il était parti (ce qu'il faisait, ou recevant l'avertissement de quelque chose digne de voir, ou changeant d'avis selon les occasions), il répondait qu'il n'allait, quant à lui, en nul lieu que là où il se trouvait, et qu'il ne pouvait faillir ni tordre sa voie, n'ayant nul projet que de se promener par des lieux inconnus; et pourvu qu'on ne le vît pas retomber sur même voie et revoir deux fois même lieu, qu'il ne faisait nulle faute à son dessein. Et quant à Rome, où les autres visaient, il la désirait d'autant moins voir que les autres lieux, qu'elle était connue d'un chacun et qu'il n'avait laquais qui ne leur pût dire nouvelles de Florence et de Ferrare. Il disait aussi qu'il lui semblait être à même ceux qui lisent quelque fort plaisant conte, d'où il leur prend crainte qu'il vienne bientôt à finir, ou un beau livre: lui de même prenait si grand

in visiting unknown countries, which he found so sweet as to make him forget the weakness of his age and of his health, he could not impress on any of his party, and everyone asked only to return home. Whereas he was accustomed to say that after spending a restless night, he would get up with desire and alacrity in the morning when he remembered that he had a new town or region to see. I never saw him less tired or complaining less of his pains; for his mind was so intent on what he encountered, both on the road and at his lodgings, and he was so eager on all occasions to talk to strangers, that I think this took his mind off his ailment.

When anyone complained to him that he often led his party, by various roads and regions, back very close to where he had started (which he did either because he had been told about something worth seeing, or because he had changed his mind according to the occasions), he would answer that as for him, he was not going anywhere except where he happened to be, and that he could not miss or go off his path, since he had no plan but to travel in unknown places; and that provided he did not fall back upon the same route or see the same place twice, he was not failing to carry out his plan. And as for Rome, which was the goal of the others, he desired less to see it than the other places, since it was known to every man, and there was not a lackey who could not tell them news of Florence and Ferrara. He also said that he seemed to be rather like people who are reading some very pleasing story and therefore begin to be afraid that soon it will come to an end, or any fine book; so he took

Travel Journal

plaisir à voyager qu'il haïssait le voisinage du lieu où il se dût reposer, et proposait plusieurs desseins de voyager à son aise, s'il pouvait se rendre seul. . . .

ROME [20 mars, 1581]. . . . Ce jour au soir me furent rendus mes *Essais*, châtiés selon l'opinion des Docteurs Moines.[4] Le *Maestro del Sacro Palazzo*[5] n'en avait pu juger que par le rapport d'aucun Frater français; n'entendant nullement notre langue; et se contentait tant des excuses que je faisais sur chaque article d'animadversion que lui avait laissé ce Français qu'il remit à ma conscience de rhabiller ce que je verrais être de mauvais goût. Je le suppliai, au rebours, qu'il suivît l'opinion de celui qui l'avait jugé, avouant en aucunes choses—comme d'avoir usé du mot de *fortune*, d'avoir nommé des poètes hérétiques, d'avoir excusé Julien, et l'animadversion sur ce que celui qui priait devait être exempt de vicieuse inclination pour ce temps; *item*, d'estimer cruauté ce qui est au delà de mort simple; *item*, qu'il fallait nourrir un enfant à tout faire;[6] et autres telles choses—que c'était mon

---

[4] According to regular practice but to Montaigne's dismay, when he first arrived in Rome (November 30, 1580), his baggage was searched and his books taken.

[5] The Master of the Sacred Palace (which exercised this censorship) at this time was Sisto Fabri (1541–94), professor of theology at the University of Rome, soon (1583) to be made general of the Dominican Order.

[6] Montaigne had often spoken carelessly of the power of fortune; he later defends this ("Des prières": 1:56). He had praised the Latin poetry of the Protestants Bèze and Buchanan ("De la présomption": II:17), and later defends this also ("De ménager sa volonté": III:

such pleasure in traveling that he hated to be nearing each place where he was to rest, and toyed with several plans for traveling as he pleased, if he could get away alone. . . .

Rome [March 20, 1581]. . . . On this day in the evening my *Essays* were returned to me, corrected according to the opinion of the learned monks.[4] The Master of the Sacred Palace [5] had been able to judge them only by the report of some French friar, since he did not understand our language at all; and he was so content with the excuses I offered on each objection that this Frenchman had left him that he referred it to my conscience to redress what I should see was in bad taste. I begged him on the contrary to follow the opinion of the man who had made the judgment, admitting in certain things—such as having used the word "fortune," having named heretic poets, having excused Julian, and the objection to the idea that anyone who was praying should be free from evil impulses at the time; *item*, esteeming as cruelty whatever goes beyond plain death; *item*, that a child should be brought up to do anything; [6] and other things of that

10). He had praised as well as condemned the emperor Julian the Apostate ("De la liberté de conscience": 11:19); demanded purity of heart in prayer ("Des prières": 1:56); twice condemned any torture (11:11 and 27) when the church approved it as a means of saving souls; and urged that a boy be fitted for anything (1:26; see above, pp. 66–7).

Only two books of *Essais* were examined, of course; the third was not yet written. The fideism of the "Apologie de Raimond Sebond" was not criticized. Montaigne made none of the changes requested—perhaps because they would have spoiled the fidelity of his portrait.

Travel Journal

opinion, et que c'était choses que j'avais mises, n'estimant que ce fussent erreurs; à d'autres, niant que le correcteur eût entendu ma conception. Ledit *Maestro*, qui est un habile homme, m'excusait fort, et me voulait faire sentir qu'il n'était pas fort de l'avis de cette réformation, et plaidait fort ingénieusement pour moi en ma présence contre un autre qui me combattait, Italien aussi.

Ils me retinrent le livre des histoires de Suisse traduit en français, pour ce seulement que le traducteur est hérétique, duquel le nom n'est pourtant pas exprimé. Mais c'est merveille combien ils connaissent les hommes de nos contrées: et le bon, ils me dirent que la préface était condamnée. . . .

. . . Le 15 d'avril je fus prendre congé du Maître *del Sacro Palazzo* et de son compagnon, qui me prièrent ne me servir point de la censure de mon livre, en laquelle autres Français les avaient avertis qu'il y avait plusieurs sottises; qu'ils honoraient et mon intention et affection envers l'Église et ma suffisance, et estimaient tant de ma franchise et conscience qu'ils remettaient à moi-même de retrancher en mon livre, quand je le voudrais réimprimer, ce que j'y trouverais trop licencieux, et entre autres choses, les mots de *fortune*. Il me sembla les laisser fort contents de moi. Et pour s'excuser de ce qu'ils avaient ainsi curieusement vu mon livre et condamné en quelques choses, m'alléguèrent plusieurs livres de notre temps de Cardinaux et religieux de très bonne réputation, censurés pour quelques telles imperfections, qui ne touchaient nullement la réputation de l'auteur ni de l'œuvre en gros; me prièrent

sort—that this was my opinion, and that they were things I had put in, not thinking they were errors; in other matters denying that the corrector had understood my thought. The said Master, who is an able man, was full of excuses for me, and wanted me to realize that he was not very sympathetic to these revisions; and he pleaded very ingeniously for me, in my presence, against another man, also an Italian, who was opposing me.

They did not return to me the book on the histories of Switzerland, translated into French, solely because the translator—whose name, however, is not given—is a heretic; but it is a marvel how well they know the men of our countries. And the best part was that they told me that the preface was condemned. . . .

On April 15th I went to say good-by to the Master of the Sacred Palace and his colleague, who urged me not to make use of the censorship of my book, in which censorship some other Frenchmen had informed them there were many stupid things; saying that they honored both my intention and my affection for the Church and my ability, and thought so well of my frankness and conscience that they left it to myself to cut out of my book, when I wanted to republish it, whatever I found too licentious in it, and among other things the uses of the word "fortune." It seemed to me that I left them well pleased with me; and to excuse themselves for having scrutinized my book so attentively and condemned it in certain details, they cited me many books of our time by cardinals and churchmen of very good reputation, censured for a few such imperfections which did not affect in the least the reputation of the author or of the

d'aider à l'Église par mon éloquence (ce sont leurs mots de courtoisie), et de faire demeure en cette ville paisible et hors de trouble avec eux. Ce sont personnes de grande autorité et cardinalables. . . .

work as a whole. They urged me to help the Church by my eloquence (those are their courteous formulas) and to make my abode in this city, at peace and without interference from them. These are persons of great authority and potential cardinals. . . .

Lettres

À SON PÈRE: *Sur la mort de La Boétie* [1]

. . . Le vendredi je le laissai encore; et le samedi je le fus
revoir déjà fort abattu. Il me dit lors que sa maladie était
un peu contagieuse, et outre cela, qu'elle était malplai-
sante et mélancolique; qu'il connaissait très bien mon
naturel, et me priait de n'être avec lui que par boutées,
mais le plus souvent que je pourrais. Je ne l'abandonnai
plus. . . .[2]

Mais deux ou trois heures après, tant pour lui conti-
nuer cette grandeur de courage, qu'aussi parce que je
souhaitais, pour la jalousie que j'ai eue toute ma vie de
sa gloire et de son honneur, qu'il y eût plus de témoins de
tant et si belles preuves de magnanimité, y ayant plus
grande compagnie en sa chambre; je lui dis que j'avais
rougi de honte de quoi le courage m'avait failli à ouïr

---

[1] The full title is: "Extrait d'une lettre que Monsieur le Conseiller
de Montaigne écrit à Monseigneur de Montaigne son père, concernant quelques particularités qu'il remarqua en la maladie et mort de
feu Monsieur de La Boétie"—"Extract from a letter that Monsieur
de Montaigne the Councillor wrote to Monseigneur de Montaigne
his father concerning certain details that he noted in the illness and
death of the late Monsieur de La Boétie." It was first published

Letters

TO HIS FATHER: *On the Death of La Boétie* [1]

. . . On Friday I again left him, and on Saturday went to see him again and found him already very worn down. He told me then that his illness was a bit contagious and moreover unpleasant and melancholic; that he knew my nature very well and asked me to be with him only for short periods but as often as I could. I did not leave him again. . . . [2]

But two or three hours later, both to keep up his great courage, and because I wished, in the zeal I have had all my life for his glory and honor, that there should be more people in his room to witness so many fine proofs of greatness of soul, I told him that I had blushed for shame that my courage had failed on hearing what he,

---

by Montaigne in Paris in 1570 at the end of a volume of La Boétie's *Œuvres*, but presumably written in 1563.

[2] La Boétie died on the following Wednesday. On Sunday, feeling that death was sure and near, he called together his wife, his uncle, and his friend Montaigne, and told them his last wishes and bequests. As he did so he looked much better.

ce que lui, qui était engagé dans ce mal, avait eu courage de me dire. Que jusque lors j'avais pensé que Dieu ne nous donnât guère si grand avantage sur les accidents humains, et croyais malaisément ce que quelquefois j'en lisais parmi les histoires; mais qu'en ayant senti une telle preuve, je louais Dieu de quoi ç'avait été en une personne de qui je fusse tant aimé, et que j'aimasse si chèrement; et que cela me servirait d'exemple, pour jouer ce même rôle à mon tour.

Il m'interrompit pour me prier d'en user ainsi, et de montrer par effet que les discours que nous avions tenus ensemble pendant notre santé, nous ne les portions pas seulement en la bouche, mais engravés bien avant au cœur et en l'âme, pour les mettre en exécution aux premières occasions qui s'offriraient; ajoutant que c'était la vraie pratique de nos études, et de la philosophie. Et, me prenant par la main:

"Mon frère, mon ami," me dit-il, "je t'assure que j'ai fait assez de choses, ce me semble, en ma vie, avec autant de peine et difficulté que je fais celle-ci. Et quand tout est dit, il y a fort longtemps que j'y étais préparé, et que j'en savais ma leçon toute par cœur. Mais n'est-ce pas assez vécu jusqu'à l'âge auquel je suis? J'étais prêt à entrer à mon trente-troisième an. Dieu m'a fait cette grâce, que tout ce que j'ai passé jusqu'à cette heure de ma vie a été plein de santé et de bonheur; pour l'inconstance des choses humaines, cela ne pouvait guère plus durer. Il était meshui temps de se mettre aux affaires, et de voir mille choses malplaisantes, comme l'incommodité de la vieillesse, de laquelle je suis quitte par ce moyen. Et puis il est vraisemblable que j'ai vécu jusqu'à cette heure avec plus de

who was suffering this illness, had had the courage to tell me. That up to then I had thought that God gave us no such great power against human calamities, and I had had difficulty believing what I had come across on this subject in the histories; but that having felt such a proof of it, I praised God that this had been in a person by whom I was so loved and whom I loved so dearly; and that this would serve me as an example, to play this same part in my turn.

He interrupted me to beg me to use it in this way, and to show in action that the talks we had had together during our health had been not merely borne in our mouths but deeply engraved on heart and in soul, in such a way as to be put into execution on the first occasions that offered; adding that this was the true object of our studies, and of philosophy. And, taking me by the hand, he said:

"My brother, my friend, I assure you that I have done many things in my life, it seems to me, with as much pain and difficulty as I do this. And when all is said, I had been prepared for it for a very long time and had known my lesson all by heart. But have I not lived enough up to my present age? I was soon to be thirty-three. God granted me this grace, that all my life up to now has been full of health and happiness. In view of the inconstancy of things human, that could hardly last any longer. Henceforth it would have been time to get down to business and to see a thousand unpleasant things, like the disadvantages of old age, of which by this means I am quit. And then it is likely that up to this time I have lived with more simplicity and less malice than I would per-

simplicité et moins de malice que je n'eusse par aventure fait, si Dieu m'eût laissé vivre jusqu'à ce que le soin de m'enrichir et accommoder mes affaires me fût entré dans la tête. Quant à moi, je suis certain que je m'en vais trouver Dieu, et le séjour des bienheureux." . . .

AU ROI HENRI IV

Au Roi [1]

Sire,

C'est être au-dessus du poids et de la foule de vos grands et importants affaires que de vous savoir prêter et démettre aux petits à leur tour, suivant le devoir de votre autorité royale, qui vous expose à toute heure à toute sorte et degré d'hommes et d'occupations. Toutefois, ce que Votre Majesté a daigné considérer mes lettres et y commander réponse, j'aime mieux le devoir à la bénignité qu'à la vigueur de son âme.

J'ai de tout temps regardé en vous cette même fortune où vous êtes; et vous peut souvenir que lors même qu'il m'en fallait confesser à mon curé, je ne laissais de voir

---

[1] Montaigne and Henry IV were old friends. As King of Navarre, Henry made him gentleman of his chamber, backed him for mayor of Bordeaux, spent two days in his château and later one evening just after his victory at Coutras, and employed him as negotiator with Henry III in Paris in 1588. When these letters were written,

484

haps have done if God had let me live until the concern with getting rich and improving my affairs came into my head. As for me, I am certain that I am going away to find God and the abode of the blessed." . . .

TO KING HENRY IV

[January 18, 1590 (?)]

To the King [1]

Sire,

It is a sign of rising above the weight and pressure of your great and important affairs to be able to stoop and lend yourself to the little people in their turn, according to the duty of your royal authority, which at every hour exposes you to every sort and condition of men and occupations. The fact, however, that Your Majesty has deigned to consider my letters and order them answered, I would rather owe to the benignity than to the vigor of your soul.

From the first I have considered you as destined for the rank you now occupy, and you may remember that even when I had to confess it to my curate I did not fail to

---

Henry iv was a Protestant king fighting hard to hold his own against the League and to win his Catholic kingdom.

For Montaigne's ambition to be a frank adviser to a king, which illness and then death kept him from realizing, see above, pp. 420–3 ("De l'expérience"—"Of Experience": iii:13).

Letters

aucunement de bon œil vos succès. A présent avec plus de raison et de liberté je les embrasse de pleine affection.

Ils vous servent là par effet, mais ils ne vous servent pas moins ici par réputation; le retentissement porte autant que le coup. Nous ne saurions tirer de la justice de votre cause des arguments si forts à maintenir ou réduire vos sujets comme nous faisons des nouvelles de la prospérité de vos entreprises; et puis assurer Votre Majesté que les changements nouveaux qu'elle voit par deçà à son avantage, son heureuse issue de Dieppe ² y a bien à point secondé le franc zèle et merveilleuse prudence de Monsieur le maréchal de Matignon; ³ duquel je me fais accroire que vous ne recevez pas journellement tant de bons et signalés services sans vous souvenir de mes assurances et espérances.

J'attends de ce prochain été non tant les fruits à me nourrir comme ceux de notre commune tranquillité, et qu'il passera sur vos affaires avec même teneur de bonheur, faisant évanouir, comme les précédentes, tant de grandes promesses de quoi vos adversaires nourrissent la volonté de leurs hommes. Les inclinations des peuples se manient à ondées. Si la pente est une fois prise à votre faveur, elle s'emportera de son propre branle jusqu'au bout.

J'eusse bien désiré que le gain particulier des soldats de votre armée, et le besoin de les contenter, ne vous eût

---

² The victory of Arques near Dieppe (September 21, 1589).
³ During Montaigne's mayoralty the loyal and astute Matignon,

look upon your successes with a distinctly favorable eye. At present, with more reason and freedom, I embrace them with my full affection.

These successes serve you up north in action, but they serve you no less down here by reputation. The reverberation strikes as hard as the blow. We could not possibly draw from the justice of your cause such strong arguments to confirm or subdue your subjects as we do from the news of the prosperity of your campaigns. And I can assure Your Majesty that in producing the new changes to your advantage that you see in these parts, your happy escape from Dieppe [2] has most opportunely seconded the frank zeal and marvelous sagacity of Marshal de Matignon,[3] from whom I like to believe that you do not daily receive so many good and signal services without remembering my assurances and my hopes.

For this coming summer I look forward not so much to the fruits that will feed me as to those of our common tranquillity, and I expect that this will spread over your affairs with the same happy tenor, dispersing, like the earlier ones, all the great promises with which your adversaries nourish the will of their men. Popular inclinations go in waves; if the leaning in your favor is once established, it will gather its own momentum and go all the way.

I would have wished, to be sure, that the individual profit of the soldiers in your army and the need to content

---

as the King's lieutenant general in Guyenne, had worked hard and closely with him to keep the peace.

Letters

dérobé, nommément en cette ville principale,[4] la belle recommandation d'avoir traité vos sujets mutins, en pleine victoire, avec plus de soulagement que ne font leurs protecteurs; et qu'à la différence d'un crédit passager et usurpé, vous eussiez montré qu'ils étaient vôtres par une protection paternelle et vraiment royale.

A conduire tels affaires que ceux que vous avez en main, il se faut servir de voies non communes. Si s'est-il toujours vu qu'où les conquêtes, par leur grandeur et difficulté, ne se pouvaient bonnement parfaire par armes et par force, elles ont été parfaites par clémence et magnificence, excellents leurres à attirer les hommes, spécialement vers le juste et légitime parti. S'il y échoit rigueur et châtiment, il doit être remis après la possession de la maîtrise. Un grand conquéreur du temps passé [5] se vante d'avoir donné autant d'occasion à ses ennemis subjugués de l'aimer qu'à ses amis. Et ici nous sentons déjà quelque effet de bon pronostic de l'impression que reçoivent vos villes dévoyées par la comparaison de leur rude traitement à celui des villes qui sont sous votre obéissance. Désirant à Votre Majesté une félicité plus présente et moins hasardeuse, et qu'elle soit plutôt chérie que crainte de ses peuples et tenant son bien nécessairement attaché au leur, je me réjouis que ce même avancement qu'elle fait vers la victoire l'avance aussi vers des conditions de paix plus faciles.

Sire, votre lettre du dernier de novembre n'est venue

---

[4] Presumably Paris, not yet besieged but attacked briefly by Henry IV on November 1–3, 1589.

them had not robbed you, especially in that principal city,[4] of the fine recommendation of having treated your mutinous subjects, in the height of victory, with more solace than do their protectors; and that you had shown that they were yours, not by a passing and usurped claim, but by a paternal and truly royal protection.

To conduct such affairs as those you have in hand it is necessary to use uncommon ways. Moreover, it has always been observed that where conquests, because of their greatness and difficulty, could not be thoroughly completed by arms and by force, they have been completed by clemency and magnanimity, excellent lures to attract men, especially toward the just and legitimate side. If rigor and punishment occur, they must be put off until after the possession of mastery. A great conqueror of the past[5] boasts that he has given his subjugated enemies as much occasion to love him as his friends. And here we already feel some promising effect from the impression received by the towns that have strayed from you when they compare their harsh treatment with that of the towns that are obedient to you. Wishing for Your Majesty, as I do, a more present and less hazardous felicity, and that you may be rather loved than feared by your people, and considering your welfare as necessarily attached to theirs, I rejoice that this same progress that you are making toward victory is also a progress toward easier conditions of peace.

Sire, your letter of the last of November has reached

---

[5] Scipio the Elder. See Livy, *History*, xxxvii, vi.

à moi qu'à cette heure, et au delà du terme qu'il vous plaisait me prescrire de votre séjour à Tours. Je reçois à grâce singulière qu'elle ait daigné me faire sentir qu'elle prendrait à gré de me voir, personne si inutile mais sienne plus par affection encore que par devoir. Elle a très louablement rangé ses formes externes à la hauteur de sa nouvelle fortune; mais la débonnaireté et facilité de ses humeurs internes, elle fait autant louable de ne les changer. Il lui a plu avoir respect non seulement à mon âge mais à mon désir aussi, de m'appeler en lieu où elle fût un peu en repos de ses laborieuses agitations. Sera-ce pas bientôt à Paris, Sire! et y aura-t-il moyens ni santé que je n'étende pour m'y rendre.

Votre très humble et très obéissant serviteur et sujet,

Montaigne

De Montaigne, le 18 de janv.

AU ROI HENRI IV

Au Roi

Sire,

Celle qu'il a plu à Votre Majesté m'écrire du vingtième de juillet ne m'a été rendue que ce matin, et m'a trouvé engagé en une fièvre tierce très violente, populaire en ce pays depuis le mois passé.

490

me only at this moment, and after the time you were pleased to set for me, when you were in Tours. I take it as a singular favor that you have deigned to make me feel that you would take pleasure in seeing me, a person so useless, but yours even more by affection than by duty. Your Majesty has very laudably adapted your outward appearance to the height of your new fortune, but you act just as laudably in not changing the good nature and ease of your inward disposition. You have been pleased to have consideration not only for my age but also for my wishes in summoning me to a place where you would be a little bit at rest from your labors and agitations. May it be soon in Paris, Sire; and there will be neither means nor health that I will not employ to come.

Your very humble and very obedient servant and subject,

Montaigne

From Montaigne, Jan. 18th.

TO KING HENRY IV

[September 2, 1590 (?)]

To the King

Sire,

The letter of July 20th that Your Majesty has been pleased to write me was delivered to me only this morning and found me caught up in a very violent tertian fever that has been popular in this region since last month.

Sire, je prends à très grand honneur de recevoir vos commandements, et n'ai point failli d'écrire à Monsieur le maréchal de Matignon trois fois bien expressément la délibération et obligation en quoi j'étais de l'aller trouver, et jusqu'à lui marquer la route que je prendrais pour l'aller joindre en sûreté s'il le trouvait bon; à quoi n'ayant eu aucune réponse, j'estime qu'il a considéré pour moi la longueur et hasard des chemins.

Sire, Votre Majesté me fera s'il lui plaît cette grâce de croire que je ne plaindrai jamais ma bourse aux occasions auxquelles je ne voudrais épargner ma vie. Je n'ai jamais reçu bien quelconque de la libéralité des rois, non plus que demandé ni mérité; et n'ai reçu nul payement des pas que j'ai employés à leur service, desquels Votre Majesté a eu en partie connaissance. Ce que j'ai fait pour ses prédécesseurs, je le ferai encore beaucoup plus volontiers pour elle. Je suis, Sire, aussi riche que je me souhaite. Quand j'aurai épuisé ma bourse auprès de Votre Majesté à Paris, je prendrai la hardiesse de le lui dire. Et lors, si elle m'estime digne de me tenir plus longtemps à sa suite, elle en aura meilleur marché que du moindre de ses officiers.

Sire, je supplie Dieu pour votre prospérité et santé.

Votre très humble et très obéissant serviteur et sujet,

Montaigne

De Montaigne, ce second de septembre.

Sire, I take it as a very great honor to receive your commands, and I have not failed to write to Marshal de Matignon three times, very expressly, of my intention and obligation to go to see him, and I even marked out for him the route I would take to go to meet him in safety if he saw fit. Having had no answer to all this, I assume that he has considered, on my behalf, the length and hazard of the roads.

Sire, may it please Your Majesty to do me the favor of believing that I will never begrudge my purse on the occasions for which I would not want to spare my life. I have never received any gift whatsoever from the liberality of kings, any more than I have asked it or deserved it; and I have received no payment for the steps I have taken in their service, of which Your Majesty has had partial knowledge. What I have done for your predecessors I will do still more willingly for you. I am, Sire, as rich as I wish to be. When I have exhausted my purse with Your Majesty in Paris, I will make bold to tell you so; and then, if you consider me worth keeping any longer in your retinue, I will cost you less than the least of your officers.

Sire, I pray God for your prosperity and health.

Your very humble and very obedient servant and subject,

Montaigne

From Montaigne, September 2nd.

Letters

Glossary

Words listed in both Mansion's *Shorter French and English Dictionary* (Heath) and *The Concise Oxford French Dictionary* are generally not given here; nor are many other words easily guessable from the context and from the French root or English cognate.

For a number of important ways in which Montaigne's sixteenth-century French differs from modern usage, see above, page xxi (Note on the Text).

accoutumer *v. i.*   to be accustomed, become accustomed.

acheminement *m.*   start.

acheminer *v. tr.*   to put on the road, start, guide.

acquêt *m.*   acquisition, gain, profit.

ains *conj.*   but.

aller *v. i.*   to go; — + *infinitive or present participle*   to be (doing), go (doing), (do).

amuser *v. tr.*   to amuse, busy, divert; s' —   to amuse oneself, busy oneself.

apparence *f.*   appearance of truth or reason, plausibility.

aucun *adj. and pron.*   some, any, someone.

aucunement *adv.*   somewhat, at all.

aventure *f.*   adventure, chance; à l' —   by chance, perhaps.

avenue *f.*   approach.

chaloir *v. imp.*   to concern, worry; *pres. ind.* il (me) chaut (I) care; *pres. subj.* il chaille.

commerce *m.*   dealings, association, intercourse, acquaintance.

cuider *v. tr.* to think; — + *infinitive* to nearly (do).

cuider *m.* presumption.

curieusement *adv.* curiously, carefully.

de ce que *conj. phr.* because.

découvrir *v. tr.* to reveal.

discipline *f.* teaching, education, training.

discours *m.* reason, reasoning, argument.

doctrine *f.* teaching, learning, message, doctrine.

duire *v. tr.* to train, accustom.

élire *v. tr.* to choose.

embesognement *m.* business, busyness, care.

embesogner *v. tr.* to busy, occupy; s' — to busy oneself;
   embesogné *a.* busy.

emmi *prep.* among, amid.

empêcher *v. tr.* to involve, occupy; **empêché** *a.* hard
   pressed, hard put to it, occupied.

entendre *v. tr.* to understand, see fit, intend, mean.

exercitation *f.* training, practice, exercise.

expérimenter *v. tr.* to experience.

feindre *v. tr.* to imagine, feign, pretend.

franchise *f.* freedom, safety.

heur *m.* good fortune, happiness.

honnête homme *m.* honorable man, good man, gentleman.

icelui, icelle *dem. pron.* this, that, it (= **celui-ci** or **celui-là**).

institution *f.* education, system of education, teaching.

joint *prep.* besides; — **que** *conj. phr.* besides (the fact)
   that.

laisser *v. i.* + *infinitive* (after à or **de**) to fail to.

librairie *f.* library.

meshui *adv.* henceforth, from now on.

nourrir *v. tr.* to bring up, foster, educate, satisfy, support.

nourriture *f.* upbringing, education.

offense *f.* harm, hurt.

offenser *v. tr.* to harm, hurt.

onques *adv.* ever.

495

ouïr *v. tr.* *(pres. ind.* j'ois, il oit, nous oyons, vous oyez, etc.; *fut.* j'orrai, il orra, etc.; *pres. part.* oyant)   to hear.
par quoi *adv. and conj.*   wherefore, therefore, hence.
patron *m.*   model.
pensement *m.*   thought.
piper *v. tr.*   to trick, deceive, fool.
piperie *f.*   trickery, deception.
plainte *f.*   complaint, pity.
pointure *f.*   prick, sting.
police *f.*   polity, government, order, society, institution, discipline.
pour *prep.*   because of; — ce que *conj. phr.*   because.
pourtant *adv.*   nevertheless, therefore, for all that.
preuve *f.*   proof, test, trial.
quand et *prep. phr.*   with; — quand *adv. phr.*   at the same time.
que *rel. pron.*   what, that which, the one who or which (= ce que or celui que); *adv.*   why . . . ?
qui *rel. pron.*   what, that which, the one who (= ce qui or celui qui); *(esp. with cond. or subj.)*   if anyone.
se ramentevoir *v. r.*   to remember.
si *adv.*   yet, nevertheless, still, moreover, so.
somme *adv.*   in short.
soudain *adv.*   immediately.
soudard *m.*   soldier.
sujet *m.*   subject, object, thing.
tant y a que *adv. phr.*   however, at all events (= tant il y a que).
tout *adj. and n. m.*   all; à — *prep. phr.*   with; du — *prep. phr.*   completely.
travail *m.*   work, travail, hardship, torment.
vertu *f.*   virtue, manliness, power.
viande *f.*   food.
voire *adv.*   true, truly, indeed, even.
voirement *adv.*   truly.

Printed in the United States
138660LV00003B/2/A